Doron Mendels (ed.)

On Memory

An Interdisciplinary Approach

PETER LANG

Oxford · Bern · Berlin · Bruxelles · Frankfurt am Main · New York · Wien

Bibliographic information published by Die Deutsche Bibliothek
Die Deutsche Bibliothek lists this publication in the Deutsche
Nationalbibliografie; detailed bibliographic data is available on
the Internet at ‹http://dnb.ddb.de›.

British Library and Library of Congress Cataloguing-in-Publication Data:
A catalogue record for this book is available from The British Library,
Great Britain, and from The Library of Congress, USA

Front cover image: Figure 7.1 Brain ingredients, page 174.
Cover design: Adrian Baggett, Peter Lang Ltd.

ISBN 978-3-03911-064-3

© Peter Lang AG, International Academic Publishers, Bern 2007
Hochfeldstrasse 32, Postfach 746, CH-3000 Bern 9, Switzerland
info@peterlang.com, www.peterlang.com, www.peterlang.net

Printed in Germany

Contents

Acknowledgements

First and foremost, I wish to thank the participants of the conference "On Memory: An Interdisciplinary Approach." The staff of the Institute for Advanced Studies at the Hebrew University of Jerusalem was helpful and kind all along. The former academic director, Professor B. Z. Kedar, as well as his successor Professor E. Rabinovici were extremely supportive and granted us a generous subsidy for the conference and its publication. Ms. Pnina Feldman, associate director of the Institute for Advanced Studies, encouraged us and helped us to realize the goal of this publication, as did Ms. Leslie Gardner of Artellus Limited, London. My thanks go also to Ms. Smadar Bergman, who drew the chart attached to my article on Günter Grass, and to Mr. Ofer Arbeli for his technical support.

Ms. Evelyn Katrak I would like to thank in particular for her efficient copy-editing and the patience she had with all of us. Special thanks to Ms. Joanna Turner who did an excellent job in converting our manuscript into book form.

Doron Mendels
Jerusalem, The Hebrew University of Jerusalem, October 2006

DORON MENDELS

Introduction

The theme of memory has become quite fashionable in historical research over the past decade or so. There has been a revived interest in the theories of the sociologist Maurice Halbwachs, and many volumes and papers have been published on different aspects of historical public memory. In this volume the reader will find a reflection of this research and various reactions to what has been done in this field, all of which has been set against the background of two papers on the biological processes that "manufacture" the memories in our brain.

This collection of essays is the outcome of a conference held at the Institute for Advanced Studies at the Hebrew University of Jerusalem in April 2005. At the conference the speakers attempted to tackle the problem of public memory from the viewpoint of various disciplines in the humanities, the social sciences and the exact sciences. Their deliberations led to many important results, some of which are presented here. I will not summarize the topics dealt with in the various chapters, as this would do an injustice to the authors, who have argued their cases extensively and with a great deal of complexity. I will just mention some of the issues that were tackled and emphasize that this volume, if read in its entirety, will give the reader some idea about the mosaic of public memory.

First and foremost, many articles in this volume clearly show that the concept of "collective memory" has sometimes been used too loosely; here it is examined cautiously and from various angles. Individual memory and the narrative of it are tackled by a psycho-therapist, showing once again that the "behavior" of memory in the individual can sometimes serve as a metaphor for the behavior of memory in the group. The relationship between individual and collective memory is discussed in some of the articles and emerges as an important facet of any form of public memory. Most scholars participating in this volume would agree that alongside aspects of memories that are collective to a group there are many subdivisions within the group that have their own memories, which are not shared by others in the larger group. These I would call fragmented memories.

On the basis of the various contributions to this volume it can be concluded that "public memory" can refer to a memory that is imbued in a national entity, or just in groups and institutions within this entity, or in both. Public memory as discussed here includes blocks of memories "belonging" to any group of people that transcend individual recall. It can be the memory of a class at school, the memory of a generation concerning some particular event it experienced, the memory that is imbued in a group that fought a certain battle, the memory that is embodied in an ethnic group or in a sect within a monotheistic religion. Individuals and groups can carry memories of the experience of others who left it as a legacy in oral or written form. Thus we can adopt the idea of Amia Lieblich concerning "primary" and "secondary" public memories.

We have tackled in various degrees and depths the problem of the *nature* of public memory and the ways in which it is connected to the society in which it is embodied. A public memory can be visible to the society, the most obvious example being the language we speak, which enfolds common memories and associations when spoken by a group. Everyone in the group has to memorize the language in order to be able to speak and understand it. A language develops and changes from decade to decade; thus people who are disconnected from their mother tongue for a while are "stuck" with an old-fashioned version of the language. But there are also public memories that are invisible. They are the memories embedded in the society's institutional structure, such as the legal system. The precedent used in the law courts is based, as Nili Cohen has argued, on the concept that a legal memory should be preserved from generation to generation. Just as individual memory can be "measured" to a certain extent, so too can public memory that is stored in its institutions. The more visible aspect of public memory is perhaps less measurable in the democratic nation-states; it can more easily be observed in the totalitarian ones.

From most articles in this volume it becomes clear that various factors have an effect on public memory. These include the *media* that create and preserve memories in societies as well as the *time* that elapses from the moment the event is memorized to its becoming public. Fashions and ideologies have an impact on the nature and durability of public memory. The nature of the regime is another crucial factor, since in autocratic and totalitarian regimes memory is largely shaped and formed for the population. Barring clandestine groups that preserve their own memories, the media in such regimes are restricted and censured in order to promote the general "collective" memory that includes made-up and filtered versions of the past as well as other experiences that are grafted onto a formal narrative. In such cases the term "collective memory" can be much more easily used than in democracies. Here the use of such a term becomes quite problematic, from the very definition of the concept of democracy; here some of us would prefer to speak of "fragments of memory" that have their own "life" in segments of the society alongside some collective aspects of memory in the entire citizen-body of the state in different time spans.

The media, as many articles in this volume show, are crucial for the creation, preservation, enhancement and destruction of public memory. The volume tackles the problems of how the media create, revive or promote certain items of knowledge that become the memories of a society (I can have a "memory" of a biblical scene from having learned it). The media may comprise radio, television, theater, cinema, the law courts, rituals and sacred places as well as religious academies. In a tight religious society or ethnic group, the media are defined and restricted regarding what the people within the group are allowed to memorize. In this context some of the authors have dealt with the issue of the communicative power of symbols and their visualization through architecture and other artifacts of art. The media in democracies and open societies can influence the impact a public memory has and the length of time it stays within the public sphere before it becomes inscribed in historiography.

Time is mentioned by most scholars, implicitly and explicitly, as a crucial factor in the "life" of a collective public memory or frag-ments thereof. How long does it take from the creation of a memory until it becomes imbued in the public mind? The processes that shape a public memory are also dealt with, as is the issue of the time it takes for memory to be transformed or translated from its oral to its inscribed or physical form. In this volume it becomes quite clear that the physical representations of experiences that were embodied in a society lose their role as soon as the generation that erected them starts to loosen its grip on these representations, which then gradually disappear from the public arena. In other words, sites are not necessarily a guarantee that a memory will be preserved for ever after. But among groups, societies and institutions that keep very strong religious memories, time has worked miracles in the preservation of sites that powerfully represent religious individuals, religious events and rituals. In such groups the memory of a physical site can also be kept in written narratives and thus become a mnemonic symbol in itself. The Hebrew Bible is full of examples of such preservation of public memory (Josh. 22:9–34).

Public memory is nourished by a canon. The Hebrew Bible is a text that nourished the collective memory of Jews and Christians for centuries; each generation memorizes its stories with the help of its filters and additional experiences. But there are also secular canons and foundational books that nourish a group that has some collective memory. A foundational event that becomes public memory needs at times also a "collective audience," as Tamar Liebes has formulated it.

The linkage between experience, the above-mentioned factors and the element of time is what creates what we call here public memory. I would like to demonstrate this point a little further. My example is drawn from the visual arts of the fourteenth and fifteenth centuries in central Italy.

Here is not the place to elaborate on this vast subject, but just to air some ideas about it.[1] It would be difficult to speculate about what people in the fourteenth and fifteenth centuries memorized. Here and there we may get a glimpse into someone's thoughts, but basically it is impossible to form an idea about this aspect of life. However, since even today much of what was painted is preserved in public places we

---

1   I hope to publish a full version of what follows in M. Blondheim and
      D. Mendels, *History and Communication*, forthcoming.

can assess what people saw and what they probably memorized as a collective audience. It was Leon Battista Alberti who in his *De Pictura*, Book II.25, said about the visual arts:

> Painting possesses a truly divine power in that not only does it make the absent present (as they say of friendship), but it also represents the dead to the living many centuries later, so that they are recognized by spectators with pleasure and deep admiration for the artist.

First, one should recall who the "manufacturers" were of the objects to be remembered in the public sphere. Those who patronized the arts were usually the strong institutions at that time, including rich merchant families, the mendicant orders, politicians and the church, as well as secular and religious institutions. True, they supported the greatest artists of that period and brought about the rise of professionalism. But it was also they who made the decisions concerning the themes to be represented (Kempers 1992). Art and politics went hand in hand and could hardly be separated at any given time. Let us view in brief the factors that shaped the public memory in central Italy at the time under consideration.

1   The Public Sphere and its Media – The Visual Arts

During the fourteenth and fifteenth centuries a vast outpouring of art can be detected in the public sphere. Every tourist on his first visit can't help but notice this. In addition to monuments there are artifacts that were placed in the public sphere: churches, public institutions, the marketplace, etc. The public would assemble in large groups for many rituals, religious as well as secular. It became an active participant, either directly or indirectly, in the governance of cities (Kempers 1992). Thus we can start with a basic assumption that the public was exposed to artifacts of art in the public sphere all the time and everywhere. Interestingly, the architectonic space that became a medium for messages for the public is also reflected in the paintings themselves and has a significant role in the memorializing role of Renaissance architecture.[2] In other words, this medium created a "bombardment" of art within the public sphere.

2   Canon of Themes

During the fourteenth and fifteenth centuries a canon of topics and subjects was formed that found expression in the visual arts, among other media (such as literature and political science). It is no accident that a more or less fixed "list" of topics and scenes was presented in the public sphere during these two centuries and beyond. Some of the recurring topics had similar fixed narratives that were only partly dependent on the Bible, either Hebrew or Greek.[3] Other paintings drew on narratives from popular literature such as the Aurea Legenda.[4] This framework of selected motifs from the canonical sources (classical mythology, the Bible and the Apocrypha) created a new canon for central Italy (as well as other parts of the country) upon which the public memory of the communities was based. One can imagine that the choice of loci and the "mass production" of public art, taken together, had a strong effect on people.

2   Examples of this abound. See for instance the use of familiar architecture by Domenico Ghirlandaio (Cadogan 2000, 77 and plate 91, 94–100; familiar architecture appears in the scene of "The Expulsion of Joachim from the Temple" and in the presentation of the Virgin in the Santa Maria Novella, 86). Or see Masaccio's "The Shadow Healing and the Distribution of Goods," in the Brancacci Chapel (Joannides 1993, pls.103–4).

3   See for instance Uccello in the Chiostro Verde: stories from Genesis (Borsi 1994, 178–87). See also the Old Testament scenes (and embellishments on them such as that of Job's) in the Collegiate Church of San Gimigniano by Bartolo di Fredi (Imberciadori and Torriti 2002, 45–60).

4   For the Aurea Legenda see de Voragine 1993. See for instance Opitz 1998, 44–59 ("Adoration of the Magi" by Gozzoli); Galli 2005, 24 ("St. Sebastian" by Piero del Pallaiuolo, pl. 23); Borsi 1994, 256–9 (the two St. George's by Uccello); the various versions of "The Massacre of the Innocents" by Matteo di Giovanni (Van Marle 1937, 16: 336–41).

3   Sending Clear Messages

In addition to the choice of location within the public sphere and the canonical framework on which the themes presented were based, the topics were well known, as were the personalities and the landscapes used for the old scenes.[5] This probably created ideal conditions for a clear message to be sent, a message that would be understood as it was meant.[6] This closed system avoided a communication method of just "speaking into the air" (Peters 1999). The messages that were visualized are of various kinds: moral messages are very strongly represented in art, e.g. a visualization of the good versus the evil man. The list of vices and good traits represented in certain works of art is a long one.[7] The symbolic and allegoric elements could be very effective in a community educated in this kind of dichotomous thinking of good and bad. In the words of Marilyn Lavin:

> Pictures of the saints and other holy personages were never meant to emulate viable reality. They were aids to memory, representation of models of perfection, maps of the road to salvation.[8]

The political message was also quite dominant in the visual arts of these centuries: the representations of good and bad government, good

---

5   Lavin rightfully argues (1990, 6) that "most spectators/worshipers knew the story and interacted with the narrative" (see her chart illustrating the interaction between narrative and spectator, ibid). For the mnemonic value of the imitatio Christi as a technique to evoke the suffering of the past, see Mills 2005, esp. 151–6.

6   For the methods used to ensure that a message would be understood as it was meant, see Katz and Popescu 2004.

7   See for instance representations of the virtues and the vices (such as hope, faith, justice, anger, idolatry, injustice) by Giotto in the Cappella degli Scrovegni, Padua (Von der Haegen-Mueller 1998, 50–3).

8   Lavin 1990, 121. For the communication value of narrative frescoes see ibid., passim.

and bad citizenship and adherence to the laws.[9] Moreover, politicians
of the time and their relatives were represented in many works of art,
sometimes in the garb of ancient classical and biblical figures, and
sometimes as people depicted in their own reality.[10] Art became such
an effective medium in shaping public memory that it was increasingly used by politicians, churchmen and influential business people.
Were it not effective, art would not have been so central in the life of
the communities, and artists would have not achieved so high a level
of professionalism.

4   Timing and the Audience

An audience at that time could be captivated by a combination of three
aspects that the visual arts provided: (1) The loci where the audience
got the exposure were the most central in the city or village – namely,
the church, the city hall, etc. (2) Many visual narratives were painted
for – and thus connected to – certain religious dates and their rituals
(Lavin 1990, 99–118). (3) Many of the painted scenes were representations of actualities and events taken from reality. Here we can
include famous battles and scenes that occurred in the past or during
the lifetime of the artist and his patron.[11] A state visit, for instance,
was thus imprinted in the public memory by the artist who painted it
in the public space.[12]

9   For good and bad government see Frugoni 2002, 201–55 (Ambrogio
     Lorenzetti); for good and bad citizenship and the reflection of the legal system
     see Kempers 1992, esp. 133–41.
10   Baetzner 1998, 50–73 (Mantegna: "The Camera degli Sposi – the Gonzaga
     Court").
11   See for instance "The battle of San Romano" by Uccello, in Borsi 1994, 212–
     31; "The battle of Maxentius" by Piero della Francesca (Lightbown 1992, 152–
     5).
12   For instance the political scenes by Pintoricchio in the Piccolomini Library in
     Siena (Luchinat 1999, 51–67).

5   Meaning

It was Gregory the Great (590–604) who argued already for the importance of pictorial representations for the (illiterate) masses (Migne, P. L. vol. 77: 1027–8). The combination of the above elements provides a fair picture as to what public memory was like in the early Renaissance, and it was effective in creating a clear and familiar message in the public sphere. Moreover, the themes, persons and historical narratives all had a significant *meaning* for the people in Italy, enabling whole communities to feel connected to the vast amount of art around them. This kind of link between communities and what they remember, and the mnemonic meanings they attach to the physical symbols around them is a central theme of this volume. Once this linkage disappears, public memory vanishes and becomes historiography – an attraction for tourists who preserve it as a vague memory of past times.

Bibliography

Baetzner, N. 1998. *Mantegna*. Cologne: Koenemann.

Borsi, F. and S. Borsi. 1994. *Paolo Uccello*. London: Thames and Hudson.

Cadogan, J. K. 2000. *Domenico Ghirlandaio: Artist and Artisan*. New Haven/London: Yale University Press.

Frugoni, C. (ed.). 2002. *Pietro e Ambrogio Lorenzetti*. Florence: Le lettere. (Article written by Maria Monica Donato).

Galli, A. 2005. *The Pollaiuolo,* translated from the Italian by Susan Wise. Milan: Continents Editions.

Imberciadori, J. V. and M. Torriti. 2002. *The Collegiate Church of San Gimigniano*. San Gimigniano: Nencini Editore.

Joannides, P. 1993. *Masaccio and Masolino: A Complete Catalogue*. London: Phaidon Press.

Katz, E. and M. Popescu. 2004. "Supplementation: On Communicator Control of the Conditions of Reception." In I. Bondebjerg and P. Golding (eds), *European Culture and the Media*. Oregon: Intellect Books, 19–43.

Kempers B. 1992. *Painting, Power and Patronage*: *The Rise of the Professional Artist in the Italian Renaissance*, translated from the 1987 Dutch version by B. Jackson. London: Allen Lane – Penguin Press.

Lavin Aronberg, M. 1990. *The Place of Narrative: Mural Decorations in Italian Churches 431–1600*. Chicago/London: University of Chicago Press.

Lightbown. 1992. *Piero della Francesca*. New York/London/Paris: Abbeville Press.

Luchinat, C. A. 1999. *Pintoricchio*. Florence: Scala.

Mills, R. 2005. *Suspended Animation: Pain, Pleasure and Punishment in Medieval Culture*. London: Reaktion Books.

Opitz, M. 1998. *Gozzoli*. Cologne: Koenemann.

Peters, J. D. 1999. *Speaking into the Air: A History of the Idea of Communication*. Chicago/ London: University of Chicago Press.

Van Marle, R. 1937. *The Development of the Italian Schools of Painting*, vol. 16. The Hague: Martinus Nijhoff.

Von der Haegen-Mueller, A. 1998. *Giotto*. Cologne: Koenemann.

Voragine, Jacobus de. 1993. *The Golden Legend*, vols 1–2. Princeton, NJ: Princeton University Press.

Chapter 1

ALEXANDER YAKOBSON

Us and Them: Empire, Memory and Identity in Claudius' Speech on Bringing Gauls into the Roman Senate

In the year 48 C.E. the Emperor Claudius spoke in the Senate in favor of admitting into that body certain notables from Gallia Comata (the "long-haired," un-Romanized part of Gaul conquered by Julius Caesar), who already held Roman citizenship. We have both the authentic speech, preserved (with two lacunae) on a bronze tablet found in Lyons, and Tacitus' version of it in *Annales* XI. 23–4. Tacitus relates the debate in the Emperor's council, which preceded the speech in the Senate, during which this measure was strongly opposed on grounds that in a modern context might be termed "nationalistic": the Senate should not be swamped by people of foreign (non-Italian) descent, even though they are Roman citizens – least of all by Gauls, with their history of hostility to Rome. This debate and the Emperor's speech, in both surviving versions, touch on fundamental questions of historical memory and national identity, the influence of the past on political decisions, and the impact of politics on the way historical past is remembered and narrated – all this in the Roman imperial context.

Using the term "national" – not to speak of "nationalistic" – in this context is of course controversial. According to a widely shared – though by no means universally accepted – view, national identities are a modern phenomenon; whatever ethnic and cultural identities existed in premodern times are not to be defined as "national." Historians of the ancient world are less likely to be concerned with this debate than modern ones, for whom modern nationalism is a

pivotal, distinctive and often deeply controversial feature of modernity. Ancient historians often use "national" terminology.[1] Late Republican Roman Italy, thoroughly Romanized culturally, whose entire free
population received Roman citizenship in the 80s B.C.E., has been
described as providing "the closest parallel found in antiquity to a
large national state in the modern sense, with a universal language and
a single system of local government and civil law" (Sherwin-White
1973, 159). Of course, "the closest parallel" still does not denote full
identity. But if, as one of the leading proponents of the "modernist"
view has suggested, nationalism has to do with the strength of the
connection between a given polity and a given culture,[2] then the extent
to which a debate on Roman citizenship and the composition of the
imperial Senate could be influenced by questions of ethnic origin,
cultural identity and historical memory – precisely at a time when the
spread of Roman citizenship beyond Italy into the provinces of the
Empire, was, as might be thought, turning it into a purely legal
concept devoid of all cultural content – is perhaps not without bearing
on the modern debate.

    Though the conventions of ancient historiography allowed
historians considerable latitude in reporting a speech, most of the
arguments in favor of admitting the Gauls into the Senate are common
to the Lyons Tablet and Tacitus' account. There is wide agreement
among scholars that the historian must have been familiar with the
speech, most probably from the *acta senatus* that he is known to have
consulted in his work. Nevertheless, the differences between the two
versions (beyond matters of style) are considerable. As for the arguments of the "opposition" among the Emperor's advisers, it is usually
assumed that Tacitus "reconstructed [them] from the authentic oration;
[they] were probably never voiced in the Senate, but the Emperor was

---

1   E.g. Mendels 1992, 13–33. Mendels rejects the view that "the Jews were the
     only specimen of a 'modern' nation to be found in antiquity" (22). As for
     "nationalism," Mendels holds that one can indeed speak of "nationalism in the
     ancient world [...] but not in the sense it has in modern times" (13).

2   See "The Congruence of Culture and Polity," in Gellner 1983. Of course, there
     are connections weaker than congruence. See Smith 2000 for a survey of the
     debate and criticism of the "modernist" view; cf. Guibernau and Hutchinson
     2004.

careful to take account of what had been said to him in council" (Griffin 1982, 414).[3]

The text on which the following discussion will be based is that of Tacitus (naturally, with references to the Tablet) – and not merely because his prose is a considerably more rewarding subject-matter for discussion than that of Claudius. It has been noted that while the Emperor's discourse (apart from its idiosyncratic Claudian traits) reads like "an advocate's speech in favour of a particular proposal," "it becomes in Tacitus a programmatic speech" in favor of admitting the best people from the provinces into the Senate. Tacitus, who was naturally less interested than Claudius in the merits of the particular claims of the Gallic chieftains, is "consistently [...] keep[ing] the debate on a general plane" (ibid., 413–14). Moreover, when Claudius deals with the general principle behind his decision in the specific case, he refers to political innovation as a time-honored tradition of the Roman state in various fields; the Roman openness to foreigners is but one example. For Tacitus, the guiding principle is, throughout, "the assimilation of foreign material" (ibid., 413; though a broader state-ment on innovation concludes his account of the speech).

The historian evidently took this opportunity to articulate the various arguments that could be heard on both sides when the process of conferring Roman citizenship on provincials, and of promoting people of provincial origin to the higher offices of state, was discussed – and, no doubt, often criticized – within the circles of the Roman elite. Moreover, by the time the *Annales* were composed (under Trajan and Hadrian, in the early second century), the integration of provincial elites had gone much further than could be imagined, or articulated, by Claudius in 48. "When Tacitus wrote, colonials and provincials from the Latin West occupied the place of the Caesars" (Syme 1958, 2:624). Indeed, the historian's version of the speech is perceptibly more "radical" in tone than the authentic one; he suppresses, as we

---

3   It seems unlikely that these arguments could have come from the record of the senatorial debate that followed the Emperor's speech and preceded the decree, since this would have meant that senators directly contradicted the Emperor on a major policy issue after he had expressed his own views forcefully and unambiguously.

shall see, Claudius' remark that accepts the superiority of Italian senators.[4] "[I]t is Tacitus' speech, not the Lyons Tablet, that can be reasonably seen [...] as foreshadowing the extension of citizenship by Caracalla [to all the free inhabitants of the Empire, in 212]" (Griffin 1982, 413). For this reason, too, the general case for the policy of bringing the provincial elites into the imperial ruling class, promoted by the Emperors – as well as the conservative objections to this policy, which changed the face of the Roman world – emerge in Tacitus' account more clearly than in the Emperor's oration.

Some of the points that appear to have been added by Tacitus may have been contained in the missing parts of the Lyons Tablet, which is "broken off horizontally at the top," so that "we have a lacuna of uncertain length at the top of each of the two columns of the inscription" (Wellesley 1954, 18–19).[5] It appears from the context that "Claudius' treatment of [the extension of citizenship and the admissibility to the Senate ...] occupied most, if not all, of the lacuna in the middle of the speech" (Miller 1956, 309). Since the speech, as inscribed in the Tablet, ends rather abruptly, it is even possible – though by no means safe to postulate – that a second tablet, and thus a third column of the text, existed,[6] providing the missing conclusion, and perhaps some remarks of a more general and "programmatic" nature. Tacitus' conclusion, at any rate, contains some of the most significant points of the speech, to which we now turn:[7]

> In the consulate of Aulus Vitellius and Lucius Vipstanus (48 C.E.), when the question of completing the numbers of the Senate was under consideration [the Emperor performing his duties as censor], notables (*primores*) of Gallia

---

4   Cf. Griffin 1982, 412. Syme argues at length that Tacitus' own family originated from either Cisalpine (Tanspadane) Gaul or from the province of Gallia Narbonensis (Syme 1958, 2: 611–24) and suggests that it was probably "native by ultimate extraction" (622).

5   Wellesley warns against attributing all the discrepancies between the two versions of the speech to these lacunae, which he does not suppose to have been extensive. Griffin argues that since the upper part of the tablet is lost, any assumption that Tacitus added substantive points of his own to the Emperor's speech is "profoundly precarious" (Griffin 1982, 405).

6   Thus Vittinghoff 1954, 364. Contra, e.g. Miller 1956, 308, n. 18.

7   Tacitus, *Annals*, Book 11:23–5. I will mainly follow the Loeb translation.

Comata, as it is termed, who had long before obtained federate rights and Roman citizenship, were claiming the privilege of holding magistracies in the capital.[8] Comments on the subject were numerous and diverse; and in the Emperor's council (*apud principem*) the debate was conducted with animation on both sides: "Italy," it was asserted, was not yet so moribund that she was unable to supply a Senate to her own capital (*urbi suae*). The time had been when a Roman-born Senate was enough for peoples [Latin and Italians allies] whose blood was akin to their own; and they were not ashamed of the old Republic. Why, even today men quoted the patterns of virtue and of glory which, under the old system, the Roman character had given the world! Was it too little that Venetians and Insurbians had taken the Senate-house by storm,[9] unless they brought in an army of aliens to give it the look of a captured town? What honours would be left to the relics of their nobility, or the poor senator who came from Latium? All would be submerged by those opulent persons whose grandfathers and great-grandfathers, in command of hostile tribes, had smitten our armies by steel and the strong hand, and had besieged the deified Julius [Caesar] at Alesia. But these were recent events. What if there should arise the memory of the men who essayed to pluck down the spoils, sanctified to Heaven, from the Capitol and the citadel of Rome? Leave them by all means to enjoy the title of citizens; but the insignia of senators, the glories of the magistrates – these they must not vulgarize.

Unconvinced by these and similar arguments, the Emperor not only stated his objections there and then but, after convening the Senate, addressed it as follows:

In my own ancestors, the eldest of whom, Clausus, a Sabine by extraction, was made simultaneously a citizen and the head of a patrician house, I find encouragement to employ the same policy in my administration, by transferring hither all true excellence, let it be found where it will. For I am not unaware that the Julii came from Alba, the Coruncanii from Camerium, the Porcii from Tusculum; that – not to scrutinize antiquity – members were drafted into the Senate from Etruria from Lucania, from the whole of Italy; and that finally Italy itself was extended to the Alps,[10] in order that not individuals merely but countries and peoples (*terrae, gentes*) should form one body under the name of the Romans. The day of stable peace at home and victory abroad came when the districts beyond the Po were admitted to citizenship, and, availing ourselves of the fact that our legions were settled throughout the globe, we added to them the

8   The local communities to which the notables belonged were "federate" – i.e. they had the status of Rome's "allies" under the terms of a treaty (*foedus*), while the notables themselves enjoyed Roman citizenship on a personal basis.
9   People from the Cisalpine Gaul beyond the Po enfranchised by Julius Caesar.
10 The grant of citizenship was made by Caesar in 49 B.C.E.; Cisalpine Gaul became part of Italy under Octavian (later Augustus).

stoutest of the provincials, and succoured a weary Empire. Is it regretted that the Balbi crossed over from Spain and families equally distinguished from Narbonese Gaul? Their descendants remain; nor do they yield to us in love for this native land (*amore in hanc patriam*). What else proved fatal to Lacedaemon and to Athens, in spite of their power of arms, but their policy of holding the conquered aloof as alien-born? But the sagacity of our own founder Romulus was such that several times he fought and enfranchised a people in the course of the same day! Strangers have been kings over us: the conferment of magistracies on the sons of freedmen is not the novelty which it is commonly and mistakenly thought, but a frequent practice of the old commonwealth. "But we fought with the Senones." Then, presumably, the Volscians and Aequians never drew a line of battle against us. "We were taken by the Gauls." But we also gave hostages to Tuscans and underwent the yoke of the Samnites. And yet, if you survey the whole of our wars, not one was finished within a shorter period than that against the Gauls: thenceforward there has been a continuous and loyal peace. Now that customs, culture and the ties of marriage have blended them with ourselves (*iam moribus artibus adfinitatibus nostris mixti*), let them bring among us their gold and their riches instead of retaining them beyond the pale! All, Conscript Fathers, that is now believed supremely old has been new: plebeian magistrates followed the patrician; Latin, the plebeian; magistrates from the other peoples of Italy, the Latin. Our innovation, too, will be parcel of the past, and what today we defend by precedents will rank among precedents.

The Emperor's speech was followed by a senatorial decree, and the Aedui became the first to acquire senatorial rights in the capital: a concession to a long-standing treaty and to their position as the only Gallic community enjoying the title of brothers of the Roman people.

Much of the debate is obviously shaped by historical memory. The "opposition" in the Emperor's council delves into distant past: the Gauls fought Julius Caesar (some hundred years before the date of the debate); moreover, the Gauls sacked Rome (in the early fourth century). These are not just historical *exempla* in the usual sense, when the lessons of history are presented as pointing to the right solution of the problem at hand – as when Claudius mentions the well-known Roman precedents for innovation and, specifically, for openness to foreigners and former enemies. Rather, history is brought to life in a much more direct way: the "sins" of their (notional) forefathers are actually visited on the present-day Gallic chieftains; historical events are adduced as an important reason for rejecting their petition. As far the "opposition" is concerned, history is not a thing of the past. Syme suggests that these arguments are in fact Tacitus' invention:

> Anger and pathos are helped out (it happens often) by the appeal to race and history, with arguments crude, feeble and spurious. So Tacitus intended. He made them up, to refute them majestically [in his version of Claudius' speech before the Senate] (Syme 1958, 2:624; Wellesley 1954, 30–1).

However, a passage in the Emperor's own speech, towards the end of the Lyons Tablet, clearly shows that he was answering, or anticipating, similar arguments. Although the point is less elaborated on here than in Tacitus' version, its position is emphatic, directly after the speaker has finally turned to the issue of Gallia Comata; the effect is strengthened if this is indeed the final passage of the speech:[11]

> But I must now plead the case of Gallia Comata with firm intent (*destricte*). If in this case anyone looks to the fact that they occupied the deified Julius in war for ten years, let him also take note of the hundred years of their constant good faith and loyalty (*obsequium*), more than tested many times when we were in difficulty. They were the ones that gave my father Drusus the benefit of safe internal peace and a secure rear when he was conquering Germany, although he was called to war while conducting a census, a practice then new and strange to the Gauls.[12]

The reference to the Gaul's loyal behavior during his father's days (apart from reflecting the personal aspect of Claudius' speech) comes close to the issue of the present-day state of the country and the attitudes of its people, which is obviously relevant when one discusses the advancement and integration of the local elites. But the length of the Gauls' resistance to the deified Julius is only relevant if the case at hand is to be decided, partially, on the (de)merits of Julius Caesar's Gallic adversaries. Of course, the Emperor's real point is that historic enmities should not be allowed to dictate imperial policy – hence his mention of Rome's wars with Italic peoples long fully integrated into the Roman state and society, and also of the ancient tradition of

---

11 But see note 6 above.
12 The English translation closely follows Braund 1985, 201. For the Latin text see *ILS* 212.

Romulus enfranchising recently defeated enemies. But he has to take into account the opposing view – whether voiced on this occasion, or generally known. This was evidently the kind of argument that could be used in opposing the political integration of people from Gaul. Tacitus' Claudius counters his advisers' arguments on the basis of the Gauls' past "offences" against Rome (including those dating back to the fourth century) both by pointing out that other historic enemies have long since became an integral part of the Roman people, and by defending the Gauls' "modern" historical record:

> And yet, if you survey the whole of our wars, not one was finished within a shorter period than that against the Gauls: thenceforward there has been a continuous and loyal peace.

That Caesar's war in Gaul was the shortest in Roman history is factually incorrect. This is hardly a "majestic refutation" of the opposition's narrow-minded "appeal to race and history"; rather, the history of the race is accepted as important enough to merit manipulation for argument's sake. The claim (in both versions of the speech) that Caesar's conquests were followed by an uninterrupted peace for a century is also wrong: it ignores the rebellion of Florus and Sacrovir described at length by Tacitus – in which the Aedui, soon to be singled out in the senatorial decree that resulted from the debate, were actively involved.[13] Even the Emperor's concluding compliment (in the Lyons Tablet) to the inhabitants of Gallia Comata for allowing his father, Drusus, to conduct a census in peace is factually wrong, or at least exaggerated. Livy (*Per.* 138) relates that this census was accompanied by disturbances, which must have been significant enough to survive in the record. Historical memory both shapes the political discourse and is shaped by it. Not just the discourse – the practical result of the discussion was a decree of the Senate under which "the Aedui became the first to acquire senatorial rights in the capital: a concession to a long-standing treaty and to their position as the only Gallic community enjoying the title of brothers of the Roman people."

13   Tac. *Ann.* III. 40–7 (21 C.E.).

This is a very old story indeed – going back to the second century
B.C.E. It is now, in 48 C.E., made the basis of a decision conferring an
important political privilege on members of this group. The political
relevance of the distant past is not merely a rhetorical device. The
decree does not directly penalize present-day Gauls for the deeds of
their "forefathers," as the "opposition" would have it – but it certainly
gives preference to some of them on precisely these grounds. The
Roman state chose to remember the Aedui, selectively, as long-
standing "allies and brothers of the Roman people," rather than as
comparatively recent rebels (under Tiberius). And yet even the more
distant historical record of that group was not unblemished from the
Roman point of view. They, too, could be charged with having fought
the deified Julius and, indeed, with treachery and ingratitude: for
having enjoyed the status of "allies and brothers" for decades – a tale
well known to every reader of Caesar's "Gallic War" – they finally
joined Vercingetorix in 52 B.C.E. (admittedly, without much enthusiasm).

One would have dearly liked to know whether ancient history in
the full sense – Rome captured by the Gauls, Juno's geese and all that
– which is prominent in Tacitus' account (of both the arguments in the
imperial council and the senatorial speech) really played a part in this
debate. Tacitus has been criticized for artificially introducing this
"hoary and time-dishonoured bogy put up to scare us by those Romans
who disliked the Gauls" (Wellesley 1954, 30; Griffin 1982, 410:
"added to discredit the opposition").[14] Whether or not they were raised
on this particular occasion, such "arguments" against Gauls were
certainly voiced from time to time; Cicero, trying to impeach the
credibility of Gallic witnesses in a forensic speech, calls Gauls "an
arrogant and faithless people [...] the true descendants of those who
burned down the Capitol."[15]

---

14   Miller 1956, 311, analyzing the structure of the argument in both texts, remarks
      that the reference to the capture of Rome by the Gauls "may just possibly come
      from the original speech" in the missing portion. Contra Griffin 1982, 406,
      n. 11.
15   Cic. *Font.* 36. Cf. *Luc.* 1. 254. For a parody of Claudius' generosity in enfran-
      chising provincials (including Gauls) see Sen. *Apocol.* 3.2; 6.1; cf. Sen. *De Ben.*
      6.19.2. On Roman attitudes to Gauls see Isaac 2004, 411–26. A hostile tradition

The Emperor's speech, in the historian's version, deals with history and identity in the same breath: it passes from the general history of the Gauls of Gallia Comata to the cultural identity of the particular Gallic notables who are asking for the privilege of starting a senatorial career:

> And yet, if you survey the whole of our wars, not one was finished within a shorter period than that against the Gauls: thenceforward there has been a continuous and loyal peace. Now that customs, culture and the ties of marriage have blended them with ourselves (*iam moribus artibus adfinitatibus nostris mixti*), let them bring among us their gold and their riches instead of retaining them beyond the pale.

A superficial reader of the passage may well get the impression that "they" – the implied subject of the second sentence (*mixti* […] *habeant*) are identical with "the Gauls" in the first one. In fact, a group of Gallic chieftains, already holding Roman citizenship for a long time (*pridem*; note also what Claudius says about their family ties with "us"), and thus, inevitably, Romanized in large measure, were asking for the privilege of holding senatorial offices.[16] Legally and to a large extent culturally, they were already "us" (*nostri*) rather than "them" (otherwise they could have no legal marriage ties with Romans "proper"). Yet, just as the opponents of the measure cast the history of Gallic wars against Rome in their teeth, the Emperor chooses to give them credit, rhetorically, for Gaul's good behavior since its conquest – or rather, for his own somewhat sanitized version of this behavior. Of course, for Claudius (and all those for whom he is made to speak here) history is not the decisive consideration. But a much stronger rhetoric-

---

accused Caesar of bringing Gauls from the newly conquered province into the Senate – Suet. *Iul.* 76.3; 80.2. But these "'Gallic' senators might be thoroughly Romanized Cisalpines" – Rawson 1994, 445.

16   Anyone coming from a non-senatorial family needed an Emperor's permission (*latus clavus*) for this. The Emperor could have accepted the petition and granted this privilege to the notables in question, as to any Roman citizen, without reference to the Senate. He chose to avail himself of the Senate's support – because of the importance of the issue, and perhaps because of the strength of the opposition.

al separation between distant past and present-day political decisions might have been expected in this context.

The decisive argument in favor of admitting these men into the Senate is the present-day level of their cultural and social integration: "now that customs, culture and the ties of marriage have blended them with ourselves (*iam moribus artibus adfinitatibus nostris mixti*)." Their legal status as Roman citizens is taken for granted. Together with their wealth, mentioned explicitly, and their free birth (we are talking about *primores*), this status constituted, in the usual practice of the Principate, sufficient grounds for granting a man of non-senatorial birth the imperial permission to stand for senatorial office. There was no formal impediment to acceding to their petition even without a senatorial decree; but the informal one – their social status as not-quite-Romans-in-the-full-sense-of-the-term – was powerful enough to necessitate the debate in the first place. The Roman "customs and culture" already adopted by the Gallic notables must have included taking a Roman name, which every Roman citizen bore, and, though this is not said in so many words, speaking Latin – as well as, no doubt, dressing and, generally, living and behaving in a civilized Roman way,[17] which will have been conducive to the establishment of the ties of marriage "with us."

The connection between the spread of Roman citizenship – first in Italy, and then, since Caesar, in the provinces – and cultural Romanization (to which the adoption of Latin was naturally pivotal) was a complicated one. No formal criteria were ever established, and there was much pragmatic flexibility in the way the Romans went about this business. Usually, however, the grant of citizenship was not just a reward for loyalty to the Roman state (and, since Caesar, to its ruler), but an acknowledgment of the fact that a certain degree of Romanization had already taken place. Once granted, citizenship was a powerful engine for carrying this process further. By the end of the Republic, Italy had been thoroughly Romanized in this way. Caesar

---

17   At least occasionally – for these men, according to Tacitus, still belonged to their "federated" – i.e. non-Roman – communities, and thus, in a sense, to two worlds.

was more cautious than is usually admitted, and followed the policy [...] of inserting a preparatory period of Latin status before the elevation of purely foreign communities to the full citizenship. The condition for a grant of Latin rights appears to have been the possession of a certain degree of Latin and Roman culture (Sherwin-White 1973, 233; cf. Strabo 3.151C).

Inevitably, with the ever wider spread of Roman citizenship under the Principate "its connection with Latin culture is gradually loosened" (Sherwin-White 1973, 222) – in the sense that Latin culture ceased to be a precondition for the bestowal of citizenship. But the citizenship did not cease to engender cultural Romanization. The final result would eventually be twofold: the bestowal of Roman citizenship on the entire free population of the Empire, and a far-reaching Latinization of its Western part (while in the Roman East the Greek language and culture held their ground).

Claudius is known to have deprived a recently enfranchised Greek of his Roman citizenship when it turned out that he could not speak Latin, holding, according to Dio, that "it was not proper for a man to be a Roman who had no knowledge of the Roman tongue" (60.17.4; cf. Suet. *Claud.* 16.2). It is clear (also from this same Dio passage) that this policy was not consistently applied: "Claudius was not putting into effect a general policy, but acting *ad hoc* on a whim." Nevertheless, "there is an attitude embodied in that whim." Generally, though there was no "official policy demand[ing] that Roman citizens should speak Latin [...] there are occasional signs of an informal ex-pectation that possessors of the *civitas* should know the language" (Adams 2003, 562).[18]

In the present case, "customs and culture" are adduced not as a reason for granting citizenship but in justification of making the people in question a fully-fledged part of the Roman elite. It is im-portant to bear in mind that this elite was not a closed caste. According to the ideology and practice of the Roman state, the Senate was open (principally through the election to senatorial magistracies) to "new-comers" – those not belonging to old senatorial families who were yet

---

18 See there 562–71 on "Latin as a language of power" and 599–608 on Latin in the Roman army. Cf. Dio 57.15.3 and Suet. *Tib.* 71 on Tiberius refusing to allow a centurion to speak Greek in the Senate.

sufficiently well-off freeborn citizens. Although the Emperor's permission was now needed for a person of non-senatorial origin to start a senatorial career, the imperial Senate was actually more representative of the higher social strata in Italy (and eventually, in the provinces) than the Republican one. To say that a whole category of citizens, defined by geography and descent, should be permanently debarred from holding offices of state was more than just an act of social exclusion: it amounted to a refusal to regard them as truly and fully Roman. In the words of the opponents, "Leave them by all means to enjoy the title of citizens; but the insignia of senators, the glories of the magistrates – these they must not vulgarize." For the opponents, the Gallic notables could never become part of "us," despite their citizenship: the weight of history – that is to say, their descent – stood in the way.

For Claudius, cultural and social integration – as well as the interests of the state – rather than past feuds, are to decide the issue. The Gallic notables were now Romans in the full sense, entitled to have this fact officially recognized – not merely, it should be noted, due to the legal fact of their citizenship, but because they have indeed become, culturally and socially, part of "us." A vestige of the distinction between "us" and "them" is still preserved in the Emperor's own words (in the historian's version), when he speaks of "their" ties of marriage with "us" (*adfinitatibus nostris mixti*), although in strict law, of course, the Gallic notables had been part of "us" since the day they were granted Roman citizenship. A clear impression is given that the passage from acquiring the legal status of a Roman to becoming a Roman in the full sense should be neither automatic, nor effortless, nor too rapid.[19] In the authentic speech, this impression is further strengthened.[20]

---

19   See Sherwin-White 1973, 240–1, on the limited scope of the actual recruitment of provincial senators under Claudius.

20   "The way that Valerius Asiaticus is reproached for having held the consulship before his native town of Vienne had attained full citizenship implies a belief in a gradual progression from enfranchisement to office holding" – Griffin 1982, 410 (with reference to II 15–17). Of course, this remark is strongly colored by the Emperor's hostility to the (recently executed) man. But the speech is

Roman civilization was famously characterized, to a remarkable degree, by a belief in the power of legal procedures and legal fictions to shape and change identity – whether in the matter of granting citizenship or "Latin rights" to non-Romans and non-Latins, or of the manumission of slaves (who also became citizens, adopting their former master's family name),.or of adoptions. But the legal procedure of enfranchisement, in and of itself, was not the whole story, as far as Roman identity, in the full sense, was concerned. It would be interesting to know whether the Gallic chieftains in question had already started adopting not just Roman laws and customs, language and names, but historical consciousness as well, regarding Rome's past (and not just that of Roman Gaul) as in some sense their own. But it is certain that the spread of Roman citizenship beyond Italy would eventually make Rome's history "an adopted past" of many people throughout the Empire.

Though Tacitus fails to report it, Claudius' own speech concedes, implicitly but unmistakably, that an Italian senator is in principle preferable:

> What then? Is not an Italian senator better (*potior est*) than a provincial one? When I come to deal with this part of my censorship, I shall then show you by my actions what I feel on this matter. But I think that not even provincials should be excluded, if only they can ornament the Senate House (*sed ne provinciales quidem, si modo ornare curiam poterint, reiciendos puto*) (II 5–9).

This is a nod to history and tradition – and to the powerful vested interests appealing to history and tradition (those who spoke in the name of "the poor senator who came from Latium"[21] in danger of being "submerged by those opulent persons" from Gaul). A traditional attitude enjoys the advantage of standing in no need of rational justification. But if one ventures to reconstruct the reasons for the Emperor's

generally more conservative and less open to provincials than the historian's rendering of it – see text.

21   Cf. Juvenile's Third Satire, probably written in the early second century, for a (satirically exaggerated) outburst of resentment against the power of rich and vulgar foreign-born people on the part of a poor authentic Roman from Rome (84–5). It is clear that many of the foreigners (principally Greeks) who have allegedly swamped the city are by now citizens and men of rank (114–20).

acceptance of this preference, they are perhaps best understood as cultural and social: an average Italian can be safely assumed to be more thoroughly and indisputably Roman in this full sense than a "newcomer" from the provinces.

Italy, at any rate, still enjoys a preference. But what is Italy? The borders of Italy (and thus of Italian descent) are not quite an "objective fact." Claudius (returning to the historian's account) recalls that in their present shape they are the result of a political decision: "Finally Italy itself was extended to the Alps, in order that not individuals merely but countries and peoples should form one body under the name of the Romans." Anyone originating from northern Italy was thus, naturally, a (potential) "Italian senator" for the purpose of this preference. Not so for the "opposition": they still speak of the appearance of "Venetians and Insurbians" (who surely stand for all the communities beyond the Po enfranchised by Caesar) in the Senate House, which they have allegedly "taken by storm," as a foreign invasion.

The whole debate is about how "we" – the Romans – should relate to "them": whether, and on what conditions, "they" should be accepted as part of "us." The Emperor's answer to the historical argument against the Gauls is to remind his audience of another well-known piece of ancient history: "We" have fought the Italic peoples – Volscians and Aequians, Tuscans (Etruscans) and Samnites, and have sometimes suffered ignominious defeats; this did not prevent "us" from enfranchising and integrating them. But, of course, as far as genealogy goes, "we" are actually "them": the Senate addressed by Claudius consisted overwhelmingly, if not wholly, of people whose ancestors, at some stage, fought Rome and were later enfranchised. This could hardly be otherwise if, as Claudius recalls, the tradition of giving citizenship to defeated enemies goes back to Romulus. The historian's rendering of the speech starts with the reminder of the foreign (once hostile) origin of the Claudian and Julian clans; the second passage of Lyons' Tablet recalls the foreign origin of some of Rome's kings (also mentioned by Tacitus). The names of the peoples mentioned in Tacitus' version include those enfranchised long before all Italy south of the Po received the citizenship in the 80s B.C.E. Arpinum, the hometown of Marius and Cicero, which had enjoyed partial citizenship since the fourth century and full citizenship (with voting rights) since 188 B.C.E., was originally Volscian. But Claudius, unsurprisingly, does not point to the absurdity of "us" – i.e. the descendants of Volscians and Etruscans (or at best, Sabines) – rejecting Roman citizens from Gaul because of Gauls' past wars against Rome. Instead, he speaks of the wisdom of "our" Roman ancestors, who strengthened Rome by enfranchising defeated foes.

Culturally, the senators who listened to Claudius were descendants of those who had fought on Rome's side in all her wars since the foundation of the city. This "cultural descent" is an important part of their identity, and both the Emperor and the "opposition" expect their behavior in the present to be influenced by it (whether by drawing the right lessons from "our" history or by carrying on, in some sense, "our" ancient feud with "them," the Gauls). But there was no secret at all about the fact that genealogically, the senators were in fact descendants of those who, at one time or another, fought Rome (naturally, those defeated and enfranchised would then go on to fight Rome's other enemies). People knew not just Rome's history, but the history of their families, and of their local "homelands."[22] The Etruscan (allegedly royal) roots of Maecenas, Augustus' powerful friend, were flaunted rather than suppressed – they were not considered as making him any less a Roman.

Roman identity was, then, more than simply a legal status. It was a collective identity – a notion of "us" – inseparably connected with the Roman state, with a strong cultural content and, as part of it, a shared (often "adopted") past. This is what today we call a national identity.

It is therefore not necessarily much more anachronistic to call the Romanized Italy of the late Republic a "nation-state" than to call it a state – using a political term than would not be coined until many centuries later. Under the rule of the Emperors, with massive grants of Roman citizenship to non-Italians, "congruence of culture and polity" could not in the long run be fully maintained (especially in the East). But the connection between the Roman polity and the Roman culture – including Roman historical memory – was not severed. The sharp

---

22   Cf. Cicero's famous passage on the *duae patriae* of every Roman of municipal origin: his local community, and the Roman state – *Leg.* 2.2.5.

distinction between "us" and "them" within the Empire became increasingly meaningless as Roman citizenship spread throughout its length and breadth, and non-Italian Emperors came to rule it. A complicated mixture and hierarchy of identities and memories emerged. It included a sufficiently strong Roman element to enable the Empire to command widespread loyalty outside Italy – notably, in Gaul (Sherwin-White 1973, 397–468). Many Romans of Gallic descent must have found it as natural to call the defenders of the Capitol in the fourth century B.C.E. "our ancestors" as French schoolchildren of non-Gallic origin have found it natural to speak of "our ancestors the Gauls."

Bibliography

Adams, J. N. 2003. *Bilingualism and the Latin Language*. Cambridge: Cambridge University Press.

Braund, D. C. 1985. *Augustus to Nero: A Sourcebook on Roman History, 31 BC–AD 68*. London/ Sydney: Croom Helm.

Gellner, E. 1983. *Nations and Nationalism*. Oxford: Blackwell.

Griffin, M. T. 1982. "The Lyons Tablet and Tacitean Hindsight." *Classical Quarterly* 32(2), 404–18.

Guibernau, M. and J. Hutchinson (eds). 2004. *History and National Destiny: Ethnosymbolism and Its Critics*. Oxford: Blackwell.

Isaac, B. 2004. *The Invention of Racism in Classical Antiquity*. Princeton/Oxford: Princeton University Press.

Mendels, D. 1997. *The Rise and Fall of Jewish Nationalism: Jewish and Christian Ethnicity in Ancient Palestine*, 2nd edition. Michigan/Cambridge, UK: William B. Eerdmans.

Miller, N. P. 1956. "The Claudian Tablet and Tacitus: A Reconsideration." *Rhein. Mus.* N.F. 99, 304–15.

Rawson, E. 1994. "Caesar: Civil War and Dictatorship." In *Cambridge Ancient History*, 2nd edition, vol. 9. Cambridge: Cambridge University Press, 424–67.

Sherwin-White, A. N. 1973. *Roman Citizenship*. Oxford: Oxford
    University Press.
Smith, A. D. 2000. *The Nation in History: Historiographical Debates
    about Ethnicity and Nationalism*. Hanover, N.H.: University of
    New England.
Syme, R. 1958. *Tacitus*, vols. 1 and 2. Oxford: Oxford University
    Press.
Vittinghoff, F. 1954. "Zur Rede des Kaisers Claudius über die
    Aufnahme von 'Galliern' in den römischen Senat." *Hermes* 82,
    348–72.
Wellesley, K. 1954. "Can You Trust Tacitus?" *Greece and Rome* 1,
    13–33.

Chapter 2

ARYE EDREI

Holocaust Memorial: A Paradigm of Competing Memories in the Religious and Secular Societies in Israel[1]

The twenty-seventh of the month of Nissan marks the day of memorial for the Holocaust, in the Jewish world, both in Israel and in the Diaspora. This day was first declared a day of memorial by the Knesset, the legislature of the State of Israel, and subsequently adopted as law.[2] The religious community in Israel known as "religious Zionist" participates fully in this day, but also commemorates the Holocaust on the tenth of the month of Tevet, as the universal day for reciting *Kaddish* (the traditional Jewish memorial prayer). In contrast, the *haredi*[3] community does not recognize the twenty-seventh of Nissan or the tenth of Tevet as Holocaust Memorial Day. This raises the question as to whether the *haredim* have an alternative day of remembrance, or if they are trying to obliterate the memory of the Holocaust. If the latter, how is it that the group that perhaps justifiably considers itself to be the group most affected by the Holocaust (Michman 1996, 616–25; Friedman 1990) does not pay attention to preserving its memory? Religious thought relating to the Holocaust

---

1   The author expresses thanks to Menahem Blondheim, Benjamin Brown, Elihu Katz, Dan Laor, Doron Mendels and Steven Wilf for their enlightening comments and thoughts; to Kimmy Caplan for his help with the bibliography, to Stanly Peerless for the translation of this article and to the Cegla Institute at the Law Faculty of Tel-Aviv University for its support.

2   The process of establishing the date for Holocaust Memorial Day in the Knesset is described in detail by Stauber 2000, chapters 2 and 4: Baumel 1992, 65–9.

3   The *Ashkenazi* (European) ultra-Orthodox community.

has been the subject of a considerable amount of research,[4] but the religious approach to memorializing the Holocaust has been marginalized. In this article, I wish to address this issue. My claim is that the religious conception of remembrance, including its goals, its content and its form, is considerably different than the accepted concept and practice in secular Israeli society. I will try to establish the fundamental distinctions between these two approaches. An understanding of the religious conception is critical to appreciating the ways in which the Orthodox community memorializes the Holocaust. I will contend that, in fact, the *haredi* community intensively memorializes the Holocaust, a claim that I will support through an analysis of the writings of rabbis and religious thinkers, and through an examination of the activities of the *haredi* community during the first few decades after the Holocaust. The degree of connection to the past and the question, to which events in the past to connect, are important values questions in every society. Yet in contemporary Israeli society, they are the fundamental issue. The debate over Holocaust remembrance in Israel in the second half of the twentieth century reflects a deep, yet often obscure, debate over the essence of remembrance, and its appropriate format. This debate concretely demonstrates the degree to which memory stands at the center of the agenda of modern Israel and reflects the competing positions in defining the essence of the State of Israel. In this context, it is important to keep in mind that every memorial incorporates forgetting as well. I will, therefore, investigate not only what each faction wished to remember, but also what they wished to forget or eradicate, and why. In the final section of the article I will suggest a unique model of Jewish remembrance that has found expression throughout Jewish history. And I will propose that the controversy in Israel is not only over the content of remembrance, but also over the very validity of this traditional Jewish model in light of the establishment of the State of Israel.

---

4   See footnote 37 below. With regard to the important variations within *haredi* society, see Caplan 2002.

1 The Lack of a "Memorial Day" in *Haredi* Society

a *"Holocaust and Heroism" or "Destruction and Redemption":*
  the Difference between the Tenth of Tevet and the
  Twenty-Seventh of Nissan as Days of Memorial

The tenth of Tevet was established as a memorial day for the Holocaust by the Chief Rabbinate of Israel in December 1948.[5] The twenty-seventh of Nissan was initiated as "The Day of the Holocaust and the Rebellion in the Ghettos" by a Knesset decision in April 1951, but was adopted as law only in 1958.[6] In spite of the similarities between these two days (Friedlander 1990), there are significant differences between them that are important for understanding the two prototypes of remembrance that will be described further on. The arguments raised in the deliberation of the Knesset and its committees by several religious leaders against the establishment of the twenty-seventh of Nissan as a day of memorial demonstrate that the argument over the date really reflects a deeper controversy.[7]

The tenth of Tevet is a fast day that has been recognized in the Jewish calendar for generations as one of the days of mourning for the destruction of the Temple.[8] The very idea of establishing a Holocaust

---

5 Although deliberations on this date, and apparently the actual conducting of ceremonies, already began earlier. See Stauber, 2000, 52–6; Steinberg 1991; Shaviv 2001. Even before the end of the war, Rabbi Yitshak Herzog, then the Chief Rabbi of Israel, wrote a letter regarding the establishment of an eternal day of memorial for the victims of the Nazis. See Hertzog 1999, 435; Hertzog 1971 Responsum 61.

6 "Martyrs and Heroes Remembrance Day Law" 1958.

7 See the statements of MK Shlomo Yaacov Gross, Protocol of Knesset session 607, March 10, 1959, 1389; MK Yitshak Meir Levin, Protocol of Knesset session 249, March 13, 1961, 13; Yitshak Meir Levin, Protocol of Knesset session 229, May 18, 1953, 1337–9 (discussion of the Yad Vashem Law).

8 According to the account in 2 Kings 25:1–3, on that day, Nebuchadnezzar, the King of Babylonia, initiated the siege of Jerusalem that led to the destruction of the First Temple. According to rabbinic tradition, the tenth of Tevet is the day mentioned in Zachariah 8:19 as the "fast of the tenth." See *Tosefta Sotah* 6:10–11; *Sifri, Deuteronomy* 6:4 (Finkelstein edition), 51. On the establishment of

memorial day on a day that was already set as a day of mourning reflects a perspective that essentially views the modern-day tragedy within the context of Jewish history as part of a sequence of Jewish tragedies during the period of the exile. Furthermore, the prototype of this memorial – the imposition of a new tragedy on an existing memorial day and the use of fasting as an instrument of memorializing – is one that has existed and has been recognized in Jewish tradition for many generations.[9] Usually, destructions and tragedies worthy of

this day as a fast day see Moses Maimonides, *Mishneh Torah, Hilkhot Ta'aniyot* 5:1–2; Yosef Karo, *Shulhan Arukh, Orah Haim* 549:1.

9   The argument that the Holocaust should be viewed as a "destruction" that is part of the series of Jewish destructions and tragedies throughout history was raised explicitly by part of the religious leadership. See the sources cited by Stauber 2005, 55–8. Rabbi Yitshak Hutner, one of the leading spokesmen of the *haredi* community in the United States opposed the use of the term "holocaust" (*shoah*), favoring instead the term "destruction" (*hurban*). In his explanation, he insists on the importance of using the traditional terminology, claiming that the use of the expression "holocaust" cuts the event off from the series of destructions throughout the history of the exile. See Hutner 1997. On the importance that the religious community attaches to viewing the Holocaust as part of the series of Jewish destructions and tragedies throughout history, see Goldberg 1998, 163–7. Rabbi Moshe Feinstein also stated that "it [the Holocaust] is in the category of all of the decrees in this long exile." See Feinstein, 1996, 57:11. See below pp. 70–1, regarding this responsum. The contrary Orthodox position found expression in the statements of Rabbi Yehuda Amital, one of the notable leaders of the religious Zionist community in the last generation, and of Rabbi Menahem Kasher, one of the most prolific writers in the *haredi* community, who is largely forgotten because his ideas did not always conform to accepted *haredi* positions. Rabbi Amital, himself a Holocaust survivor, wrote: "If a person doesn't feel that the *Book of Lamentations* and the elegies pale in contrast to the Holocaust – it means ignoring the Holocaust" (Maya 2002, 118). The following statement of Rabbi Kasher, also a Holocaust survivor, is recorded by Rabbi Yisrael Rosen from his recollection of a public address: "I am no longer able to say the elegies on Tisha B'Av. They do not speak to me after the awesome holocaust in Europe. It is impossible to cry over the martyrs of Meinz, Worms, and Spira, and to forget and debase the cry of the blood of our brothers from Auschwitz, Meidanik, and Treblinka" (Rosen 2000). Emil Fackenheim also insisted on the uniqueness of the Holocaust in relation to the other tragedies in Jewish history. See Fackenheim 1988. Kimmy Caplan discussed the interesting changes that took place in *haredi* society with regard to the Holocaust, as demonstrated by the penetration of the term "holocaust" in *haredi*

remembering were observed on the ninth of Av, the date that traditionally marks the destruction of both temples. One who studies the book of elegies for the ninth of Av will find not only lamentations for the destruction of the first and second temples, but also poems memorializing victims of the crusades, the Spanish expulsion and other tragedies.[10] In contrast, the twenty-seventh of Nissan has no significance in the traditional Jewish calendar. It was chosen because of its connection to the outbreak of the Warsaw Ghetto uprising.[11] The significance of this connection was clear from the very declaration of this day as a Holocaust memorial day: "The first Knesset declares and establishes the twenty-seventh of Nissan as an annual Day of the Holocaust and the Rebellion in the Ghettos – an eternal day of memorial for the House of Israel."[12] The deliberations over the name

parlance. See Caplan 2002 and Schwartz 1986. The recent changes in *haredi* society with regard to the Holocaust are demonstrated in Farbstein 2002. With regard to the use of the term "holocaust," she writes in an apologetic manner: "The emphasis on the connection between Jewish existence before the Holocaust and during the Holocaust is part of the general worldview that sees the destruction of European Jewry as part of the flow of Jewish history, as a terrible link in the ongoing chain of destruction that began with the destruction of the Temple. The use of the term 'holocaust' does not imply that it is an anomalous and unique event in Jewish history, but rather to emphasize the awesome proportions of this tragedy" (Farbstein 2002, 9).

10   On the structure of history in the rabbinic perspective see Yerushalmi 1982, 25. On days of memorial and the imposition of other events on these days see Yerushalmi 1982, 40–1 and footnote 19. An interesting question is why the rabbinic council preferred the tenth of Tevet to the ninth of Av. See Steinberg 1990. Perhaps the ninth of Av was considered too congested to attach to it an event of the proportions of the Holocaust. It is interesting that the idea of remembering the Holocaust on the ninth of Av was already raised at Yad Vashem in 1946. See Stauber 2000, 50. In the latter part of the 1970s, Prime Minister Menachem Begin revisited this proposal.

11   For a comprehensive and orderly discussion of the history of establishing the date see Stauber 2000, 56–60. See also, Ben Amos 1999; On the gap between tenth of Tevet and the twenty-seventh of Nissan See also Steinberg 1990 and 1991.

12   The Protocol of the Knesset, April 12, 1951. The Knesset decision was not adopted as law and had little impact. Only in 1958 was the decision adopted as law: "Martyrs and Heroes Remembrance Day Law." The law includes explicit guidelines as to how the Holocaust should be memorialized.

of the day clearly reflect the centrality of "heroism" in the creation of a Holocaust memorial,[13] and the difficulty that it raised for a portion of the religious community.[14] Similarly, it appears that the connection of the twenty-seventh of Nissan is not only to the ghetto uprising but also to Israel Independence Day, which falls one week later, reflecting a clear perspective that views the establishment of the State of Israel and of Jewish self-defense as a "response" to the Holocaust.[15]

In comparing the two approaches to Holocaust memorial, geographical location also has significance. The place chosen by the Chief Rabbinate for a Holocaust memorial was Mount Zion in Jerusalem,

13   See Stauber 2000. A fascinating detail in this regard is the competition over the name of the day of memorial until the name was established as the "Martyrs and Heroes Remembrance Day Law" in 1958. To that point, the day of memorial on the twenty-seventh of Nissan was called by a number of names by Yad Vashem, such as "The Day of the Ghetto Uprising" and "The Day of Memorial of the Holocaust and the Rebellion." See idem. This was true even though the phrase "Holocaust and Heroism" was set already in the "Martyrs and Heroes Commemoration (Yad Va-Shem) Law" in 1953. The argument appeared again explicitly in later Knesset deliberations. See the Protocol of the Knesset, session 262, March 27, 1961, 1505; see also the statement of Yitshak Zuckerman cited by Stauber 2000, 140.

14   In 1951, the Chief Rabbinate published a "prayer book" in advance of the twenty-seventh of Nissan entitled "Prayer Book for the Twenty-Seventh of Nissan – The Day of Holocaust and Mourning"! The prayer book can be found in Baumel 1992, 155. The benefit of the expression "Holocaust and Heroism" as opposed to the name originally adopted ("Holocaust and the Ghetto Uprising") is that it leaves the expression "heroism" open for interpretation. The religious Zionists could interpret it in the traditional Jewish sense as martyrdom to sanctify the name of God. There were those who opposed this name for that very reason, so that it not be given that interpretation. See the statement of MK Rabbi M. Nurock of the National Religious Party and the opposing stance of MK Emma Talmi of the left wing Mapam party in the deliberation on the law in the Knesset plenary in the Protocol of the Knesset, session 607, March 10, 1959, 386.

15   The interior minister, Ben Yehudah, who introduced the legislation for a Holocaust memorial day, stated as follows in the deliberations: "This proposal is worded in light of another law that was adopted previously by the Knesset in the context of another event that is worthy of being etched in the memory of our people – Israel Independence Day" (Protocol of the Knesset from 10 March, 1959, 1385).

near the traditional burial site of King David.[16] There is no doubt that Friedlander is correct in asserting that the selection of this site derived from the perspective that the State of Israel is the first stage of messianic redemption. The setting establishes a connection between the Holocaust and the redemption,[17] which is symbolized by the "Messiah, the son of David." In addition, Mount Zion and King David are associated not only with the future redemption but also with the Temple that was destroyed. As such, this placement creates an unequivocal link between the Holocaust and the essence of ancient Jewish history.[18] In contrast, the placement of Yad Vashem, the official Holocaust memorial, opposite Mount Herzl, expresses the connection between holocaust and rebirth. Both the twenty-seventh of Nissan and the placement of Yad Vashem lack any connection to Jewish tradition. Looking toward a new Jewish future characterized by Jewish independence and self-defense, in contrast to the prototypical

16   Mount Zion was transferred to the authority of the Ministry of Religion immediately after it was liberated in 1948. Minister Y. L. Maimon appointed the Director General, S. Z. Kahane, as the one responsible for the holy sites including Mount Zion. Rabbi Kahane was the son of the last rabbi of Warsaw and was highly motivated to create a memorial for the Holocaust, an effort in which he was involved already in 1946. He therefore initiated the move to turn Mount Zion into a Holocaust memorial. In 1949, the ashes of victims of the Holocaust were brought to Israel and buried on Mount Zion, a point that contributed to turning the site into a Holocaust memorial. Indeed, the Hall of the Communities on Mount Zion was for many years the focal point for conducting prayers and activities to memorialize the Holocaust, and served as a meeting place for survivors on various memorial days for particular communities. See Stauber 2000, 136.

17   See *Agadat ha-Sorfim ba-Esh*, which was written by Rabbi Kahane, the founder of the site (mentioned in the previous note), at http://moreshet.co.il/kahane/ tavnit2.

18   In those years, Jerusalem was divided and Mount Zion was the closest place from which to see the Temple Mount, the site of the destroyed Temple. Many Jews came there, particularly on holidays, to see the Temple Mount, to pray and to perform an act of remembrance for the commandment of the festival pilgrimages.

"exile Jew," they find in the ghetto uprising the historical anchor onto which the "new" Jew can grasp.[19]

The gap between the past and the future hovers between the tenth of Tevet and the twenty-seventh of Nissan – an attempt to create a memorial for the Holocaust that views it as part of the continuity of Jewish history versus an attempt to create a memorial that views it as a cataclysmic event representing the beginning of a radically new era in Jewish history. It is a gap between "holocaust and redemption" and "holocaust and heroism," between divine redemption and human strength, between the Davidic messiah and Herzl. It is a gap that pits tradition and continuity against rupture and change.

b   Haredi Opposition to Holocaust Memorial

While the religious Zionist community observes both of the official Holocaust memorial days, the *haredi* community, as mentioned earlier, observes neither. Neither day is mentioned in *haredi* journalism, in *haredi* synagogues or in *haredi* educational institutions. It is easy to understand *haredi* opposition to the twenty-seventh of Nissan, since it clearly has no connection to Jewish tradition.[20] Why, however, do the *haredim* reject the tenth of Tevet, which reflects a traditional approach to memorializing. Even if we assume that the opposition is based on the "innovation" of imposing the Holocaust on the tenth of Tevet rather than on the ninth of Av, or on a challenge to the authority of the Chief Rabbinate of Israel, we are left with the compelling question of why the *haredi* community did not establish an alternative date to remember the Holocaust. The liturgy – the elegies of Tisha

19   For comprehensive research on the discussion regarding the relationship between the Holocaust and the rebirth of the State of Israel, see Gorny 2003.

20   In 1983–5, two *haredi* educators in the United States contributed articles to *The Jewish Observer* that constituted a reformulation and finalization of Rabbi Hutner's article in 1977. These articles summarized the points of opposition to the twenty-seventh of Nissan: that no mourning is permitted in the month of Nissan, that the date emphasizes the physical heroism aspect rather than the spiritual and that it hints at a connection to Israel Independence Day. See Baumel 1992, 81.

B'Av and other penitential poems – is recognized in the *haredi* community as a medium for preserving collective Jewish memory (Yeruṣhalmi 1982, 43–5). Why, then, did the Holocaust not find expression, at least, in the elegies of the ninth of Av?

In fact, quite a few elegies were written on the Holocaust. The first was apparently the well-known liturgical poem *"Eli, Eli, Nafshi Bekhi"* (Oh God, my God, my soul cries), which was written by Yehudah Leib Bialer in Warsaw in 1948 (Bialer 1957, 45). In addition, notable rabbinic figures composed elegies on the Holocaust, including Rabbi Shmuel Wazner, one of the important rabbis in the Bnei Brak community, and the Rebbe of Bobov, Rabbi Moshe Halberstam.[21] Nevertheless, these works were not included in the elegies of Tisha B'Av, nor did they find their way into printed prayer books. In places where these elegies were recited, they were read from printed sheets that were distributed among the congregation. Even the significant pressure from lay and rabbinic leaders to have them included in published prayer books was rebuffed.[22] It seems to me that the most important factor that prevented the inclusion of these works in prayer books was that a number of notable rabbis expressed explicit and forceful opposition to the recitation of elegies on Tisha B'Av in memory of the Holocaust. The stature of the rabbis who took an oppositional stance was much greater than those who supported the formal adoption of these elegies. Those who expressed their op-

21   The most complete collection of elegies written for the holocaust can be found in Mayer 2002.
22   On the attempts of Rabbi M. Kasher see Rosen 2000. On the pressure exercised by Uri Haim Lifschitz in the mid-1970s, see Mayer 2002. On the pressure exerted by Pinchas Hertzka and his correspondence on the matter see Hertzka 1984. On requests to the Hazon Ish to establish a memorial day for the Holocaust, see Brown 2003, 429–31. On the discomfort with the lack of a process of memorial and mourning for the Holocaust see Schwartz 1986 (esp. 282–9). In this context, it is important as well to see the comments of the Rebbe of Slonim, who writes: "Should we not fear that God will, heaven forbid, take revenge on the great scholars and enlighteners of Israel who denied tens of thousands of victims a proper eulogy?" See Brazovsky 1987, 15–16. For a summary of the arguments that appear in halakhic literature against the establishment of a process of mourning and memorial for the Holocaust see Mayer 2002, 10–11, although his approach is to try to prove the opposite.

position included some leading rabbis: Rabbi Avraham Yeshayahu Karlitz, the Hazon Ish (Karelitz 1939, 1: 96); Rabbi Yitshak Zev Soloveitchik, the Brisker Rav in Jerusalem (Sternbuch 1989, #721); and Rabbi Menachem Shach, head of the Ponovitz Yehiva (Schwartz 1986, 288); also prominent Chassidic leaders: Rabbi Menachem Mendel Schneerson, the Rebbe of Lubavitch;[23] and Rabbi Yekutiel Yehudah Halberstam, the Rebbe of Klausenberg (Mayer 2002); and even Rabbi Joseph B. Soloveitchik, the unquestioned leader of modern Orthodoxy in America (Arazi 1972). These rabbis were without a doubt the most influential personalities in the Orthodox world in both Israel and the United States in the latter half of the twentieth century. Since they were from the generation of Holocaust survivors, their authority on this issue had additional weight. Many of them experienced the horrors of the Holocaust and lost their families. For example, Rabbi Yitshak Zev Soloveitchik lost his wife and four children, and the Rebbe of Klausenberg lost his wife and her eleven children. The opposition of these rabbis precluded any possibility that the attempt to include memorials to the Holocaust among the elegies of the ninth of Av, and even more so those of the tenth of Tevet, would succeed. This opposition is surprising and begs for explanation.

It was not only the recitation of elegies in memory of the Holocaust that was rejected. Other methods of memorializing – such as the establishment of an eternal day of memorial, a collective period of *shiva*, etc. – that were proposed both by Holocaust survivors and by rabbis who had a particular affinity to this issue were also unable to overcome the opposition of the rabbinic leadership.[24] As a result, no

---

23   See Rosen 2002. Rabbi Jacob Hecht, one of the prominent figures in the Chabad movement, explains his opposition to the composition of a new elegy for the Holocaust. Among other arguments, he claims: "We have enough elegies. [...] What we need now is healthy Jews, both physically and emotionally whole, who conduct their lives and their households according to the Torah, happy to do the will of their creator [...]." (cited in Baumel 1992, 42). See also on the Chabad Internet site, *The Laws of Tisha B'Av* by Rabbi Y. Ginzberg.

24   See note 21. The discomfort of the *haredi* community with regard to the lack of a memorial day for the Holocaust is evident in Schwartz 1986. See also Weinberg 1998, vol. 2, section 31: "In my opinion, it is appropriate to establish a day of memorial for the rabbis and the martyrs who were killed, slaughtered,

traditional memorial was established or organized by the *haredi* community.[25]

The nature of the rabbinic opposition to Holocaust memorial is even more surprising when we consider that during the period that Jews lived in Europe, they established a number of memorial days in the Jewish calendar on which were observed the same traditional practices of mourning as those practiced on days of mourning for the destruction of the Temple. Thus, for example, the twentieth of Sivan was observed as a day of prayer and public fasting until the outbreak of the Holocaust. This day was established by Rabbeinu Tam in memory of those who perished in the Edict of Bloish in 1171.[26] On this same date in 1648, the Nemerov pogroms took place, in which thousands of Jews were killed by the troops of Bogdan Chmielniczki. In 1650, the date was established by the Council of the Four Lands as a day of memorial for the victims of the Nemerov Decrees (Halperin 1945, 78). Once again, a new day of memorial was imposed on an

and burned to sanctify the name of God, and to remember the souls of these martyrs on this day."

25 It is interesting to note in this context the more popular manner in which memorials were created in the course of time without the approval of the great religious authorities. See, for example, the article by Baumel 1995, who surveys the various ways that individuals and groups chose to memorialize the Holocaust in a private, unofficial manner. One of the methods was the publication of memorial volumes for communities, similar to the *Memoir Bukh* (Memory book) that was the custom in the Middle Ages. Baumel surveys 300 volumes of this sort.

26 *Sefer Hazekhirah* (Memorial volume) written by Rabbi Ephraim of Narvonne is quoted in Haberman 1997, 126: "On Wednesday, the twentieth of Sivan 4931 [=1171], all of the communities in France, distant counties, and the Rhine accepted upon themselves a day of eulogizing and fasting on their own accord and in fulfillment of the directive of Rabbeinu Yaacov ben Harav R. Meir (Rabbeinu Tam), who wrote correspondence about it and informed them that it would be appropriate to establish a universal fast day for all of our people, that would be greater than the fast day of Tzom Gedaliah ben Ahikam, for 'it is a day of atonement.' This is the language of our master, and so he wrote, and it is correct, and so it has been accepted by the Jews. The liturgical poem '*Hatanu Tsureinu*' is based on this." See Urbach 1980, 111–12. On this entire matter see also Yerushalmi 1982, 48.

existing day, "a day on which the troubles multiplied."[27] The authority
of the rabbis to establish memorial days was clearly recognized, not
only in practice, but also in Jewish legal literature. Thus, for example,
Rabbi Yoel Sirkus wrote:

> The positive commandment [of reciting prayers at times of need] includes a
> commandment to cry out and fast on days on which decrees were issued and
> great troubles occurred, even after the trouble has passed. This is also a
> component of repentance, that all should know that these horrible events took
> place because of their inappropriate behavior.[28]

The "Magen Avraham," one of the prominent commentators on the
Shulhan Arukh who himself experienced the Chmielniczki pogroms,
writes of the custom to fast, to afflict oneself, and to say penitential
prayers that were composed to memorialize the Decrees of 1648–9:

> On Friday of the week in which the Torah portion of *Hukkat* is read, some
> individuals fast because on that day, twenty wagons filled with holy books were
> burned in France [...] and also in the year 1648, two large communities were
> destroyed on the same day as recorded in the penitential prayer composed by
> the *Siftei Kohen*. There is also a custom to fast on the twentieth of Sivan in the
> entire Kingdom of Poland.[29]

---

27   It is an interesting fact that at the beginning of the discussion on Holocaust
     memorial, the twentieth of Sivan was suggested as an appropriate day by Dr.
     Yom Tov Levinsky. See Stauber 2000, 50–2. Similarly, it is a fascinating fact in
     this context that, because of the censor, Haim Nahman Bialik called his essay
     on the Kishinev Pogroms in 1903 "*Masa Nemirov*" and only later changed it to
     "*Mi-gei Ha-harigah*" (From the Valley of Death).
28   The Bakh (one of the great Jewish legal authorities in Poland during the
     sixteenth and seventeenth centuries), *Tur, Orah Haim* 580.
29   Rabbi Avraham Avli Halevi Gumbiner (Poland, 1637–83), *Magen Avraham,
     Shulhan Arukh, Orah Haim*, 580:8; the *Siftei Kohen* mentioned here is the
     Shakh, Rabbi Shabtai Kohen (Lithuania, 1621–62), one of the important legal
     authorities, who also experienced the Chmielniczki pogroms and wrote elegies
     on the events. See also Rabbi David Halevi, *Taz* on *Shulhan Arukh, Orah Haim*,
     566:2.

Armed with these arguments and this tradition, many survivors turned to the rabbis to request the creation of a memorial for the Holocaust, but their request was refused.[30]

A *haredi* writer who addressed this issue, expressing criticism of the lack of a day of Holocaust memorial in *haredi* society was Rabbi Yoel Schwartz. In spite of the conspicuous criticism, he writes:

> Not all of the scholars of the generation agreed with the Hazon Ish on this matter (see, for example, the response of Rabbi Yehiel Weinberg, Responsa *Sridei Esh*, Vol. II, p. 53). Nevertheless, it is clearly understood that it is impossible to enact any enactment without the agreement of the greatest scholars of the generation. The very opposition of great scholars such as the Hazon Ish inherently nullifies any possibility of establishing a memorial day for the Holocaust (Schwartz 1986, 287).[31]

The Hazon Ish, Rabbi Avraham Yeshayahu Karlin, was the unquestioned leader of the *haredi* community in the 1940s and the early 1950s.[32] Schwartz's point was precisely correct: the opposition of the Hazon Ish silenced the discussion. His decisive stance prevented the entry of elegies for the Holocaust into the prayer book, the establishment of a day of Holocaust memorial, or any other traditionally accepted form of memorial. The Hazon Ish not only prevented memorial of the Holocaust in the modern Israeli fashion, he prevented any expression through the liturgy or other accepted forms of Jewish memorial. In response to a person who requested the establishment of a halakhically acceptable day of mourning for the Holocaust, the Hazon Ish wrote:

---

30   On the despair of Rabbi M. Kasher because of the refusal of the rabbis to cooperate with him in his attempt to establish elegies for the Holocaust on the ninth of Av see Rosen 2000.

31   Schwartz is one of the prolific writers in the *haredi* community, but his writings are not stereotypical. His reflective look at *haredi* society and his veiled criticism of the rabbis is an unusual phenomenon. See as well his discussion of the connection between Zionism and the Holocaust, 122–37. On Schwartz and his discussion of the Holocaust see Caplan 2002, 144–58.

32   On the central position of the Hazon Ish in fashioning the character of *haredi* orthodoxy in Israel see Brown 2002, 2003.

Halakhic matters are established by the Torah, where the fundamental principles are recorded in written form and are explained in the Oral Law. Even a prophet is not allowed to innovate something without some reliance on the Torah. Just as a failure to fulfill a commandment is an aberration, so too an addition beyond the commandments of the Torah is an aberration.

On this basis, one must ask a legal question of a scholar whether it is appropriate to observe seven days of mourning for the terrible troubles that we experienced. If we are obligated, we do not need confirmation. But if we are exempt, we must take care to observe the exemption, because it is the Torah that exempts us, and "to obey is more important than offering a sacrifice." The suggestion to gather, establish and do, decree, and fulfill is to deal flippantly, heaven forbid, with the foundation of Jewish law. It is appropriate to remove it from the agenda before it is raised.

So too, the establishment of a fast day for generations is considered a rabbinic commandment, which could only be done at the time that we still had prophecy. How can we be so brazen, a generation that should remain quiet, to consider establishing things for the generations. Such a suggestion testifies that we rebuff all of our sins and our lowliness, at a time when we are sullied with our sins and transgressions, poor and empty of Torah, and naked of commandments. Let us not make ourselves greater than we are. Let us examine our ways and repent. This is our obligation, as it is stated: "Is this the fast that I have chosen?" (Greinimann 1939, 111; Brown 2003, 426).

The words of the Hazon Ish reflect a total rejection of any idea relating to the creation of a memorial to the Holocaust. On the surface, the argument of opposition is anchored in the belief that our generation is not capable of innovating, and should not aspire to do so. Indeed, there is no doubt that in the modern period, there has been a great sensitivity in rabbinic circles to any innovation. Orthodox Judaism was built on opposition to the modern aspiration to reconstruct and innovate, and was therefore cautious of any innovation, even if it was halakhically legitimate and had a precedent (Samet 2005; Katz 1992). In the context of memorializing the Holocaust, this viewpoint found expression in the positions of other rabbis as well.[33]

---

33   It is possible that in the age of renewed Jewish sovereignty, this concern took on an added dimension. The addition of a special day to the Jewish calendar could have been seen as identification with the religious Zionists, who sought to initiate holidays relating to the Jewish state, such as Israel Independence Day, as religious holidays. Yet it is important to note that the fierce opposition of the Hazon Ish came to expression as early as 1945, when Chief Rabbi Herzog

For example, Rabbi Joseph B. Soloveitchik said with regard to adding an elegy for the Holocaust as follows: "Who in our generation can be arrogant enough to compose new prayers?" (Arazi 1972, 324). Rabbi Shach also gave explicit expression to this view in strongly opposing the recitation of elegies for the Holocaust on the ninth of Av: "This constitutes a breaking of boundaries and provides a precedent for those who wish to restructure and reform to utilize for justifying further reforms."[34]

Nevertheless, it seems to me that in spite of the validity of this reasoning, it is not sufficient or convincing enough, particularly given the awesome proportions of the Holocaust. The Hazon Ish, in his previously mentioned correspondence, deals directly with the aforementioned commandment to establish fast days in memory of the destruction. His response, that it "could only be done at the time that we still had prophecy," is both weak and unclear. It would seem that the opposite is the case, that the prophet might not innovate while the rabbis were entrusted with the power to issue enactments, particularly with regard to additions and stringencies as opposed to leniencies. In fact, the rabbis did so throughout the generations (Brown 2003, 428–9). In reality, in spite of the unquestioned status of the Hazon Ish, his position with regard to the Holocaust was subject to halakhic challenge by a Holocaust survivor who served as a rabbi in the United States, an individual whose stature was much below that of the Hazon Ish (Spitz 1980; Brown 2003, appendix 28: 195). This critique, and the fact that it received a respectable voice, is an unparalleled phenomenon. It is difficult to find another subject on which such a strong attack was waged against the opinion of the Hazon Ish. This fact strengthens the argument that the *haredi* community felt uncomfortable with the positions of its leaders. At the same time, this

---

proposed to organize a day of mourning or memorial for the Holocaust. See Brown 2003, 425.

34 Cited in Schwartz 1986, 288. See also the discussion of Rabbi Yissachar Goldstein, in Goldstein 1989 #40. Rabbi Goldstein was one of the radical *haredi* rabbis who waved the banner of opposition to innovation. Therefore, in his support for the recitation of elegies for the holocaust, he dealt explicitly with the problem of innovation. The concern with regard to innovation in this context has a unique and important quality.

reaction seemed to strengthen the resolve of the leadership, in spite of the criticism and the internal lack of comfort.

In reading the previously cited quote from the Hazon Ish, I also get the strong impression that the argument against innovation actually conceals the real reason for the ruling, which is not explicitly stated. First, the response is not an orderly halakhic discussion, characteristic of the Hazon Ish, and in fact, it relies on no halakhic sources.[35] In addition, the statements of the Hazon Ish are characterized by an undercurrent of denigration for the request to create a memorial for the Holocaust. One example is his use of the terminology "to gather, establish and do, decree, and fulfill." Similarly, the biblical verses that he quotes also imply a denigration of the very suggestion proposed.[36] Benjamin Brown, in his thesis on the Hazon Ish, suggests that the opposition of the Hazon Ish derived from the difficulty that the *haredi* community faced in dealing with the Holocaust on an ideological level. First, is the theological problem of how to explain God's involvement in the world in the face of such a great destruction of Jews. Second, is the problem of how to explain the failure of the great Torah scholars to help save their people, especially in light of accusations raised by the Zionists. Brown claims that the Hazon Ish, and many other rabbis, wished therefore "to lessen the memory of the Holocaust and the difficulties inherent in it" (Brown 2003, 432). Brown admits

35   In contrast, see the halakhic discourse of Chief Rabbi Herzog, Herzog 1999, 435.

36   The first verse is taken from 1 Samuel 15:22: "And Samuel said: 'Has the Lord as great delight in burnt-offerings and sacrifices, as in hearkening to the voice of the Lord? Behold, to obey is better than sacrifice, and to hearken than the fat of rams'." It expresses sarcasm toward those who believe that it is possible to atone for an external action by not following the true word of God. The second verse, quoted from Isaiah 58:5–7, also expresses sarcasm toward those who believe that fasting rather than good deeds are the essence: "Is such the fast that I have chosen? The day for a man to afflict his soul? Is it to bow down his head as a bulrush, and to spread sackcloth and ashes under him? Wilt thou call this a fast, and an acceptable day to the Lord? Is not this the fast that I have chosen? To loose the fetters of wickedness, to undo the bands of the yoke, and to let the oppressed go free, and that you break every yoke? Is it not to deal your bread to the hungry, and that you bring the poor that are cast out to your house?" See Brown 2003, 426–7.

that this sense remains only a speculation, since it does not emerge from the text, but he contends that it is not without foundation (Brown 2003). It seems to me that Brown's contention is unconvincing, at least as a sole argument. *Haredi* literature does in fact deal specifically with both of these issues in a broad manner. The theological problem is the classical issue of "the righteous person who suffers," which has been discussed at length by Jewish thinkers throughout the ages. The subject was also dealt with extensively in religious literature in the wake of the Holocaust.[37] The issue of the behavior of the great Torah scholars was also addressed, although to a lesser degree and somewhat apologetically (Caplan 2002; Friedman 1990).[38] Paradoxically, the *haredi* community viewed the Holocaust as a theological victory of sorts, since they utilized it to attack modernity after previously having been on the defensive against modernity before the Holocaust. The question posed was not "Where was God in the Holocaust?" but "Where was man"? – where were humanistic ethics and progress? (Schwartz 1986, 138–79). This viewpoint was even expressed by Rabbi Yehudah Amital, a modern Orthodox rabbi:

> Can we believe in mankind after what the Nazis and their collaborators did to our people? [...] It is not possible to have faith in man after this. Furthermore,

37   In reality, this subject was already addressed during the time of the Holocaust. The most famous person to deal with it was Rabbi Kalonymus Kalmish Schapiro, the Rebbe of Pietsesna who was one of the most influential spiritual leaders in the Warsaw Ghetto. See his book, written in the ghetto during the Holocaust and preserved and published after he perished, Kalonymus 1960; Farbstein 2002, 429; Michman 1996; Schweid 1996. On religious thought after the Holocaust, see Berkowitz 1973; Schweid 1996; Fackenheim 1989, 65. Fackenheim rails against any attempt to find a theological "explanation," a reason, or meaning for the Holocaust. Rather, he emphasizes in his writings the Jewish will to live, and the dedication of the Jews to their people and faith, which came to expression in the establishment of the State of Israel as a manifestation of commitment to the continuity of Jewish history. See Schwartz 1986, 37–137. A fascinating and important religious approach is that of Rabbi Yehudah Amital: Maya 2002, 116. See the analysis of Maya 2002, 42–50. On the position of Rabbi Tsvi Yehudah Kook, see Rosen-Zvi 2002. See also Berkowitz 1979; Fackenheim 1978.

38   Among other things, they launched an attack against the Zionists and their "collaboration" with the Nazis. See Porat 1994.

[…] they say that they believe in man and that is what gave them the power. We saw to what depths man is able to sink. Happy are we, and how good is our lot, that we believe in God (Maya 2002, 103; Wolf 1980, 192).

From the perspective of the believing Jew, the world of those who cast their fate with man and his ethics, with equal rights and the enlightened culture, was shattered.[39]

---

39   One explanation that arose for opposition to any type of memorial for the Holocaust was that the depth of the pain did not allow for it to be expressed in words. It is difficult to be convinced that this is not an apologetic argument. An excellent example of this position is the statement of the Rebbe of Slonim, whose positions will be discussed further on. With regard to the holding of prayer services or days of mourning and the like, he writes: "Not only that no memory remained of the martyrs, may God avenge their blood […] but that also after the Holocaust, their deaths and memory were not given an everlasting memorial. […] The heart languishes that after such a vast destruction, no memorial, eulogy or lament was established, as was done following the edicts of 1648–49 – the establishment of the 20th of Sivan as a day of fasting and penitential prayer – which was relatively a much smaller tragedy, or the way that elegies were written regarding the massacres in the Middle Ages and the Crusades […] When Jews sit on the floor on the ninth of Av and lament the destruction of the Temple, they pour out their hearts for these tragedies as well, and in this manner their memory is preserved among the Jewish people. How are the decrees of the Holocaust different from these other decrees? Without a doubt, it would be appropriate to establish for them a day of fasting and lamentation" (Brazovsky 1987, 15–16). The response of the Rebbe is that silence is preferable, in the same sense that "Aaron was silent" (after the deaths of his two sons – Leviticus 10:3), in that there are no words that are capable of expressing the depth of the pain.

2 The Function of Memory: Renewal of the Continuity of the Generations

a   Building or Rehabilitation: The Holocaust and the Jewish World in its Wake

I would like to suggest alternative reasons for the rabbinic opposition to memorializing the Holocaust, be it in the format accepted by Israeli society or even in the more accepted traditional formats discussed above. I will try to demonstrate that this difference of opinion reflects a gap between different objects of memory, that the past that the *haredi* leaders wished to preserve was fundamentally different than the past that Israeli society sought to preserve. This distinction mandates different formats of memorial. My claim is that both Holocaust memorial day and traditional days of memorial share the desire to remember the tragedy and to preserve consciousness of the destruction and its catastrophic implications. I argue that the rabbinic leaders did not want to memorialize the Holocaust in this manner. They wished to focus not on the destruction and the destroyers, but rather on the world that was destroyed. Following the Holocaust, the religious community felt that its world had been shattered, and that memorializing this destruction was a privilege that it could not grant itself at this stage. The existential imperative was to awaken memory of the world that was destroyed. Clearly, this memory focused on a very specific aspect of that world. In order to strengthen its importance, it was necessary to forget other aspects of the Jewish world that was destroyed. This approach does not differ in its perception of the enormity of the catastrophe but derives from the sense of urgency, that most energies had to be directed toward restoration and rebuilding. For this purpose, the function of remembering was to preserve the memory of the world before the destruction, so that its image could serve as the blueprint for the world that was to be built.

The State of Israel in its very essence sought to create a new Jewish world, a world that constituted a response to the Holocaust.

Certainly, the memory of the Holocaust served this goal. The Holocaust represented the great crisis, the turning point from the old order to the new. The memory of the Holocaust represented a paradigm of the suffering of the Jews in dispersion, the injustice that was perpetrated against them and their helplessness in the absence of a homeland of their own and the ability to protect themselves. Whether consciously or unconsciously, the Holocaust became a moral justification for the state. It validated the aspiration to create a new reality of Jewish sovereignty in which Jews would be able to defend themselves. In contrast, the rabbinic leadership wanted to rebuild the old world, to piece together the shards of the world that had been shattered, a world that was from their perspective a living and vibrant spiritual world.

While Israeli society wished in its memory of the Holocaust to emphasize the catastrophe as a contrast to the new Jewish world that was in the process of being built, *haredi* society wished to deemphasize the catastrophe in order to claim that it was rebuilding a world that was a direct continuation of the world that was. Each society sought in the collective memory a legitimization for the world that it wished to create – for Israeli society, the catastrophe and the helplessness; for *haredi* society, the memory of the rich spiritual world that was destroyed.

b   *"At Least Let Us Save Their Spirit": Memory of the Holocaust or Memory of the World That Was Destroyed*

Rabbi Shalom Noah Brazovsky (d. 2000), the Rebbe of Slonim, one of the important and prolific leaders and thinkers in the post-Holocaust Hassidic community, dealt a great deal in his writings and speeches with the Holocaust, its meaning, its implications, and the means of preserving its memory. A number of his writings and speeches on the subject were collected and published in one volume (Brazovsky 1987). The collection opens with an article entitled "Remember What

Amalek Did to You," which deals with the biblical commandment to remember:[40]

> And behold, it is distressing that from year to year what Amalek did to us in our generation is increasingly forgotten. Even if forgetting is a natural process, for such a horrible catastrophe the likes of which have not been witnessed since the creation of the world, the process of forgetting is much too rapid. This will lead to a new generation that will not know at all what took place there, and what great Jews lived in that generation (Brazovsky 1987, 7).

We see that the forgotten memory that so disturbed the Rebbe was the memory of "the great Jews who lived in that generation." The Rebbe continues and elaborates:

> The imperative to remember includes firstly what we find in the Torah – that a Jew is obligated to always remember what Amalek did. Amalek represents the evil forces of creation [...] at one time Amalek and Agag, at another time Haman or Hitler, may his name be blotted out [...] The intent is to delve into it and understand, but even if it is impossible to grasp,[41] you must remember what Amalek did *to you* [emphasis in the original text], what we lost. The fact that we lost in our generation a complete link in the chain of the generations, a complete generation lost, an especially great generation, with outstanding people and spiritual giants. The meaning of remembering includes an aspect of study – to follow in their footsteps and learn in their ways (ibid., 7–8).

The original interpretation of the Rebbe with regard to the biblical commandment to remember, "Remember what Amalek did to you," is that he transferred the emphasis from the word "Amalek" to

40   Amalek was a nation that attacked the Israelites just after they were liberated from Egypt. The Torah includes a commandment to remember what Amalek did. The use of the term "Amalek" to refer to the Nazis is significant, as it demonstrates the desire to view the Holocaust within the accepted historical contexts, and to see it as part of the continuity of Jewish history. It also implies that its remembrance is associated with the biblical commandment. See note 9, above.

41   The intent is that it is impossible to understand the Holocaust using the usual instruments of thought and faith, and that perhaps there is therefore no reason to deal with it. In the beginning of the article, the Rebbe stated in this context as follows: "The history of the Jewish people is filled with difficult chapters that are impossible to understand and grasp, but there is one chapter that is completely closed, and that is the very appropriate expression for the horrible destruction [...]" (Brazovsky 1987, 7).

the word "you." The commandment to remember Amalek does not relate to Amalek at all, but "the meaning of remembering includes an aspect of study." Memory does not relate to the destruction, and certainly not to the destroyers, but rather to what was lost. The method of preserving the world that was lost is "to follow in their footsteps and learn in their ways" – in other words, restoration and reconstruction.

In his introduction to the section cited above, the Rebbe indirectly negates an alternative method of remembering the Holocaust:

> Six million Jews, among them one million children and infants who had not tasted of sin, were murdered in abnormal ways, publicly burned alive in fiery ovens. The mind and heart of man are limited in the amount of pain that they are able to tolerate, and they cannot internalize more than their measure. There is no expression that can express the tragedy, there is no brain that can grasp it, and no heart that can feel the depths of the pain (ibid., 7).

It is clear from his words that there is no sense in dealing with something that cannot be fathomed. Although we are not capable of handling the depths of the pain of what was lost, the same is not true of the recognition and understanding of the world that was lost. In another place, the Rebbe addresses the commandment to remember Amalek in the concrete context of the Holocaust:

> This commandment is placed on the conscience of every Jew in our generation – to remember and not to forget. Let us awaken and exalt the memory of "Jerusalem," the memory of the source of holiness with which we were blessed during our exile in Europe, that was wiped out with such awful brutality without a remnant. We will pass on to the coming generation the imprint of this most glorious period, a time in which Torah Judaism and Hassidism were at the pinnacle of their development and growth: we will tell them about the spiritual giants, the cedars of Lebanon and the pillars of Torah who enlightened our people (ibid., 1987, 17).

In using the term "Jerusalem," the Rebbe is referring to Lithuania, which he viewed as the penultimate Jewish community. The summary and essence of remembering is that we "pass on to the coming generation the imprint of this most glorious period." Therefore, the "source of holiness" that was wiped out, the "imprint of the period," and the "spiritual giants" are the objects of our memory. By remembering them, we fulfill the biblical commandment to "remember what Amalek did to you."

In the continuation of his speech, the Rebbe explains the essence and importance of transmitting the story to future generations. This is, in my opinion, the essence of his approach:

> This remembering serves as the foundation for the spiritual standing of coming generations. For the continuity of the generations is based on the concept of *"mekablin dein min dein"* ("receiving one from another"). It is like a chain in which each link is intertwined with its neighbor. This connection is the basis of its existence. The great difficulty for the generation after the Holocaust is how to bind the chain together [...] For when one link of the chain is loosened, the two sides can no longer be joined. How will the next generation receive the light that comes down from generation to generation? (ibid., 18)[42]

The validity and vibrancy of a tradition is in its power to serve as "a chain in which each link is intertwined with its neighbor, and this connection is the basis of its existence." The Sages placed great importance on the claim of continuity of the tradition of Oral Law from which their power derived: "Moses received the Torah at Sinai and passed it on to Joshua, and Joshua to the Elders [...]" (Mishnah Avot 1:1). There is no question that the narrative of preserving continuity and the transmission of Torah occupied a central position in all of the generations, for inherent within it is the basis of the authority and validity of Jewish law (Yerushalmi 1982, 31–2). The argument of the Rebbe is that the force of the Holocaust grants it a significance that transcends the tragic deaths of millions of people. The Holocaust severed the continuity of the generations that is the source of the vibrancy of the Jewish people and its culture, and thus threatened the continued spiritual existence of the people: "how will the next

---

42   The amazing thing is that the Rebbe made comments of this sort at a gathering of Slonim Hassidim at the very end of the war in May 1945: "We have gathered here, the remnants of our people – shaken, dazed, broken, and neglected from enormity of destruction of our people, to strengthen ourselves and comfort one another, those who God left as a remnant, to restore our ruins and strengthen our holy society, and to continue the golden chain from generation to generation" (ibid., 9).

generation receive the light that comes down from generation to generation?" From this, we can understand why remembering has such importance and spiritual significance: "it serves as the foundation for the spiritual standing of coming generations." Remembering has the potential to restore and renew the continuity of the tradition:

> The memory of the destruction and annihilation obligates us. If we were not able to save these martyrs physically, it is our obligation to at least save their spirit. [...] The special role of our generation is to establish anew the legion of the King that was destroyed and to dedicate our best energies to the education of the new generation. [...] The memory of the Holocaust awakens us to this task (Brazovsky 1987, 18–19).

In these comments, the Rebbe placed upon his followers a difficult and responsible role. Yet, he also aroused enthusiasm and inspiration to save the world that was destroyed from oblivion: "to at least save their spirit." Their role is to be the next link in the chain of tradition – "to establish anew the legion of the King," "to know the great responsibility to establish the future generation."[43] Toward that end, it is necessary to reconnect to the chain the link that was so damaged. In order to achieve this goal, the Rebbe suggested, among other things, to make the survivors of the Holocaust talk, so that they would tell their stories:

> The remnant, the survivors who still merited to see the light, must serve as a conduit to transmit the flame that shined in previous generations to the youth of the new generation. [...] This heritage will provide a small degree of balm and healing to the broken of our generation, and will help to connect the two ends of the chain, so that our new generation will inherit its path from our glorious past (ibid., 18).

The encouragement of Holocaust survivors to tell their stories is well known to us today. Its goal is to give testimony to the horrors of the Holocaust. In contrast, the Rebbe wished to achieve, through the testimony of the survivors, a completely different goal. He viewed the survivors of the Holocaust as those "who still merited to see the light,"

---

43   Brazovsky, ibid., 10, delivered at the gathering of Hassidim at the very end of the war.

the light of the world that preceded the destruction. The Rebbe would not even consider encouraging survivors to talk about where they were and what they experienced during the Holocaust, nor apparently would he consider it important. Rather, he viewed it as crucial to hear the stories of the survivors about the world that they experienced prior to the destruction. This story serves as the "conduit" that transmits the light from the generation before the holocaust to the generation after. It connects "the two ends of the chain." If the popularly recognized slogan of Holocaust memorial is "Never again!" the slogan of the Rebbe would be "Again, forever!" – we will continue to live and restore the world that was destroyed.

One of the central motifs in the religious, and particularly the *haredi*, narrative of the Holocaust is that of *Kiddush Hashem*[44] (the sanctification of God's name) during the Holocaust, the story of Jews who struggled to continue the observance of a few of the commandments, even at the gates of hell.[45] Not only is the heroic struggle to continue the observance of commandments stressed in this literature, but also the preservation of faith, prayer and trust in God – clinging to

44   The concept of *Kiddush Hashem* in Jewish tradition relates to giving up one's life rather than saving oneself by forfeiting one's faith. See Maimonides, *Sefer ha-Mitzvot*, Positive commandment 9: "This is the commandment of *Kiddush Hashem* that all Jews are commanded to follow – that is, allowing ourselves to be killed by force because of our love of God and our belief in His unity." In other words, it is giving up of one's life for the sake of religious belief, a practice that has a long tradition and is deeply ingrained in the memory of Ashkenazi Jewry from the Edicts of 1096, known as the Crusades. Nevertheless, we must remember that the Holocaust was not a religious struggle per se and could not be escaped by forfeiting one's religious beliefs. Therefore, the concept of *Kiddush Hashem* was actually transformed, with regard to the Holocaust, to refer to the readiness to accept difficult sacrifices for the sake of dedication to the Torah and its commandments.

45   See Eliach 1988. Eliach analyzes the significance of observing tradition as the acquisition of spiritual freedom – the creation of a meaningful life within the reality of slavery in which they found themselves. It is important to note that this idea is found in the tradition of the Sages, who spoke about the fact that the Children of Israel in Egypt preserved their identity through spiritual freedom.

faith in spite of the great tribulations.[46] The Rebbe of Slonim wrote in
the previously mentioned volume as follows:

> These will I remember – also the lights in the fog that shone within the
> darkness, specifically in the days when vision terminated, [...] the unvan-
> quished holy ones whose natural Jewish spirit was not broken and did not
> surrender [...] The essence of their war of opposition was not expressed in
> terms of temporal rebellion. [...] Therefore, they went to the altar with an
> exalted spirit of pride and exalted holiness (ibid., 23–4).

Amos Goldberg, who studied this phenomenon in the *haredi*
press, claimed that the *haredi* use of *Kiddush Hashem* as the dominant
theme in the memory of the Holocaust served three functions: (1) it
provided meaning to the Holocaust within traditional categories; (2) it
emphasized the standing of the believing Jew within the supreme
challenge posed by the Holocaust; and (3) it established a myth of
heroism to compete with the Zionist myth of physical heroism
(Goldberg 1998, 167). Although I concur with all three of Goldberg's
points, I believe that there is an additional and very important point
that must be added, as I will explain.

In her book entitled *Be-Seter Ra'am: Halakhah Hagut u-
Manhigut bi-Yemei ha-Shoah* (*Hidden in Thunder: Perspectives on
Faith, Theology, and Leadership During the Holocaust*), Esther
Farbstein, a *haredi* educator and historian, attempts to shed light on
another dimension of the Holocaust – traditional life in the ghettos and
camps, the heroism of dedication to faith and tradition.[47] The book
demonstrates that the concept of *Kiddush Hashem* in the Holocaust is
apparently the central concept of the memory of the Holocaust in
haredi society, and that it is designed to accomplish the goals outlined
by Goldberg. Nevertheless, it seems to me that the author has an
additional, and perhaps even more important, goal – that by projecting
the image of the Jew who remains true to his heritage in the face of the

---

46   For examples of this literature, see Aibeshits 1975; Eliav 1965; Prager 1980;
     Prager 1974. For examples of Jewish legal response literature, see Oshry 1983;
     Meisels 1954; Efrati 1947; Efrati 1960; Fuchs 1995. For research in this area,
     see Michman 1988; Eliach 1988; Caplan 2002; Avneri 1982.

47   See Farbstein 2002. The publication of this book represents a prime example of
     the increased scope in dealing with the Holocaust in *haredi* society in recent
     years. See Caplan 2002.

Holocaust, the author wishes to penetrate into the Jewish world that existed before the destruction. She wishes to foster the memory of a world that was, in her opinion, forgotten or erased, a world in which Torah and faith were the central components.

Elsewhere, Farbstein wrote a programmatic article on the teaching of the Holocaust, the goals and methods for teaching about Jewish life during the Holocaust.[48] The point of departure of the article is that research and instruction "ignore the reaction and experience of a large and vital part of the Jewish population that responded in its own way to the tragedy." The author surveys three existing methods of dealing with this area, and suggests a fourth method. The approach that she proposes is called the "integrative approach," which "integrates the study of religious life and spirituality into every chapter on the Holocaust." In explaining the preferability of this approach, she writes:

> They [the methods] have to uncover before the students a world of reaction that derives from their common past, to at least provide a small window to the rich Jewish world that the enemy was unable to defeat and that flowed through the ocean of troubles, and thus to strengthen the Jewish identity of the student and the pride of his belonging to the Jewish people. In this manner of teaching, religious life during the Holocaust will achieve its proper place in history, in which they were intertwined even during times of distress.

We clearly see here the deep-seated desire to utilize the Holocaust as a window for understanding the collective Jewish past, for understanding the spiritual components that the Jews brought to the Holocaust, those components that "the enemy was unable to defeat." The power of these Jewish components, rather than the power of the enemy, constitutes in the eyes of the author the object of remembering the Holocaust. The discussion of Jewish life during the Holocaust is essentially designed to understand the spiritual world that accom-

---

48 See E. Farbstein, *"The Unique Perspective of the Center for the Teaching of the Holocaust,"* which appears on the Internet site "Zachor: Jewish Faith during the Holocaust" at www.zachor.org.il. This site is administered by the Center for the Teaching of the Holocaust of the Michlalah College for Women in Jerusalem, a seminary for religious teachers. Ms. Farbstein is the founder and current head of the institution.

panied the Jews to the Holocaust. The real goal is to penetrate and observe the world that was destroyed in the Holocaust through a recognition of the "alternative heroism" – the response of the believing Jew to the horrors of the Holocaust. This is a good medium for achieving this goal, since the various "religious responses" were the direct result of the preparation and values that preceded the Holocaust.[49]

Rabbi Ephraim Oshry, the Rabbi of the Kovno Ghetto, who survived the Holocaust, subsequently published the religious questions that were addressed to him during the Holocaust and his responses. In this book, as well, the very difficult events that the rabbi experienced are generally mentioned only when they are relevant to the Jewish legal issue being discussed. In the introduction to his book, Rabbi Oshry indicates that it took him 15 years after the end of the war to review all of the materials that he had from the war:

> And I saw the possibility of creating with them outstanding and very valuable material that would give a comprehensive picture of the spiritual life of the prisoners of the ghetto against the backdrop of daily life during the war. And I said to myself, "this was from God" – to record responses and establish through them a memorial to the righteous and pure souls that sanctified the name of heaven in their lives and in their deaths, to be a remembrance and a remnant of

---

49   See Esh 1973, 240. As a historian, Esh speaks about the need to bring to light the character of the Jewish collective before the Holocaust in order to understand its responses to the events: "We must recognize the character of each segment of the Jewish community – its demographic and economic profile, its social and cultural activities, its degree of political consciousness, and its religious life. By doing all of this, we will open a window for understanding the reactions of each group when placed in distress." Farbstein goes in the opposite direction: she claims that by studying the *Kiddush Hashem* of the Jews during the Holocaust, we will thus know their world before the Holocaust. These different goals are achieved through different methods. To understand reactions to the Holocaust, Esh studies the Jewish world just before the outbreak of the Holocaust, including the spiritual background that each group brought to it. Farbstein, on the other hand, studies the behavior of Jews during the Holocaust in order to penetrate and know the world before the Holocaust. Clearly, Farbstein is interested only in one particular dimension of life before the Holocaust.

the Jews of Lithuania, a Judaism that was rooted in its glorious academies and its outstanding rabbis (Oshry 1983, vol. I: Introduction).

According to the statement of Rabbi Oshry, the spiritual heroism of the Jews in the ghetto that comes to expression in his book is not designed to create an "alternative heroism." Rather, it is designed to enable the reader to decipher the life and values of the Jews before the outbreak of the war: "Judaism that was rooted in its glorious academies and its outstanding rabbis." Indeed, he states this more explicitly in his introduction to the fourth volume of his work:

> And this was essentially the goal that I set before myself when I published the three volumes of *Mi-Ma'amakim* (*Out of the depths*) – that just as the impact of the Jewish community of Lithuania on the larger Diaspora community was recognized because it served as a sanctuary of Torah, wisdom and ethics, so its destruction should be projected in the pages of this book (ibid., vol. IV: Introduction).

3   Restoring the Continuity of Torah Learning

a   The Yeshivot *(Talmudic Academies) as Realms of Memory*

As mentioned above, the memory of the destruction of the Holocaust in Israeli society constitutes the cornerstone for the building of a new world, a different world, in which the Jews know how to deal with such threats. In contrast, in the *haredi* community, the memory of the world that was destroyed serves as the cornerstone for the restoration and reconstruction of the lost world. During the first decades after the establishment of the State of Israel, the central claim of the *haredi* community, whether explicit or implicit, was that that they were involved in restoring the world of Torah that was lost in the Holocaust.

A central and fundamental component in this process was the reestablishment of *yeshivot* that were destroyed. Both the *haredim* and the religious Zionists viewed the restoration of the *yeshivah* world as the true monument to the world that was destroyed. The *yeshivah* was perceived and projected as the symbol of the world that was lost, a world in which Torah learning was the primary spiritual, intellectual and religious activity. Furthermore, the *yeshivah* as an institution of Torah learning was viewed as a symbol of the continuity of the generations. As such, the reconstruction of the *yeshivah* world was viewed not only as the reconstruction of the world that was lost in the Holocaust, but also as the restoration of the continuity of the chain of tradition.

One of the outstanding *yeshivot* in Israel during this period was the Ponevitch Yeshivah in Bnei Brak, which was founded by Rabbi Yosef Kahanaman (1886–1969), who prior to the war had been both the head of the *yeshivah* and the rabbi of the town of Ponevitch in Lithuania. At the time of the German occupation, Rabbi Kahanaman was on a mission of salvation outside of Lithuania and was thus able to find refuge and survive. He subsequently moved to Israel and reestablished his *yeshivah*, which became the most important and influential *yeshivah* in Israel. The building of the *yeshivah* was accomplished with the complete support, encouragement, and cooperation of the Hazon Ish. Ten years after its founding, after the *yeshivah* began to flourish and its reputation was established, Rabbi Kahanaman succeeded in completing its permanent building. He set the date for the dedication of the building on the twenty-seventh of Sivan 5713 (10 June 1953), the day on which the Nazis entered Lithuania. The dedication ceremony took on the character of a memorial ceremony, opening with the reading of the traditional memorial prayer in memory of the martyrs of the Holocaust. In the opening address at the founding of the *yeshivah*, Rabbi Kahanaman stated:

> This day, the 27th of Sivan, is a bitter and violent day on which the Nazis occupied Lithuania. [...] And thank God, on that very day we are standing here in the Holy Land, and dedicating this great and holy abode, that will serve as an eternal memorial to the students of my *yeshivah* in Ponevitch, [...] an eternal living memorial in the Holy Land (Koll 1970, 426).

Rabbi Kahanaman described the occasion of the setting of the cornerstone, ten years earlier, as follows:

On the day of the setting of the cornerstone of the Ponevitch Yeshivah in the Land of Israel – in memory of the *yeshivah* that was destroyed in Lithuania – we did not drink juice, we drank tears. The Hazon Ish and I recited two Psalms, we poured a shovel of cement, and with this everything was concluded (ibid., 355).

The biography of Rabbi Kahanaman records the following story:

Once, [Rabbi Kahanaman] was invited by a group of Lithuanian immigrants in Israel to a memorial service for the martyrs of Lithuania and Latvia. The speakers that preceded [Rabbi Kahanaman] said that the martyrs of Lithuania should be remembered by naming streets after them and by planting forests in their memory. The exiled Rabbi of Ponevitch reacted as follows: "The true memory of the martyrs of Lithuania will be honored and eternalized only if we build the spiritual values of their Judaism" (ibid., 392).

Thus the *yeshivah* is the ultimate memorial to the martyr of the Holocaust because it restores "the spiritual values of their Judaism." Consciously and explicitly, the *yeshivah* was built "as a memorial to the *yeshivah* that was destroyed in Lithuania," and consciously and explicitly, it constitutes "an eternal living memorial."

Approximately twenty years after the founding of the Ponevitch Yeshivah, Rabbi Kahanaman established a branch in Ashdod, a new city that was being established in the southern part of the country. The *yeshivah* was not named the Ashdod Yeshiva, nor was it called the Ponevitch Yeshivah, for it was already memorialized. Rather, it was called the Grodna Yeshivah. At the ceremony for setting the corner stone, on the fifth of Kislev 5724 (11 November 1963), in the presence of the leading rabbis from various parts of Israel, Rabbi Kahanaman stated:

I saw my goal and my mission in life to establish a name and a remnant for the essential image of Lithuanian Jewry. [...] The crowning glory of the memorial activity will be the establishment of eighteen *yeshivot* in the Holy Land, in memory of the eighteen *yeshivot* that were destroyed in Lithuania, that have not yet merited to have their names and memory established (ibid., 485).

This motif repeats itself again and again. The *yeshivot* are the "essential image of Lithuanian Jewry," and they constitute the memorial for that Judaism. The memorial is accomplished by establishing them anew, to "establish their names."

At the same event, Rabbi Yehezkiel Avramsky, the president of the Council of the Heads of Yeshivot and one of the outstanding rabbinic leaders at that time, spoke as well. In his words, he compared the activities of Rabbi Kahanaman with those of Isaac in the Book of Genesis:

> "And Isaac dug again the wells of water, which they had dug in the days of Abraham his father; for the Philistines had stopped them after the death of Abraham; and he called their names after the names by which his father had called them" (Genesis 26:18). The Nazis, may their names be blotted out, not only sealed the wells, but also filled them in with dirt so that they never function again. But the Rabbi of Ponevitch returned, dug them again, and called them by their original names. Thus, *yeshivot* and fortresses of Torah, synagogues, and schools are being established in the Holy Land, and are called by the names that our ancestors called them. As our sages already said: "The synagogues and academies of Babylonia will in the future be established in the Land of Israel" (ibid., 488).[50]

50   The source cited at the end of the citation regarding the academies of Babylonia is taken from the Babylonian *Talmud, Megillah* 29a. S. Y. Agnon, the Nobel laureate Hebrew writer, chose this same quote as the conclusion of his outstanding novel *Ore'ah Nata la-Lun* (*A guest for the night*). The novel, which deals with the crisis faced by Polish Jewry as a result of World War I, was written after Agnon visited his hometown of Buczacz in 1930. It is somewhat ironic that the book was first published at the time of the outbreak of World War II. As demonstrated by Dan Laor, the biographer of Agnon, this led the critics to view the book as an elegy to the Jewish towns that were about to disappear. Indeed, although Agnon describes the collapse of the village, he mourns the loss of the world that it represented and its values. As stated, he chose to end the novel on an optimistic note and, one might say, a Zionist note as well: "I know that a person does not get excited about the key of our old house of study. But I said to myself, since in the near future our house of study will be re-established in the Land of Israel, it would be good for me to have the key in my possession" (Agnon 1968, 444). Indeed, there is no doubt that Agnon not only wanted to create an elegy for the destruction of European Jewry, but essentially saw himself as one who could, by virtue of the key he possessed, open up a clear window to the world of Polish Jewry before the destruction. In addition, he presents the rebuilding of the Land of Israel as the ideal place for establishing Jewish life. See also Laor 1995, 82–5.

The sense of restoration, reconstruction and continuity is clear, emanating from the words of the rabbi and all of the other speeches at the ceremony. The academies of Babylonia, and in this instance the academies of Lithuania, were being re-established in the Land of Israel. The continuity of the generations was restored and was moving forward. The image of the wells of Isaac in the comments of Rabbi Avramsky was not utilized by chance. The character of Isaac in the Book of Genesis was not that of a revolutionary. Rather, he was essentially involved in restoration, preservation and fortification of the revolution that was initiated by his father, Abraham.

The climax of the biography-hagiography of the Rabbi of Ponevitch is the description of an encounter that took place at the end of the 1960s, toward the end of his life, with a Holocaust survivor who had remained in Lithuania and just recently immigrated to Israel:

> Just a few days ago, he visited the graves of his ancestors in Ponevitch and took leave of his city, thinking that he would not return to see them forever. [...] The houses of study of Ponevitch were dormant and padlocked. [...] He walked deliberately to the porch leading to the hall of the *yeshivah*. His connection to the place increased. No, he was not a dreamer – his feet were standing once again on the site that bears the name Ponevitch. There too, in that distant village, the roof of the *yeshivah* was once elevated. [...] Here too, in Bnei Brak on the heights of the Ponevitch Yeshivah, the same landscape of old of houses of study is visible. Here too, the chant of the *gemara* wafts. A half century ago, the destroyer rose up against Ponevitch. But see what a wonder: the ruins have been restored anew. [...] He stood in the new Ponevitch – restored, flourishing, and spreading its ideology – and he began to cry. [...] And he concluded in a passionate Lithuanian Yiddish: "Ponevitch has been resurrected!" (ibid., 513–14).

"Ponevitch has been resurrected!" is a slogan that is heard regarding the establishment of *yeshivot* in Israel and in the United States. Each *yeshivah* is designed to be a monument to a world lost, a monument to one of the *yeshivot* that was destroyed in Europe. Rabbi Aaron Kutler, who was the head of the Klotsk Yeshivah before the war, immigrated to the United States and reestablished his *yeshivah* in the city of Lakewood, New Jersey. The Yeshivah of Chachmei Lublin was rebuilt in Bnei Brak by one of its students, Rabbi Shmuel Wozner. The Telshe Yeshivah was re-established in the United States in

Cleveland, Ohio, in the same format as it existed in Europe before it was destroyed.[51] There are, as well, many other, similar examples. The *yeshivot* are places of memory (Mendels 2004, chapter 1). They are the place that the world that was lost is remembered, and in addition, they declare a loyalty and dedication to that world.[52]

Rabbi Moshe Feinstein, one of the most important Jewish legal authorities in the second half of the twentieth century, who moved from Lithuania to the United States, wrote a responsum entitled: "There is an obligation to place a monument on a grave, establishing a monument in memory of a mother and father whose burial place is unknown, and the reason why a set day of fasting was not established to memorialize the Holocaust" (Feinstein 1996, vol. IV: #57). With regard to erecting a monument in memory of victims of the Holocaust whose burial places are not known, he wrote:

51   In 1976, a volume entitled *Jubilee Volume of the Telshe Yeshiva: On the 100th Anniversary of the Founding of the Yeshiva, 1875–1975* was published (no author). The message of the book is clear, as indicated in the title, that the Telshe Yeshivah that was closed and destroyed in World War II was essentially not destroyed. It continues to exist in the United States. At the end of the book, the history of the *yeshivah* is recorded by Rabbi Avraham Shoshana. He describes the founding of the *yeshivah* in America at the end of the war by a number of refugees as follows: "They began to try feverishly to find a suitable framework in which they could restore the spirit of the *yeshivah*, a framework that would preserve the character of the *yeshivah* in Lithuania without an American influence. They did not want to create a new *yeshivah*, but to restore the old one, to revive in the United States the concept of Torah study in the manner that it was understood and realized in the great Lithuanian *yeshivot*."
52   Rabbi Shlomo Volbe (1914–2004), one of the well-known spiritual counselors of the Israeli *yeshivah* world, himself a Holocaust survivor, published a book after the Yom Kippur War entitled: *Bein Sheshet le-Asor – Hartsa'ot u-Ma'amarim Bein Shtei ha-Milhamot* (*Between the Six and the Tenth: Lectures and Articles between the Two Wars* (the Six-Day War and the Yom Kippur War)). In the book, he discusses the essence of Judaism in contemporary times, and the responsibility placed upon "faithful" Judaism. One of the chapters in the book entitled "The [Contemporary] Period" is divided into four sections. The second section is entitled "The Depths of the Holocaust" and the third section is entitled "The Yeshivah". The *yeshivah* is presented as the response to the Holocaust.

> With regard to those who were killed in Europe during the Holocaust and their place of burial is unknown, [...] should their children set up a monument here [...] in America where the children live? As far as I know, we do not find this idea in the *Gemara* or the Jewish legal codes, nor is it mentioned in passing in other literature. We have also not heard of Gaonim who instructed to do this (ibid.).

The brevity of his words is designed to berate the very idea. We have not found this idea anywhere in halakhic literature, and this apparently ends the discussion. However, immediately following, Rabbi Feinstein begins a lengthy discussion on the nature of the monument of Avshalom, the son of David, as described in the Book of Samuel – that he established as a monument for himself, a monument of stone. Avshalom's actions must be understood from a Jewish legal perspective. How can they be reconciled with Rabbi Feinstein's contention that there is no precedent in the tradition for a monument that is not on a grave?[53] From among the various biblical commentators, he chose to adopt the interpretation of Rashi, who explains the biblical verse "In order to memorialize my name, I will establish for myself a monument of stone" as follows: "It was an important building."[54] On the basis of this interpretation, Rabbi Feinstein concludes:

> It is certainly appropriate to create a memorial to honor his mother and father. [...] The building constructed to honor the deceased should be an important building. It is certainly not important if it is an empty building, but that it be for a specifically beneficial purpose such as Torah study or for charity. This is clearly a very important memorial and monument (ibid.).

In the continuation of his response, Rabbi Feinstein led the questioner, who wanted to build a monument to the memory of his parents who perished in the Holocaust, to the conclusion that only the

53 At the beginning of his comments, Rabbi Feinstein also relates to the monument that Jacob placed on the grave of his wife Rachel, as described in Genesis 35:20. For the "organic" rabbinic reading of biblical texts – i.e. understanding the text in light of Jewish law as they knew it in their time and place – see Heinmann 1974, 8–13.

54 The commentary of Rashi on 2 Samuel 18:18. He could have said that Avshalom intended to be buried there and that it was therefore a monument on a grave.

building of a *yeshivah* could be considered, and that the *yeshivah* constitutes "a very important memorial."

In another place, Rabbi Feinstein was asked about the building of a *yeshivah* high school that would include general studies in its curriculum, in a particular city in the United States. His response included the following remarks:

> We must internalize in our hearts that the great destruction of Torah perpetrated in the world places a huge obligation on Torah students to try to become *gedolei Torah* (Torah giants) and *yirei shamaim* (fearers of heaven) in their stead. This matter is a requirement for all Jews (Feinstein 1996, vol. III: #82).

The staunch opposition of Rabbi Avraham Yeshayahu Karelitz, the Hazon Ish, to any type of Holocaust memorial program was mentioned above. It seems to me that that the question regarding his opposition cannot be detached from the fact that the Hazon Ish was the "father of the *yeshivot*," as demonstrated by his absolute determination in the years following the Holocaust to establish *yeshivot* in Israel (Brown 2002, 390–400; Cohen 1966, 217–69). This connection can be clearly seen in the following letter, which the Hazon Ish wrote to the head of the Slonim Yeshivah, when he embarked on a fundraising campaign for a new *yeshivah* building:

> Behold, it is a labor of great value that the one who increases the honor of our Torah, may he be granted long life, is participating in building the academies of Babylonia in the Holy Land. [...] It is special to us to call the *yeshivah* the Slonim Yeshivah, for the name reminds us of the powerful drive and the strong valor dedicated to maintaining the tablets of the Torah in the bitter and violent exile that we experienced. And we have returned it to its place from where it came, to a place of rest and inheritance, in its beauty and wonderful brilliance, that all of the clouds of the exile could not dim its light or weaken its flavor. [...] I wish you luck on your journey to the United States in order to give our brothers there the merit to participate in this great commandment – to give a lasting memorial to the Slonim Yeshivah (Cohen 1966, 218–20).[55]

The concept of the continuity of the Torah discussed above finds clear expression in these comments of the Hazon Ish. At the conclusion of the letter, the Hazon Ish blesses the head of the *yeshivah* for

---

55   For an additional discussion of other parts of this letter, see p. 83.

going out to raise funds in order "to provide a memorial for the sheltering walls of the Slonim Yeshivah." Furthermore, even though at the beginning of the letter the Hazon Ish speaks specifically about the fact that in the wanderings of the Jewish people from exile to exile, the names of *yeshivot* were changed, he praises and strongly encourages the preservation of the names of *yeshivot* from Eastern Europe in their transfer to Israel. "It is special to us to call the *yeshivah* the Slonim Yeshivah." The reason for this preference is very important: "For the name reminds us of the powerful drive and the strong valor dedicated to maintaining the tablets of the Torah in the bitter and violent exile that we experienced." In other words, the preservation of the name of the *yeshivah* as the name of a city in White Russia is designed to remind us of the drive for Torah study in Eastern Europe. The purpose of Holocaust remembrance is clearly to restore and revive that world.

It is very interesting that this letter was written by the Hazon Ish on the eleventh of Tevet 5709,[56] the day after the first observance of the tenth of Tevet as a Holocaust memorial day as dictated by the Chief Rabbinate of Israel. It is difficult to be certain of the connection, but it is also difficult to ignore the significance of the timing. It is reasonable to suspect that perhaps the Hazon Ish saw this letter and the ideas expressed in it as a response to the idea fostered by the Chief Rabbinate – the establishment of a day of mourning and memorial, an idea that he strongly opposed.

b *Jewish Religious Literature on Alternative Methods of Remembering*

The issues discussed above came to expression as well in the realm of literature. In the years immediately following the Holocaust, the primary focus of *haredi* literature throughout the community was the publication of the Torah insights of notable rabbis who perished. The following example is characteristic, in my opinion, and explains the significance that was attributed to this process. Rabbi Avraham Borenstein (1839–1910), the founder of the Sokachov hassidic

---

56   A photocopy of the original letter can be seen in Cohen 1966, 221.

dynasty, and author of *Aglei Tal* and *Avnei Nezer*, died decades before
the Holocaust. His Hassidic insights on the Torah were preserved
orally by his followers. After the war, the Borenstein family decided
to publish these insights. In the introduction to the book, his grandson,
the publisher, raises the dilemma of publishing writings that the author
himself chose not to publish so that they would remain an oral tradition:

> Words from the hidden realm, words transmitted from mouth to ear, with a
> tumultuous heart and fear of the holy, at a propitious moment (Borenstein 1976,
> 7).

The strength of oral tradition is that the words are transmitted
with the emotion and atmosphere that accompanied them originally,
an element that is lost in the written word. Nevertheless, he explains
why, in spite of this, it was decided to publish them:

> The aversion of our fathers [...] was justified at its time [...] before, as a result
> of our sins, Polish Jewry, and the Hassidic centers that were there, were
> destroyed, [...] when Hassidic life was still in place and the bearers of the
> banner stood at their head and continued to actively guide those who yearned
> for the word of G-d [...] Then there was not a great need for books [...]
> However, now, in our impoverished generation, after the holocaust came upon
> us with Divine fury [...] and the Torah may conceivably be forgotten among the
> Jews, G-d forbid, the publication of the remnants that remain as a vestige is like
> saving something from the fire that G-d ignited in his wrath. It is better that the
> words of Torah should be collected, even if not with the comprehensiveness and
> depth required, than to be forgotten completely. Between the two choices,
> insolence or the sinking of the words into the depths of oblivion, we prefer the
> former (ibid., 8–9).

The writer recognizes the fact that the Rebbe's decision not to
publish his writings was a principled decision, based on his view that
Hassidic Torah is a living tradition that loses its uniqueness and
perfection when committed to writing and detached from the context
in which it was delivered. Nevertheless, the expropriation of these
works from the original aspirations of their author, was a calculated
decision based on a recognition of the tremendous change that had
taken place as a result of the Holocaust. The essence of the change
was the disruption of the living and vibrant tradition, the cessation of

the possibility for an active and natural continuity. Committing the words to writing out of responsibility and fear that they would be lost, apparently reflects a concern for an impending severance of the chain, for "the sinking of the words into the depths of oblivion." In my opinion, however, it also, and perhaps primarily, reflects a sense of beginning – not a feeling of despair, but an unbelievable revival of creativity. The book that was published was designed to be the corner-stone for a new building, for the restoration of the courtyard that had to be built on the pillars of the one that had been destroyed (Meisels 1954).

The Jewish bookshelf is graced by additional literary genres that essentially constitute "memorial literature" in the sense that we are discussing (Baumel 1995) – books that try to return to "the moment before" and to etch it into our memory so that it will be possible "to grasp onto it" and to reconnect the chain, as in the metaphor of the Rebbe of Slonim. A number of examples are as follows: literature on customs, a genre that was not well-known before, particularly in the Hassidic world; books of lectures that recreate the academic ap-proaches of the *yeshivot*; and new editions of books by the heads of the *yeshivot* of previous generations who perished in the Holocaust or who died in decades preceding the Holocaust. These types of works reflect the sense that the Jewish life of Poland and Lithuania must be remembered and bequeathed to future generations.[57]

A particularly characteristic and interesting example of this phe-nomenon is a book published by the *Hevrat Shas de-Kehillat Yere'im* community in Budapest, Hungary. The jubilee anniversary of this community fell in 1944. Obviously, the celebration of this event did not take place as planned. Nevertheless, after the war, the remnant of the community gathered to belatedly "celebrate" the founding of the destroyed community. Not surprisingly, the event was marked by the publication of a book entitled: *The Inheritance of the Refugee: A Collection of Responsa from the Great Scholars of Hungary, Most of*

---

57 For a survey of halakhic literature see Piekaz 1972, 485. Similarly, an important literary genre is one that studies the biographies of great rabbis who perished in the Holocaust. See for example: Levin 1956–72; Unger 1969; Zeidmann 1970; Mirsky 1955.

Whom Died as Martyrs for Kiddush Hashem during the Edicts of 1944, May God Avenge Their Blood. In the introduction to the book, the editors survey the history of the community, describe the rabbis who led it and recount what happened to it during the Holocaust. The motivation to publish the book is explained as follows:

> The holy responsibility now falls upon us – the surviving remnant that remained, a small minority of the many – to save for the coffers of Israel the strewn pearls that were cast into the ashes of the hearth. Is this book not a brand snatched from the burning fire? It seems that it would not be possible to celebrate this belated jubilee in a more appropriate and pleasing manner than to publish the Torah insights of the greatest scholars of the country, almost all of whom died as martyrs for *Kiddush Hashem*, may God avenge their blood, and to establish for them an eternal memorial within Torah Judaism. [...] And now, behold this book of ours is a remembrance of a period that began in ascent and ended in decline. [...] And our prayer rises to the heights, that just as we merited to conclude this period, we will merit to begin a new period of everlasting ascent (Yerushat ha-Pleitah 1946, Introduction).

One who reads these words is amazed that a Jew could stand in Budapest in August 1946 and declare: "we merited to conclude this period." It is important to realize that the intent of the comment was that "we merited" to publish a book of Torah insights from scholars of the previous generation, and as such to conclude the period by saving it from oblivion. The writer is very aware that he stands at the end of one period and the dawn of a new one. He wants to "save for the coffers of Israel" the legacy of the previous generation, their Torah insights, so they might be "an eternal memorial" for the people of the generation, and so they might serve as a cornerstone for those who come "to begin a new period."

4 Competing Memories: Jewish Memory and Israeli Memory

I will now examine the *haredi* format for remembering the Holocaust within two comparative contexts: one in relation to the format and content of Jewish remembrance as reflected in Jewish culture and tradition, and the second against the backdrop of changes and developments in the Jewish world in the age of modernity. Within these two contexts, I will try to explain the *haredi* approach to remembrance that developed in Israel, and the tension between it and the Zionist approach to remembrance, as functions of adherence to and rejection of traditional Jewish models of remembrance. I will also discuss the divergence of *haredi* Holocaust memorial from traditional models of remembrance as a function of the tension between late nineteenth-century orthodoxy and the secularized Jewish world. In conclusion, I will do a comparative survey of Israeli and *haredi* approaches to Holocaust memorial, with a focus on the deep significance of these competing memories.

a   *The Prototype of Jewish Remembrance:* Zekher Le-Hurban *(Remembrance of the destruction) and* Zekher Le-Mikdash *(Remembrance of the Temple)*

One understanding of the connection between *haredi* forms of remembrance in Israel and traditional forms of Jewish remembrance relates to the prototypes for remembering the destruction of the Temple in rabbinic literature. The two concepts that are well known to us from rabbinic literature regarding the memory of the Temple are *Zekher Le-Hurban* (Remembrance of the destruction) and *Zekher Le-Mikdash* (Remembrance of the Temple). In the generation immediately following the destruction of the second Temple, the rabbis dealt with remembrance in an intensive manner. Mourning for the Temple and the events of destruction were not themselves the focus of the remembrance. With regard to the destruction, they said:

It is impossible to mourn too much, and it is also impossible not to mourn. Rather, this is what the Rabbis said: "A person should paint his house with whitewash, and leave a small place [unpainted] as a remembrance of Jerusalem."[58]

The main focus of the rabbis was to remember the Temple in its glory. Toward that end, they initiated two processes that were different, and perhaps even in conflict with each other. On the one hand, they tried to preserve the memory of the Temple and its ritual service. At the same time, they created ritual substitutes for the Temple rituals. The daily prayer service, the Sabbath prayer service, all of the holidays and even Yom Kippur were fashioned anew into a format that constitutes *zekher le-mikdash* (Alon 1970, 1:163–6; Aderet 1990, especially 28–30).[59] Even as they continued to pray and beg for the rebuilding of the Temple, it was paradoxically not the destruction of the temple that stood at the center of the religious discourse, but rather its existence. The rabbis dealt with filling in the gap, with creating a presence of the Temple in the present. The worship of God that was centered in the Temple was lost in its destruction, and the rabbis toiled to create alternate methods for serving God, and to convince their followers that these substitutions were valid because of their similarity to the worship service in the Temple. These substitutes were the cornerstone for the building of a new world, for the building of a new Judaism based in the synagogue and the house of study where the worship of God was expressed through prayer and Torah study (Elbogen 1971, 189–90; Safrai 1994, 133–53; Gutman 1980).

The Rebbe of Slonim, whose insights into memorializing the Holocaust were discussed above, was certainly aware of this distinction, and even related to it explicitly:

This remembrance [of the martyrs of the Holocaust] is an important foundation for the spiritual standing of the coming generations. It is similar to the remembrance of the destruction of Jerusalem, the memory of the source of our holiness

58 *Tosefta Sotah* 9:12, (Leiberman edition, 244). See also Babylonian *Talmud, Baba Batra* 60b.
59 On pages 37–158 the writer discusses ways of *Teshuva* and repentance, as developed after the destruction. See also Aderet 1993; Mor 2003; in the matter of prayer see Fleischer 1989 and more recently Knohl 2005.

that we had previously in this world through the revelation of God's presence in the Temple. Even after its destruction, our emotional bond to it was not severed by virtue of the continuous memory of it that a Jew mentions countless times each day in his prayers, his meals, and above all his joyous occasions. […] The special significance of the memory of the holy martyrs is similar to that (Brazovsky 1987, 17).

The Rebbe explains that the great amount of attention to the memory of the Temple in Jewish tradition is designed to preserve the Temple itself as a living entity in the consciousness and daily experience of the Jew: "Our emotional bond to it was not severed by virtue of the continuous memory of it." The remembrance of the Temple, from the Rebbe's perspective, tries to create an existential reality, to continue the existence of the Temple itself in the present. This remembrance tries to transfer the sense of belonging to the Temple of the past to a current sense of belonging.

There is a dialectic tension concealed in his comments – that even though the rituals created by the rabbis certainly represent a new and different prototype for the worship of God, they also create a direct and vibrant continuity through the medium of memory. Through the use of motifs and symbols taken from the Temple, the tremendous calamity is slightly blurred, and the new service of God is fashioned as continuity and stability. It seems to me from his comments that the Rebbe was cognizant of this tension. He saw remembrance as the spiritual foundation of the coming generations because it contains the basis for the continuation of the past generations.

b   *"Remembrance of the Torah": The Content of Jewish Remembrance*

There is, I believe, another similarity between traditional Jewish remembrance and *haredi* remembrance of Holocaust. Many scholars have taken note of the fact that in the postbiblical period, historiography almost disappeared completely from the cultural and spiritual world of the Jews. In spite of the importance and centrality of remembrance in the Bible and in the normative Jewish legal system, historical events were generally not recorded in the postbiblical period

(Yerushalmi 1982; Herr 1977). Nevertheless, it is important to note that even though they did not record historical events, the Jews were very committed to recording their spiritual creativity. Torah insights were recorded and were passed on to future generations. Yerushalmi discussed the fact that the rabbis

> salvaged what they felt to be relevant to them, and that meant, in effect, what was relevant to the ongoing religious and communal (hence also "the national") life of the Jewish people. They did not preserve the political history of the Hasmoneans, but took note of the conflict between the Pharisees and Alexander Jannaeus (Yerushalmi 1982, 25).

These comments must be understood in a broader context. "The advancement of religious life," according to the rabbis, was not manifested in the preservation of practical *halakhah*, but rather in the preservation and transmission of their Torah learning. They perceived the advancement of religious life as their Torah study, and its growth, development, preservation and transmission to future generations.

Babylonian Jewry bequeathed to us the most monumental work in the history of Jewish communal life, the Babylonian *Talmud*, which served as the foundation for all subsequent Jewish spiritual creativity. Nevertheless, one who might wish to write a book on the centuries of Babylonian Jewish history would find himself practically without sources. It is a fact that, in spite of its tremendous scope, the Babylonian *Talmud* preserved only the Torah insights of its sages. It recorded in an obsessive manner their teachings, interpretations and development of Jewish law, and their deliberations regarding faith and ethics. These were meticulously arranged and edited, and passed from generation to generation. When the *Talmud* arrived in Europe, it became the cornerstone for the scholarship of Sefardi (Spanish and North African) and Ashkenazi (Western and Eastern European) Jewry during the Middle Ages. Although we are aware of the martyrdom for *Kiddush Hashem* during the crusades from the writings of the scholars of Ashkenaz, and even that these events were etched into the collective memory of Ashkenazi Jewry, a chronicle of the events of the crusades was never written by a Jewish scholar. What was essentially preserved in the memory and collective consciousness of the Jewish community was the spiritual creativity of that period. For example, the works of the Tosafists was well preserved and became an invaluable asset for Torah learning in subsequent generations. In this type of remembrance, there is a clear hidden message that the truly significant events that took place of the banks of the Rhine River during the eleventh to thirteenth centuries were the writing of Rashi's commentaries on the Bible and the *Talmud*, and the commentaries of his followers, the Tosafists. The same is true for Sefardi Jewry as well. The monumental work of Rabbi Yosef Caro, the *Shulhan Arukh* that was published in the generation after the Spanish expulsion, became an invaluable asset in Sefardi Torah study and jurisprudence. In practical terms, the *Shulhan Arukh* represents a summary and codification of Torah learning and halakhic rulings written in the previous five centuries in Spain. It is a fact that with the expulsion of the Jews from Spain and the final severance of the continuity of the vibrant and creative tradition of Sefardi Torah interpretation, Rabbi Yosef Caro collected and edited this tradition, thus eternalizing it and enabling it to serve as the cornerstone for continued creativity in future generations. It is beyond the scope of this paper to deal with the question of why the Jews did not record the history of their years in exile. It seems to me, however, that the vast preservation and transmission of Torah learning communicates clearly the message that Torah learning was the primary accomplishment of the Jewish community during the exile that was worthy of being remembered. It should be noted that this prototype of Jewish remembrance contains within it a comforting and supportive message for a wandering people that was not able to find a resting place. Even in the absence of political power, territory, and a structured national life, the national culture was alive and vibrant, and served as the heart of the existence of the Jewish people. The intellectual enterprise associated with Torah learning constituted the most important event, and one might say the only event, worthy of preservation.

The *haredi* leadership in Israel after the Holocaust tried to function within this model of remembrance and to continue it. It is important to note that this model was strongly challenged from the beginning of the Enlightenment. That challenge grew significantly with the growth and success of the Zionist movement that wanted to create a new collective Jewish memory. It tried to revive lost mem-

ories of the homeland and of Jewish political autonomy, with all of
their implications, and to obliterate memories of life in exile that were
still in force. The Holocaust and the establishment of the State of
Israel increased the challenge that faced the *haredi* leadership. It
appeared that the focus of their memory had lost its validity. They
therefore dedicated their efforts to its restoration, and forcefully neg-
ated anything that could draw attention away from it or that reflected
any identification with the opposition. As both the content and format
of Holocaust memorial were nationalized, the *haredi* leadership
opposed any form of remembrance that was adopted by the other side,
even if its source was in Jewish tradition, such as reciting elegies on
the ninth of Av or the establishment of a day of mourning on the tenth
of Tevet.

Although the *haredi* approach to Holocaust memorial is similar
in some ways to traditional forms of remembrance, as we have seen, I
believe that there is another important dimension to *haredi* remembrance that distinguishes it from traditional forms of remembrance.
This dimension will add to our understanding of the *haredi* opposition
to the application of some traditional forms of remembrance to
Holocaust memorial.

c   *Rejection of the Dimension of Time: The Distinction between
    Jewish Remembrance and* Haredi *Remembrance in Israel*

In an effort to create the presence of the Temple and its service in
daily religious life after the destruction, the Rabbis enacted numerous
laws that were "*zekher le-Mikdash.*" Yet, it was clearly impossible to
create an identical world to the world that existed before the destruction. The rabbis wished to create continuity, not by creating an
identical world but by creating a new world that reflected the old
world that was destroyed and its values. This approach was evident
also in the study of Torah and its transmission, where the rabbis were
careful to distinguish between the historical layers in the text. Thus the
traditional page of the *Talmud* is structured as an intergenerational
dialogue – the *amoraim* interpret the tannaitic material, and Rashi and
the Tosafists interpret the Talmud. There is continuity in the ongoing

study, but the boundaries between the various levels are clear. It seems that this perspective did not exist in the *haredi* world after the Holocaust. In the previously mentioned letter that the Hazon Ish sent to the head of the Slonim Yeshivah, he wrote:

> And behold, during the centuries that the Babylonian *yeshivot* wandered, paving the way for their return to the land from which they were exiled, the ruins of the *yeshivot* that were destroyed in Babylonia were rebuilt in foreign countries – Spain, France, and Germany. Their names were changed, but not their spirit. This is the Torah that was driven into ten exiles, and built its home in the land of Shinar, and was then exiled from Babylonia to western countries. This is the Torah that now returns from the destroyed plains of the west to the "Land of the Deer," the Holy Land that was given to our forefathers as an everlasting inheritance, which was its residence when it came from Sinai to appear with its rays of light in the midst of Israel.[60]

"The Torah that was driven into ten exiles [...] that now returns." The academies of Babylonia, where the Babylonian *Talmud* was created, are the ones that wandered throughout all of the exiles, changing their names but not their spirit. From an existential stand-point, the Hazon Ish describes an absolute identification between these institutions and the Torah that was studied within their walls. The identification is preserved with their return to Israel. The very same Torah went into exile two thousand years ago, and it returns "to the 'Land of the Deer,' the Holy Land that was given to our forefathers as an everlasting inheritance."[61] This constitutes a clear attempt to blot out any possibility for change and development.

Even Rabbi Joseph B. Soloveitchik, the central personality of modern Orthodoxy in the United States, strikes a similar chord. One of his followers committed to writing some comments that he heard from Rabbi Soloveitchik during the recitation of elegies on the ninth

---

60   See p. 72.

61   It is worthwhile to note that the Hazon Ish does not view the building of *yeshivot* in Israel as another station in their wanderings, but as a return to the inheritance. Similarly, it is important to note that the wanderings of the people throughout the generations is described as the wanderings of the Torah and the *yeshivot*. The thing that wanders is the Torah, the essence and central aspect of the people's existence.

of Av. Rabbi Solovetchik opposed the writing of elegies for the Holocaust on the grounds that we are not authorized to introduce innovations in our times, certainly not in the prayer service. The essence of the argument is concealed in his claim that there is no need for new elegies since remembrance of the Holocaust is contained within the existing elegies relating to previous tragedies. The model of the destruction of the Temple repeats itself. In other words, the Holocaust is another catastrophe in a long line of catastrophes that the Jewish people experienced in exile. When speaking about the elegy for the destruction of the communities of Worms, Meinz and Spire,[62] Rabbi Soloveitchik said:

> When I read the *kinnot* (elegies) on the destruction and martyrs of Spire, the destruction of the community of Meinz, and cries of the shattering of glorious Worms, I think of Warsaw, Vilna, and Kovno. Tisha B'Av is a memorial day for all of the tragedies of Israel. There is no need to need to create a special day for them or to write new *kinnot* (Arazi 1972, 324).[63]

A close reading of Rabbi Soloveitchik's comments reveals that his argument is much deeper than that the various destructions are similar. Rather, he claims that the destructions are identical, and even that the communities that were destroyed are identical, as well. Warsaw is Spire, Vilna is Worms, and Kovno is the glorious Meinz. Without even mentioning the communities of Warsaw, Vilna, and Spire, they are memorialized significantly in this elegy. They are remembered by us in the image of Spire and Meinz. What is important to remember is that the communities that were destroyed in the Holocaust were identical to Jewish communities throughout the generations. They represented a link in the chain of tradition. The practical message in Rabbi Soloveitchik's words is that this identification must continue, that it is an ongoing process in our time. The destroyed community of Meinz was rebuilt in Kovno, and the destroyed com-

---

62 These were celebrated Torah centers in Germany that were destroyed during the Crusades.

63 Compare the opposite position expressed by Rabbi Kasher and Rabbi Amital in note 9, above. For the same concept in Rabbinic Thought see Yerushalmi 1982, 21–2.

munity of Kovno is being rebuilt in New York, Boston, Jerusalem and Bnei Brak.

In reality, the replication of destroyed communities is not a realizable goal. The Holocaust was so powerful that the world that is rebuilt in its wake must in any case be a different world than that which preceded it. Nevertheless, it is precisely against this fact that the *haredi* remembrance of the Holocaust acted. It tried to blur and minimize the catastrophe that took place. *Haredi* remembrance not only focused on the world that was, but, in an attempt to create continuity, it focused only on a particular aspect of that world – the world of Torah. It claimed that it was restoring the exact world that was destroyed, a point that differentiates it from the traditional model of remembrance. "Ponevitch is resurrected."[64] This phenomenon can be explained by understanding the essence of Orthodoxy and its struggle against modernity.

There is a well-known slogan of Orthodoxy in the modern era that was coined by the Hatam Sofer: "Innovation is prohibited by the Torah." On the surface, this slogan apparently reflects a strategy against the innovations introduced by the Reform movement and other more moderate modern Jewish movements. However, this slogan actually has a deeper and more significant meaning. It actually reflects a reaction to the serious and real challenge that modernity and enlightenment presented to traditional Judaism – the introduction of the dimension of time to the study of sacred texts. Historical thought represented a break with traditional Jewish thought. It sought to describe the development of Jewish religious literature and Jewish history as dynamic processes that instituted changes in accordance with the circumstances of time and place. Rabbi Nachman Krochmal's book, which was the first Orthodox attempt to deal with this challenge, tried to release text study from the restrictions of dogma, and to understand each text in its historical context. The title that he chose for the book – *The Guide for the Perplexed of the Time* – emphasizes the fact that the confusion experienced by the religious community in the modern period is the result of the introduction of time to Jewish consciousness (Schorsch 1994, 178–9; Rawidowicz

64   See above, p. 69.

1961). In the premodern period, scholars could preserve their traditions within a context of historical layers without feeling threatened. New interpretations were never viewed as products of the time, but rather as the products of pure investigation of the text. The development of commentaries was perceived as the result of an ongoing process of Torah study. The contemporary reader in each generation became completely engaged with the text, and approached it from a subjective, rather than an objective, perspective (Heinemann 1974, 2–14). The Babylonian *Talmud* opens its discussion of every law in the *Mishnah* with the following question: "From where do we know this?" – or in other words, what is the source of this law? The answer always relates to extrapolation from a biblical verse. The new law is viewed as a natural outgrowth of an older source, derived through a natural and coherent process of study and interpretation. In contrast to the desire to criticize the past and to implement change that characterizes modern society, traditional society is characterized by a rejection of innovation. Rather, change is always viewed as a function of the past and innovation is always presented as a natural outgrowth of an older source. Modern scholars seek a different answer to the Talmudic question: "From where do we know this?" They seek an answer that is rooted in the dimension of time.[65] While traditional commentators in the premodern period were not bothered by historical layers and did not entertain the possibility of external influences, modern scholars try to uncover the impact of historical influences on Jewish law. The modern approach not only challenges the authority of the Jewish legal codes, it also limits the ability to claim that new innovations are actually rooted in older sources.

I believe that this distinction helps us understand the difference between traditional and modern Jewish models of remembrance, and the opposition of the *haredi* leadership to the use of traditional forms of remembrance, such as elegies, to memorialize the Holocaust. Focusing on the horrors of the Holocaust supports the fact that the world that was destroyed will never return, that the new society being created is really not a continuation of the old society. The perspectives of modern society forced the *haredi* leadership to fight even against

---

65   For further elaboration see Harris 1995.

the traditional model of remembrance. The rabbinic leadership wanted to resurrect the world that existed before the Holocaust, to preserve the image of the old world in the here and now.

d   Competing Memories

Every memory chooses what it wants to save from being forgotten. In our case, is it the memory of a smitten community torn to pieces without hope of salvation, or alternatively, an active and vibrant culture that was destroyed? Each of these pictures particularizes its pain and is fashioned as well by what it chooses to forget. Each remembrance also serves the immediate needs of its group. One emphasizes the catastrophic nature of the Holocaust in order to differentiate the new period from the period before the Holocaust, and to use it to establish a moral justification and historical imperative for the building of a new world. The other tries to achieve the opposite – to know and understand the world that was destroyed in order to build the new world in its image, as an authentic continuation of the old world. The struggle between various groups in Israeli society regarding the content and format of Holocaust memorial is a good example of the use of collective memory as a social force that can be controlled and transmitted in a calculated fashion by leaders or a social elite to achieve particular goals and objectives.[66]

Collective Jewish memory occupied a central role in Zionist thought. Zionism wished to forge a new Jewish identity. Toward that end, it had to establish anew the collective memory of the Jewish people, to determine what should be remembered and what should be forgotten. Some current memories were obliterated, while other long forgotten memories were retrieved from the abyss of oblivion (Zerubavel 1995; Luz 2003, 37–41). This fact, along with the proximity between the Holocaust and the birth of the State of Israel, gave

66   This is similar to the argument of Maurice Halbwachs, an influential researcher on the topic of remembrance. On the importance of his work with regard to Jewish remembrance see Yerushalmi 1982, 5–6; Zerubavel 1995, 3–12; Goldberg 1998.

Holocaust memorial a central place, both implicitly and explicitly, in the public discussion regarding the essence of the Jewish state, its goals and objectives (Gorny 2003). The focus on the destruction of European Jewry at the expense of the memory of the culture and values of the world that was destroyed served the Zionist agenda and its goals for the state. First, it sharpened and strengthened the Zionist argument negating the viability of Jewish life in exile, and the culture and values inherent in the old world mentality. Second, it projected the State of Israel as an alternative model of Jewish existence – a Jewish world based on nationalistic values that are fundamentally different than the religious values that prevailed in the exile. Third, it projected the value of normalized sovereignty as a deterrent to such catastrophes that were the result of life in exile.

In contrast, the *haredi* community wished to preserve an alternative collective memory. The *haredi* leadership sought to remember the world that was destroyed and to emphasize its vitality. It distanced itself from the ideas inherent in the Israeli model of remembrance, and could certainly not accept the negation of the culture that developed in the exile. As we have seen, they viewed the Holocaust as part of a continuum of catastrophes that have occurred to the Jewish people throughout the exile, and perhaps more importantly, they projected the new society that they were building as a continuation of the world that existed before the Holocaust. As in all remembrance, this remembrance also included forgetting, at times consciously and deliberately. Any aspect of that society that was not connected to Torah was erased from their consciousness. The elements of the society that did not enter the halls of the *yeshivah* or the courtyards of the *Hassidim* were completely forgotten (Caplan 2002, 147).[67] Also, the image of the

---

67 Caplan cites the criticism of Schwartz (1986) regarding this phenomenon: "While previous generations did not hesitate to proclaim 'because of our sins we were driven from our land,' 'our fathers sinned and are no longer alive,' and 'we and our fathers have sinned,' our generation has idealized the generation of the Holocaust as a generation in which everyone was holy, pure, and without sin" (147). Schwartz is critical of this phenomenon and calls for change, but he accurately describes the phenomenon. It seems to me that one of the most interesting examples in this context is the perpetuation of the names of cities and villages in Eastern Europe in the names of *haredi* cities, neighborhoods streets

helpless Jew in exile was omitted from the picture because it would arouse sympathy for the claims of the opposite paradigm of Holocaust memorial. On the contrary, the place of the martyr who sacrificed himself for *Kiddush Hashem*, the true Jewish hero, was emphasized. In addition, the destruction itself did not occupy an important place in the remembrance, unless it served to enhance the understanding of Jewish values before the Holocaust. The *haredi* leaders projected the old world as a perfect world of Torah and *Hassidut*, to the exclusion of other elements that characterized Jewish life immediately before the Holocaust. Ironically, they sought to create in their own communities, and in Israeli society in general, the memory of the world that was destroyed in the image of the one they were now building.

The content of remembrance certainly influences the format as well. *Haredi* remembrance saw itself as a defensive remembrance. Israeli remembrance of the Holocaust sought to excise the religious element of the picture by eliminating any memory of *Kiddush Hashem* in the Holocaust or the fact that the Jewish world that existed before the Holocaust was essentially a vibrant and creative religious world from a spiritual and intellectual standpoint. As such, the *haredi* remembrance could not adopt the official Israeli model of Holocaust memorial. In those years, a conflict with the dominant sector of society over the format of public Holocaust memorial, utilizing the very same instruments – ceremonies, assemblies and texts – was doomed to failure. They therefore turned to completely different formats, to models that have deep roots in Jewish tradition. The *yeshivot* became the place of remembrance, and books recording the insights of Torah scholars from the period just before the Holocaust took the place of elegies or other texts that were used at public memorial gatherings.

The battle over the memory of the past provides a window through which to observe the values conflict between the *haredi* and

---

and institutions in Israel. It is clear why a street would be named after the Rebbe of Gur; but it is not clear why Matersdorf, a village in Hungary, should have its name perpetuated in the name of a *haredi* neighborhood in Jerusalem. The answer lies in the disregarding of any element of the society that is not connected to Torah. Matersdorf is remembered because, in the minds of the *haredim*, it was a village that was totally dedicated to Torah.

Zionist segments of contemporary Israeli society. At the same time, in spite of the fundamental differences between these communities and the goals that they are trying to advance through remembrance of the past, there is an important common denominator between their models of remembrance. Both express a strong concern for the vitality of the Jewish collective, and both express a dedication to the continuity of Jewish existence and Jewish history. Also, the common goal of both groups is the building of a new Jewish world. In this regard, there is an additional element of commonality that lies beneath the surface. The *haredi* claim that it is rebuilding a world that is identical to the Jewish world before the Holocaust must in reality be understood in a more limited sense. A close look at the texts reveals a realization that while it is possible to create continuity with previous generations, replication is in actuality not possible. The surprising and most stirring expression of this reality is found in the writings of the Hazon Ish. He stated that the *yeshivot* that were established in Europe were the *yeshivot* of Babylonia that had wandered for centuries – "their names were changed, but not their spirit."[68] Yet, he did not view the establishment of the *yeshivot* in Israel after the Holocaust as just another station in the wanderings of the Torah. Rather, this anti-Zionist leader expressed the phenomenon as follows: "This is the Torah that now returns from the destroyed plains of the west to the 'Land of the Deer,' the Holy Land that was given to our forefathers as an everlasting inheritance." The Torah is no longer wandering, it has returned to its home. Thus these two competing memories share not only a concern for the Jewish collective but also an appreciation of the significance of the return to the Land of Israel. Yet this commonality cannot obscure the unbridgeable gap between the two visions of what must be built – a new and different Jewish world or a restoration and reconstruction of the Jewish world that was lost.[69]

---

68   See above pp. 55–6.
69   A number of years ago, there was a heated scholarly debate over the position of
      David Ben-Gurion regarding Holocaust memorial. In spite of some different
      nuances, the disagreement was not over the facts but rather over their inter-
      pretation. It is clear that Ben-Gurion was not excited about the establishment of
      Yad Vashem, and throughout the 1950s, he never participated in Holocaust
      memorial programs or visited memorial sites. Eliezer Don-Yehiya claims that

Bibliography

Aderet, A. 1990. *From Destruction to Restoration: The Mode of Yavne in the Re-Establishment of the Jewish People* (in Hebrew). Jerusalem: Magnes Press.

—. 1993. "Masekhet Eduyot k-Edut le-Darkhei ha-Shikum veha-Tkuma" ("Tractate *Eduyot* as a Tesimony for the ways of Restoration and Revival"). In A. Oppenheimer, I. Gafni and M. Stern (eds), *Jews and Judaism in the Second Temple, Mishnah and Talmud Periods* (in Hebrew). Jerusalem: Yad Ben-Zvi, 251–65.

Agnon, S. Y. 1968. *A Guest for the Night*. New York: Schocken Books.

Ben-Gurion's approach was driven by his vision of Jewish sovereignty. According to this approach, he wished to develop a "Land of Israel ethos" that would project the important place of the state in contemporary Jewish history, and primarily the development of a national culture, without dealing with the values of the exile. Accordingly, Ben-Gurion believed that it was necessary to focus the national memory on events that could contribute to the unification of the Jewish people and could motivate them toward the goals of the Zionist enterprise and the formation of the state (see Don-Yehiya 2000; Don-Yehiya 1993; Stauber 2000, 64, 266). In contrast, Anita Shapira claims that Ben-Gurion, as all of the leaders of state at that time, was involved in acting on immediate needs: "We are talking about the early years of the state. On the agenda of the government and the Knesset were important questions such as the law of public education, the law of military service and security, the establishment of a legal system, in addition to the absorption of large waves of immigration, securing living quarters, work and education within systems that were exploding from overload. [...] The establishment of Yad Vashem as well as other spiritual and symbolic issues were important, but there were other things that were more important" (Shapira 1999, p. 43). In spite of the fundamental differences between these two interpretations, they do share some perspective. Whether based on principle, as Don-Yehiya claims, or on practicality, as Shapiro claims, Ben-Gurion wished to focus on building the state from a "forward looking perspective." It turns out, ironically, that there is some similarity between the *haredi* opposition to Holocaust memorial programs and Ben-Gurion's absence from them. Both wished to focus on building the Jewish future, and viewed that as the essential focus of remembrance.

Aibeshits, Y. 1975 (5736). *Bikdusha ubi-Gvura: Pirkei Kiddush Hashem u-Mesirat Nefesh, Asufa Teudit al ha-Emuna ke-Gorem Mashpia be-Tkufat ha-Shoah* (*With Holiness and Heroism: Chapters in Martyrdom and Self-Sacrifice, a Testimonium on Belief as an Influential Factor during the Holocaust*) (in Hebrew). Tel Aviv: No publisher mentioned.

Alon, G. 1970. *Toldot ha-Yehudim be-Tkufat ha-Mishna* (*The History of the Jewish People in the Mishnaic Period*), vol. 1. (in Hebrew). Jerusalem: Hakibbutz Hame'uhad.

Appelfeld, A. 1998. "Zikaron Ishi ve-Zikaron Kibutsi-siha" ("Personal and Collective Memory – An Interview") In Y. Rappel (ed.). *Memory and Awareness of the Holocaust in Israel* (in Hebrew). Tel Aviv: Ministry of Defence, 11–17.

Arazi, R. L. 1972 (5733). "Be'Kinot' im ha-Gaon Rabbi Y. D. Soloviechik" ("Lamentations with the Gaon Rabbi Y. D. Soloviechik") (in Hebrew). *Shana be-Shana*. Jerusalem: The Chief Rabbinate of the State of Israel, 320–6.

Avneri, Y. 1982. "Safrut ha-Halakhah be-Yemei ha-Shoah" ("Halakhic Literature during the Holocaust") (in Hebrew). *Sinai* 92, 172–88.

Baumel, J. T. 1992. *A Voice of Lament: The Holocaust and Prayer* (in Hebrew). Ramat Gan: Bar Ilan University Press.

—. 1995. "In Everlasting Memory: Individual and Communal Holocaust Commemoration in Israel." *Israel Affairs* 1 (3), 146–70.

Ben Amos, A. and I. Bet-El. 1999. "Ceremonies, Education and History: Holocaust Day and Remembrance Day in Israeli Schools." In R. Feldchai and E. Etkes (eds), *Education and History: Cultural and Political Contexts* (in Hebrew). Jerusalem: The Zalman Shazar Center for Jewish History, 469–74.

Berkowitz, E. 1973. *Faith after the Holocaust*. New York: KTAV Publishing House.

—. 1979. *With God in Hell*. New York: Hebrew Publishing Co.

Bialer, Y. L. 1957. *Ashdot Yamim: Shirim* (*Ashdot Yamim: Poems*) (in Hebrew). Jerusalem: Mossad Harav Kook.

Borenstein, Avraham ben Menachem Ze'ev. 1976. *Sefer Ne'ot ha-Desheh* (*The Book of Ne'ot Desheh*) (in Hebrew). Collected and edited by A. Y. Borenstein. Tel Aviv: No publisher mentioned.

Brazovsky, S. N. 1987 (5748). (*Haadmor mi-Slonim*) *Kontres ha-Haruga Alekha: Asufat Ma'amarim al Hashmadat Yahadut Europa be-Shnot ha-Shoah (1939–1945) ve-Inyanei Galut ve-Geula* (*(Hassidic Rabbi of Slonim): A Collection of Articles on the Annihilation of European Jewry in the Holocaust (1939–1945), and Matters of Exile and Redemption*) (in Hebrew). Jerusalem: No publisher mentioned.

Brown, B. 2002. "From Political Isolation to Cultural Enrichment: Hazon Ish and the Path of Israel's *Haredi* Society (1933–1953)." In M. Bar On and Z. Zameret (eds), *On Both Sides of the Bridge* (Hebrew). Jerusalem: Yad Ben Zvi, 364–413.

—. 2003. "The Hazon Ish: Halakhic Philosophy, Theology and Social Policy As Expressed in His Prominent Later Rulings" (in Hebrew). Jerusalem: The Hebrew University (Unpublished Doctoral Dissertation).

Caplan, K. 2002. "The Holocaust in Contemporary Israeli *Haredi* Popular Religion." *Modern Judaism* 22 (2), 142–68.

Cohen, S. 1966. *Pe'er ha-Dor: Prakim mi-Masekhet Hayav ve-Yetzirato shel Gaon Dorenu Maran Rabbi Avraham Yeshaayahu Karelitz Zt"l, Baal Hazon Ish* (*Pe'er ha-Dor: Chapters from the Life and Work of the Gaon of our Generation, the Late Rabbi Abraham Yeshaayahu Karelitz, Author of Hazon Ish*) (in Hebrew). Bnei Brak: No publisher mentioned.

Don-Yehiya, E. 1993. "Memory and Political Culture: The Israeli Society and the Holocaust." *Studies in Contemporary Jewry* 9, 139–62.

—. 2000. "Mamlakhtiut, Shoah ve-Mesarim Hatrani'im" ("Statehood, Holocaust and Conspirational Messages") (in Hebrew). *Alpayim* 20, 81–106.

Efrati, Rabbi Shimon. 1947 (5708). *Sefer me-Emek ha-Bakha: Responsa, Berur le-Or ha-Halakhah shel She'elot she-Nithavu le-Regel ha-Ason* (*The Book of me- Emek ha- Bacha: Responsa to Halakhic Questions that were caused by the Catastrophe*) (in Hebrew). Jerusalem: Mossad Harav Kook.

—. 1960 (5721). *From the Valley of Death* (in Hebrew). Jerusalem: No publisher mentioned (Hebrew).

Elbogen, Y. M. 1971. *Hatfila be-Ysrael ve-Hitpathuta ha-Historit* (*Prayer in Judaism and its Historical Development*) (in Hebrew). Tel Aviv: Dvir.

Eliach, Y. 1988. "The Holocaust – A Response to Catastrophe within a Traditional Jewish Framework." In Y. Gutman and G. Greif (eds), *The Historiography of the Holocaust Period.* Jerusalem: Yad Vashem, 719–35.

Eliav, M. 1965. *Ani Maamin: Eduyot al Hayehem ve-Motam shel Anshei Emunah be-Yemei ha-Shoah* (*I Believe: Testimonies about the Life and Death of Believers in the Holocaust*) (in Hebrew). Jerusalem: Mossad Harav Kook.

Esh, S. 1973. *Studies in the Holocaust and Contemporary Jewry* (in Hebrew). Jerusalem: Yad Vashem.

Fackenheim, E. 1978. *The Jewish Return into History; Reflections in the Age of Auschwitz and a New Jerusalem.* New York: Schocken Books.

—. 1989. *Essays* (Hebrew). Jerusalem: Hasifriyah Hatziyonit.

Farbstein, E. 2002. *Hidden in Thunder: Perspectives on Faith, Theology, and Leadership during the Holocaust* (in Hebrew). Jerusalem: Mossad Harav Kook.

Feinstein, Rabbi Moshe. 1996. *Responsa Igrot Moshe, Yoreh De'ah*, translated by Moshe Dovid. NJ: No publisher mentioned.

Fleischer, E. 1989–90. "On the Beginning of Obligatory Jewish Prayer" (in Hebrew). *Tarbitz* 59 (3–4), 397–441.

Friedlander, S. 1990. "The 'Shoah' between Memory and History." *Jerusalem Quarterly* 53, 115–26.

Friedman, M. 1990. "The *Haredim* and the Holocaust." *Jerusalem Quarterly* 53, 86–105.

Fuchs, A. 1995. *Holocaust in Rabbinic Sources (Response and Sermons)* (in Hebrew). Jerusalem: No publisher mentioned.

Goldberg, A. 1998. "The Holocaust in the Ultra Orthodox Press" (in Hebrew). *Yahadut Zmanenu* 11–12, 155–205.

Goldstein, Rabbi Isachar. 1989 (5750). *Responsa Ohel Isachar* (in Hebrew). Jerusalem: No publisher mentioned.

Gorny, Y. 2003. *Between Auschwitz and Jerusalem.* London: Vallentine, Mitchell.

Greinmann, S. 1989 (5750). *Kovetz Igrot* (*A Collection of Epistles*) (in Hebrew). Bnei Brak: No publisher mentioned.

Gutman, Y. 1980. "Motsao shel Beit ha-Knesset" ("The Origin of the Synagogue") In Z. Safrai (ed.), *The Ancient Synagogue: Selected Studies* (in Hebrew). Jerusalem: Merkaz Shazar, 47–8.

Haberman, A. M. 1970 (5731). *Sefer Gzeirot Ashkenaz ve-Tsarfat: Divrei Zikhronot ve-Piutim* (*The Book of Decrees in Germany and France: Recollections and Poems*) (in Hebrew). Second edition. Jerusalem: Ofir Publishing.

Halperin, Y. 1945. *The Records of the Council of the Four Lands* (in Hebrew). vol. 1. Jerusalem: Mossad Bialik.

Harris, J. M. 1995. *How Do We Know This: Midrash and the Fragmentation of Modern Judaism*. New York: SUNY Press.

Heinemann, Y. 1974. *Darkhei Aggada* (*The Ways of the Aggada*) (in Hebrew). Jerusalem: Magnes Press.

Henkin, Y. H. 1991 (5752). "Yom ha-Zikaron le-Hurban Yahadut Europa ve-Haim Hakhameha tau be-Hanhaga" ("A Memorial Day for the Destruction of European Jewry. Were its leaders Wrong?") (in Hebrew). In *Shana be-Shana*. Jerusalem: The Chief Rabbinate of the State of Israel, 291–310.

Herr, M. D. 1977. "The Conception of History among the Sages." *Proceedings of the Sixth World Congress of Jewish Studies* (in Hebrew). Vol. 3. Jerusalem: World Union of Jewish Studies, 129–42.

Hertska, P. 1984. *Divrei Drisha ve-Hitorerut le-Amirat Kinah be-Yom Tisha be-Av: Le-zekher Kedoshei Yisrael she-Nishmedu be-Europa be-Shnot 1939–1945* (*A Sermon Urging the Uttering of Lamentations on the Ninths of Av in Memory of the Martyrs that Perished in Europe during the Years 1939–1945*) (in Hebrew). New York: Vaad ha-Meorerim le-Amirat Kinah le-Kedoshei Europa.

Hertzog, Rabbi Isaac. 1971 (5732). *Responsa Heikhal Yitshak, Orah-Haim* (in Hebrew). Jerusalem: Mossad Harav Kook.

—. 1999 (5759). *Kol Kitvei Maran Hagaon Rabbi Yitshak Aizic Halevi Zt"l* (*The Collected Works of the Gaon, the Late Rabbi Yitshak Aizic Halevi*) (in Hebrew). Psakim ve-Ktavim, vol. 2, Responsa Orakh-Haim. Jerusalem: Mossad Harav Kook.

Hutner, Y. 1997. "Holocaust." *The Jewish Observer* 12 (8), 1–9.

Kalonymus, K. S.1960 (5720). *Esh Kodesh (Fire of Holiness)* (in Hebrew). Jerusalem: No publisher mentioned.

Karelitz (Hazon Ish), A. Y. 1939 (5750). *Kovetz Igrot Maran Hahazon Ish Z"l (Collected Epistles of the Late Hahazon Ish)* (in Hebrew), S. Greinmann (ed.). Bnei Brak: No publisher mentioned.

Katz, J. 1992. *Halakhah in Strait: Obstacles to Orthodoxy at Its Inception* (in Hebrew). Jerusalem: Magnes Press.

Knohl, Y. 2005. "Bein Kol ve-Demama: Ha-Tfila veha-Pulhan ha-Mikdashi, be-Mikra be-Kumeran vebe-Safrut Hazal" ("Between Sound and Silence: The Prayer and the Temple Cult in the Bible and in Qumranic and Rabbinic Literature") (in Hebrew). *Mehqare Talmud* 3,748–53.

Koll, S. 1970. *Ehad be-Doro: Korot Hayav, Ma'avako u-Fo'olo shel Rabbi Yosef Shlomo Kahanaman (The One and the Only is his Generation: The Life, Struggle and Deeds of Rabbi Yosef Shlomo Kahanaman)* (in Hebrew). Tel Aviv: Orot Publishing Tel Aviv.

Laor, D. 1995. *S. Y. Agnon: New Perspectives* (in Hebrew). Tel Aviv: Hakibbutz Hame'uhad – Sifriat Poalim.

Levine, Y. 1956–1972. *These Will I Remember: A Collection of the Biographies of the Martyrs of 1940–1945* (in Hebrew). Vols 1–7. New York: The Institute for the Research of the Haredi Community.

Luz, E. 2003. *Wrestling with an Angel.* New Haven: Yale University Press.

Maya, M. 2002 (5762). *A World Built, Destroyed and Rebuilt: Rabbi Yehudah Amital Confronts the Memory of the Holocaust* (in Hebrew). Alon Shvut: Tevunot Publication.

Mayer, M. 2002 (5763). *Elegies in Memory of the Holocaust for the Ninth of Av* (in Hebrew). Jerusalem: Orachot Publication.

Meisels, H. 1954 (5715). *Responsa Mekadshe ha-Shem (Responsa of the Martyrs)* (in Hebrew). Chicago: No publisher mentioned.

Mendels, D. 2004. *Memory in Jewish, Pagan and Christian Societies of the Greco-Roman World.* London/New York: Continuum and T&T Clark.

Michman, D. 1988. "Research on the Problems and Conditions of Religious Jewry under the Nazi Régime." In Y. Gutman and

G. Greif (eds), *The Historiography of the Holocaust Period.* Jerusalem: Yad Vashem, 737–48.

—. 1996. *The Impact of the Holocaust on Religious Jewry: Major Changes within the Jewish People* (in Hebrew). Jerusalem: Yad Vashem.

Mirsky, S. K. 1955 (5716). *Mosdot Torah be-Europa be-Bniyatam uve-Hurbanam (Torah Institutions in Europe, their Foundation and Destruction)* (in Hebrew). New York: Ogen Publishing.

Mor, S. 2003. "The Laws of Sacrifice or Telling the Story of the Exodus?" (in Hebrew). *Zion* 68, 297–311.

Oshry, E. 1983. *Responsa from the Holocaust.* New York: Judaica Press.

Piekaz, M. 1972. *The Holocaust and Its Aftermath: Hebrew Books Published in the Years 1933–1972* (in Hebrew). Jerusalem: Yad Vashem.

Porat, D. 1994. "'Amalek's Partners': Ultra-Orthodox Anti-Zionist Accusations in Israel in the 1980s against Zionism during the Period of the Holocaust" (in Hebrew) *Zionism* 19, 295–324.

Prager, M. 1974. *Sparks of Glory,* New York: Shengold Publishers.

—. 1980. *Those Who Never Yielded: The History of the Chassidic Rebel Movement in the Ghettoes of German-Occupied Poland,* translated by Y. Leiman. New York: Lightbooks.

Rawidowicz, S. (ed.) 1961. *The Writings of Nahman Krokhmal: Introduction.* London: Ararat Publishing Society.

Rosen, Rabbi Yitzhak Yehuda. 2002. "Lama Lo Lomar Kinot Al Yom ha-Shoah" ("Why not Say Lamentations for the Holocaust?"). *Kfar Chabad,* 17 July.

Rosen, Y. 2000 (5760). "Kinot ha-Shoah le-Tisha be-Av: Parashah Alumah be-Mifaalo shel ha-Rav M. M. Kasher Zt"l'" ("Lamentations for the Holocaust on the Ninth of Av: An Unknown Episode from the Life of the Late Rav M. M. Kasher") (in Hebrew) *Tzohar* 6, 153–64.

Rosen-Zvi, Y. 2002. "The Holocaust in the Thinking of Rabbi Zvi Yehuda Kook" (in Hebrew) *Democratic Culture* 6, 165–209.

Safrai S. 1994. *In Times of Temple and Mishnah: Studies in Jewish History,* vol. 1. Jerusalem: Magnes Press.

Samet, M. 2005. *Chapters in the History of Orthodoxy* (in Hebrew). Jerusalem: Merkaz Dinur.

Schorsch, I. 1994. *From Text to Context: The Turn to History in Modern Judaism*. MA: Brandeis University Press.

Schwartz, Y. and Y. Goldstein. 1986 (5747). *Leket Dvarim be-Nosei Hurban Yahadut Europa (1939–1945) Mitoch Aspaklaria shel Torah* (*A Collection of Essays Concerning the Destruction of European Jewry through the Lens of the Torah*) (in Hebrew). Jerusalem: Hamossad Leidud Limud Hatorah.

Schweid, E. 1988–9. "Is the Holocaust an 'Unprecedented Event'?" (in Hebrew). *Iyyun* 37 (3–4), 271–85.

—. 1994. *Wrestling until Day-break*. Lanham: University Press of America; Jerusalem: Jerusalem Center for Public Affairs.

—. 1996. "The Impact of the Holocaust on *Haredi* Thought" (Hebrew). *Avar Ve'Atid* 3 (1), 44–55.

Shapira, A. 1999. "Ha-historia shel ha-Mitologia- Kavim la-Historiografia al Odot Ben Gurion veha-Shoah" ("The History of Mythology: outlines of the Historiography of Ben-Gurion and his Attitude Towards the Holocaust") (in Hebrew). *Alpayim* 18, 24–53.

Shaviv, Y. 2001 (5762). "'Zikaron la-Shoah: Yom Hazikaron-Yom Hakadish Haklali" ("Remembering the Holocaust: The Memorial day – The General day of the Kaddish Recitation") (in Hebrew). In A. Warhaftig (ed.) *Ha-Rabanut Ha-Rashit Le-Yisrael Shivim Shana le-yisudda*. Vol. 2. Jerusalem: Hechal Shelomo, 445–71.

Spitz, A. L. 1980. "Al Kvi'at Yom Ta'anit al Harugei ha-Hurban" ("On the Announcement of a Day of Fast in Memory of the Holocaust Victims") (in Hebrew). *Hamaor* 32 (5), 13–18.

Stauber, R. 2000. *Lesson for This Generation: Holocaust and Heroism in Israeli Public Discourse in the 1950s* (in Hebrew). Jerusalem: Yad Ben-Zvi Press.

—. 2005. "The Jewish Response during the Holocaust: The Educational Debate in Israel in the 1950s" (in Hebrew). *Shofar* 22 (4), 57–66.

Steinberg, Y. A. 1990 (5751). "Asara be-Tevet: Yom Ha-Shoah she-Hafach le-Yom ha-Kaddish ha-Klali (Korotehah shel Takanah)" ("The Tenth of Tevet: The Holocaust Memorial day which became the General day of Reciting the Kaddish") (in Hebrew). *Shana be- Shana.* Jerusalem: The Chief Rabbinate of the State of Israel, 378–85.

—. 1991 (5752). "Asara be-Tevet ke-Yom ha-Shoah (Ha-Takanah ha-Mekorit shel ha-Rabanut ha-Rashit Nokhah Kvi'at ha-Knesset), Iyyun Ra'ayoni" ("The Tenth of Tevet as a Memorial Day for the Holocaust. (The Original Enactment of the Chief Rabbinate of the State of Israel as against the Decision of the Knesset)" (in Hebrew). *Shana be-Shana.* Jerusalem: The Chief Rabbinate of the State of Israel, 311–20.

Sternbuch, M. 1989(5749). *Responsa Teshuvot ve-Hanhagot* (in Hebrew). Vol. 2. Jerusalem: Agudat Netivot HaTorah Ve-Hahesed.

Unger, M. 1969 (5729). *Admorim she-Nispu ba-Shoah (Hassidic Leaders who Perished in the Holocaust)* (in Hebrew). Jerusalem: Mossad Harav Kook.

Urbach, E. E. 1980. *The Tosaphists: Their History, Writings and Methods* (in Hebrew). Jerusalem: Mossad Bialik.

Weinberg, Rabbi Yehiel and Y. Weinberg. 1998 (5759). *Responsa Sridei Esh* (in Hebrew). Vol. 2. Jerusalem: Mossad Harav Kook.

Weitz, Y. 1995. "Political Dimensions of Holocaust Memory in Israel during the 1950s." *Israel Affairs* 1(3), 129–45.

Wolf, A. 1980. " Divrei Raboteinu al Gzeirot Europa" ("The Sayings of Our Ancestors on the Decrees of Europe") (in Hebrew). *Hashkafoteinu* 4, 192–5.

Wolowelsky, J. B. 1989. "Observing Yom Hashoah." *Tradition* 24 (4) 1989, 46–58.

Yerushalmi, Y. H. 1982. *Zakhor: Jewish History and Jewish Memory.* Seattle: University of Washington Press.

Yerushat ha-Pleitah: Kovets Teshuvot mi-Gdolei Medinat Hungaria Asher Rubam Nehergu al Kedushat Hashem be-Sha'at ha-Gezerah 1944 (The Inheritance of the Deceased: A Collection of Responsa from the most Outstanding Leaders of Hungary, most of whom Perished as Martyrs in the Holocaust of 1944) (in Hebrew) (no author). Budapest: No publisher mentioned.

Zeidmann, H. 1970. *She-Hicarti: Dmuyot me-Avar Karov be-Mizrah Europa* (*Those whom I Knew: Figures from the Near Past from Eastern Europe*) (in Hebrew). Jerusalem: Mossad Harav Kook.

Zerubavel, Y. 1995. *Recovered Roots: Collective Memory and the Making of Israel.* Chicago: University of Chicago Press.

Chapter 3

JEFFREY ANDREW BARASH

Analyzing Collective Memory

What is collective memory? The attempt to respond to this question, which has been subject to lively debate over the course of the past decades, faces very different and even disparate kinds of response according to the ways in which it is analyzed in the various disciplines of the humanities and in the social and cognitive sciences. In each case the term "collective memory" signifies the transmission of shared experience that has been retained by a group. But even this rudimentary qualification raises difficulties that immediately come to mind: first, memory necessarily refers to the original sphere of personal experience, to the intimacy of personal life; to speak of "collective memory," then, necessarily presupposes a principle of cohesion of singular personal memories within an overarching whole. The definition of this principle is by no means an easy task. Second, when one refers to group experience into which personal life is interwoven, memory takes on a completely different perspective in relation to a small group, such as a family or a professional association, in contrast to a more extended collectivity, such as the public sphere of national commemoration. Often comprehension of the word "memory" is obscured when it is applied indifferently to personal or collective experience, on the one hand, and to small or very large groups, on the other. It is in this light that the question concerning the meaning of "collective memory" and the "place" in which it might be found arises. One is reminded of St. Augustine's famous description of personal memory in quest of its hidden source in book X of the *Confessions*, in which he likened memory to the soul itself ("Hic vero, cum animus sit etiam ipsa memoria") (St. Augustine 1988, vol. II, Bk X, 110–11) and described it as being in a "place which is not a place" ("interiore loco, non loco") (ibid., 100–1). And beyond the personal sphere, this same question of "place," of "locus," is all the more complex in relation to collective memory.

An initial phenomenological attempt to locate collective memory aims to situate it at different levels, according to whether it is shared by smaller or larger groups. At the most elementary level one can speak of the experience of a family, of a school class or of a professional group. Here the description of shared memories may be quite simple: an important event, for example, may characterize the personal reminiscences of each of the members of the group over the course of their lives. Beyond memories retained by small groups, one may refer to memories shared by larger collectivities which recall events that draw on collective practices much older than any of the members of the group and, as such, constitute a fundamental source of the identity of each of its members. One may take as examples political or religious ceremonies, which follow symbolic patterns of behavior. As a sign of patriotism, the members of a group who share the same nationality, upon hearing the national anthem of their country, rise to their feet. The Pesach Seder enjoins each of the participants to reenact in memory the flight from Egypt, by which a mighty hand led the Jewish people to freedom. Similarly, the members of a Christian church celebrate the ritual of the Eucharist in remembering the words of Christ: "This is my body, which is for you, do this in memory of me." In such examples, the identities of smaller groups, whether family or other gatherings, incorporate the memories of larger preexisting groups and draw on symbolic practices that are at the root of all collective experience as such.

In terms of a phenomenological description such as this, the characterization of collective memory, in spite of the variety of levels at which it may be situated, indicates in a preliminary way that the possibility of referring memory beyond the sphere of personal experience arises in the communicative power of *symbols*. It is in deploying potent symbols that flags in the political sphere or wine in religious ritual evoke collectively meaningful reminiscence. Our phenomenological investigation of the locus of collective memory must thus proceed by clarifying the relation between personal memory and the collective forms of remembrance conveyed by means of symbols. This will be done in two steps: first, by elucidating what is taken to be a phenomenological description of collective memory; second, by arguing in favor of the *primacy* of such analysis, which will be considered in relation to the challenge presented by psychoanalytic, neurocognitive and sociohistorical methods, which to my mind are the predominant methods of approach to the phenomenon of collective memory in the contemporary human, natural and cultural sciences.

1

To present an initial phenomenological elucidation of the relation between personal memory and symbolically elaborated collective remembrance, I draw on an example that seems particularly appropriate for this task: the famous speech of Martin Luther King Jr, "I have a dream."

Martin Luther King delivered this speech on 28 August 1963, during the "March on Washington," which rallied nearly 250,000 participants. The demonstration was called in the name of the civil rights movement, which was protesting against the conditions of political and social inequality to which black Americans were subjected. This event also marked a commemoration: assembled before the Lincoln Memorial, it recalled the centenary of the famous Emancipation Proclamation by which President Abraham Lincoln, in the midst of the American Civil War, proclaimed the liberation of the black slaves. Martin Luther King called attention to this commemoration in his speech, and also reminded his hearers that the promise of equality made by Lincoln had never been kept.

However, the evocative power of Martin Luther King's speech stems not only from the fact that he reminded his hearers of this unkept promise. At another level, the Protestant pastor recalled something else, which stood at the heart of Lincoln's own speech: the idea of equality upon which the American nation, beginning with the Declaration of Independence of 1776, was founded: "We hold these truths to be self-evident, that all men are created equal," as we can read in this document, cited by Lincoln and evoked once again by Martin Luther King. More important still, the founding fathers of the United States did not limit themselves to a purely *political* legitimation of this principle of equality; they also grounded it in what they considered to be a divine sanction. Lincoln did not hesitate to refer to this religious foundation of the principle of equality, and Martin Luther King recalled with singular eloquence its profound eschatological source. Thus, after envisioning the end to racial strife in the American South and the possibility that black and white children might walk peacefully hand in hand, the Protestant pastor evoked the prophetic vision – drawing on the New Testament's Gospel of Saint Luke, which explicitly recalled the Old Testament words of the prophet Isaiah: "The glory of the Lord shall be revealed, and all flesh shall see it together" (Luther King 1998, 226).

This example permits the establishment of an important distinction, which is necessary for the elucidation of the phenomenon of collective memory. At one level of analysis, one can elicit the collective memory retained by those who listened to the speech on 28 August 1963. I recall how vividly this discourse moved me as a young schoolboy, as I watched it on television. I remember the tense context in which it was presented in that year, which, less than three months later, would witness the assassination of John F. Kennedy. With this example in mind, a first "locus" of collective memory may be identified: the recollection of shared experience that a group retains. On this day, 28 August 1963, the demonstrators, the schoolboy who viewed it on television and the contemporaries who learned of the event through the other media all remembered it, albeit in different ways and at various points of distance from the event itself. Maurice Halbwachs, in his pioneering works, *Les cadres sociaux de la mémoire* and *La mémoire collective*, defined the phenomenon of collective memory in similar terms, as the experience that a group shares and retains. For Halbwachs, collective memory lasts only as long as the group that remembers the shared experience and disappears as soon as all of its members have passed away. At this point, collective memory gives way to historiography and to its quest for traces of a past that living individuals no longer retain (Halbwachs 1997, 97–142).

When defined in these terms, however, the phenomenon of collective memory still remains at a preliminary level of analysis. It would have been possible, indeed, to listen to the speech without comprehending its significance. One might have failed to pay attention to its words, as many often do while listening to political utterances that are for them a source of infinite boredom. One might in such a case recall ancillary or even trivial phenomena – the beautiful sun that illuminated the August sky, the unusually large number of the police forces called in for the occasion, or the tension that could everywhere be felt on this momentous occasion. To my mind, it is essential to distinguish between the direct recall of an event and another moment with which it is often confused, its *symbolic embodiment*. Symbolic embodiment as a collective phenomenon precedes and distinguishes itself from historical narrative, which seeks to grasp the event following the disappearance of all living memory. In its fluidity and immediacy it also differs from what we commonly refer to as "tradition," with which it is often confused. If imagination accompanies the activity of remembrance (it would reach beyond the present analysis to examine this point in detail), it is *a fortiori* an essential moment in the symbolic embodiment of collective memory. For this reason, symbolic embodiment may very well arise in the direct experience of the event, forming the core of subsequent recollection: contemporaries who appreciated the theologico-political depth of Martin Luther's speech initially grasped the importance of the event and the contribution of Martin Luther King, which is today the object of official commemoration on a national scale. This is not to deny the existence of different and even contradictory manners of symbolically embodying an event: southerners hostile to the message of the black pastor or the head of the FBI, J. Edgar Hoover, who evinced an implacable hostility toward Martin Luther King and toward his cause, accorded a very different symbolic significance to the event than did his supporters. In this sense, collective memory is, from the very point of its genesis, fragmented memory (Mendels 2004, 30–47). At the same time, it is in each case the symbolic force that permits collective memory to constitute a source of temporal continuity of group identities, which, as it is codified, lends itself to the formation of what we normally call "tradition."

Here a distinction needs to be drawn that is essential to the discussion. I distinguish between the multitude of perspectives retained by personal memories of a collectively experienced event and the symbolic embodiment of memory, constituting a collectively identifiable locus for past experience. And the point I seek to make is that "collective memory" can be reduced to neither one nor the other of these moments but gravitates between them as modes of recall of the remembered past. At one extremity is found the singularity of perspective that roots all collectively significant experience in the web of personal remembrance; at the other extremity symbolic embodiment raises remembrance beyond personal experience to confer upon it significance and communicability in the collective sphere. At one extremity, it is possible to limit remembrance so completely to the realm of personal experience that its collective significance is blurred (the beautiful sun that illuminated the August sky, the unusually large number of the police forces called in for the occasion, the tension that could everywhere be felt on this momentous occasion); at the other extremity, even after all personal, living recollection of the event has vanished, its symbolic embodiment in a specific event can be recalled and reenacted to lend significance to later collective experience (Martin Luther King declaring: "I have a dream"). It is in the thickness of its many stratifications that symbolic embodiment confers on collective memory a perdurability extending well beyond the lives of those who directly experience a moment in its ongoing and changing articulation. And this perdurability indicates a dimension of symbolic embodiment of language and gesture that constitutes a metapersonal fount of personal and interpersonal interaction.

2

Described in such a manner, the phenomenon of collective memory would seem to lend itself to straightforward analysis. The problematic status of collective memory becomes apparent, however, as soon as the phenomenological description is abandoned and one attempts to account for it through methodologies that locate its source beyond the scope of experience. Three such methodologies, above all, serve to orient current conceptions of collective memory: those inspired by psychoanalysis, by the neurocognitive fields and by the sociohistorical disciplines. Each of these methodologies presents an approach to collective memory that is difficult to reconcile with the others. Which of them, therefore, is most capable of situating the phenomenon of collective memory? Let us briefly examine the claims of each method as a means of bringing our conception of collective memory more clearly into focus.

Much of the recent literature dealing with collective memory has drawn its inspiration from psychological and psychoanalytic research, most directly stemming from the work of Sigmund Freud and his school. According to Freud's well-known theory, all human relations are founded on the dynamics of the individual's early experiences in the nuclear family, in which the mechanisms of repression of un-acceptable unconscious wishes, as well as of traumatic experiences, are constitutive of both individual and group relations. All relations are characterized by repressed desires and repressed experiences con-tinuing to operate tacitly and condition everyday behavior in ways not readily brought to awareness that commonly operate in the form of symptoms. And it is in this light that symbolic meaning is analyzed. Symbols are of importance insofar as they can be related to psychic functions, above all in their quality as symptoms of unconscious pro-cesses that can be therapeutically treated. Other types of symbols, most notably in the spheres of politics and religion, come into view to the extent that they mirror psychological processes. Hence, for ex-ample, in *The Interpretation of Dreams*, Freud established a parallel between the work of dream censorship in the dreams of the sleeping individual, which through symbolization and related psychic mechanisms hides the unacceptable content of repressed desires expressed in the dream, and the work of the political writer who, through similar tactics, conceals the explicit content of a political message before the watchful eyes of the political censor (Freud 1953, 141–2). Here, as elsewhere in Freud's work, the notion of collective memory as repressed memory is conceived of in terms of a theory of psychological drives and anxieties. Likewise, in later works such as *The Future of an Illusion*, the content of religion comes into view to the extent that it corresponds to a psychological function derived from primal family relations: at once from the infantile belief in the father as an omnipotent protector and from distant recollections of the archaic killing of the primal father, subsequently resurrected as a divinity. For Freud, it is in this sense that "the store of religious ideas includes not only wish fulfillments but important historical recollections" (Freud 1961, 42). Religion for Freud expresses an essentially illusory symptom of repressed wishes. In the theoretical treatment of both political and religious themes, as of conscious experience more generally, symbols come under consideration to the extent that they express unconscious drives, recollections of an archaic past in which they were once enacted and which are subsequently subjected to the mechanisms of sublimation or repression. They are expressed, "remembered," in the form of symptoms revealing present sources of anxiety, tension and illness that the therapist seeks to remedy. As a central part of the dynamics of this process, repressed memories need to be taken beyond their symptomatic expression as repressed experience and consciously worked through. "Remembering, Repeating and Working Through" is indeed the title that Freud gave to his famous paper on this subject, which, in recent years, has aroused particular interest in studies in philosophy and the human sciences (Freud 1958).

The doubts I raise concerning the pertinence of this method for an understanding of the phenomenon of collective memory in no way bring into question the significance of psychoanalysis as a therapeutic method, nor deny the phenomenon of repressed collective experience and the need for a therapeutic working out of past trauma at a collective level. My doubt concerns the capacity of the psychoanalytic method to reveal the full significance of the symbol – what I have termed the symbolic embodiment of experience in collective memory. Certainly it would be possible to characterize the movement of Martin Luther King in psychological terms, underscoring the traumatic collective experience of centuries of slavery, followed by a century of injustice during which blacks were deprived of elementary civil rights. Subsequent to the changes in legislation, in large part due to the moral persuasiveness of this movement's non-violent tactics, one might continue to underscore the ongoing inequalities that have persisted following the institution of political equality. Or one might signal what certain authors have described as an "abuse" of memory and, in extrapolating from Freud's theory (albeit not always in accord with Freud's intentions), support their arguments on the basis of assumptions drawn from collective psychology. In this vein, following the initial success of the civil rights movement, the principle aim of the black minority might appear to be to convert a situation of past injustice into a new privileged status. Did Martin Luther King himself, in his "I have a dream" speech, not proclaim that the American people had a debt to pay to black citizens and that he had come to Washington to "cash a check"? And once civil rights have been granted, is it not all the more convenient to be able to "place oneself in the position of the victim" ("la prétention à s'installer dans la posture de la victime") in order to legitimate further claims to reparation? As Tzvetan Todorov writes, applying the psychology of family therapy to the political domain: "To have once been a victim gives you the right to complain, to protest and to make demands" ("Avoir été victime vous donne le droit de vous plaindre, de protester, et de réclamer") (Todorov 1995, 56). And in adopting a similar psychological perspective in his recent work, *La mémoire, l'histoire, l'oubli*, Paul Ricoeur, while stressing that he does not want to overstate this point, hardly questions Todorov's claim that the posture of the victim "creates an exorbitant privilege, which places the rest of the world in a situation of being holders of a debt" ("Cette posture engendre un privilège exorbitant, qui met le reste du monde en position de débiteur de créances"). This is why Ricoeur abandoned the idea of a "duty to remember," preferring instead, in accord with his interpretation of the Freudian terminology he adopts, a "working through" of the collective memory of past trauma (Ricoeur 2000, 104–11; Ricoeur 2000a, 1ff).

But, whether we are referring to black Americans or to any other minority group (Todorov and Ricoeur have most immediately in view the posterity of Jewish victims of the Shoah), does this concentration on the psychological dimension of collective memory provide us with the best mode of access to this phenomenon? By strictly applying the analogy of individual psychic processes to collective recollection, do we not risk obscuring the symbolic depth and long durability of those experiences specific to larger collectivities, which emerge into view only in the space between personal reminiscence and symbolic inscription?

Given Ricoeur's earlier work on Freud and on the limitations of the Freudian reference to symbolism largely in the framework of an analysis of symptoms, the paucity of his description of the phenomenon of symbolism is noteworthy. Ricoeur had earlier illustrated that if symbols are indeed, as Freud claimed, the material of symptoms, a too exclusive insistence on their symptomatic character risks obscuring the multiple significations of the symbol. In one sense – regressive – the symbol may be symptomatic of an illness; in another context – progressive – it may give birth to a work of art, a religious doctrine or a new political foundation (Ricoeur 1970, 514–43). And it is rather the importance of this eminently phenomenological insight that the present analysis seeks to underline.

3

It is well known that Freud maintained a lively interest in the somatic sources of psychological processes, even if he limited his clinical work to the psychological explanation of mental phenomena. The cognitive scientist, who relies on the description of neurological functions underlying experience, takes such somatic sources to be the central focus of investigation. Among the theorists in this field, the work of Gerald M. Edelman is particularly important since he focuses directly on the phenomena of personal and collective memory, while providing cogent philosophical commentary on his method of analysis. His neurophysiological theory has had wide influence on this theme not only in the United States but in Europe, notably among the members of the school of Jean-Pierre Changeux. Edelman's underlying philosophical presuppositions can be summarized by a quote from the book *Quiddities* by Wilfred Quine, which is placed in epigraph at the beginning of Edelman's major work, *The Remembered Present: A Biological Theory of Consciousness* (1987, 8): "Whatever it precisely may be, consciousness is a state of the body, a state of nerves." By this statement Quine, and with him Edelman, do not simply seek to reduce the faculties of consciousness – memory, imagination, perception, reflexion – to bodily functions, but to conceive of mind and body as a unity and thus to "repudiate mind as a second substance, over and above body." What is important here, however, is less the question concerning the substantial composition of this unity than the conclusion Edelman draws from it: the possibility of rigorously explaining it in terms of its natural function. In line with this argument, Edelman asserts that memory and individual consciousness, as well as language and collective modes of understanding – consequently, all that might be placed under the heading of collective memory – are means of natural adaptation of human organisms to their environment. The capacity to remember past events and to communicate them collectively through language are naturally useful, and they favor adaptation in permitting humans to liberate themselves from the constraints of the immediate temporal moment and recall past experience as a basis for deliberating future action. The temporal consciousness with which the development of memory is intrinsically connected constitutes a uniquely human capacity that Edelman terms "higher order consciousness." And he attempts to account for the emergence of this capacity through the biological and neurological laws of natural selection that govern the process of human evolution. In his words:

> With higher-order consciousness, the ability to plan a series of actions, more or less free of immediate time constraints, must have enhanced fitness. In hominids, at least, primary consciousness must have had evolutionary efficacy, insofar as it is required for the development of a self-concept and of language (ibid., 248).

This critique of Edelman's attempt to explain the workings of consciousness, and more precisely the phenomenon of collective memory, does not dispute the central place of neurophysiological functions in accounting for memory; what I question is the claim of these methods to scientific validity, and even to philosophical plausibility, when they are extended beyond the purview of empirical science into the domain of speculation. In this vein, the claim to reveal neurophysiological preconditions *necessary* for explaining the physical capacity to represent and to retain images or sounds, as well as for their communication, may well be an empirically grounded conclusion. But the hypothesis that the laws of natural selection or, for that matter, any general laws of nature, might provide *sufficient* grounds to account for personal consciousness, and thus for collective experience and collective memory, is highly speculative, to say the least. Even where speculative propositions are dressed up in scientific language, we are dealing not at the level of empirical science but with metaphysical hypotheses that allow of no scientific proof. Edelman himself has shown willingness to admit the speculative nature of his theories and the fact that they involve materialist presuppositions. And here he oversteps a principle source of his philosophical inspiration, the theory of Quine. Quine, indeed, always refused to account for consciousness, and the phenomena of memory, imagination or perception, in neurophysiological terms. He explicitly adopted Donald Davidson's principle of "anomolous monism," signifying that in considering mind to be an expression of body, he doubted the possibility of accounting for a complex of mental events in physiological or neurological terms (Quine 1987, 132–3). And Davidson himself made a decisive point in this regard in his essay "Mental Events," in *Essays on Actions and Events*, when he emphasized among mental events moral properties that, in his opinion, defy reduction to physical or neurological processes. He acknowledged that

> dependence or supervenience [of the mental in regard to the physical] does not entail reducibility through law or definition: if it did we could reduce moral properties to descriptive, and this there is good reason to *believe* cannot be done (Davidson 1980, 214).

In dealing with this distinction between the mental and the physical, I would above all underscore the principle of the *validity* of normative standards in the mental sphere, which no logically coherent theory can reduce to biological function or to natural law. From this perspective, the neurophysiological claim to account for consciousness, and, more specifically, for the phenomenon of memory, discounts what is most fundamental: the premise according to which symbolic structures, the locus of embodiment of collective memory, possess an inherent truth that is valid independently of any consideration of its neurophysiological preconditions. The symbolism of social justice is ultimately convincing by virtue of this intrinsic significance, and any attempt to attribute its development to the invisible hand of natural law necessarily skirts this question of its inherent validity. (The most convincing and systematic discussion of this idea of validity is still to be found, in my opinion, in Husserl's *Logical Investigations*, but it would reach beyond the scope of the present investigation to take up this point in detail.)

4

The sociohistorical approach to collective memory, which has also exercised great contemporary influence in the study of this phenomenon, shares little common ground either with psychoanalysis or with neurocognitive theories. The socio-historical method rejects any attempt to understand collective memory in terms of extrahistorical models, whether psychological or evolutionary. Against such models, the socio-historical method presupposes the radical historicity of human experience and of the modes of collective remembrance of the past. From this perspective, the role of memory changes in relation to its social function. This school of analysis has focused above all on the devaluation of the role of collective memory following the rationalization and urbanization of the predominant sectors of modern society. This development has brought in its wake the decline of rural com-

munities over the past centuries and the disappearance of its oral traditions, which were a primary source of collective memory in the
premodern context. Walter Benjamin provided salient insight into this
phenomenon in his famous essay "The Storyteller" (Benjamin 1991, 2:
438–65). And in adopting a parallel idea of the historicity of collective
memory in his preface to the multivolume work *Les lieux de mémoire*,
Pierre Nora has elaborated on this assumption concerning the radical
divergence in the function of memory between premodern and modern, between traditional rural and modern rationalized forms of society. It is this premise concerning the radical break with the past
inaugurated by modernity that led Nora to underscore the fragility of
collective memory in the contemporary context. With the decline of
the social function of collective memory, the lines of continuity
linking the present to an ongoing, living memory and to the past it
retained are severed: "One speaks so much of memory," says Nora,
"only because it no longer exists" (Nora 1984, xvii). The disappearance of collective memory, according to Nora, not only corresponds to
the decline of its social function due to the urbanization of modern
society; urbanization and rationalization also signaled its secularization. Collective memory in traditional society is sustained by the
continuity provided by ongoing religious practices, by the rituals and
liturgies that are an integral part of traditional life; the rationalization
of all conditions of human existence typical of the modern world
engenders a radically different approach to the past: in the chasm left
by the demise of collective memory and of the religious practices that
kept it alive, modernity seeks to resurrect the past through historical-
critical methods of analysis that hold such practices at a distance.
"Memory," as Nora writes, "situates recollection in the sphere of the
sacred [...]. History, as an intellectual and secular operation, elicits
analysis and critical discourse" (ibid., xix).

Here, however, we wonder if Nora's assumption that the decline
of important sectors of rural society and of oral traditions that were a
living source of collective memory can be generalized to such an
extent. Collective memory and the symbolic meanings it embodies ex-
hibit a vitality that is in no way restricted to traditional rural environ-
ments and, as the speech of Martin Luther King attests, shows an

ongoing capacity to revitalize past religious and political experience in the contemporary world.

If, therefore, I level a general critique against the three orientations elicited here, it is to call for a renewal of the phenomenological approach to collective memory that seeks its locus in the space between personal recollection and symbolic embodiment.

Bibliography

Augustine, St 1988. *Confessions*, translated by William Watts, 2 vols Cambridge, MA: Loeb Library, Harvard University Press.

Benjamin, W. 1991. *Aufsätze, Essays, Vorträge, Gesammelte Schriften*, II, 2. Frankfurt am Main: Suhrkamp.

Davidson, D. 1980. *Essays on Actions and Events*. Oxford: Clarendon Press.

Edelman, G. M. 1989. *The Remembered Present. A Biographical Theory of Consciousness*. New York: Basic Books.

Freud, S. 1953. *The Interpretation of Dreams, The Standard Edition of the Complete Psychological Works of Sigmund Freud*, vol. 4, part 1. London: Hogarth.

—. 1955. *Beyond the Pleasure Principle. Group Psychology and Other Works. The Standard Edition of the Complete Psychological Works of Sigmund Freud*, vol. 18. London: Hogarth.

—. 1958. "Remembering, Repeating and Working Through," *The Case of Schreber. Papers on Technique and Other Works. The Standard Edition of the Complete Psychological Works of Sigmund Freud*, vol. 12. London: Hogarth.

—. 1961. *The Future of an Illusion. Civilization and Its Discontents and Other Works. The Standard Edition of the Complete Psychological Works of Sigmund Freud*, vol. 21. London: Hogarth.

Halbwachs, M. 1994. *Les cadres sociaux de la mémoire*. Paris: Albin Michel.

—. 1997 [...] *La mémoire collective*. Paris: Albin Michel.

Husserl, E. 1992. *Prolegomena zur reinen Logik.* Vol. 1, *Logische Untersuchungen*; vol. 2, *Werke.* Meiner: Hamburg.

Luther King, M. 1998. *Autobiography.* New York: Warner Books.

Mendels, D. 2004. *Memory in Jewish, Pagan and Christian Societies of the Graeco-Roman World.* London/New York: Continuum and T&T Clark International.

Nora, P. 1984. "Entre mémoire et histoire. La problématique des lieux." *Les lieux de mémoire.* vol. 1, *La République.* Paris: Gallimard.

Quine W. 1987. *Quiddities.* Cambridge, MA: Belknap Press.

Ricoeur, P. 1970. *Freud and Philosophy: An Essay on Interpretation*, translated by Denis Savage. New Haven: Yale University Press.

—. 2000. *La mémoire, l'histoire, l'oubli.* Paris: Éditions du Seuil.

—. 2000a. "L'écriture de l'histoire et la représentation du passé." *Le Mond*, 15 June.

Todorov, T. 1995. *Les abus de la mémoire.* Paris: Arléa.

Chapter 4

Yoram Bilu

Saint Impresarios in Israel as Agents of Memory

1   Introduction

In recent years Israel has witnessed a proliferation of holy sites and cultic practices related to saint worship. Old-time saints' sanctuaries are glowing with renewed popularity; new ones are being added to the native "sacred geography," and the list of contemporary charismatic rabbis acknowledged as *tsaddiqim* (holy, pious men) is growing (Bilu 2004; Gonen 1998). While this revival appears too widespread to be the monopoly of one particular group, Jews from Morocco have emerged as a major force behind it, impregnating the cult of the saints in contemporary Israel with a distinctive Maghrebi flavor (Ben-Ami 1984).

The Maghrebi revival of the cult of the saints, in all forms and manifestations, is an impressive testimony to the tenacity and durability of traditional practices under conditions of massive social change. The focus of this chapter, however, is on one particular manifestation of saint worship where issues related to the dynamics of cultural remembrance are most acute: the "symbolic translocation" of *tsaddiqim* through dreams. Two attributes make this dream-based undertaking all the more pertinent to issues of memory. First, since many of the projects included here involved saints transferred from Morocco to Israel, this was the only pattern daringly aiming at a full-blown *restoration* of the Moroccan past. All other contemporary forms of Maghrebi saint worship in Israel may be viewed as *compensatory* alternatives for the Moroccan saints' sanctuaries that remained remote and difficult to access since the massive immigration of Moroccan Jews to Israel in the 1950s and 60s. Second, since we deal here with individually based initiatives inspired by visitational dreams (Bilu 2000a; Bilu and Abramovitch 1985; Crapanzano 1975), issues related to the interface of individual and collective memory come to the fore. These issues are all the more pressing against the epistemologically precarious status of dream messages, even in cultural settings congenial to otherworldly apparitions, and the plebeian background of the dreamers. As inspiring as the nightly encounters with the saints have been, the new shrines that these encounters bred could not be sustained without a community of believers.

Concentrating on the dreamers, who were the prime movers behind the new shrines, I view these saint impresarios as agents of memory *par excellence*. Consequently I seek to deploy their projects in a wider, memory-driven context through the following steps: first, I examine the Jewish Moroccan traditions of saint veneration as forms of cultural memory. Second, I discuss the dialectics of forgetting and remembering in the vicissitudes of these traditions following immigration and the massive break with the past it generated. Focusing on the accounts of the saint impresarios, the emphasis here is on the critical links between biography and community, individually recalled experiences, and social and public forms of memory. Third, shifting my gaze to macro-level processes in present-day Israel, I seek to account for the constitution of saint-based "landscapes of memory" (Kirmayer 1996) and "mnemonic communities" (Zerubavel 1996) in Israel's urban periphery. These developments are explored in terms of the politics of memory and identity in contemporary Israel and the challenges it poses to the master commemorative narrative of Zionist ideology. Taking into account that the new shrines are historically situated, I conclude by evaluating their durability or "shelf life" in the densely populated and highly contested sacred geography of Israel.

2   Jewish Saint Worship in Morocco: Identity, Community and Memory

Saint worship played a major role in the lives of many Jews in traditional Morocco and constituted a basic component of their ethnic identity. In form, style and prevalence this cultural phenomenon clearly bears the hallmarks of indigenous saint worship, perhaps the most significant feature of Moroccan Islam (Eickelman 1976; Geertz 1968; Gellner 1969; Munson 1993). At the same time, however, it was also reinforced by the deep-seated conception of the *tsaddiq* in classical Jewish sources (Goldberg 1983; Stillman 1982).

Most of the Jewish Moroccan saints were depicted as charismatic rabbis, distinguished by their erudition and piety. These rabbis were believed to possess a special spiritual force, which did not fade away after their death. This force, akin to the Moroccan Muslim *baraka* (Rabinow 1975; Westermarck 1926), could be utilized for the benefit of the saints' adherents. In contrast to their Muslim counterparts, most of the Jewish Moroccan *tsaddiqim* were identified as such only after their death. Therefore their miraculous feats were usually associated with their tombs. In fact, as befitting oral traditions, some of these *tsaddiqim* were devoid of any historical marker and endowed with a highly stereotypical life story. At the same time, however, the strong sense of inherited blessedness associated with the Jewish notion of *zekhut avot* (literally, the virtue of the ancestors) allowed for the emergence of some dynasties of *tsaddiqim*, the most well-known of which were the Abu-Hatseras, the Pintos and the Ben-Baruchs (Ben-Ami 1984).

Virtually every Jewish community, including the tiniest and most peripheral, had one or more patron saints. While the popularity of most of these saints was quite circumscribed, some of them acquired reputations and followings that transcended regional boundaries. As mentioned, some of the saints were well-known historical figures, while many others seemed to be legendary characters, recognized as blessed with holiness only after a posthumous apparition, most typically in dreams.

Generally speaking, the presence of the saints was a basic given in the social reality of Moroccan Jews, a central idiom for articulating a wide range of experiences. In this sense, the folk-veneration of *tsaddiqim* in traditional Morocco constituted an organic *milieu de mémoire,* in Pierre Nora's terms (Nora 1984). The past blended easily with the present through a wide variety of "mnemonic tools." The legends of the saints, orally transmitted, were widely shared; the saints' shrines, ordinarily situated in the local cemetery or in the familiar environs, served as salient anchors of memory bolstered by many practices and rituals. The main event in the veneration of each saint was the collective pilgrimage to his tomb on the anniversary of his death and the *hillulah* (celebration; plural *hillulot*) there. In the case of the more renowned saints, thousands of pilgrims from various regions would gather around the tombs for several days, during which they feasted on slaughtered cattle, drank *mahia* (arak), danced and chanted, prayed and lit candles. All these activities, combining marked spirituality and high ecstasy with mundane concerns, were conducted in honor of the *tsaddiq.* Thus *hillulot* at the shrines functioned as Bakhtinian *chronotopes,* strengthening the cultural schema of the *tsaddiq* in the devotees' life space through the convergence of holy place, holy time and exciting ritual activity.

In addition to collective pilgrimages, visits to saints' sanctuaries were made on an individual basis in times of plight. As intermediaries between God Almighty and the believers, the problems that saints were considered capable of solving included the whole range of human concerns. The presence of the saint was also strongly felt in daily routine, as people would cry out his name and dream about him whenever facing a problem. At home, candles were lit and festive meals (*se'udot*) were organized in his honor and his name was conferred on male newborns. In many cases the relationship with the saint amounted to a symbiotic association spanning the entire life course of the devotee.

For devoted members of the cult of the saints, the internalized cultural representation of the *tsaddiq* (Spiro 1987) was a Janus-faced personal symbol, at once personal and collective, private and public, internal and external (Kracke 1994; Obeyesekere 1981, 1990). Through the cultural idiom of the saint, inchoate experiences and painful feelings could be articulated and objectified. Hence the "landscapes of memory" associated with the saints were both extra- and intra-personal. The saints were conspicuously represented in the shrine-dotted outer landscapes; but as strong personal symbols mediating cultural idiom and private experience, the saints were also strongly registered in the believers' mental landscapes. The work of memory was multifaceted, involving semantic, biographical memory (e.g. engaging personal episodes related to saintly interventions) but also embodied memory, manifested in highly emotional responses and encoded bodily gestures of awe and deference.

Beyond the ahistorical character of many *tsaddiqim*, the folk system of saint worship defied chronology, as old and new saints were aligned together, without much attention to historical differentiation. In fact, some of the most popular figures in the Jewish Moroccan pantheon of saints were latecomers, discovered only in the twentieth century. Rather than a frozen set of cultural vestiges, Jewish Maghrebi saint worship was a dynamic system, accommodating to shifting circumstances, in which new saints and shrines successively emerged, sank and resurfaced. The 1940s and 50s, decades of rapid modernization in Morocco, were also the golden period of saint worship among Moroccan Jews. The rapid social changes wrought by the French during their Protectorate (1912–56) – manifested in massive migration, urbanization, and secularization – shattered the traditional Jewish communities. Under the resultant growing disorientation, the salience and appeal of the traditional dispensers of solace and protection had been growing. Following colonial-enforced pacification, communication and locomotion between the Jewish communities became affordable and, with it, the accessibility of the shrines. The improved economic and political conditions facilitated organizational efforts that resulted in drawing large numbers of visitors to the tombs of the saints. At the same time, notwithstanding the growing popularity of *hillulot*, one could track changes in the cult of the saints that corresponded to Nora's proposed (admittedly overschematic) transition from *mileux de mémoire* to *lieux de mémoire*. The massive migration of Jews to Casablanca and other urban settings, where most of the saints' sanctuaries were located, and the rapid social changes that entailed, corroded the central place of the saints in daily reality.

The emerging break with the past, weakening the traditional moorings of family and community, has dialectically accentuated the role of *hillulot* as public events, bounded and ceremonial, situated in territories where Jewish presence was dwindling and celebrating traditional forms of life gradually receding. Anticipating their function in Israel in the late twentieth century, *hillulot* in mid-twentieth-century Morocco served to cultivate a sense of group identity and ethnic distinction in times of rapid social changes.

3   The Lives and Times of Saint Impresarios

The social fabric of Moroccan Jewry, including their saint worship traditions, was ruptured following the massive waves of immigration from Morocco to Israel during the 1950s and 60s. To the predicament of homecoming, fed by cultural shock and enormous economic difficulties, one could add the painful disengagement from the saints whose tombs had been left behind. Veteran members of the cult of the saints remained attached to the *tsaddiqim* of their past in the first years after immigration, but the *hillulot* of these *tsaddiqim* underwent a process of diminution and decentralization, being now modestly celebrated at home or in the local synagogue (Ben-Ami 1984, 208; Stillman 1995; Weingrod 1990). Once the newcomers became more rooted in the local scene and more confident in their Israeli identity, hagiolatric practices were forcefully revived as emblems of ethnic pride, compatible with the resurgence of ethnic sentiments in many immigrant-absorbing countries (Bennett 1975; Eisenstadt 1980; Novak 1979). The sites established by the saint impresarios I studied were modest in comparison with the popular shrines of local old-time *tsaddiqim* such as Rabbi Shimon Bar-Yohai and Rabbi Meir Ba'al-Ha-Ness, or new ones such as Rabbi Israel Abu-Hatsera (Baba Sali) and Rabbi Hayim Houri (Bilu and Ben-Ari 1992; Weingrod 1990). But as mentioned above, some of them were particularly audacious in seeking to resolve the cultural problem of the "abandoned" Maghrebi saints by relocating them in the local landscape. A transplanted *tsaddiq* figures in the first of the two dream-based projects I am discussing here.

(1) *The House of Rabbi David u-Moshe*. The sanctuary of Rabbi David u-Moshe, one of the most popular Jewish saints in Morocco (Ben-Ami 1981; Bilu 1987), is located in Tamezrit near Agouim in the Western High Atlas. In 1973, a 40-year-old forestry worker named Avraham dedicated a room in his modest apartment in Safed to Rabbi David u-Moshe following a dream series in which the tsaddiq indicated his wish to leave Morocco and reside with him. Drawing pilgrims from all over the country, the shrine has emerged as the most successful among the new sites.

(2) *The "Gate of Paradise" and Elijah the Prophet*. According to a Talmudic legend, the entrance to the Garden of Eden in its terrestrial form is located in the town of Beit She'an in the central Jordan Valley.[1] In 1979 a leader of a cleaning team in the local municipality named Yaish announced that he had discovered the Gate of Paradise in the backyard of his house. Elijah the Prophet, the protagonist of Yaish's visitational dreams that precipitated the discovery, was declared the patron of the site. While the traditions associated with the shrine in Beit She'an were local rather then imported, the vicissitudes of the Gate of Paradise were strongly related to issues of individual and collective remembering and their interface.

The childhood memories of Avraham and Yaish were suffused with close encounters with *tsaddiqim*. Avraham grew up on stories glorifying the miraculous feats of two of his ancestors, Rabbi Shlomo Timsut and Rabbi Ya'aqov Timsut. According to the family myth, Rabbi Shlomo was brutally murdered by the wife of a local *kaid* (governor) after declining her sexual advances, and his body was clandestinely entombed in the wall of her house. To expose the perpetrator

---

1   "With regard to Gan Eden, Reish Lakish said: If it is in Eretz Israel, Beit Shean is its entrance" (Babylonian *Talmud, Eruvin* 19a, New York: Mesorah Publications, Ltd, 1990).

of the heinous crime, the disappeared rabbi told his wife in a dream who had killed him and where his body was interred. Consequently, the governer's wife was executed and Rabbi Shlomo was reburied in the cemetery of Marrakech, where he acquired a name as a popular *tsaddiq* (Ben-Ami 1984, 563–5). While the historical basis of this story appears tenuous, it should be noted that two cardinal themes in the narrative – dream revelation and relocation of a burial site – resonate with the later apparition of Rabbi David u-Moshe in Safed.

A more specific link to Avraham's later project seems to have been encoded in the death legend of his great grandfather, Rabbi Ya'aqov Timsut. One month after the deceased rabbi had been buried in Marrakech a letter came from Jerusalem announcing the marvelous emergence of a tombstone with the name of Rabbi Ya'aqov Timsut in the Mount of Olives Cemetery. Thus a model for the transfer of a Jewish saint from Morocco to Israel, a very rare theme in Jewish Moroccan hagiography,[2] had already been in existence as a family tradition prior to the Safed project.

While Avraham's impressions of his late ancestors were formed by oral accounts transmitted in the family, his recollections of his maternal grandfather, still alive and well when Avraham was a child, were vivid, direct and suffused with subjectivity. The circumstances of the death of the grandfather, to whom Avraham was fondly attached, were particularly pertinent to the later initiative. The old patriarch died far away from home, in the coastal town of Essaouira (Mogador), where he had been receiving medical treatment. The Jews of Essaouira, well aware of the piety and blessedness of the late rabbi, hastened to bury him in the local cemetery, thus depriving young Avraham and his family of a place to visit and commemorate the deceased. It should be noted, in light of Avraham's later initiative, that this particular predicament was similar to the one that confronted many other Moroccan Jews in Israel, following the painful disengagement from the Maghrebi abodes of their *tsaddiqim*. Avraham was among the first to assuage this problem by bringing Rabbi David u-Moshe to his home. It might be speculated that in building the shrine

---

2   In Ben-Ami's vast compilation of saints' legends it appears only once (1984, 562).

for Rabbi David u-Moshe, a saint Avraham initially claimed not to have known before the first dream revelation, Avraham unconsciously compensated for the vacuum created by his grandfather's disappearance. The original situation, in which the family *tsaddiq* was appropriated by others, to be buried afar, was reversed and rectified by bringing into the house a "foreign" *tsaddiq*, hitherto unknown, from afar.

Yaish's line of pious ancestry was no less impressive than Avraham's. His great grandfather, a renowned healer, was believed to have gained absolute control over the *jnun* (demons). Yaish's grandfather, Rabbi Issakhar Amar, was considered so pious and devout that he could stop a flowing river with his prayer. Living in an adjacent house, he served for young Yaish as an exemplary model of piety. Thus it appears that the intimate liaison of Avraham and Yaish with Rabbi David u-Moshe and Elijah the Prophet, respectively, was informed by their vivid childhood memories of family *tsaddiqim*. The analytic framework of personal symbols alerts us to the possibility that they both cast the images of their patron saints in the mold of their beloved grandparents and other pious ancestors.

The nostalgic affection that marked Avraham's and Yaish's memories of family *tsaddiqim* extended to reminiscences related to other spheres of their childhood. Consider Yaish's portrayal of his childhood village, Oulad Mansour in southern Morocco:

> Everything was plentiful there. We had beans, pears, grains; we used to fill up sacks with all sort of fruits and dry them. From the river we brought large quantities of fish. [...] People were strong and healthy, and happy too. The water was pure, the air fresh and clear. Nothing got spoiled there. All the inhabitants of Oulad Mansour, Jews and Arabs, were like brothers.

Given the idealized nature of the account, it is tempting to suggest that in establishing the Gate of Paradise in his house, Yaish may have sought to restore the lost Paradise of his childhood. It should be noted that such Arcadian depictions of the Maghrebi past were ordinarily colored by strong spiritual hues, as both Avraham and Yaish have stressed the piety and religious devotion that characterized Jewish life in their communities of origin. This spiritual ambience, bolstered by religious studies in the local synagogue (*sla*) under the close supervision of the local rabbi, was weakened upon immigration to Israel. Again, it is interesting to note how Yaish, who was eleven years old upon immigration, contrasted his Moroccan school experience with learning in Israel:

> Here it was free and easy, without authority. I became less and less conscientious. There we were strong. We studied all day long as we were supposed to do. In any case, the rabbi would not let us deviate from the course of study.

It is no wonder that the negligent atmosphere in the local school, coupled with the family's harsh economic situation, led Yaish to abandon permanently the path of learning after just one year in the new country, when he was twelve years old. For years Yaish lamented his truancy and sought actively to undo it by maintaining a life style of piety and learning, and by running a *Talmud Torah* (religious school) for wayward youth in the sacred site he had established. Yaish was well aware that in building and running the school he was healing his own past wounds.

Even though the theme of Paradise lost and regained was peculiar to Yaish's project, it could be extended metaphorically to Avraham (and other saint impresarios) as well. In both cases, personal memories of the Maghrebi past have transpired into the shrines: the spiritual ambience corroded by immigration and secularization was reinstated there, and so were the forsaken family *tsaddiqim* – under the guise of the shrines' patron saints (as personal symbols). In addition, painful memories of significant losses – the "disappearance" of Avraham's saintly grandfather, Yaish's abandonment of the path of learning – could be redressed and rectified in the new shrines. As mentioned earlier, the restoration of the past was most straightforward in the House of Rabbi David u-Moshe, which became the Israeli home of a popular *tsaddiq* from the Moroccan High Atlas. Significantly, Avraham claimed at first that he had not known Rabbi David u-Moshe in Morocco, but he later retrieved a lost childhood memory, in which he had collected money for the saint's *hillulah*. Such fluctuations in memory may be viewed as part of the struggle of members of an émigré community against the cultural amnesia imposed on them by the hegemonic group. Consider Yaish's contrasting school experiences in Morocco and Israel. In his native village he was deemed an exemplary student, according to his account, due to high motivation and excellent rote memory. But the move to Israel led to no less than an identity-erasing transformation:

> When we came here, we *forgot* the whole world […]. The nonsense one heard at school in Beit She'an was entirely unrelated to religion, this way I *forgot* everything; we learned what they taught us and *forgot* all else we knew

Thus, the secular curriculum in the public school produced massive forgetting tantamount to amnesia. In bringing Elijah home and establishing the Gate of Paradise, Yaish was able to create a *lieux de mémoire*, a storehouse for the saint worship traditions and spiritual ambience that the hegemonic authorities in the new country tried to suppress.

As the psychocultural vehicle for revelation, the dreams that triggered the erection of the shrines partake of the same dialectics of remembering and forgetting. Ordinarily, most dreams are not remembered at all, and the few that are registered in consciousness tend to fade away without active attempts at elaboration and recall. Indeed, Avraham and Yaish both reported that at first, they tended to ignore the nightly messages of the *tsaddiqim*. Only after repeated exposure to these messages did they accept them as veracious communications from otherworldly figures. Thereafter, they spared no effort to transform the dream-narratives into written texts and circulate them on a wide scale. The active process of dream recall was thus metonymic to the cultural salvage work of retrieving saintly traditions and reinstalling them in Israel. Moving from process to content, the theme of abandonment and forgetting was most forcefully invoked by Rabbi David u-Moshe in his first dream encounter with Avraham: "Why have those who left Morocco forsaken me and deserted me?" The *tsaddiq*'s complaint lies at the interface of individual and collective memory and may be taken as the key for understanding the role of Avraham and other saint impresarios as cultural brokers and agents of memory.

On the individual level, the reproach may have been generated by Avraham's covert sense of guilt for altogether forgetting Rabbi David u-Moshe, for whom he had collected money as a child. Psychodynamically, in line with the argument that Rabbi David u-Moshe was personally reconstituted by Avraham in the mold of his holy ancestors, the saint may have given voice to the "forsaken" family *tsaddiqim* from whom Avraham had been disengaged upon immigration. Group sociodynamics, however, appears no less important here than individual psychodynamics, for the complaint resonated with the generalized "Moroccan experience" in Israel, reflecting the collective mood of many ex-devotees who had also been dissociated from their once-cherished saints after immigrating to Israel. In recalling Rabbi David u-Moshe, Avraham was probably acting out and redressing his own painful memories; but at the same time he also touched upon a collective predicament – the "desertion" and "forgetting" of the Jewish Moroccan community of saints following immigration to Israel.

The use of visitational dreams as conduits for eliciting and reviving past traditions entailed a distinctive culture-based epistemology of memory. The articulation of the relation of past to present, as reflected in the recalled experiences of the dreamers, was not based on distanced objectification but rather on direct engagement, even embodiment. In the dreams, the past was reconstituted through engaging in dialogues with *tsaddiqim*. Many of these dreams were *transchronic* in nature, as they brought together *tsaddiqim* from different periods of time. In some of Avraham's dreams, for example, the biblical prophet Elijah, the talmudic sage Rabbi Shimon bar-Yohai and the nineteenth-century founder of the Abu-Hatsera family, Rabbi Ya'aqov, appeared on a joint mission with Rabbi David u-Moshe. Such dreams constituted a simultaneous display of successive temporalities (Lambek 1998). Following Fabian (1983) and Bird-David (2004), it might be argued that visitational dreams portray not the past in the present but past figures as *coeval*. In other words, the *tsaddiqim* do not appear synchronously, as co-occurrences in the same physical time, but rather "occupy" the same intersubjective time. This condensation within the space of the present does not necessarily mean that the voices of the dream protagonists are altogether flattened or confused. Still, it resonates with processes of cultural recollection, where the creative realignment of past sediments defies neat historical periodization.

4   Hierophany at the Margins: The Social Context of Cultural Remembering

In seeking to situate the renaissance of Maghrebi saint worship in the wider context of contemporary Israeli society, the fact that most of the arenas for this revival were situated in the urban periphery of Israel, and particularly in "development towns" (*ayarot pituah*), appears highly significant. The peak of the population dispersion policy initiated by the Israeli government in the early 1950s coincided with the first massive waves of immigration from the Maghreb. Consequently, many Moroccan Jews found themselves relegated to these hastily built, "planted" communities on the periphery of Israel, where they were assigned pioneering roles that veteran Israelis were unwilling to assume (Inbar and Adler 1977). As the largest ethnic group placed in development towns, Moroccan Jews' partaking of the Zionist dream was marred by the many ills of these disadvantaged communities. These ills included limited occupational opportunities due to an under-developed infrastructure and reliance on one type of industry based on manual, low-paying jobs; an almost total dependence on government services; a poor educational system; and a high rate of population turnover, in which the more resourceful, upwardly mobile inhabitants left the towns while the poor and the less able tended to stay (Aronoff 1973; Semyonov 1981).

Because of these chronic problems the development towns were depicted derogatorily as "residual communities" or "sinks" for the less resourceful immigrants. Many of the socioeconomic and political ills that characterized these towns in the 1950s and 60s still haunted them at the turn of the century. At the same time, however, the inhabitants who did stay in the towns, despite the social and economic difficulties, have slowly developed a genuine attachment to the locality. The growth of these "natural" sentiments of belongingness to and rooted-ness in the local community found expression in and was further enhanced by recalling the saints in these communities. The process whereby past traditions of "forsaken" *tsaddiqim* were revived and deployed in the new locales granted metahistorical depth to places that were without a recognized and validated past, thus making them a more integral part of Israel. The *tsaddiq* endowed the town with an aura of sanctity, and the residents' sense of attachment was placed within a larger meaning-giving system, based on the idioms encoded in their revived Maghrebi traditions. As agents of memory revitalizing key cultural symbols, which many ex-members in the cult of the saints painfully missed, the saint impresarios managed to strike a collective chord. Their dreams accounts were therefore answered with scores of dreams in their respective communities, culminating in a lively dream discourse among the believers around the shrines (Bilu 2000).[3]

This process, whereby sacred sites were being added to the country's landscape, was strongly associated with the changing context of ethnic consciousness in Israel. The folk veneration of saints (along with the preservation or revival of other practices associated with Middle Eastern and North African Jews, such as ethnic festivals and ethnic music) provided many Maghrebi Jews with a set of cultural means to deal with their situation (Deshen 1994). By discovering and establishing sacred sites associated with the saints, they expressed their integration into the Israeli society. In this sense, the *hillulot* at various sites partake of the nature of "ethnic renewal ceremonies" (Weingrod 1990). They reflect the growing confidence of an émigré group in being part of the contemporary Israeli scene while, at the same time, indicating a strong sense of ethnic distinctiveness and a proud search for Maghrebi roots.

A leading Israeli social scientist has designated the renaissance of Maghrebi-based saint worship in the new country a "symbolic diasporization" of Israel (Cohen 1983). This designation makes sense insofar as the repressed or suppressed traditions are coming back and being placed within the mnemonic communities of veteran members of the cult of the saints. Note, however, that in planting the cult of the saints in the contemporary scene, the *tsaddiqim* were reconstituted in a life reality quite remote from traditional Morocco. They were attuned to the major concerns of present-day Israelis – not the least of which were security issues related to the Israeli-Palestinian conflict. The

---

3   Elsewhere I designated this emergence of dream discourse "oneiroicommunity" (Bilu 2000b).

local landscapes of memory and mnemonic communities thus generated were strongly informed by the Maghrebi past, but at the same time they were shaped and reshaped by the current Israeli reality.

To conclude, the fit between the impresarios' life events and the generalized Moroccan experience in Israel generated an impressive resonance between individual and cultural remembering, resulting in new sanctuaries for local and imported *tsaddiqim*. But this fit is historically situated and therefore quite bounded. Looking at the vicissitudes of our two sanctuaries since the 1970s, it is interesting to note that it is the House of Rabbi David u-Moshe, hosting an imported (or rather migrant) *tsaddiq*, that survived, while the Gate of Paradise, based on a local tradition, ceased to exist at the turn of the century.

While both sites functioned as *lieux de mémoires,* giving focus to unsituated and suppressed cultural memories related to *tsaddiqim*, I suspect that the grandiose nature of Yaish's initiative, and the consequent reluctance of the local rabbinical and municipal authorities to endorse and support it, contributed to its final demise. In contrast, Avraham's initiative, which gave back to the believers a once-venerated *tsaddiq* whom they acutely missed, appears fairly established and the House of Rabbi David u-Moshe is enjoying a steady flow of visitors all year round. Acknowledging the flexible, dynamic processes underlying cultural remembering in general and the volatile history of saints' sanctuaries in particular, it is an open question how the House of Rabbi David u-Moshe and its like will fare after the current generation of veteran members in the Maghrebi cult of the saints dies out.

Bibliography

Aronoff, M. J. 1973. "Development Towns in Israel." In M.Curtis and
    M. S. Chertoff (eds), *Israel: Social Structure and Change.* New
    Brunswick, NJ: Transaction, 27–46.
Ben-Ami, I. 1981. "The Folk-Veneration of Saints among Moroccan
    Jews, Traditions, Continuity and Change: The Case of the Holy
    Man, Rabbi David u-Moshe." In S. Morag, I. Ben Ami and
    N. Stillman (eds), *Studies in Judaism and Islam.* Jerusalem:
    Magnes Press, 283–345.
—. 1984. S*aint Veneration among the Jews in Morocco* (in Hebrew),
    Folklore Research Center Studies 8. Jerusalem: Magnes Press,
    1984.
Bennett, J. W. (ed.). 1975. *The New Ethnicity: Perspectives from
    Ethnology.* St. Paul: West Publishing.
Bilu, Y. 2000a. "Dreams and the Wishes of the Saint." In
    H. E. Goldberg (ed.), *Judaism Viewed from Within and from
    Without: Anthropological Exploration in the Comparative Study
    of Jewish Culture.* New York: State University of New York
    Press, 285–314.
—. 2000b. "Oneirobiography and Oneirocommunity in Saint Worship
    in Israel: A Two-Tier Model for Dream-Inspired Religious
    Revivals." *Dreaming* 10(2), 85–101.
—. 2004. "The Sanctification of Space in Israel: Civil Religion and
    Folk-Judaism." In U. Rebhun, and C. I. Waxman (eds), *Jews in
    Israel.* Lebanon, NH: Brandeis University Press, 371–93.
Bilu, Y. and H. Abramovitch. 1985. "In Search of the Saddiq:
    Visitational Dreams among Moroccan Jews in Israel." *Psychiatry*
    48(1), 83–92.
Bilu, Y. and E. Ben-Ari. 1992. "The Making of Modern Saints: Manu-
    factured Charisma and the Abu-Hatseiras of Israel." *American
    Ethnologist* 19(4), 29–44.
Bird-David, N. 2004. "No Past, No Present: A Critical Nayaka Per-
    spective on Cultural Remembering." *American Ethnologist* 31,
    406–21.

Cohen, E. 1983. "Ethnicity and Legitimation in Contemporary Israel." *Jerusalem Quarterly* 28, 111–24.

Crapanzano, V. 1975. "Saints, Jnun, and Dreams: An Essay in Moroccan Ethnopsychology." *Psychiatry* 38, 145–59.

Deshen, S. 1994. "The Religiosity of the Mizrahim: Public, Rabbis and Faith" (in Hebrew). *Alpayim* 9, 44–58.

Eickelman, D. 1976. *Moroccan Islam: Tradition and Society in Pilgrimage Centers*. Austin: University of Texas Press.

Eisenstadt, S. N. 1980. "Some Reflections on the Study of Ethnicity." In E. Krausz (ed.), *Migration, Ethnicity and Community*. *V*ol. 1. New Brunswick, NJ: Transaction, 1–4.

Fabian, J. 1983. *Time and the Other: How Anthropology Makes Its Object*. New York: Columbia University Press.

Geertz, C. 1983. *Islam Observed: Religious Development in Morocco and Indonesia*. Chicago: University of Chicago Press.

Gellner, E. 1969. *Saints of the Atlas*. Chicago: University of Chicago Press.

Goldberg, H. E. 1983. "The Mellahs of Southern Morocco: Report of a Survey," *The Maghreb Review* 8 (3–4), 61–9.

Gonen, R. (ed.) 1998. *To The Tomb of the Righteous: Pilgrimage in Contemporary Israel*. Jerusalem: The Israel Museum.

Inbar, M. and C. Adler. 1977. *Ethnic Integration in Israel,* New Brunswick, NJ: Transaction.

Kirmayer, L. 1996. "Landscapes of Memory: Trauma, Narrative, and Dissociation." In P. Antze and M. Lambek (eds), *Tense Past, Cultural Essays in Trauma and Memory*. London: Routledge, 173–98.

Kracke, W. H. 1994. "Reflections on the Savage Self: Interpretation, Empathy, Anthropology." In M. M. Suarez-Orosco, G. Spindler and L. Spindler (eds), *The Making of Psychological Anthropology*. Vol. 2. Fort Worth, TX: Harcourt Brace, 195–222.

Lambek, M. 1998. "The Sakalava Poiesis of History: Realizing the Past through Spirit Possession in Madagaskar." *American Ethnologist* 25 (2), 106–27.

Munson, H., Jr. 1993. *Religion and Power in Morocco*. New Haven: Yale University Press.

Nora, P. 1998. "Between Memory and History: Les Lieux de Mémoire." *Representations* 26, 7–25.

Novak, M. 1979. "The New Ethnicity." In D. R. Colburn and G. E. Pazzetta (eds), *America and the New Ethnicity.* Port Washington, NY: Kennikat Press, 15–28.

Obeyesekere, G. 1981. *Medusa's Hair: An Essay on Personal Symbols and Religious Experience.* Chicago/London: University of Chicago Press.

—. 1990. *The Work of Culture.* Chicago: University of Chicago Press.

Rabinow, P. 1975. *Symbolic Domination: Cultural Forms and Historical Change in Morocco.* Chicago/London: University of Chicago Press.

Semyonov, M. 1981. "Effects of Community on Status Attainment." *Sociological Quarterly* 22, 359–72.

Spiro, M. E. 1987. "Collective Representations and Mental Representations in Religious System Symbols." In K. Benjamin, and L. L. Langness (eds), *Culture and Human Nature.* Chicago: University of Chicago Press, 161–84.

Stillman, N. A. 1982. "Saddiq and Marabout in Morocco." In I. Ben-Ami (ed.), *The Sephardi and Oriental Jewish Heritage Studies.* Jerusalem: Magnes Press, 485–500.

—. 1995. *Sephardi Religious Responses to Modernity.* Luxembourg: Harwood Academic Publishers.

Westermarck, E. 1926. *Ritual and Belief in Morocco.* London: Macmillan.

Zerubavel, E. 1996. "Social Memories." *Qualitative Sociology* 19 (3), 283–99.

Chapter 5

NILI COHEN[1]

Memory and Forgetfulness in Law

Memory is of cardinal value to the life of a person, a community or a nation. Could we even imagine science without the contribution of memory to academic achievement? What would our lives be without memory? But can memory be harmful at times? Is forgetfulness a necessity from time to time? These questions play a central role in the debate on personal and collective consciousness. They also play an important role in the life of each organism. Avram Hershko and Aaron J. Ciechanover received a Nobel Prize for the discovery of Ubiquitin – a small protein that targets proteins for destruction – the cell's own forgetfulness device. Do these questions have any relevance for law?

The acclaimed Argentinian author and Jerusalem Prize laureate Jorge Luis Borges wrote a short story called "Funes, His Memory" (*Collected Fictions*, 131). The protagonist is Ireneo Funes, a Uruguayan who, after falling off his horse at the age of nineteen, finds he is unable to forget anything.

> Funes perceived every grape that had been pressed into the wine and all the stalks and tendrils of its vineyard. He knew the forms of the clouds in the southern sky on the morning of April 30, 1882, and he could compare them in his memory with the veins in the marbled binding of a book he had seen only once, or with the feathers of spray lifted by an oar on the Rio Negro on the eve of the battle of Quebracho [...]. He was able to reconstruct every dream, every daydream he had ever had [...]. Two or three times he had reconstructed an entire day [...]. Funes remembered not only every leaf of every tree in every patch of forest, but every time he perceived or imagined that leaf [...]. He had effortlessly learned English, French, Portuguese, Latin (ibid., 135–7).

---

[1]   I wish to thank advocates Yael Simonds-Yoaz and Maya Lakstein for their excellent assistance in preparing this article.

Funes's shadow hovers above all of us. We, laymen and academics, long for an infallible memory, that would enable us to collect details and acquire knowledge; that would help us remember and learn everything with ease. However, perhaps so as not to torment ourselves too much, Borges tells us at the end of the story that he suspects Funes

> was not very good at thinking. To think is to ignore (or forget) differences, to generalize, to abstract. In the teeming world of Ireneo Funes there was nothing but particulars – and they were virtually *immediate* particulars (ibid., 137).

Funes's story, which begins ostensibly as a song of praise to memory, soon becomes a lament upon its curse. Excessive detail – the inability to filter, to separate the wheat from the chaff – makes it difficult to formulate ideas and comprehensive rules. Funes demonstrates the gravity of memory, the burden of full sensory grasp, and shows us why we need a forgetting mechanism to act upon the cognitive and emotional spheres.

"Funes, His Memory" is part of Borges's attempt to examine the existence of the world and the impressions of the senses and the consciousness through which we experience it. Within this same undertaking Borges tells another tale (ibid., 402), "Dr. Brodie's Report," the story of a Scottish researcher who, during his travels, came across the Yahoos. This tribe possesses almost no memory. Even the witch-doctors of this tribe have little memory. They can remember only what happened that morning or last evening. However, they possess the ability to predict the immediate future – the next ten or fifteen minutes – with great accuracy. Borges is not very impressed with this ability. He notes that "philosophically speaking, memory is no less marvelous than prophesying the future" (ibid., 405). In any case, since the Yahoos are devoid of memory, their history doesn't cast a shadow over them. In fact, it is not part of their world. Their legal system is not based on proof, argument or reasoning. What is the point of trying to prove the occurrence of events no one can remember?

What is the lesson of Borges's tales? Is a world without memory better than a world that remembers everything indiscriminately?

Borges dismisses both scenarios. He diagnoses Funes the Memorious as an incompetent thinker, and he regards the Yahoos as a once civilized tribe that degenerated over time. Borges tells us what we actually all know: our world can consist of both past and future, but to the appropriate extent. A world solely of the past is subject to destruction: Funes dies at the age of twenty-one. The burden of the past defeats him. A world with no past may not be problematic, but it is lean, vacant and degenerate.

The tension between past and future is fertilizing and indispensable. It creates our private and collective consciousness. It is an engine for our aspirations and development. How does this tension materialize in law?

One of the major functions of courts is to determine what happened in the past, and this determination is an essential part of the ruling. In this matter, the judge acts as a historian (of the old school), according to Leopold von Ranke's imperative to tell everything the way it really happened (*wie es eigentlich gewesen*; Weinryb 1987, 12),[2] using the personal memories of witnesses and other evidence. In criminal law the prosecution has to prove that the defendant murdered, stole or embezzled. In private law one has to prove that a contract was signed between Rachel and Leah, according to which Rachel made a loan to Leah. All these are judicial conclusions based on facts. Constructing the facts is based on a reconstruction of the past. As individuals our memory is flawed:[3] our memory is poor and limited. We

---

2   Of course there are those who disagree with von Ranke on the question of whether it is possible to know what really happened and whether this is indeed the goal of history. For this debate see Novick 1988; Appleby et al. 1995; Evans 1997.

3   On the deceits of memory see Schacter 2001. The sins of memory listed in the book are transience, which refers to a weakening or loss of memory over time; absent-mindedness, which involves a breakdown at the interface between attention and memory; blocking, which entails a thwarted search for information that we may be desperately trying to retrieve; misattribution, which involves assigning a memory to the wrong source; suggestibility, which refers to memories that are implanted as a result of leading questions, comments or suggestions when a person is trying to call up a past experience; bias, which reflects the powerful influences of our current knowledge and beliefs on how we remember our past; and persistence, which entails the repeated recall of disturbing information or events that we would prefer to banish from our minds altogether.

forget what we would have been happy to remember, and remember what we may have been happy to forget. The memory of one is unlike that of the other, and even when a number of people witness an incident, each one will register it in a different way (see the story of Rashomon; Almog 2001, 297, 316–19). Indeed, Funes testifies that before falling off the horse, "he had been what every man was – blind, deaf, befuddled, and virtually devoid of memory [...] he looked without seeing, heard without listening, forgot everything, or virtually everything" (*Collected Fictions*, 134–5).[4]

Had we been granted Funes's legendary memory, there would be no problem with our accuracy in reconstructing the past: we would know exactly what happened beforehand – that A pulled the trigger and shot B, or what was said in the moments before making the loan. Funes could have made a decisive contribution to the personal history of each of us and to the collective history of all of us. However, court proceedings, already lengthy, would have lasted many days and become even more exhausting due to Funes being unable to separate the wheat from the chaff, his memory being all-inclusive without distinction. Furthermore, burdensome precision and dwelling upon details would have blurred the whole picture and perhaps even impinged upon an understanding of the circumstances that led in one case to the death of a person, or in another case to the signing of a contract.

Funes stands in complete opposition to the Yahoos, who are devoid of memory and lack a personal and collective past, yet still manage to operate a social system, and a judicial one within it. But what is law without memory? Memory is vital for law not only in order to reconstruct the past for purposes of deterrence, and maybe even for revenge, it is also vital for building a culture comprised of the norms, customs and traditions upon which the laws are founded. This memory is a collective memory, and it is mainly composed of an accumulation of legislation and legal cases.

I will focus here on legal cases. A judgment is a court's decision, and it operates on two levels: the first is that of *the litigant parties –*

---

4   On the difficulties of searching for truth in both history and law, see Cohn
     1986, 35 and especially 77–9.

the judgment resolves the dispute, it binds the parties and cannot be reopened; the second level is that of *the rest of the world* – the verdict is a ruling that becomes part of the legal rules of the relevant society (Barak 1990, 267).

Our legal system adopted the principle of legal precedent (*stare decisis*), which we accepted from the Common Law (Tedeschi 1959, 92; Heiner 1986, 227).[5] What is binding and becomes part of the legal rules is the section of the verdict that drove the judge to decide what she decided, the *ratio decidendi*, differing from the *obiter dictum*, which has no binding force (Tedeschi 1964, 99).[6] Therefore, in its judicial action the court binds itself to the past, settles the dispute at hand in the present and creates a general norm for the future (Barak 2000a, 821). However, the principle of legal precedent, formally applied, is not without its problems. Why be bound to a ruling only because it was given in the past? Why be bound to a ruling the court might regard as erroneous?[7] In other words, the principle of legal precedent may serve as an example for the subjugation of the present to the past. It also opposes one of the central concepts of law, a striving for truth – not only the factual truth, but the legal truth. In this respect, the principle of legal precedent does not align with other scientific theories. Should we accept the physics of our ancestors, the ancient epistemology or mathematics of the past? The answer, of course, is negative. Hobbes, in his *Leviathan* noted that in law, as in geometry, only the rules of reason deserve respect (Hobbes 1946, 21, 27). In this spirit, Holmes noted that it is outrageous to think there is

5   For the application of principle in the Common Law see Freeman 1994, 1261–
     3. On the Continent, at least historically, there is no obligating status for court
     rulings, only a guiding power by which great importance is granted to doctrine
     – that is, interpretations of laws in scholarly writings. For further reading on the
     distinction between the two systems, see Tedeschi 1959, 99–
     102, 111–12; England 1990, 127.
6   For the question of how to determine what the *ratio decidendi* is see Raz 1979,
     180–209. However, the question is complex, and there are those who claim that
     in practice the distinction is not made. See Cohn 2001, 415.
7   For the problem of compliance with (or adherence to) past decisions in the
     general context of decision-making theory see Tamir 2004, 211, 226. This com-
     prehensive and interesting essay discusses the problems with the principle of
     legal precedent in general, with a special affinity to Israeli law.

no better reason to justify a legal rule than the fact it was made in the days of Henry IV (Holmes 1920, 167, 187). In other words, according to Holmes's view, in order for a legal rule to be binding, it is not enough that it was decreed in the past. Whenever one wishes to apply it, one should reexamine it and only then, provided that it fits the new circumstances, should one bestow on it binding power. In Holmes's view, the justification for the affirmative enforcement of a rule does not lie in the past, but in the present: in its suitability to operate in the current circumstances (Kronman 1990, 1029, 1034–5).

After this short review we may feel deterred by and perhaps contemptuous towards the principle of legal precedent. Does everyone share this view? Is this a universally shared opinion? Is there a rational reason that justifies the principle of legal precedent?

The principle of legal precedent has gained renewed support in recent years. Legal scholars from various standpoints have justified it (Shauer 1987, 571; Maltz 1988, 367). Two main types of rationale support the principle of legal precedent: the first is utilitarian, the second is moral. The *utalitarian* rationale is based on a series of secondary ones. One of these is that past decision, which creates a legal rule after examining its justification, is an efficient and cost-effective mechanism for creating binding rules. Another is that the principle of legal precedent promotes the value of certainty of the law: it mitigates planning of *future* action and *in retrospect* it facilitates foreseeing the outcome of the legal hearing. In addition, the principle of legal precedent helps to create consistency in the body of rulings of the courts and to establish the credibility of the judiciary. In short, even if, in some regard, a certain precedent is incorrect, it is worth adhering to because the cost of deviating from a precedent is many times higher than the cost of adhering to a precedent even if it is not a very good one.[8] These are the utalitarian reasonings.

Alongside them stands the *moral* rationale, the gist of which is the principle of equality. The implication of this principle is that every litigant party is subject to the same legal rules as any other litigant in a similar case. However, these two types of rationale disregard the con-

---

8   For an economic analysis of the principle of legal precedent see Kornhauser
     1898, 63; Lee 2000, 643.

tribution of the past, whose strength lies in a respect for tradition, and they examine the past merely from the point of view of its intellectual influence on the present. Yet, can the past in itself justify the principle of legal precedent? Some think the answer is in the affirmative (Kronman 1990, 1029, 1043–7).

Law is culture – that is, an accumulation of knowledge, thought, ideas. It is as a building constructed gradually, brick by brick, by different builders, by different judges in different eras.[9] The rulings or verdicts are a vital component in the building blocks of the law. They constitute collective memory.

The memory of the past requires preservation mechanisms. Preservation is the link between past and future generations.[10] Every generation acts as a trustee of its predecessors and its successors. Thus it is in environmental preservation and in cultural preservation. The culture of the past – in this case the judgments of the past – is a gift from our previous generations, and the preservation of the past is not only an act of gratitude toward our predecessors but also a message to the following generations. We will be able to believe that following generations will make the effort to preserve our judicial heritage only if we succeed in preserving the legacy of our predecessors. The principle of legal precedent is part of the same preservation mechanism that enables the law to operate as a continuous cultural and social creation.[11]

However, the question that still remains to be asked is the following: why are the mathematician and the physicist free from subju-

9   Barak 2000b, 724: "Judicial production, like writing a serialized book, is an endless task. The judges who are no longer presiding [...] wrote the previous chapters. The presiding judges write its sequel [...] while relying on the past. It is all written in continuity [...]"

10   Chapter 1 of *Sayings of the Jewish Fathers* (*Pirqe Avot*) clearly demonstrates the idea of the halakhic chain, which survives generations and connects them: "Moses received the Torah from Sinai, and he delivered it to Joshua, and Joshua to the elders, and the elders to the prophets, and the prophets delivered it to the men of the Great Synagogue" and so on through the pairs and ending with Raban Shimon Ben Gamliel.

11   This is the reasoning of Kronman 1990, 1029, who emphasizes that beyond the utilitarian and moral rationales stand respect for tradition and esteem of the past as the bases for the commitment to the principle of legal precedent.

gation to the past, whereas the jurist is obliged to it? (Kronman 1990, 1029, 1057–64). The answer is that the mathematician and the physicist act within different realms than those of the world of justice. The mathematician acts within the realm of pure reason whereas the physicist acts within the realm of nature. Neither nature nor pure reason are bound to the insights of the past. Surely the insights of the past may assist the mathematician and the physicist in decoding those secrets of the universe and of reason that have yet to be discovered, as acknowledged by Newton's confession to Robert Hooke that if he is able to "have seen further it is by standing on ye shoulders of Giants".

However, the insights of the past, of themselves, cannot enslave either nature or mathematics, since the rules of nature and of logic are not dependent upon the eye of the observer. Indeed, the insights of the past did not bind Newton. The new rules he discovered became the binding rules of science until a new paradigm appeared and in turn changed those. In short, the foremost imperative in science is the search for truth, and the past's insights are not binding assumptions.

Nevertheless, law is not only a scientific theory. It is a tool designated to fulfilling a social end. Law was created by humankind to enable a communal life based on justice and fairness. The quest for truth is one of the purposes of law, but not the only one. Alongside it the law seeks to establish long-lasting order and stability.[12] The principle of legal precedent, which codifies the accumulations of past rulings while continuously acting upon them, creates a foundation for the realization of social order and stability.

Does this mean that law resembles Funes the Memorious? Is the legal system obligated to collect all the judgments ever made and act upon them without exception?

One should distinguish between law as a cultural phenomenon and law as an active social system. The legal historian who documents law of centuries past may be glad to have Funes's memory, which will enable him to reconstruct the rules of the past with absolute accuracy.

---

12   For a discussion regarding the basic values of law see Elon 1998, 269; Barak 1996, 11. For the rules of evidence that limit the admissibility of evidence that may shed light on a case in order to protect higher values see Zaltzman 2001, 263. On the purposes of law see Barak 1992, 264–6.

(Incidentally, the historian of mathematics or physics might also appreciate such a capacity.) However, this is not the case regarding the binding rules. A social system, not unlike any organic system, cannot remain static. The preservation of legal culture through the principle of legal precedent does not mean intransigent conservatism. Every social body harbors an intensive dynamic of destruction and construction, whereby flawed components are removed and new ones created, while non-deficient ones remain intact. Maintenance and renovation sometimes require at least partial demolition of what exists, in order to protect the entire edifice. Indeed, Funes's destiny shows that unqualified adherence to the past oppresses and retards appropriate development. Funes lacks a forgetting or erasing mechanism, which would have enabled him to rid himself of the burdens of the past for the sake of a balanced and proper continuation of his life. This mechanism should not effect total or near total erasure, as in the case of the Yahoos. Without memory there can be no culture. However an erasing or abolishing mechanism is needed to help free us from an unnecessary attachment to the past and facilitate growth in the future. As noted, adherence to precedents is founded on utalitarian and moral arguments, as is the need to sometimes contravene precedents. Adherence to faulty rulings merely because they have been made might lead to a vain waste of resources and damage to actual litigants. Reluctance to follow an erroneous and inefficient ruling might necessitate ignoring it in order to avoid the need to openly refute it. But blurring the truth about the decision-making process in the courts would surely not add to the credibility of the judiciary.

How can we guarantee that the legal past, sometimes based upon different values, will not mortgage future generations?

One means of evading the chains of binding legal precedent, although not without difficulty, is the creation of a distinction: what remains binding is that part of the verdict which compelled the judge to rule the way she did. When one wants to create a distinction one notes, for example, a new material fact that does not exist in the original binding legal precedent. This might lead to the conclusion that this is not a similar case and therefore there is no need to apply the same rule. The principle of equality, fundamental to the principle of legal precedent, is irrelevant when the case in question is different.

Another possibility is to stretch the distinction between the *ratio decidendi* and the *obiter dictum* so that what would apply to the case at hand is the *obiter dictum*, which in any case is not legally binding.[13] However, both the distinction doctrine and the overstretching of the *obiter dictum* do not deal directly with the difficulty, as they assume in advance that the precedent does not apply to the case at hand – because it can be distinguished or because it is not subject to what was actually expressed only as an *obiter dictum*.

Article 20 of the Basic Law: judicature provides a direct solution to the problem.[14] The law states that a rule laid down by the Supreme Court shall be binding upon any court other than the Supreme Court.[15] In other words, the legal precedents of the Supreme Court are binding upon lower courts, but the Supreme Court itself can deviate from them for any reason.[16] One may compare these forgetting devices to the mechanism within the living cell that targets proteins for destruction. The power to deviate from a binding legal precedent is the law's Ubiquitin.

The Supreme Court frequently deviates from its own rulings. Yet this move requires reasoning and persuasion. Thus any deviation from a precedent is done with maximum forethought. In the conflict between truth and stability, sometimes the value of truth triumphs and sometimes the value of stability defeats truth.

> Only when the weight of the considerations that support the new rule ascends the weight of the considerations supporting the old rule and the damage that will be brought about by the change, should the court deviate from an old precedent.[17]

---

13   It goes without saying that if the case is heard before a higher court, which in any case is not bound by the precedent, it can nullify it. For evading techniques, see Tamir 2004, 229–30.
14   *Laws of the State of Israel* vol. 38, 1983–4, 101.
15   According to the same law a rule laid down by a District Court shall guide only a Magistrate's Court.
16   The law does not say that the Supreme Court is guided by its own rulings.
17   Barak 2000b, 307. For the tendency of the court to stick to its own precedents and criticism see Tamir 2004, 249, footnote 177. Amongst the considerations for deviating from a legal precedent or adherence to it: prevention of miscar-

Memory and forgetfulness are two faculties we possess, and the contest between the two contributes to the formation of our character as individuals and as a community. This contest is universal and occurs of course not only in Borges's imagination. In the summer of 1934, Berl Katznelson said:

> Had the world had nothing but memory, what would have been our fate? We would have succumbed to the burden of memories. We would have become slaves to our memory [...] the image of our faces would be a copy of past generations. And if forgetfulness would have defeated us completely – would there have been place for culture, science, self-awareness, or spiritual life? Dark conservatism wants to divest us of our power to forget, and pseudo-radicalism regards any remembrance of the past as "the enemy" [...]. An innovative and creative generation does not cast the heritage of the past onto a pile of ashes. It examines, checks, removes and brings nearer. [18]

The principle of legal precedent is the arena of combat between memory and forgetfulness, between conservatism and radicalism.[19] The principle of legal precedent – says Justice Barak – is an expression of the honorary debt that the present owes the past (Barak 2000b, 737).

In the temple of science, where we all owe a debt to the past, I conclude by saying: it seems one can understand Justice Aharon Barak's words as a paraphrase of Newton's humble confession. Even if one may bring about great changes in law it is due only to the fact that those who do it stand on the shoulders of giants.

---

riage of justice, damage to stability, legislative change, the age of the rule; see Tamir 2004, 260–7.

18 *The Writings of Berl Katznelson, Examination, Conversations with Educators* 6 (Mifleget Poalei Eretz Israel (Land of Israel Workers' Party) Publishing, 1947), 389–90. I thank my colleague Professor Dan Laor who brought this to my attention.

19 For the tension between tradition and reform in the Hebrew Law, see Edrei 2003, 193, 203–7.

Chapter 6

DAN DINER

From Society to Memory: Reflections on a Paradigm Shift

"The Age of Society." That is the title the historian Gerhard Schulz gave his volume of collected essays published in 1969. It was subtitled "On the Political Social History of the Modern Period" (Schulz 1969). If you consider the very broad arc covered by the essays gathered together in that book, the word "society" elevated in the title into a kind of emblem of an entire epoch, as an overriding theme seems, to put it mildly, somewhat overdone, exaggerated. The topics dealt with range from the history of the genesis of bourgeois society, imperialism in the nineteenth century, German Social Democracy and the idea of international balance, and Eduard Bernstein's importance and impact; on to such topics as interest groups in Germany since the onset of industrialization, measures of state support in the Eastern territories, the national clubs of 1919, questions of political resistance, nationalism and totalitarianism. "The Age of Society" as a blanket term to cover this? One may wonder. Basically, the papers presented there, most published in the 1950s and first half of the 60s, center on a key problem that preoccupied West German historiography at that specific time – namely, the Weimar Republic and the pre- and post-histories of its failure. Maybe the only exception is the excellent introductory essay, framed in the tradition of intellectual history, on the genesis of bourgeois society, *bürgerliche Gesellschaft*. Schulz's brief note informing readers that the first part of this essay appeared in the 1969 festschrift for Hans Rosenberg, the emigré social historian on the faculty in Berkeley, suggests that the choice of the title "The Age of Society" was likely something else – namely, a gesture of respect, an expression of homage – to the father of the social-historical school in Germany, teaching at UC Berkeley (Schulz 1970, 3–65).

This is a sufficient explanation for the choice, but not really a satisfactory one. I think more relevant here is indeed the date of publication: 1969. It seems as if Schulz, a historian based at Tübingen University, had an almost seismographic sense for the emerging hegemonial importance of a current in historiography, very much imbued with the zeitgeist, which soon would become a veritable vogue in West Germany and beyond – namely, social history. When viewed this way, the title "The Age of Society" is not some sort of diagnostic label for a past era. Rather, I suspect it is meant as a *prognosis*, a reference to what was to come. It doesn't conclude an assessment but augurs an agenda for the future.

And indeed, beginning about 1969, we can note an element in the historical sciences that seems to promise a kind of breakthrough of the paradigm of social history. It is true that four years before, in 1965, Hans-Ulrich Wehler edited and introduced the collected essays of Eckard Kehr, one of the early pioneers in what later came to be known as social history or *Gesellschaftsgeschichte*. That publication certainly bore the earmarks of a new beginning: methodologically, the traditionally dominant primacy of foreign policy in the historical sciences was to be rejected. It would be replaced by a new emphasis on home affairs, domestic policy (Kehr 1965 (1977)).

Since the 1960s, the historical social sciences have been attracting ever greater academic attention, with ever more palpable impact. At the high tide of the old Federal Republic, in the 1970s, these historical social sciences established themselves as a dominant subdiscipline within the field of history. This circumstance was probably due in large part to that quiet affinity which the social-historical school bore to the old Federal Republic, a state and polity that were in effect predicated on a thoroughly *social* semanticization of the political.

In any case, from that point on, there was no real question about the central significance of the historical social sciences. Their effect was felt everywhere – until, after some two decades of uninterrupted centrality in historical discourse, their beacon function was apparently dimmed by a cascade of events in the wake of watershed year 1989, and they began quite visibly to lose their dominant position. Such a retreat from the high ground of hegemony, brought about by the circumstances of the time and its zeitgeist, down onto the crowded lowlands, where a multiplicity of equal historical subdisciplines compete for influence, and insight does not occur in a vacuum. This demotion in rank has apparently been accompanied by the powerful even impetuous emergence on the scene of a competing paradigm: the paradigm of memory (Assman 1992; Halbwachs 1980).

This paper attempts to trace a paradigm shift from *society* to *memory* visible today throughout the historical sciences. It will do so by looking back on the sequencing in the formation of historical paradigms. In addition, proceeding on the basis of such a suspected paradigm shift, I will try to sketch a prognosis, plausible in terms of a diagnostics of our time, for the historical sciences in the new European context now emerging. My general presupposition here is that historical paradigms should best be seen as delayed modes of interpretation of historical processes that have preceded them. They form an arsenal of semantizations that seek to correspond to the specific importance of their object in the life-world. In the time frame of the past two centuries or so, roughly speaking, there has been a sequence involving a shift from the paradigm of the *state* to that of *society*, and more recently to the paradigm of *memory*. Thus "state" signifies the vessel of rule and its vertically structured hierarchical architecture of power, which evolved from the premodern circumstances of the *ancien régime*; "society" signifies a more horizontal structuration appropriate for modernity and increasingly respondent to the demands of equality; "memory" stands for the shattering of a previous mode of homogenization, perhaps best characterized as postmodern. That homogenized structuration was generated via state *and* society, grounded on the notion of nation common to them both. Distinguished from this, memory could stand more abstractly for what might be subsumed as "difference."

Historical reality and historiography are strikingly divergent. Often the historiographical paradigm does not catch up with the historical reality that preceded it until much more than a generation or so later. One can even gain the impression that the historical paradigm has a retarding function: it serves to block or slow down an emerging

development in tune with the zeitgeist. Such a delay in the historical
sciences was noticeable right from the start – namely, when the
fledgling field of history seized on the *state* as a self-evident paradigm
precisely at a point in historical reality when it was challenged in its
traditional monopoly by a swiftly crystallizing *society*.

This was specifically the case when Leopold von Ranke – who in
the received view can arguably be regarded as the father of history as
a scientific discipline – elevated the state via the primacy of foreign
policy to the level of an individual subject acting on the historical
stage. This move transformed power and rule into fundamental categories of history (Mommsen 1988). In this way, the newly established political historiography – i.e. a writing of history semanticized
in terms of the state and its power – participated as a factor in the
temporary hedging in of a form of society sprung from the conceptual
arsenal of the Enlightenment, *societas civilis sine imperio*. Meanwhile,
the absolutist state, which had earlier evolved from the matrix of a
neutralization of the wars of religion as religious *civil wars*, furthered
a conceptual universe that, materialized as society, would soon come
to dispute the state's former undisputed hegemony in promoting peace
on earth. Or to make use of a later image in political iconography:
society began here to disembowel Leviathan, to eviscerate it piece by
piece (Schmitt (1938) 1982; Koselleck 1988). That is a development
quite in keeping with the events of the nineteenth century. Earlier on,
fed by the ideas of the Scottish Enlightenment and the French ency-
clopedists Ferguson and Smith, Condorcet and Diderot, society was
semanticized in terms of the *language of class* and social organization
– i.e. over and beyond the previously hegemonial emblematics of the
state and the social estates. As this trend was politicized, the semantics
of the social was totally revolutionized. The linguistic inventory of the
ancien régime was discarded as unneeded detritus; the space opened
up by this discursive housecleaning was then occupied by a secular
imagery of the social that apparently viewed itself as materialistic –
and infused with some of that special verve reminiscent of religious
energy otherwise unique to the sacred realm.

Lynn Hunt recently commented on how the French Revolution
had converted religious energy into social energy (Hunt 2003). That
transformation was already inscribed in Rousseau's *Contract Social*.

The convention concluded there sanctified the social order springing from it and shaped by human hand. In Hunt's view, the semanticizing of the social was permeated by a religious enthusiasm that was apparent only in contradiction with its social sobriety. In this way, the interpretive power of the social expanded to take on a more inclusive significance, oriented to the total complex. In particular, the axiom of class loomed forth in emblematic form from the available semantic conceptual field of society – inscribed with a telos anchored in the philosophy of history.

In any event, the hiatus between state and society constitutive for the nineteenth century was omnipresent. Proceeding from the Paris revolts of 1830 and 1848, the language of class spread beyond the borders of the land of revolution. And, as a result of the situation and developments in France, the concepts and metaphors were imbued with a long duration. Karl Marx contributed to this turn, as did, most especially Lorenz von Stein. Stein thought he could discern in those events what was a world-historical movement approaching its end: bourgeois society had achieved definitive control over the state (von Stein 1972; Schnur 1978).

An unresolved tension between state and society remained a characteristic feature of Germany's political history. Its axial impact is visible in the central events of Prussian-German history: extending from the Prussian constitutional conflict of 1862 until the October reforms of 1918 and the associated final parliamentarization of the Reich. Down to the October reforms, the executive enjoyed a prerogative reminiscent of semi-constitutional relations. Thus during the Wilhelmian period, an era of mounting modernity, there were systematic efforts to hamper any transposing of parliamentary formation of will into governmental power in conjunction with the balance of forces in the Reichstag. The rising social forces were deemed incapable over the long term of forming a coalition. The constantly expanding Social Democracy was effectively surrounded, hemmed in. In Weimar, in turn, the *ancien régime* disavowed as a result of the end of the war sought to refortify its position: it dug in behind article 48 of the Weimar Constitution of 1919 as protection, awaiting a state of emergency that would favor it.

In a comprehensive review of developments in this subfield, the American-based historian of the social history school Geoff Eley has noted that the period when "class" was in high esteem as a category of scholarship extended from roughly 1860 to 1930 (Eley 1996). And this quite over and beyond the importance of this time period for the political periodization of German history. In view of the rise of mass society, radicalized by the rifts and faults opened up by the great global economic Depression, this concept forfeits its diagnostic value and ability to mobilize. In addition, fascism and National Socialism forced the few social scientists and social historians who occasionally were prepared to speak up academically to withdraw into silence. Their protagonists avoided a confrontation and retreated into exile.

It is highly likely that if Weimar had survived it would have brought the paradigm of society to full fruition, both historically and in the sense of a diagnosis of the era. That by the way would also have meshed well with the efforts of Carl Heinrich Becker. Becker, an Orientalist at Heidelberg University, was closely allied with Max Weber and was for many years Prussian minister of culture. Instead, there was a total semantic inversion. The code of society was fatefully replaced by a code of biologism. The administrative violence unleashed by the National Socialists was geared to the absolute destruction of the body. Its negative apotheosis reached its apogee in stark and sheer physical destruction. And that led to a denial of the encompassing social framing, which sought to provide comprehensive readings for the entirety of human reality. In the fires of Auschwitz, the epistemological meaning of the social dimension evaporated.

After 1945, the social returned under strange circumstances. The milieu of its comeback was the Cold War. The antipodal binarism of political freedom and a literal notion of social equality, embodying a fundamental antagonism of values, West versus East, drew on different evolving semantic arsenals of the Enlightenment. The associated primacy of the social made it possible for sociology to establish itself as a leading, even paradigmatic, discipline in the human sciences. In the West, it emerged split down the middle in terms of fundamental weltanschauung. The fierce struggle over positivism in German sociology in the 1960s points this up with great clarity: on one side, there were the empirical social sciences; on the other, an encompassing social perspective seeking to offer a totalizing explanation applicable to society as a whole. Differing, even antipodal, definitions of modernity and modernization collide here. One is arrayed in the armor of the philosophy of history; the other repudiates any orientation to history's philosophy, either overt or covert.

The era of the Cold War was an age of neutralization. And the expression of this neutralization in the academic sphere was precisely that very hegemony of the social sciences. The particularist memories of Europe, interspliced in World War II, were neutralized. After the temporal smelter beginning in 1989, strata of events previously considered closed files pressed once again to the surface. This temporal rewind, so to speak, is the manifestation of those epistemic phenomena that are of central salience for memory's manifestations – namely, the binding of time to place. In the return of historical spaces unfolding since the 1989 watershed, the historical times bound up with these spaces are necessarily reinvoked. And as the memory of the Cold War fades, almost as if it had never even occurred, the times that preceded it appear to move ever nearer. That may be due to the fact that World War II was a preeminent foundational event, comparable in its magnitude to the Reformation or French Revolution. Here are happenings of such sheer weight and density that the times preceding and subsequent to them are drawn into the pull of their vortex. In its impact, World War II becomes something like a time jam. That jam increasingly appears to be breaking up, dissolving into the future.

At the core of such a time jam lies the Holocaust. That was not always the case. Even a couple of decades ago, it was quite possible to write a history of World War II without even mentioning the Holocaust. This may be connected with the circumstance that the mass murder was carried out totally beyond the space of diplomacy and combat. Later inquiry into the Holocaust took a direction which cast the Holocaust as an event that seemed totally external to the events of the war and battlefront. Yet quite apart from questions in research strategy shaped by and beholden to circumstances of the time and zeitgeist, it is necessary to ask what has helped to elevate the Holocaust into an object of such comprehensive and intense attention – although that attention did not surface until the late phase in the Cold War and its distinctive chemistry of neutralizing memory.

The special status of Event Auschwitz may be bound up with the disconcerting sense generated by the Holocaust, that here was the destruction of fundamental even anthropological certainties of human society. And that not only did the industrial destruction of human beings without any discernible reason or purpose obliterate that core of utilitarian fundamental assumptions about rational behavior, it also contaminated that arsenal of interpretations of the world qua totality. Dealing with the Holocaust thus cut a kind of channel into the solid memory-neutralizing time block of the Cold War. And it did so at a time when there could not yet be any talk about decoding World War II, in terms of the history of memory, as a cataclysmic foundational event.

So this was the one aspect of the Holocaust: a kind of window opening onto that foundational event which the war was to become. But in the perception of other dramas that came to pass in the war, the Holocaust also had another aspect. One that was more bound up with closure. Closure in that Event Auschwitz, by dint of its hyper-radicality, is infused with an extraordinary level of negative epistem-ics. First of all, the Holocaust, in contrast to other, sub-events within the foundational macro-event of the war, is unable to generate any appropriate historical narrative. It lies in a space beyond narrativity. That has certain consequences for chains of chronology and causality associated with questions of representation. To that extent, it is not surprising when the Holocaust or the description of the National Socialist mass murder is associated, in a very intuitive and pre-theoretical manner, with the metaphor of memory. There is in any event a striking affinity between historically guided interest in the Holocaust on the one hand, and the significance of memory on the other – a memory triggered by this event, as it were, and demanding ever more validity. The metaphor of memory stands for a phenomenon of simultaneity. Paradoxically perhaps, a simultaneity of times and their strands that chronologically are not simultaneous. The Holocaust evokes this phenomenon because the repetitive character of industrial murder, involving repeated application of the same process of destruc-tion, can be represented in statistical terms. Numbers can be given. But such a representation refuses to fulfill the demands of historical narrativity. A narrative that might befit the sheer gravity of the Event can succeed only if it draws the narrative *tempora* preceding and subsequent to the Event into its force field. And the temporal volume of this expanse of narrative time necessarily far exceeds the extremely short chronological duration of the actual Event. The consequence is that often baffling phenomenon of a genuine contamination. Times preceding and subsequent are contaminated by an Event whose duration seems determined by a half-life period on the apparent *increase*. In any event, it is striking that event and memory diverge, indeed necessarily must diverge. Or as Hans Blumberg phrased it: the morphology of memory is not cognizant of any pure factual meaning (Blumenberg 1991).

The time smelter of the Cold War dissolves the time jam intrinsic to the memory of World War II. Released from the blockade of neutralization, the contexts of events associated with the history of the war and its consequences are re-stratified, reconfigured. Links becomes visible that were barely predictable in their impact – such as the affinity of memory and restitution – widening the perimeter of historical memory.

While from the late 1940s on the collectivizations in Soviet-controlled Eastern Europe contributed to a socially semanticized forgetting of the respective prehistories, private property, restored to its own right after 1989, has necessarily helped forge a kind of reconstruction of the past. This is a natural consequence of the anthropological affinity between memory and property. Thus the cadastral property register comes to function as an arsenal of legally binding memory, open to public inquiry and arching beyond the biological life of the given owner. In the process, the duration inherent in the world of objects approaches the validity of historical temporal horizons. The restored property begins to seek out its rightful owner. This catalyzes efforts to reconstruct past relations of ownership and to provide restitution.

The recent debate that has flared about the proper forms of inquiry into and remembrance of the fate of German expellees and refugees in the final phase of the war and thereafter was also catalyzed by that time smelter of 1989. The shifts this debate is engendering may not provide an occasion for the redrawing of borders, as might have once been feared. But they will contribute to a revision of the

boundaries of memory in the respective histories of relations of the
collectives that took part in the events. Also contributing to this has
been another phenomenon across the globe – namely, a discourse of
suffering, very much oriented to human rights and thus prone to non-
historical argumentation. In order to gain sway, this discourse makes
use of the arsenals of imagery and analogy of World War II elsewhere,
even beyond Europe. By contrast, due to the inherent historical assessment such discourse contains, people are less ready to note the
context-bound historical dimension here, and are wont to ascribe
causes and apportion guilt. The most recent publications focusing on
the Allied bombing war and the destruction of German cities are
exemplary for a view framed solely in terms of a history of suffering,
with little concomitant consideration for the respective historical context. The horror of individual fates here fused en masse, as reflected in
the images of death and devastation, necessarily brings with it another
anthropological perspective of the past, as the history of the collective,
now calling for responsibility to be determined and blame assigned.
Be that as it may, the impact of World War II as a European foundational event continues unabated. After forty years of neutralization, the
various European memories now have the option of balancing off their
respective legacies of remembrance. Such a process proceeds in keeping with the emergent procedures of the histories of relations of the
collectives with one another. And such histories are essentially guided
by memory.

The paradigm of memory and a conjunct pluralization of European historical narrative has one taproot in the phenomenon of the
time jam, so significant for the memory of World War II. A second
lies across the Atlantic in the U.S. There, beginning in the 1980s and
under the aegis of French post-structuralism, a pluralization of the
conceptions of history began to take hold in the academy. It allegedly
functioned to undermine the entire concept of history. Important here
is the fact that America's identity presupposes far less history than
Europe's self-understanding. In actuality, Europe in contrast to the
United States is *the* historical continent. History is a profoundly European invention. Hegel already attributed a special character to North
America: in his eyes, it was a bourgeois society without a state. He
thus chose to exclude it from his systematics in the philosophy of

history. Ultimately, Europe is dominated by the primacy of spatiality, America by that of temporality. Europe is stamped by the emblem of origin, America by the emblem of the future. Compounding the circumstance that America is more bound up with time than space and Europe vice versa, there are further factors that undermine the existence of history with a capital H in the States.

There is for example the pluralism of Protestant denominations imported from the mother country, England – this was a constellation that structurally presupposed a condition fundamental for life in America: *e pluribus unum*. In the 1970s and 80s, the form of this original religious pluralism was replenished and filled by other, externally visible special identities – namely, ethnic diversity, in a space somewhere beyond the political. For those very same systematic reasons, this serves to sweep away the very underpinnings from beneath a monistic history essentially oriented to the homogeneous nation as history's primary subject. Despite a certain weakening in its intensity, that monistic mold has continued to claim validity in the European context. Right from the start, it would seem, the historical circumstances for history were very different in America and Europe. As if the writing of history were following the dictates of differing styles of thought here and there. In the past and in individual cases, this may not have been too noticeable, due simply to the fact that the academic world tends to be universal and international. But it was discernible in questions of preferred method and privileged modes of approach. In Europe, there was the impress of monism, a dominance of history; across the Atlantic, pluralism ruled, a dominance of culture.

With the advent of the cultural turn, the pluralizing differenti-ation of the historical canon in the States was strengthened, extending all the way to a kind of non-recognizability. In America, dominated by the triad of the paradigms of class, race and gender, central to cultural studies and originally conceived in a historical frame, few master narratives exist. In the European context, these narratives are generally oriented to have a direct impact on the public sphere and thus on political life and action. This has far-reaching consequences for ques-tions of canonization and the formation of corpus. While in the U.S., canon and corpus are suspected of abetting the homogenizing or hierarchizing pretensions of one or another tradition of narrative or interpretation, the formation of canon is probably compelling for traditional societies such as those of Europe. Ultimately, in contrast to the more truncated memory of American contemporary culture, sprung from the womb of Enlightenment, they must administer a memory extending over centuries.

As a historical continent, Europe can bid adieu to history with a capital H only at the cost of forfeiting its own panoply of identities. The fact that the European histories, decked out in national guise, have little to proclaim beyond their arguably formidable cultural achievements is of course another story. Just think of the history of maritime expansion, the religious civil wars, nationalism, imperialism and colonialism, the history of the world wars – and the history of institutional, total power in the form of fascism and communism, so significant for the cataclysmic twentieth century. Nonetheless, Europe can look to times signaling a further *differentiation* and *pluralization* of images of history that previously were in the main national and homogeneous.

Let me make a rather apodictic assertion: European unity cannot come about in analogy to the creation of the German Reich in the nineteenth century. Yet the public statements of many historians in the Federal Republic on the questions of Europe may give rise to such an impression. These are historians whose forte is a social history closely bound up with the paradigm of the nation-state.

Despite all the evident effort to repeatedly proclaim and vaunt Europe's diversity, the analogy intuitively based on the history of German unification in the nineteenth century leads to an image of Europe that, like a reiteration of Bismarck's foundation of the Reich, takes on the contours of a unitary polity. But if it wants to succeed, the tendency toward unifying the continent will have to pursue another avenue, privileging soft forms of integration. While carefully preserving difference, common shared features will be grounded by pursuing procedures in which consensual elements are balanced off by majority decision. Unity and difference will thus have to reconcile themselves as structural constants in the configuration of Europe. Traditions of such a communicative architecture can be sought in the arsenals of the European memories. Moreover, it is not the nineteenth century and modernity, with their static structures oriented to homogeneity and centralization, that can serve as a meaningful armature for a functioning European architecture – but rather, perhaps paradoxically, precisely that which is *pre-modern*. Of course not the material circumstances and frames of pre-modernity: the principle of equality and the associated phenomena of national homogenization and social stratification in the sense of progress and human welfare have ensured there can be no return to those hard realities. Yet planners for the future might turn their attention to a number of the structural features of the pre-modern. And this not only because the pre-modern and post-modern would seem to share a certain affinity. Rather, what I have in mind is the epistemologically relevant character of various *pre-modern* phenomena for a *post-modern* future in Europe.

The historical sciences would be well advised to loosen up the continuing quasi-subliminal effect of a perspective guided by an entrenched canon. That perspective constantly seeks to engage the constitutive character of the French Revolution, the homogenizing nation-states and the paradigm of the social obligated to the ideal of equality.

By means of alternative agendas, new perceptions could be crystallized open to the interrupted and never fully exploited potentials of pre-modernity for a Europeanist post-modernity. One could, for example, draw on little interpreted elements of tradition in multinational imperial states. Such states, in view of the dominant telos of modernity in the historical sciences, are rarely deemed a source for new notions about the future, alone by dint of their dynastic structure of legitimacy, their smoldering questions of nationalities, their stunted agrarian conditions and postponed democratization. So it would indeed be a great mistake to assume that the imperative of the hour is to rejuvenate elements of tradition thought meaningful from empires long sunk into landscapes of political ruin. Rather, important for perspectives beyond the received nation-state is the exploratory attempt to sound out and tap those pre-modern historical elements of experience in regard to their *epistemic value* for a post-modern view of the world. In any event, the epistemic profit that would accrue would be a heightened awareness of and sensitivity to (1) heterogeneous structures and (2) consensual procedures. Moreover, this would also highlight phenomena of imperial integration antipodal to the nation-state, such as trans-territoriality and trans-nationality. Or forms of a composition of belonging moored to emblems of diversity that do not correspond to patterns of ethnic homogeneity and associated dimensions of participation in the state and polity – a hybridity *avant la lettre*, so to speak, before the term existed.

To expand the canon of the historical sciences by the addition of a genuinely Europeanist perspective requires opening up a historical horizon of interpretation beyond the realm of the national. To move beyond the national would mean going beyond the efforts of ultimately comparativistic approaches characteristic of the perspective of inquiry into so-called *entangled histories* or *histoires croisées*. Elements of such an approach can be found where they encounter historical phenomena that have been pushed aside and crowded out by the weight of the paradigms of state and society moored to the notion of the national, and have thus fallen into desuetude. We must thematically revitalize such residues of the supra-national. This does not mean exacerbating the ever deeper and more frequent fissures running through the historical sciences. It does not entail an inflationary particularization. On the contrary, what it calls for is the need to aspire once more to a unity of the historical narrative. But a unity of such narrative on the very basis of diversity. Not a return to the *grand récit*, but an intention that can be formulated anew in attempting to achieve a kind of *integrated* history. This approach ought to befit the old continent, a territory where history is inscribed as an unmistakable trait of character. And if such an approach also helps to further political integration, well then all the better.

Bibliography

Assmann, J. 1992. *Das kulturelle Gedächtnis. Schrift, Erinnerung und politische Identität in frühen Hochkulturen*. Munich: C. H. Beck.
Blumenberg, H. 1991. *The Legitimacy of the Modern Age*. Cambridge, Mass.: MIT Press.
Eley, G. 1996. "Is All the World a Text? From Social History to the History of Society Two Decades Later." In T. J. McDonald (ed.),

The Historic Turn in the Human Sciences. Ann Arbor: University of Michigan Press.

Halbwachs, M. 1980. *The Collective Memory.* New York: Harper Row.

Hunt, L. 2003. "Presidential Address: The World We Have Gained: The Future of the French Revolution." *American Historical Review* 108(1), 1–19.

Kehr, E. 1965, 1977. *Der Primat der Innenpolitik*, H. U. Wehler (ed.). Berlin: de Gruyter. English edition: 1977. *Economic Interest, Militarism, and Foreign Policy.* Berkeley: University of California Press.

Koselleck, R. 1988. *Critique and Crisis: Enlightenment and the Pathogenesis of Modern Society.* Oxford: Berg.

Mommsen, W. J. (ed.) 1988. *Leopold van Ranke und die moderne Geschichtswissenschaft.* Stuttgart: Klett-Cotta.

Schmitt, C. (1938) 1982. *Der Leviathan in der Staatslehre des Thomas Hobbes. Sinn und Fehlschlag eines politischen Symbols.* Hamburg: Hanseatische Verlagsanstalt.

Schnur, R. (ed.) 1978. *Staat und Gesellschaft- Studien über Lorenz von Stein.* Berlin: Humboldt.

Schulz, G. 1969. *Das Zeitalter der Gesellschaft. Aufsätze zur politischen Sozialgeschichte der Neuzeit.* Munich: Piper.

—. 1970. "*Die Entstehung der bürgerlischen Gesellschaft.*" In G. A. Ritter (ed.), *Entstehung und Wandel der modernen Gesellschaft: Festschrift für Hans Rosenberg zum 65. Geburtstag.* Berlin: de Gruyter, 3–65.

Stein, L. von. 1972. *Gesellschaft, Staat, Recht.* E. Forsthoff (ed.). Berlin: Propyläen Verlag.

Chapter 7

Idan Segev

What Changes in the Brain When We Learn

We have, in the next place, to treat of Memory and Remembering, considering its nature, its cause, and the part of the soul to which this experience, as well as that of Recollecting, belongs.
Aristotle in his treatise *On Memory and Reminiscence*

Abstract

In many ways we are the albums of memories we have collected in our brain. The creation of this ever-changing brain album is made possible because of the amazing tendency of the neuronal substrate to constantly change following new experiences. These physical changes undergo progressive stabilization in the brain, sometimes forming long-term memories. What are the physical changes underlying memory in our "brain machine"? The developments of new optical, electrical and molecular technologies enable one, for the first time ever, to view the living brain while it changes and learns. The major recent advances in this fascinating field of research are briefly summarized herein. A brief introduction to the brain "life-ware" is provided, followed by a highlighting of the main modifiable (plastic) neuronal mechanisms that may support learning and memory in the brain. It is worth emphasizing that when the unique learning mechanisms that brains utilize are eventually unraveled, we could then help to cure memory deficits, expand our memory capacity and begin building learning machines that will successfully behave in, and adapt to, the ever-changing environment that surrounds us.

1   The Substrate for Learning in the Brain – Nerve Cells and Synapses

Each of the 10 billion nerve cells (neurons) that compose our brain is an independent electrical entity ("microchip," Fig. 7.1, lower left). When stimulated (e.g. by sensory input, by direct electrical stimulation or by other neurons connected to it, see below) it generates a series of prototypical electrical signals called "spikes" (Fig. 7.1, lower right). Each of these spikes has a rather constant shape and amplitude. It is therefore of a digital type – it either exists (in full amplitude and a fixed duration) or it does not exists at all. When a sensory stimulus arrives (e.g. a word appears on the paper you now read), millions of neurons in your visual system fire a series of such spikes. These spikes represent (encode) the sensory (e.g. visual) stimulus. Similarly, when you hear a piece of Bach music, million of neurons in the auditory system fire spike trains and, collectively, this firing in the activated network of neurons (Fig. 7.1, top right), represents this piece of music in your brain. When you move your hand, millions of neurons in the motor system of your brain fire trains of spikes, thus representing (and planning) the movement. In other words, the internal language of the brain is composed of specific groups of neurons that fire, at a particular time, a series of spikes, thus representing an item (a face, an emotion, a memory, an idea) that is being processed by the brain at that time.

Most neurons are not connected electrically to one another. Rather, they interact with each other via a unique apparatus called a "synapse" (originating from the word "synapsis" – meaning clasp (or grip) in Greek; Fig. 7.1, schematic dots in lower left and Fig. 7.2 in colour plate section). The synapse forms a tiny physical gap between the synaptically connected neurons and is unidirectional (i.e. a given synapse connects cell 1 to cell 2 but not vice versa). When a spike occurs in neuron 1, a chemical (a neurotransmitter) is released at the synapse, and this neurotransmitter binds to specific receptors in cell 2. The latter then responds to the neurotransmitter with a small electrical signal, called a "synaptic potential." Unlike the "all-or-none" nature of the spike, the synaptic potential is an analog (rather than digital) in nature – it may be very small (a tenth of a millivolt) or larger (several millivolts) and, for a given synapse, it may attain either a positive sign ("excitatory" synapse) or a negative sign ("inhibitory" synapse). The synapse is therefore a chemical device that transforms digital signals (spikes) in one cell (the pre-synaptic neuron) to an analog signal – the synaptic potential – in the other cell (the post-synaptic cell). The strength of the synapse (the efficacy of the synaptic connection) may vary; yet each synapse typically retains its signs, it is either excitatory or inhibitory.

How does the synaptic potential (the input to a neuron) generate an output in the form of a spike train in this neuron? When many (hundreds) of excitatory synapses bombard a given neuron (and not too many inhibitory synapses act at the same time) then individual potential of each synapse sums up with that of other synapses and, if a certain positive voltage threshold is reached, then the receiving (post-synaptic) neuron responds with a spike (or a series of them, Fig. 7.2 in colour plate section). The neuron is therefore an input-output electrical device that transforms (via its synaptic connections) the analog synaptic signals that it receives (over its receptive, or input, region – the *dendritic* tree, Fig. 7.2) from many other neurons to a series of digital signals – a series of spikes (generated on the neuron's output process – the *axonal* tree, Fig. 7.2).

2   What Changes in the Brain During Learning?

What, then, could change in the brain "life-ware" described above –
the neurons and their synapses – when we learn? Some possible
neuronal mechanisms that are not mutually exclusive come to mind:
(1) *New* nerve cells may grow (and new neural networks are then
formed) when we learn something new. (2) The strength of *existing*
(synaptic) connections changes, thus functionally changing the con-
nectivity (and the activity) within the *existing* neural networks in
response to a sensory stimuli. (3) New synapses are formed between
neurons that were not connected before, thus effectively creating new
networks of neurons that, when active, represent a new memory.

a   New Neurons for New Memories?

Although in recent years it was found that in some regions of the adult
mammalian brain new nerve cells do grow, this growth is rather
sparse, and it is unlikely that our new memories are stored by these
new nerve cells. An interesting counter example of this is the brain of
songbirds, where the males during the courtship period generate a
typical song and, only during this period, a large number of new nerve
cells grow and were shown to play a key role in the generation of the
song. These cells then die, and the singing of the song subsides until
the next courtship period. This fascinating example, in which physically new networks serve a new function, is the oddity rather than the
rule.

b   Adjusting Synaptic Strength for New Memories?

The strength of the synaptic connection can indeed change very
rapidly. It was shown that when synapses are repeatedly activated,
their resultant post-synaptic potential might become larger or smaller,
thus effectively changing the strength of this synaptic connection.

Indeed, synapses are probably the most modifiable (plastic) elements in the nervous system. Furthermore, after a short period of activation, the change in synaptic strength may last for hours and days (long-term potentiation, LTP, or long-term depression, LTD, in the synaptic strength), and probably even longer (the question of whether one needs to "replay" memories by reactivating the neural networks involved – e.g. while dreaming – in order to stabilize the changes that correspond to the new memory is an issue under investigation). But what are the rules that "decide" when a synapse will become stronger or weaker following its activity?

The Canadian psychologist Donald Hebb (1949) was the first to formalize a tentative rule for changes that may occur in the connection between nerve cells:

> When an axon of cell A is near enough to excite cell B or repeatedly or consistently takes part in firing it, some growth or metabolic change takes place in one or both cells such that A's efficiency, as one of the cells firing B, is increased." One may succinctly summarize the "Hebb learning rule" as stating that "when cell A persistently participates in firing cell B, then these cells are more strongly connected to each other.

Indeed, recent experiments in pairs of synaptically connected nerve cells demonstrate that, in many systems, the Hebb rule does hold true. Furthermore, in many cases the "anti-Hebbian" rule also holds. Namely, if cell A is consistently not involved in firing cell B, then the synapse between them is weakened (Fig. 7.3 in colour plate section).

c   *Forming New Synapses for New Memories?*

The development of the two-photon microscope in recent years enabled one to follow a given synaptic connection day after day in the living brain and explore how stable this connection is and whether new synapses are formed. It was recently found that new synapses are constantly formed (by creating a very small new protrusion – called a dendritic spine – that forms a synapse with a nearby axon, see Fig. 7.4), and old synapses may disappear. In other words, in our densely packed nervous system, a slight shuffling in its fine anatomy (without changing its gross anatomy – e.g. adding neurons or growing new long branches) enables the formation of new contacts between preexisting neurons. This relatively new discovery has shifted our thinking about memory storage in the brain. Whereas it was previously thought that most of the changes associated with memory rely on changing the strength of *existing* synapses, it is presently believed that the formation of *new* synapses may play a key role in learning and, in particular, in stabilizing long-term memories.

Whatever the biological mechanism, whether it is the growth of new synapses or the strengthening or weakening of old synapses, both mechanisms establish functional new networks that *when active*, could, in principle, represent (store) new memories (e.g. new learned capabilities). Repeated imaging of the brain while one rehearses a given practice in order to learn a new skill (e.g. playing the piano) shows that the brain region that represents the acquired skill (e.g. the region representing the movement of the fingers) "grows." This growth implies that a larger neural network (more neurons are now more tightly connected to each other) is involved in the refined (and more coordinated) learned movement of the pianist fingers. To the best of our knowledge, no new nerve cells are added to the brain of an expert pianist. But more nerve cells are recruited (via the strengthening of the synaptic connections in the network or by adding new synaptic connections to it) following acquisition of a skill. The capacity of the brain to constantly rewire itself is so vast (the number of its synapses is on the order of 10^{14}), that establishing new functional networks while we learn does not necessarily destroy old memories. Indeed, with such a huge number of synapses in a single human brain (10,000 times larger than the number of people in the world), we can learn much more than we do.

It should be emphasized that the physiological changes in the synaptic strength as well as the morphological changes (the formation of new synapses) are all supported by sophisticated genetic machinery that is responsible for generating and maintaining these changes. The molecular basis for memory is a very active field of research today, and its details are beyond of the scope of the present article (Dudai 2004). The interested reader is advised to dive into the fascinating Nobel lecture by Eric Kandel (winner of the 2000 Nobel Prize), entitled *"The Molecular Biology of Memory Storage: A Dialog between Genes and Synapses"* which can be found at http://nobelprize.org/ medicine/laureates/2000/kandel-lecture.html.

Epilogue: Emotional learning, sleep and memory, and brain-inspired learning theory

The problem of the biological basis of memory in the brain has many facets, and only a few were summarized above. One intriguing question is the neural basis for emotional learning and memory. A specific brain region called the amygdala is known to be involved in emotional responses and, in particular, in fear conditioning and the formation of long-term memories of fear associations. Synaptic mechanisms such as LTP were implicated as being the basis for such associations (Ledoux 2003). But why is it that emotions are so powerful and so hard to control and relearn (especially those that cause behavioral disorders)? What is it, at the synaptic level, that makes it so hard to forget (get rid of) strong emotions, whereas we tend to rather easily forget names or faces or other skills that we have acquired but stopped practicing them? This puzzle remains yet to be unraveled.

Another intriguing question is, what the role is of different brain areas – from the hippocampus to the cortex to the limbic systems – in the process of acquiring and storing memories. The hippocampus is considered to be the brain region where new facts and events are initially processed and stored, whereas certain neocortical regions are believed to store this information for a longer time. Retrieval of old memories activates other brain regions. So it seems that different aspects of memory are distributed over different brain regions and, indeed, a local damage may yield specific loss of one aspect of memory (e.g. damage to the hippocampus may destroy the capability to acquire new memories, but old memories are retained). Importantly, new molecular techniques pave the road for a deeper understanding of the cellular mechanisms that underlie memory consolidation and retrieval. In this context it is worth mentioning the growing behavioral, electrophysiological and molecular studies demonstrating that sleep contributes to memory consolidation. A good review on the aspects mentioned above can be found in a special issue of the journal *Neuron* (2004) that is fully dedicated to the question of memory in its many facets.

But what is still missing for providing a real breakthrough in understanding how memory is represented and stored among distributed networks of neurons and their synapses, and how these memories are retrieved (e.g. via associations), is a *learning theory* (a mathematical model) that will incorporate the experimental data into a comprehensive picture. Without such a theory we will remain with a collection of (very important) experimental facts that will not provide the deep understanding that is required for describing as complex a system as the learning brain. Indeed, without such a theory we cannot say, "We understand how the brain works."

Happily, in the last two decades, many powerful theoreticians, physicists, mathematicians and computer scientists have joined this endeavor. New mathematical theories are being developed to describe: how memory is distributed in neuronal networks? What is the memory capacity of such networks? How do such networks retain memory while facing the constant death of cells and synapses? and How does the brain make predictions based on old memories, and consequent changes when these predictions are proven to be successful? (see Dayan and Abbott 2001; Hopfield and Brody 2004; Gutig and Sompolinsky 2006).

We are at an age of "brain-renaissance," in which a variety of disciplines – biology, physics, psychology, computer science – and many brains join forces to try and develop such a theory. There are good reasons to believe that the big "brain-eureka" is just around the corner.

Bibliography

Dayan, P. and L. F. Abbott. 2001. *Theoretical Neuroscience: Computational and Mathematical Modeling of Neural Systems.* Boston: MIT Press.

Dudai, Y. 2004. *Memory from A to Z: Keywords, Concepts, and Beyond.* Oxford: Oxford University Press.

Gutig, R. and H. Sompolinsky. 2006. "The Tempotron: A Neuron That Learns Spike Timing-Based Decisions." *Nature Neuroscience* 9(3), 420–8.

Hebb, D. O. 2002. *The Organization of Behavior: A Neuropsychological Theory.* Mahwah, NJ: Lawrence Erlbaum Associates, Inc., new edition, June 15.

Hopfield, J. J. and C. D. Brody. 2004. "Learning Rules and Network Repair in Spike-Timing-Based Computation Networks." *Proceedings of the National Academy of Science* (USA). 101(1), 337–42.

Ledoux, J. 2003. *Synaptic Self: How Our Brains Become Who We Are.* New York: Penguin Books

Neuron. 2004. 44(1) (30 September). Cell Press.

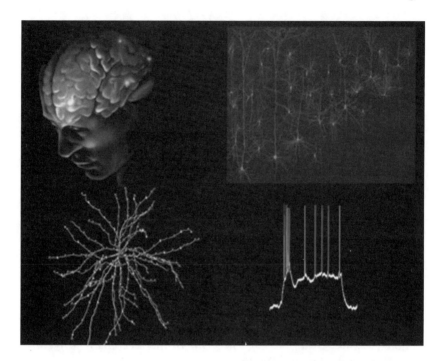

Figure 7.1 Brain ingredients. Our brain is a home for billions of inter-connected nerve cells (top right). Each individual nerve cell (lower left) is a tiny input-output electro-chemical microprocessor with a tree-like structure (the dendritic tree). It receives over its surface many thousands of synaptic contacts (schematic color circles) originated from axons of other nerve cells. When these synaptic contacts are activated (e.g. in response to a sensory input) the cell fires an output in the form of a train of prototypical electrical signals, called spikes (lower right). Our thoughts and feelings, our sensory perception and motor actions are all represented in the brain by a code that is carried by these spikes and is distributed among neuronal networks comprising of large number of nerve cells.

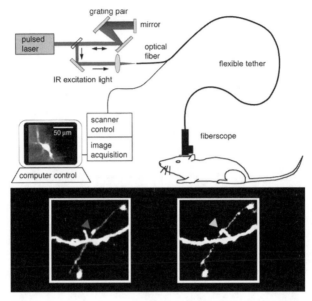

Figure 7.4 An optical view on anatomical changes in the living brain. Schematic drawing of the two-photons microscope system containing a small microscope stage, mounted on the head of a mouse, with a laser beam entering the brain via a small hole in the skull. This system enables one to repeatedly view the same location at a μm resolution (the size of a single synapse). The lower left picture shows an axon (thin white line) of one nerve cell crossing nearby (but not contacting) a dendrite (thick white line) of another cell. Several days later, a synaptic contact is formed at that same location between the axon and the dendrite (see arrowhead). This anatomical re-arrangement of synaptic contacts during behaviour is thought to be one of the several physical bases for learning and memory processes in the brain.

Chapter 8

BIANCA KÜHNEL

Memory and Architecture: Visual Constructions of the Jewish Holy Land[1]

The Jewish practice and notion of pilgrimage have characteristics and a rhythm of their own. Although at times sharing some patterns with Christian pilgrimage, Jewish pilgrimage developed along completely different paths and at a different pace, its aims and purposes stemming from the supreme position of Eretz Israel in Jewish life and thought.[2]

Eretz Israel is holy to the Jews on the strength of the Bible. According to a midrashic concept, there are several degrees of holiness, and Jerusalem and the Temple enjoy the highest one (Ginsberg 1909, 1:12; 1925, 5:14, note 39). One can argue that the given holiness of the Land of Israel as a whole was the reason that Jews for a very long time did not develop a concept of individual holy places, and why, for still longer, no consistent pilgrimage patterns came into existence (Reiner 1988). To that, should be added the specific opposition in Judaism to tomb cult, which played such an important and formative role in the early stages of Christian pilgrimage. Moses' unknown burial place is a classic example of biblical origin (Deuteronomy 14), repeated over and over again by midrashic sources (Safrai 1987, 2:303–13). According to a couple of early midrashim, Jacob asked to be buried in Eretz Israel to prevent the Egyptians from turning his tomb into a pagan cultic spot. The Halakha declares that it is forbidden

1 A first draft of this study was presented at the conference "Architecture and Pilgrimage 600–1600" held at CRASSH (The Cambridge Centre for the Arts, Social Sciences and Humanities) in July 2005.
2 On the dichotomy between the Jewish memories of a central Land stemming in the Second Temple period and the reality, as emerging from memories left by pagan neighbors, see Doron Mendels 2004, esp. chapter 7, 89–102.

to build a structure above a righteous one's grave, because "their sayings are their memories" (ibid., sources in notes 8 and 10).[3] Generally, and not only regarding prominent figures, Jewish graves are required to be deep in the earth, so that nobody will be tempted to pray over them or worship the defunct.

In the absence of a variety of holy places, it is understandable that Jewish pilgrimages did not take place for a long time. The three obligatory annual visits to the Temple, as postulated by the Bible, were not pilgrimages but participation in festivals.

This situation changed radically under the influence of the Crusades (Reiner 1988; Prawer 1988, esp. chapters 6 and 7). The waves of Christian pilgrims coming from Europe set an example and worked as an incentive to European Jews. But, more than that, the powerful renewal of the Christian hold on the Holy Land and the reassertion of the Christian *loca sancta* probably aroused a sense of envy and competitiveness on the part of Jews, whether local, Eastern or Western. The change that took place in the aftermath of the Crusades only partly resided in the increasing number of visitors to Eretz Israel (including the famous, such as Yehuda Halevy and Benjamin of Tudela) and in the beginnings of pilgrimage writings, as often noted in the scholarly literature. But to my mind these are only symptoms of a more comprehensive and significant, though gradual, process – namely, that of transforming Eretz Israel into the Jewish Holy Land.

What does this mean? First of all, the beginning of the documentation of the Land of Israel as a holy land, which led to the concretization and dissemination of holiness from the Temple of Jerusalem throughout the whole country; second, a departure from the abstract concept of sanctity emanating from one central holy place, to approach more closely the (Christian) concept of many holy places, determining the borders of the Holy Land.

What are Jewish holy places? They are places associated with biblical figures, with sages of the Mishna and Talmud as well as their schools and academies, and with places believed to be the tombs of biblical heroes. These sites concretized into a historical collective

---

3   Ibid., sources in notes 8 and 10.

portrait of the country as described in the Bible, in the two Talmuds and in the midrashic literature – a portrait that could be copied, multiplied and transported to the diaspora. This paper deals with one such channel of the dissemination of the holiness of Eretz Israel: a unique channel operating through visual images of architectures perpetuating the significance of a site in time.

The formative process of the Jewish Holy Land was accompanied at all stages by written descriptions of pilgrimage, which acted as the main channel in maintaining the bond between the visitor, or immigrant, and his community at home. The illustrious pilgrims of the twelfth century (Yehuda Halevy, summer 1140; Benjamin of Tudela, in the second half of that century; Petahyah of Regensburg and Jacob son of Nathaniel Cohen from France), all left literary testimonies of their impressions of Eretz Israel.[4] Already then, if not even earlier, a different genre developed in the shape of lists of holy places, no doubt with the initial aim of guiding the traveler in the quickest and most efficient way. One such list was attached to Benjamin of Tudela's travel description.

During the thirteenth century there are clear indications of streams of travelers (for example: "the immigration of the three hundred Rabbis" from France) and many other pieces of evidence – of itineraries and of the establishment of rituals at the holy places (one of the itineraries, for example, certainly originated before 1291, since it started and finished at Acre). At the same time, various patterns of immigration developed; communities of Eastern and Western immigrants established themselves in Eretz Israel and were at first economically independent. During the fourteenth century local communities developed a network of relationships with their home country communities, who became increasingly aware of their responsibilities toward the immigrants, as keepers of the holy places in their name. Fundraising began, through regular emissaries (*shadarim*) from Eretz Israel to the countries of origin. Pilgrimage records and travel lists played an important role in this undertaking as documents and representatives of the holy places. This role gained importance during subsequent cen-

4   For bibliographical references, see Reiner 1988 and Prawer 1988. See also Prawer 1946, 43–50.

turies, with the growing influx of pilgrims and immigrants due to the Black Death in Europe and the persecutions in Spain. Immigration lost its elitist and intellectual character, and the way was opened to new forms of representation.

The illuminated lists of holy places that are the topic of this paper constitute one of these new forms that developed during the sixteenth century. They mark two new developments in the history of Hebrew pilgrimage literature and art (I will refer to them as art, noting that the few scholars who have paid attention to the illuminations preferred to label them folk art): first, emancipation of the lists of holy places, which began to be circulated on their own; second, the visualization of holy places through architectural representations. Jointly, these two developments led to the crystallization of a phenomenon unique in the history of Jewish (and Christian) pilgrimage art.

Seven such illuminated lists so far are known, all of them from the sixteenth century (Zucker 1996, 3–15; Reiner 2002, 9–19; Sarfati 1987, 21–9). Three, the most beautiful and best preserved, are in the collection of the Jewish National and University Library in Jerusalem (JNUL),[5] another is in the Meir Benayahu private collection in Jerusalem[6] and one is in the Jewish Theological Seminary library in New York;[7] two fragments are in Princeton;[8] an unfinished manuscript is in Moscow,[9] and another is in the Cecil Roth collection in Leeds Uni-

5   I am extremely grateful to Rivka Plesser, Head of the Manuscripts and Archives Department at the Jewish National and University Library in Jerusalem, not only for allowing me to study the scrolls, but also for sharing with me her expertise in related written and visual material kept in the library's collections.

6   Tempera and ink, 62 x 89cm. The colophon in the middle of the last column names the scribe Moshe b. Aaron Trigero, gives the date 1549–50, and reveals the place of production, Jerusalem.

7   New York, JTS, Mic.3598, Italian origin, tempera and gold powder on parchment, width 12, Sarfati 2002, pl. 19.

8   Princeton University Library, Garrett Hebrew Ms 4, watercolor and ink, 40.5 x 12.5cm (two fragments of a parchment are rolled up widthwise). Ibid., pl. 21.

9   Moscow, The Russian National Library, Ginzburg collection, no. 579. Ink on paper, unfinished. Ibid., pl. 14.

versity Library.[10] With the exception of this last one in Leeds, which is a codex, and the one in the Benayahu private collection in Jerusalem, which is one rectangular sheet of parchment divided into four columns, all the exemplars are scrolls, the great majority of them parchment scrolls, on which writing and illumination were done in ink and tempera. The anachronistic use of scroll, parchment and manuscript illumination in a period when printing was more than one hundred years old has to be considered intentional, and as such it helps outline the purpose of these illuminated lists.

This paper is mainly based on two scrolls in the Jewish National and University Library in Jerusalem (JNUL 8° 6947 and JNUL 8° 1187), which were produced in Eretz Israel and are representative of the whole group. Being 19.5cm wide and 219.3cm long, JNUL 8° 6947 is the largest scroll known to date (Figs. 8.1 and 8.2 in colour plate section). JNUL 8° 1187 is somewhat smaller (12.2 x 140cm) and very elegant, with a list of places and illuminations that is similar although not identical to those in JNUL 8 6947 (Figs. 8.3 and 8.4).

JNUL 8° 6947 is not only the largest, but also the most detailed and best documented of the preserved lists. A colophon gives the name of the copyist, Uri b. Simeon of Biella; the date, 1564; and the place of production, Safed (Zucker 1996; Sarfati 2002, pl. 13, 16). Details concerning the history of this scroll are also known: in 1574 or 1575 it was taken to Italy and possibly copied in Venice, although no evidence exists. A printed version, Cippi Hebraici, containing the Hebrew text and its Latin translation, was produced in Heidelberg in 1659 and again in 1662 by the German theologian and Hebraist Johann Heinrich Hottinger. One page of copper etchings with illuminations is now in the Gross family collection in Tel Aviv (Sarfati 2002, pl. 15; Sarfati 2002, 22). Contacts between Safed and Italian communities are well documented, especially after the influx of Jewish travelers from Italy during persecutions there in the second half of the sixteenth century. For example, a letter by David de Rossi sent from Safed to Italy as early as 1534 tells that his sister will be bringing lists

10   Leeds University Library, Ms Roth 200, published by Cecil Roth in facsimile in 1929. The colophon mentions Casale Monferrato as place of production, and the date 1597–8. Ibid., pl. 18.

of tombs and holy places in the country, drawn up by Jerusalem authors, on her way back to her home in Italy (Sarfati 2002, 23, 28).

Before the actual list of holy places begins, the Tabernacle and Temple implements are elaborately depicted in their own frame, in a way familiar from the thirteenth – fourteenth-century Sephardic Bible manuscripts – such as the Farhi Bible in the Sassoon Collection, JNUL Ms 368, from the second half of the fourteenth century (1366–82) (Narkiss 1992, 99, color pl. 16) (Fig. 8.5). Then a title in its own frame announces the list to follow: "Yihus ha-avot ve ha-neviim ve ha-zadikim…" (The genealogy of the patriarchs and the prophets and the righteous…). This is mainly a list of tombs of the righteous, arranged from south to north, from Hebron to Galilee. An additional title follows, explaining:

> Those are the travels of the people of Israel who go from place to place, to kneel on the tombs of the righteous, to pray and ask for mercy for themselves and for their brethren in the diaspora. God, blessed be he, will receive their prayers and will bring us closer to our salvation.

The itinerary starts in Hebron at the tombs of the patriarchs, where one can read "Adam and Eve, Abraham and Sarah, Yitzhak and Rebecca, Jacob and Leah"; it continues with the tomb of Prophet Jesaja at Halhul and Rachel's tomb near Bethlehem. The tombs are depicted as small arched aediculae in a combined outer and inner view in which hanging lamps are very prominent. JNUL 6947 and 1187 differ in the shape of the tombs, 1187, being more elaborated than 6947.

The depiction of Jerusalem that follows is clearly dominated by the representation of the Temple Mount. The two scrolls present two different methods of showing the Temple Mount. JNUL 6947 presents a bird's-eye view of the enclosure seen from the East, with the Dome of the Rock at the center and al-Aqsa shown in a corner (Fig. 8.6). In JNUL 1187, the main components of the Mount are depicted separately (Fig. 8.4): the Dome of the Rock and al-Aqsa are seen in a kind of isometric view, with the relative proportions between the two maintained: the Dome of the Rock has a larger dome over a centralized building; al-Aqsa is longer, with the dome covering only part of the building, the other part having a flat roof.

The other holy places depicted in Jerusalem are (Fig. 8.2 in colour plate section): the tombs of the kings of the House of David (locations mentioned: Zion, David's palace); the tomb of the Prophetess Hulda (only in JNUL 6947, lacking in 1187) on the Mount of Olives (there also, at the top, a platform (אצטבא) is mentioned, where the Shekhina stood when it took off for the ten journeys); and the tomb of Zechariah and Absalom's memorial in the Kidron Valley (evoking the shape of the real tombs) (Fig. 8.7). "Opposite Jerusalem" a mountain is mentioned (Ramah) and a place from which Abraham saw and revered Mount Moriah. Between Jerusalem and that mountain are the tombs of Shimon ha-Zadik and the seventy Sanhedrin: JNUL 6947 shows an elaborate building with a pointed dome and five arches, one of which contains the entrance to the building; the other four tombs and hanging lamps, representing the tombs of the seventy; and the tomb of Shimon ha-Zadik, which is a much smaller, independent building.

On the Ramah, the tombs of the Prophet Samuel and of his mother, Hannah, are listed and depicted (that of his father, Elkana, is also mentioned but not shown). The text says that Samuel's actual grave cannot be seen, but that the "Ishmailim" built a monument there, hence the crescent above the aedicula containing his tomb. Behind the monument one can see a red-domed synagogue with Torah scrolls inside (JNUL 1187 has a different arrangement).

From Jerusalem, which occupies approximately half of the entire scroll, the itinerary takes the northern route to Samaria, the Jordan Valley, the Galilee and the Carmel. The illuminations (Fig. 8.2 in colour plate section) are less detailed than in and around Jerusalem. They include the tombs of Joshua and his father, Nun; Caleb ben Jephuneh; the tomb of the Rambam in Tiberias; and a few other stereotyped tombs of Galilean rabbis.

To sum up: half the scroll is occupied by monumental representations of the Tabernacle and Temple implements and of Jerusalem. JNUL 1187 has an additional depiction, that of the labyrinth of Jericho, which represents the beginning of the conquest of Eretz Israel.[11]

---

11   The Italian scroll in JNUL 2370, 12 x 145cm, tempera and gold powder on parchment, shows only the Jericho labyrinth at the opening, no Tabernacle and

The other half of the scroll is a more or less stereotypical rendering of tombs through an arch and a hanging lamp, documenting the itinerary from Jerusalem to the Galilee. Local details are emphasized by text and illumination, their role being to support the authenticity of the holy places. This combination of stereotyped elements with authentic details is well known in Christian art from the fourth century onward (Kühnel 1987; Ousterhout 1990).

What do these illuminated itineraries have to tell us in general? What do they contribute in the context of memory?

It is clear that in being so elaborate in material and decoration, the sixteenth-century Hebrew scrolls departed from the merely functional itineraries; they certainly fulfilled a representative role. I would not go so far as Elchanan Reiner does in assuming that these scrolls were hung on the wall as an alternative to *zekher la-hurban* (the place left bare on the wall near the entrance to a house to commemorate the destruction of Jerusalem), but I assume that they were displayed in synagogues to support the work of the *shadarim* in their fundraising campaigns. They were most probably kept in synagogues and homes to represent the Jewish Holy Land and keep it alive in the collective memory of diaspora communities.

It can hardly be a coincidence that the lists of holy places acquired an independent status and became illuminated immediately after the change from Mameluke to Ottoman rule in Eretz Israel. The new government raised the hopes of both local and diaspora Jews for a better life and easier access to the holy places. At least one of the scrolls, JNUL 6947, expresses great admiration for Sultan Suleiman the Magnificent's building activities and the improvement in basic living conditions in Jerusalem, most of all the modernization of the water supply system. Besides, a change of hands in general could have been taken as a good opportunity to reassess the country's Jewish identity, especially during what appeared at first to be a favorable and tolerant regime. The new spirit may have raised the level of expectations and hopes for the rebuilding of the Temple. The crescent above the buildings of the Temple Mount clearly indicates that the Jews were

Temple implements. This scroll, the third in the JNUL collection, is attributed to Italy, according to the style of the buildings which is Classical-Renaissance.

aware of the buildings' Muslim identity, but that this fact was not considered an impediment to their being legitimate representatives of the *locus* of the Temple. The same applies to the monument over Samuel's grave on the Ramah.

The atmosphere of tolerance at the beginning of Ottoman rule must also have been instrumental in inspiring Jewish illuminators who obviously drew from the illuminated Hajj certificates documented from the end of the twelfth century on (Aksoy and Milstein 2001, 101–34). The scroll shape, the architectural representations of holy places and tombs, their arrangement one after the other separated by lines of text, even such details as the shape of the buildings and their arches and hanging lamps as well as the coloring – these are all arguments supporting a linkage between illuminated hajj certificates and the Hebrew lists of holy places.

The visualization of the holy places certainly heightens their symbolic quality and is indicative of layers of meaning and emphases not highlighted by the text alone. The Tabernacle and Temple implements as well as the labyrinth of Jericho are not required by the itinerary list; both were added by the illuminator to enhance the Jewish identity of the Holy Land, by referring to history and to the divine determination of the bond between the people and the land of Israel. The use of scroll and parchment reflects the same function of added authority drawn from the past and the permanent and thus, through association with the Torah scroll, to a holy text.

The menorah is singled out among the Temple utensils and identified with that of Zechariah's vision, being part of the prophecy of rebuilding the Temple. The identification is made through a caption from Zechariah 4:2–14 and through the image of the dome above the menorah inscribed *gullah* (a bowl for oil), a reference to the same vision, according to which oil is being poured without human agency. The comparison with the illumination to this chapter in the Cervera Bible in Lisbon, dated to 1300,[12] speaks for itself (Figs. 8.8, 8.9).

Messianic hopes are part and parcel of the Jewish bond with Eretz Israel. Some specific conditions may support this aspect of our scrolls. From the end of the thirteenth century onward a concept crys-

12   Lisbon, Biblioteca Nacional, Ms.Ill.72, fol. 316b. Narkiss 1992, 79, pl. 6.

tallized concerning the immigration of the pious (the Hasidim) – namely, that they go to the Holy Land to hasten the end of days. During the fourteenth and fifteenth centuries, the time of the Black Death and the Spanish persecutions, the movement gained some additional messianic coloring, as messianic fervor developed in Europe, especially in Spain.

From both a historical and an art historical point of view, the scrolls represent a novelty in the Jewish approach to holy places. Before the sixteenth century attention was dedicated exclusively to representations of the Temple; in the scrolls many other holy places are added, so that conceptually and visually a comprehensive itinerary is developed, covering the entire Holy Land and not deriving its effect from one focal point alone. Until then, the Temple was represented through scattered implements, referring more to the cult and its continuity through the synagogue than to the *locus* itself. In the scrolls, the role of representation is on the contrary taken by the architecture commemorating the place.

These sixteenth-century scrolls, then, represent a turning point in Jewish pilgrimage and art, being the first to show collective icons of the Holy Land. The architecture depicted in them documents a sharp and significant change in attitude from total indifference to careful attention to detail.

Bibliography

Aksoy, S. and R. Milstein. 2001. "A Collection of Thirteenth-Century Illustrated Hajj Certificates." In *Ugur Derman 65th Birthday Festschrift*. Istanbul: Derleyen.

Ginsberg, L. 1909, 1925. *The Legends of the Jews*. Philadelphia: Jewish Publication Society of America, vol. 1, 1909; vol. 5, 1925.

Kühnel, B. 1987. *From the Earthly to the Heavenly Jerusalem: Representations of the Holy City in Christian Art of the First Millennium.* Vienna/Rome/Freiburg: Herder.

Mendels, D. 2004. *Memory in Jewish, Pagan and Christian Societies of the Graeco-Roman World.* London/New York: Continuum, T&T Clark International.

Narkiss, B. 1992. *Hebrew Illuminated Manuscripts*, 3rd ed. (in Hebrew). Jerusalem: Keter.

Ousterhout R. (ed.) 1990. *The Blessing of Pilgrimage.* Urbana/Chicago: University of Illinois Press.

Prawer, J. 1946. "The Jews in the Latin Kingdom of Jerusalem" (in Hebrew). *Zion* 11, 43–50.

—. 1988. *The History of the Jews in the Latin Kingdom of Jerusalem.* Oxford: Oxford University Press.

Reiner, E. 1988. "Pilgrims and Pilgrimage to Eretz Israel 1099–1517" (in Hebrew). PhD diss., Jerusalem, The Hebrew University.

—. 2002. "Traditions of Holy Places in Medieval Palestine – Oral versus Written." In R. Sarfati (ed.), *Offerings from Jerusalem: Portrayals of Holy Places by Jewish Artists.* (Published subsequent to the exhibition at the Israel Museum, Winter-Summer 1996.) Jerusalem: The Israel Museum, 9–19.

Safrai, Z. 1987. "Tombs of the Righteous and Holy Places in Jewish Tradition" (Hebrew). In *Zeev Vilnai Jubilee Volume.* Jerusalem: Ariel, 2: 303–13.

Sarfati, R. 2002. "The Illustrations of Yihus ha-Avot: Folk Art from the Holy Land." In R. Sarfati (ed.), *Offerings from Jerusalem, Portrayals of Holy Places by Jewish Artists.* (Published subsequent to the exhibition at the Israel Museum, Winter-Summer 1996.) Jerusalem: The Israel Museum, 21–9.

Zucker, S. 1996. "'Yihus ha-Avot' or 'Those Are the Travels': The Scroll of the Holy Places in the Collections of the National and University Library" (Hebrew). In *About Books and People*, Newsletter of the National and University Library in Jerusalem 10, 3–15.

Figure 8.3 JNUL 8° 1187, detail.

Figure 8.4 JNUL 8° 1187, detail.

Figure 8.5 JNUL Ms 368, Sassoon Collection, The Farhi Bible.

Figure 8.6 JNUL 6947, detail.

Bianca Kühnel

Figure 8.7 The tombs of Zechariah and Absalom in the Kidron Valley.

Figure 8.8 JNUL 8° 6947, detail.

Figure 8.9 Lisabon, Cervera Bible

Chapter 9

DAN LAOR

How Are We Expected to Remember the Holocaust? Szenes versus Kasztner

The year 2004 was the sixtieth anniversary of the destruction of Hungarian Jewry. It is a well-known fact that the Holocaust reached the Jews of Hungary at a relatively late phase of World War II and was completed within a very short time: the Nazis occupied Hungary on 19 March 1944, preparations for the "Final Solution" began in April, and from 15 May to 9 July, a period of only eight weeks, 434,351 Jews were sent to Auschwitz. Thus by mid-July, all of Hungary, except for the capital Budapest, was *Judenrein* (Cohen 2001). The anniversary of these tragic events was marked by scientific conferences, commemoration ceremonies, radio and television programs, and numerous publications. Quite naturally, the various controversies about the destruction of Hungarian Jewry re-emerged.

The aim of this paper is to speak of two prominent figures associated with the Holocaust period in Hungary: Hannah Szenes and Israel (Rudolf, or Rezsö) Kasztner. However, discussion will not focus on the events involving Szenes or Kasztner in the course of World War II, but will examine the attitudes to the two figures that have crystallized in Israeli society over the years and been represented in a wide variety of channels and modes of representation.

Hannah Szenes, born in Hungary, daughter of the author Bela Szenes, immigrated to Eretz Israel on the eve of World War II and joined kibbutz Sedot Yam. She volunteered to fly out to Europe with a group of paratroopers and was dropped over Yugoslavia in March 1944. After staying for a few months with the partisans, she crossed the border into Hungary in June, was captured, and was imprisoned in Budapest. Brought before a Hungarian military court and accused of spying, she was cruelly tortured; on 7 November 1944 she was executed by a firing squad, without having saved a single Jew. Szenes was a gifted poet and, though only twenty-three years old when she died, left an impressive literary legacy. In 1950 her remains were brought to Israel and she was reinterred on Mount Herzl (Masters 1972).

Israel Kasztner, journalist and lawyer, was deputy chairman of the rescue committee established in Hungary during the war. After the Nazi occupation, he participated in negotiations conducted by Adolf Eichmann and other S.S. officers with the elected leaders of the Jewish community. These negotiations, known as *"Blut für Ware"* (Blood for goods), were instrumental in rescuing many Jews: 1,684 Jews were saved in the "Kasztner train," and probably the lives of many thousands of additional Jews were saved as a result of other actions taken by Kasztner. After immigrating to Israel in 1947, Kasztner became a well-known public figure. His world collapsed during and after the "Kasztner trial," held in 1954–55, at the close of which the president of the Jerusalem District Court, Benjamin Halevi, declared that "Kasztner sold his soul to the devil." About a year and a half after the end of the trial, largely owing to the influence of the verdict, Kasztner was shot by an assassin. In 1955 the Supreme Court essentially overturned Justice Halevi's verdict (Bauer 1990).

Both Szenes and Kasztner enjoyed high visibility after the Holocaust, each of them being identified, and rightly so, with a different code of behavior in regard to the Jewish response to the German death machine. In that connection, the poet Natan Alterman coined the phrase "Two Paths" (*Shtei ha-Derakhim*): the path of revolt and active resistance, as against the path of cooperation and negotiation (Laor 1995). One may thus describe the structuring of the memory of the Holocaust in Israeli society as a process centered on the contest between Szenes and Kasztner as to which of them is the legitimate representative of that period.

In the summer of 1955, following the verdict in the Kasztner trial, an article was published by author Matti Megged, formerly a member of the Palmah, exposing the dichotomy between Szenes and Kasztner and, as a result, the moral dilemma that is represented by these two figures:

Whoever "forgives" Kasztner – thereby also obliterating the memory of Anielewicz and Tenenbaum, or placing the rebels and the intercessors on the same level – is not forgiving Kasztner the man; he is shaping the face of the nation, its path, its moral stand, today and tomorrow [...].

No, we are not commanded to remember and mention Kasztner the man. We have one single memory from those days, the days of the Holocaust in Hungary, and we should bear it constantly in mind: the memory of Hannah Szenes.

Both phenomena are not part of the past; they cannot be the subjects of a conciliatory, forgiving, false discourse. We are called upon to remember both, in order to award the victory to only one of them (Megged 1955).

Of the thirty-two paratroopers who participated in the mission to Europe, it is Hannah Szenes who has utterly captured the national imagination, and she has been commemorated on a grandiose scale: her writings have been published and put to music; she is the subject of a large literature; places and streets have been named for her; her name is perpetuated in ceremonies and gatherings, in drama and theater, in the press and the media, in school textbooks and children's literature. The beginnings of the "myth" of Hannah Szenes go back as far as 1945; one early manifestation was a ceremony held at kibbutz Sedot Yam on the first anniversary of her death, which continued with the publication of a commemorative anthology, mainly featuring the speeches given at the ceremony. Of special interest was the speech delivered by the writer Aharon Megged (Matti's brother), a member of Kibbutz Sedot Yam and a close friend of Hannah Szenesz. It is Aharon Megged who then played a major role in the formation and cultivation of the myth:

In every generation, Jewish heroism gushes forth in its own channels, choosing its heroes, the human embodiments of that generation's core desires, the epitome of its spirit. Hannah's generation, the generation of "illegal" immigrants and conquerors; the generation of pioneers, settlers, and defenders of their enterprise; the generation of catastrophe and destruction; the generation that lost millions of compatriots – that generation chose as its hero the emissary and pioneer who risked her life on her way from this country to the Diaspora, to snatch her brethren from the jaws of death (Megged 1945, 71).

The obsession with Hannah Szenes is not surprising, given the tendency then prevalent in the *Yishuv*, and later in the young state, to identify with acts of heroism and revolt, implying disapproval of the typically passive response of the Jewish masses and the functioning of Jewish leadership. The widespread admiration for the Warsaw Ghetto revolt can serve as an example. As noted by many scholars, the understanding of the Holocaust, and, in particular, criticism of Jewish behavior during the Holocaust have been nourished by the ethos of heroism and struggle cultivated in Israel, which was largely a natural corollary of the concept of "negation of the Diaspora," on the one hand, and of the existential circumstances dictated by life in the land of Israel, on the other (Stauber 2006). Hannah Szenes was, as it were, sucked into this vacuum; her personal fate and her actions seemed from the start to be wonderfully commensurate with the archetypal "New Jew," who rejects the Diaspora and penetrates deep into the Valley of Death, carrying the torch of heroism in his or her own hands and embodying the ideal of resistance and revolt.

Megged's rhetoric was maintained and backed up in further publications during the 1940s, under the auspices of Ha-Kibbutz Ha-Me'uhad publishing house, established by the left-wing faction of the Kibbutz movement. Two books were published almost simultaneously: a collection of the oeuvres of Szenes herself, edited by Moshe Braslavski, and the personal memoir written by Yoel Palgi (Palgi 1946). In his book Palgi, also a paratrooper, gave evidence of Hannah Szenesz's fate in Hungary, supplying details – some of them may have been imaginary – of the interrogation, the torture and, in particular, the execution:

> Hannah did not allow them to bind her eyes. Perhaps she wanted to see the sky, stretching above this cursed prison, for a few more moments. Or perhaps she wanted to fix her burning gaze on this officer and his three soldiers standing ready to shoot her, so that her blue eyes would follow them as long as they lived, giving them no rest.
> The captain gave the command in a hoarse voice. The soldiers fired. She sank, bleeding, to the sand (Palgi 2003, 207).

Moshe Braslavski, one of the leading intellectuals of Ha-Kibbutz Ha-Me'uhad movement, had compiled a collection of Szenes' poems and diaries, presenting a poet and a writer hitherto unknown. Szenes' writings, introduced by the editor, were followed by memoirs written by two of her fellow paratroopers, Yoel Palgi and Reuven Dafne. The newly revealed poet was introduced to the public not just as a literary talent but as a national heroine: "All the details of her life, mission and death" – wrote Braslavski – "add up to a sublime epic of a singular personality, with a brilliant crown of Hebrew heroism" (Braslavski 1944). Later revised and enlarged, this book has since gone through fifteen editions, publicizing the highly talented writer and poet in the context of her great mission.[1]

Szenes-worship continued apace in the years following the foundation of the state, during which the "heroism" (*"Gevurah"*) dimension was strongly emphasized in public discourse, at the expense of the Holocaust dimension (*"Shoah"*). The evidence of this worship was seen and felt everywhere: Szenes' remains were brought to Israel and re-interred in the national pantheon on Mount Herzl; her name has been commemorated again and again in the public space; the story of her life has been extensively featured in official and semi-official literature; her name was brought up repeatedly in schools; and the annual assemblies held in her memory at kibbutz Sedot Yam have been honored as state occasion (Tidor-Baumel 1996).

Against this background, Aharon Megged's play *Hannah Szenes*, staged by Habimah National Theater in 1958, is particularly striking (Megged 1993). While Megged based his text on personal acquaintance with Szenes and on evidence he collected (among others, from her mother, Katarina Szenes); he was no less inspired by George Bernard Shaw's play *Saint Joan was* staged by the Tel Aviv Chamber Theatre back in 1954. This play provided Megged with the necessary tool for the presentation of Hannah Szenes as a martyr, burned at the stake for her devotion to the supreme mission she had undertaken, till the bitter end. The show itself was an unprecedented theatrical event: The best actors were assembled for the occasion (among them the legendary Hannah Rovina, in the role of Szenes' mother); the press and radio covered the event extensively; and its commercial success

---

1   New editions were published long after Braslavsky's death in 1961. For the last edition (no. 15) see *Hannah Szenes: Shirim, Yomanim, Eduyot* (*Hannah Szenes: Poems, Diaries, Testimonies*) (in Hebrew). Tel Aviv: Ha-Kibbutz Ha-Me'uhad, 1994. For an English edition see: *Hannah Senesh: Her Life and Diary*, translated by Marta Cohn, London: Vallentine, Mitchell 1971.

was considerable for those days (116 stagings). The production took on the dimension of an important public and state occasion: political leaders attended the opening night, special performances were put on for soldiers and youth, and the theater remained open for a performance even on Holocaust Day – when theaters are closed by law – to enable the public to see the play (Laor 1998).

Critics also joined forces to market the play, which they thought to be of national significance. Lea Porat, the refined theater critic, had her reservations about Megged's competence as a playwright. Nevertheless, she felt committed to encourage the public to go and see the show. She wrote:

> How loathsome is the task of the theater critic, who is obliged to find fault, in relation to this play. Indeed, it is a long time since we have seen a play that is so important to see, so good to identify with, a play concerning which one wants to say: go *en masse* to see it, for it is part of yourselves, your own flesh and blood, a ring of pure gold in the chain of your history (Porat 1958).

It was no accident, then, that the victimization of Kasztner by Israeli society – the justice system, the press, "public opinion" – took place in the mid-1950s, at the very time the cult of Hannah Szenes was reaching its peak. The Gruenwald-Kasztner trial, heard before the Jerusalem District Court beginning in April 1954, was ostensibly a libel suit brought by the Attorney General of Israel to defend Kasztner against the slanders written by Malkiel Gruenwald in a locally published pamphlet that he edited. However, the maneuvering of the defense attorney, Shmuel Tamir, with the backing of the bench, converted Kasztner from witness to accused; almost imperceptibly, Kasztner found himself before an Israeli court, publicly accused of collaborating with the Nazis in occupied Budapest, thus, as argued by Gruenwald's attorney, blocking any attempt at resistance and revolt, and abandoning Hungarian Jewry to its fate (Segev 1993, 255–320; Weitz 1995; Bilski 2004, 19–82).

Moreover, the well-orchestrated assault on Kasztner proceeded largely in the shadow of the Hannah Szenes myth, in the sense that her personal example was to a large extent the yardstick against which Kasztner's personality was measured and judged. This trend was clearly expressed throughout the trial: in Shmuel Tamir's arguments

and rhetoric, where he repeatedly spoke of Kasztner and the paratroopers; in the impressive testimony of Hannah Szenes's mother
Katarina, which was largely instrumental in virtually turning Kasztner
into the accused party; and, of course, Justice Halevi's acceptance in
his verdict of most of Tamir's argument in regard to his attitude to the
paratroopers, in fact stating bluntly that Kasztner had "abandoned"
Hannah Szenes when she was imprisoned in Budapest. The press
eagerly followed suit, especially Shalom Rosenfeld, who in his reports
in the daily *Ma'ariv* – his articles turned later into a book – backed
Tamir and Halevi to the hilt, exploiting to the full the potential of the
polarized presentation of Hannah Szenes as a symbol of devotion,
heroism and self-sacrifice, as against Israel Kasztner, whom he
described as a symbol of demeaning intercession and collaboration.

After listening to Katarina Szenes's evidence, Rosenfeld wrote:

> A great wind blew that day in the hall of the Jerusalem court, bringing down
> with it the wondrous spirit of that young woman, when she parachuted onto
> enemy territory, when she descended into her Jewish brethren's Vale of Tears,
> with assurance, calm, much love, and endless devotion (Rosenfeld 1955, 163).

This rhetorical manipulation did not take place in a vacuum:
Israel in the 1950s was dominated by a stereotypical perception of the
millions of Jews who had perished in the Holocaust as having gone to
their deaths "like sheep to the slaughter," and the concomitant treatment of the established Jewish leadership and the *Judenräte* as collaborators. However, the recognized heroes of the Holocaust in Israel
were at the time not the members of the youth movements that had
headed the revolts and in fact paid with their lives, but the Palestinian
paratroopers, chief among them Hannah Szenes.

The denunciation of Kasztner reached its peak on 22 June 1955,
when Benjamin Halevi read the verdict – which took him fourteen
hours to complete. As Rosenfeld wrote:

> Halevi's voice is calm and hushed, but the sentences are like stone courses,
> great hewn blocks laid upon and alongside one another. There is no break, no
> space between them. His far-reaching, cold logic and factual analysis is tem-
> pered with phrases from the realm of literature and the realm of symbolism, like
> the one that a few hours later shocked the whole country from the pages of the
> newspapers: "Kasztner sold his soul to the devil" (Rosenfeld 1955, 405).

Following Halevi's controversial verdict, the Attorney General – under the direction of the Israeli government – submitted an appeal to the Supreme Court of Justice. This was done in January 1957, but on 3 March of that year Kasztner was shot by an assassin at the entrance to his home at 6 Emanuel Street, Tel Aviv. Twelve days later, he died of his wounds. Thus, in the *Memorbuch* for the Holocaust then taking shape in the Land of Israel, whose characters were sharply divided into heroes and villains, Hannah Szenes was put on a pedestal under a shining halo, a kind of Israeli Joan of Arc, whereas Israel Kasztner, who had actually rescued Jews (as even Halevi had to admit), was condemned to play the role of the villain.

A shift in attitudes to Kasztner seemed to have occurred by the time the Supreme Court made its decision. The verdict – which was announced in 1958 – was written by Justice Agranat, who allowed the state's appeal and essentially quashed Justice Halevi's position on most counts. Pninah Lahav, in her biography of Agranat, wrote:

> Perhaps at this stage in his life, Agranat had come to accept the notion that the fervent Zionist goal of "becoming a normal people," if translated into the admiration of sheer physical prowess, was itself a sign of abnormality [...] Perhaps the best sign of normality was a coming to terms with the past, an empathizing with rather than a judgment of the millions of victims. Humility, not fiery rhetoric, was needed (Lahav 1997, 143–4).

This, she believed, was the rationale underlying Justice Agranat's judicial opinion in his closely reasoned verdict, whose 194 pages had taken him six months to write. As to the Supreme Court's judgment, set against the background of its time, Lahav makes the following statement:

> Like all of Agranat's major decisions of the period, his Kasztner opinion was ahead of its time. His version of the history of the Holocaust of Hungarian Jewry, which he carefully detailed, declined to echo popular opinion. Today Agranat's version is widely considered standard history (ibid., 128).

A similar view, though from a different vantage point, was offered by Yehiam Weitz, who later wrote a biography of Kasztner. At a debate held at Yad Ben-Zvi in 1992, he said:

The significance of the verdict on appeal was internalized and understood only years later [...]. In 1958, the discrepancy between it and the image of the Holocaust was so great that it could not really be digested or intelligently discussed in its various aspects (Weitz 1993).

Yet the real shift in the representation of Kasztner took place in the course of the 1980s. It may be explained against the background of the maturing of Israeli society in all aspects of its view of the Holocaust. The first signs of the process may be dated to the Eichmann trial, consisting primarily in a diminution of the importance attached until then to the "heroism" aspect, increased empathy toward the victims, and an ability to understand the Holocaust in immanent terms rather than through the prism of Zionist and Eretz-Israel experience. The process was clearly ripening toward the end of the 1970s and the beginning of the next decade, when Israeli society's attitudes toward Jewish leadership during the Holocaust showed signs of changing.

The first inkling of a shift in relation to Kasztner was a documentary series aired on Israeli television in 1982, produced by Yehudah Kaveh.[2] The series reconstructed both parts of the Kasztner affair: the Hungarian part (entitled *Kofer Nefesh (Ransom)*) and the Israeli part (*Pesak Din (Verdict)*), with the participation of all those who had been involved. Shmuel Tamir's repeated condemnations of Kasztner as "the greatest collaborator with the Nazis" was confronted by a formidable battery of speakers who threw cumulative light on the other side of the coin: Kasztner as a courageous Jewish leader, acting sincerely to rescue the Jews of Hungary, who had become a victim of Israeli society, especially of the press and the judicial system. The chief commentator of this series was historian Yehuda Bauer, who has paved the way through his academic work for a new understanding of the Holocaust, criticizing the simplistic cult of heroism and by and large defending the role of Jewish leadership under Nazi occupation. In his comments, Bauer accused the judicial system as well as the public for having failed in their understanding of the Holocaust in general and of the destruction of Hungarian Jewry in particular. The final scene of the film was a well-staged reconstruction of the assassination of Kasztner,

2   Israeli Television Archive (Channel 1), Jerusalem.

followed by a televised passage from the Supreme Court verdict, which had been suppressed for years by Israeli society and was now, as it were, rediscovered.

Gradually, the ground was prepared for the conversion of Israel Kasztner, the villain of the 1950s, to a kind of "hero of our times," a perfectly legitimate representative of the Holocaust – a category that had long been reserved for heroes of the Szenes stamp. One explicit expression of the new trend was the play *Kasztner* by Motti Lerner, staged by the Chamber Theater, of which the premiere took place in July 1985; this was in a way a late response to Aharon Megged's *Hannah Szenes*. The plot was based on an as yet unpublished book by Dov Dinur, a Holocaust survivor from Hungary, who treated the Kasztner affair from a whole new perspective (Dinur 1987). The location of the drama was Budapest under Nazi occupation. It cleverly depicts Kasztner's heroic struggle with Eichmann, on the one hand, and the community leaders, on the other, describing Kasztner himself as obsessed by the need to save Jews. Only the prologue and epilogue take place in Eretz Israel, and they refer directly to the famous trial. The final scene depicts the dead Kasztner mocking Justice Halevi's verdict, at the same time bitterly attacking the "myth of heroism" carefully cultivated by the *Yishuv* and the State. Kasztner, played in the Chamber Theatre production by Oded Te'omi, declares:

> Of course, it was cooperation with Kasztner that made the annihilation possible. Kasztner is the explanation for the Holocaust. In contrast to Kasztner, there were other people who had a monopoly on heroism [...]. The names of these heroes are inscribed in block capitals on the monument of our national honor. How many Jews did these heroes save? What was the object of their heroism? And the man who managed to rescue from the Germans a train with 1,684 living Jews – he is a collaborator (Lerner 1993).

Lerner's play attracted considerable attention in the press. Played to full audiences, it was chosen by the Chamber Theater to represent it in festivals abroad. In 1986 the producers of *Kasztner* were awarded the Aharon Meskin award for the best show of that year at a ceremony held in the presence of Yitzhak Navon, Israel's former president and minister of education. Ironically, the ceremony took place in the hall of the Habimah Theater in Tel Aviv, the very place where Megged's play *Hannah Szenes* had been staged some thirty years before.

The reception accorded Lerner's play paved the way for Israeli television's production of a documentary drama, entitled *Mishpat Kasztner* (*The Kasztner trial*), which constituted yet another highly significant step in the reinstatement of Kasztner's public image. The series, based on a script by Motti Lerner and directed by Benni Barabash, was aired in 1994, this time with the help of historian Yehiam Weitz, who was on the verge of publishing a biography offering a clearing of Kasztner's name (Weitz 1995). In *Mishpat Kasztner* – which was structured along the well-tried lines of the "trial drama" – the playwright-scriptwriter transferred the scene of action from Hungary to Israel, enabling him to directly confront Israeli society and its institutions: mockery of the judicial process; touching scenes of what was happening outside the court; and, above all, a scene of Kasztner dying in the hospital – all these inevitably stirred up feelings of empathy toward the hero-victim, who was again received with sympathy and understanding by the press and public opinion. Incidentally, the production of the series was one of the most heavily financed projects in the history of Israeli television: it was aired in three parts, enlisted the participation of the best actors and was accompanied by a special film about its preparation; the Broadcasting Authority even published a special pamphlet including the entire script, with an introduction by the series adviser, Yehiam Weitz, who offered it the backing of a professional historian (Lerner 1994). Ironically, the series was aired in November 1994, the month in which the fiftieth anniversary of Hannah Szenes' murder occurred. Inspection of the Israel Television archives reveals only marginal reference to that event, in a program on religious and traditional affairs. This program included selections from the play by Aharon Megged, performed by a group of relatively unknown actors.[3]

---

3   Both programs are available at the Israeli Television Archive (Channel 1), Jerusalem. It is interesting that in the same year, 1994, composer Arie Shapira completed the production of an electronic opera in which the libretto (rendered also in English) presents, by and large, a pro-Kasztner position. See "The Kasztner Trial: Electronic Opera in 13 scenes" (1991–4) – Compact disc published by

However, it was Lerner and Barabash – very much against their
wish – who managed to bring Hannah Szenes back to the headlines,
following a long period in which the public interest in the national
heroine had gradually waned.[4] Shortly before the series was screened,
the press reported that the new film included a scene in which
Kasztner pronounces serious accusations against Hannah Szenes for
the "betrayal" of her paratrooper comrades (Palgi and Goldstein), in
fact causing their capture. Indeed, the Chamber Theater production
had also criticized the cult of heroism, as an integral and logical part
of a strategy to legitimize the figure of Kasztner. But as they approached the television series, the writers had decided to go one step
further by combining the clearing of Kasztner's name with an open
delegitimization of Hannah Szenes. Lerner himself, in an article published after the controversy was over, explained his motives as
follows:

> I do not have, and never had, any interest in defaming the memory of Hannah
> Szenes, whom I consider to be a great heroine. […] By placing the two charac-
> ters – Kasztner and Szenes – in contrast with each other I meant no provocation,
> but an attempt to find out how it happened that Szenes, the intrepid, utterly
> pure, paratrooper, became a national heroine, though she had not saved a single
> person from death; whereas Kasztner was condemned to perdition, despite
> having rescued many thousands directly and hundreds of thousands indirectly.
> The presentation of Kasztner and Szenes one against the other is aimed to
> examine the system of values of Israeli society, which created this paradox
> (Lerner 1999).

Whether one accepts Lerner's explanations or rejects them, the
struggle for commemoration had been defined by one of its engineers
as a direct confrontation between two heroes of the Holocaust of Hungarian Jewry, Szenes and Kasztner.

---

the Society of Authors, Composers and Music Publisher in Israel (ACUM),
ca.no. As-001.

4   It has waned, but never really perished: this is well reflected by the semi-
official welcome given in Israel to Menahem Golan's film "Hannah's War"
(1988). There were also few attempts to treat Szenes from a personal point of
view, which was also a way to challenge the semi-official narrative (Laor
1998).

Paradoxically, this move proved itself to be absolutely futile, as it led to a reaffirmation of the public debt to Hannah Szenes, and to a reinforcement of her weakening position in Israel's collective memory. This was largely expressed by the press, which came up with in a series of pro-Szenes publications, and later in the Knesset, which responded in its session on 9 November 1994 to three urgent proposals for a debate. One member, Eli Goldschmidt (Labor), came up with a long speech in defense of Szenes, quoting in full her well-known poem, which was performed when President Clinton visited Yad Vashem: "God – may there be no end/ to sea, to sand,/ water's splash,/ lightning's flash/ the prayer of man." And then he said:

> There is no mentally sound Jew who is not moved to tears upon hearing the song of a young girl, walking barefoot in the sands of Sedot Yam, who decides to go on a mission from which there is no return. A nation that denies its symbols denies itself.
>
> The story of Hannah Szenes, for me – and, I believe, for every Israeli Jew – expresses the very essence of Jewish and Israeli being in all its heroism and tragedy.[5]

It is particularly interesting to consider the position taken by the Supreme Court, which turned down a suit brought by Giora Szenes, Hannah's brother, and other parties, who demanded the omission of the controversial elements. However, a special appeal was made by the judge to the Broadcasting Authority to consider their omission. The request was responded to positively, and the offending passages were finally omitted. Yet the reasons for the verdict were published only five years later, on 26 July 1999. Justice Aharon Barak gave a length explanation of the majority opinion, which permitted the passages to be aired even if their content was in fact false; whereas Justice Cheshin, who was in the minority, explained why they should be excised. Nevertheless, each of them, in his own way, declared their deep commitment to the memory of Hannah Szenes. Justice Barak wrote:

---

5   *Diverei ha-Knesset* (*The Knesset Protocols*), 1994/5, Vol. IV, 6: 1594–607. HCJ 6126/94 Senesh v. Broadcasing Authority, 53(3) P.D 817.

Had I written the play, I would have refrained [from the problematic passage]. The possible denigration of the myth of Hannah Szenes is regrettable. But a democratic society does not safeguard myths by eroding freedom of speech and creation. On the contrary, a myth must emerge from a free exchange of opinions and outlooks. It cannot be the outcome of state restrictions on the freedom of expression and creation. The myth of Hannah Szenes will subsist and prosper by virtue of genuine freedom, not of the silencing of falsehood. It is Hannah Szenes' poems and heroism that consolidate the myth.

Justice Mishael Cheshin wrote an epilogue to the verdict, in which he expressed a dissenting opinion:

Hannah Szenes was a warrior-poet or, should we say, a poet-warrior – poet, warrior, and dreamer. Hannah loved life. Wandering barefoot in the golden sands of Caesarea beach, a girl of about twenty-one, she prayed to God: "God – may there be no end [...]" And even in those darkest of dark days, blood-red times, shortly before she ventured into the inferno, she sang of revolt, of death, of honor [...] "Blessed is the match consumed/in kindling flame [...]/ Blessed is the heart with strength to stop/ its beating for honour's sake." Hannah Szenes' heart knew how to die with honor. No-one can take Hannah Szenes' honor and her good name from her, neither by words nor by action.[6]

The need to defend Hannah Szenes and, even more, the attempt to safeguard her place in collective memory, were clearly expressed in a memorial ceremony held at Kibbutz Sedot Yam on 5 November 2004, on the sixtieth anniversary of her death. Speeches by the president of Israel (read out in his name), former Prime Minister Shimon Peres, the I.D.F. Chief of Staff, the commander of the Para-troopers, and the secretary of the kibbutz referred to the heroic heritage and to Jewish resilience; these tributes were interspersed with vocal numbers and recitations of Hannah Szenes's poems and writings. "A voice called. I went./ I went, for it called [...]" – her words were read with emotion by the kibbutz secretary, Shimon Buber. However, those present could not avoid the impression that the highly emotional production, held under the auspices of the Association for the Perpetuation of Hannah Szenes' Mission and Heritage, was quite unlike the traditional ceremonies held in the past at the same kibbutz; it had been a formal, well-designed ritual, forcefully expres-

6   HCJ 6126/94 Senesh v. Broadcasting Authority, 53(3) P.D. 817.

sing the myth of Hannah Szenes and the special status of "heroism" in the Israeli system of values.

The diminished status of the ceremony in recent years is a late reflection of the change in public attitude toward Hannah Szenes, which has set the ground for the shaping of a new attitude towards Kasztner and for the shift of his position in the commemorative hierarchy. Yet one cannot ignore the occasional attempts that challenge this version of events. Various initiatives to put Kasztner name on streets or public places either in Tel Aviv or in Haifa have so far been confronted with strong opposition, as if he had never been rehabilitated. The same has happened also in writing: for example, in his posthumous autobiography, Gruenwald's attorney, Shmuel Tamir, who later became Israel's Minister of Justice, dedicates no less than 838 pages of his book to the historical trial, in which he repeats with utmost fervor his old-time arguments about Kasztner, whom he still sees – in the late 1990s – as one of the greatest collaborators with the Nazis (Tamir 2001); similarly, Ruth Linn, a Professor of Education at Haifa University and a long time devotee of Rudolf Vrba, has more recently condemned what she considers to be the systematic suppression of the story of Vrba's escape from Auschwitz and his composition of the "Auschwitz Report." In her reading, this suppression has been motivated by no less than the desire of the Israeli political establishment to defend Kasztner's failure to publicize this report, which, she believes, might have minimized the extent of the Holocaust in Hungary (Linn 2004).[7]

On 1 July 1955, a few days after the verdict in the Kasztner trial had been handed down, the author Mati Megged, writing in *La-Merhav*, appealed to his readers not to forgive Kasztner: "We have one single memory from those days, the days of the Holocaust in Hungary, and we should bear it constantly in mind: the memory of Hannah Szenes [...]." But he went on to temper his message somewhat: "We are called upon to remember both [= both 'phenomena,'

7   Prior to the publication of her book in the U.S., Linn made a similar argument in a Hebrew publication (2004). It was followed by a counter argument made by Yehuda Bauer, ibid., 185–9. The book itself was made public in Israel through an article by Uri Deromi (2004).

Szenes and Kasztner] in order to award the victory to only one of them" (Megged 1955). Megged was right to revise his demand and call for both Szenes and Kasztner to be remembered; but his uncompromising demand to award the victory to Hannah Szenes alone was quite wrong, and it surely has not withstood the test of time. Much more to the point was a poem published by Nathan Alterman during the trial ("*Yom ha-Zikaron veha-Mordim*" ("Memorial Day and the Fighters")), in which he called for a moderation of the cult of heroism, for a just treatment of "the masses of Israel," for a reconsideration of those he called "the heroes [of the community] who negotiated or complied" with the Nazis, and for recognition of the fact that the Jewish revolt in the ghettos and camps – which maintained such a central place in the Israeli consciousness – is no more than "a feature" of the whole affair.[8] This outlook seems to be more in keeping with our patterns of memory as they have crystallized in the last decades, and as we tend to view them from the perspective of fifty or sixty years.

Bibliography

Alterman, N. 1989. "The Remembrance Day – and the Rebels," translated by Vivian Eden. *The Jerusalem Post Magazine*, 28 July.

Bauer, Y. 1990. "Kasztner Rezso." In *The Encyclopaedia of the Holocaust*. New York/London: Macmillan, 2: 787–90.

Bilski, L. 2004. *Transformative Justice: Israeli Identity on Trial*. Ann Arbor: University of Michigan Press.

Braslavski, M. (ed.) 1945. *Hannah Szenes: Haye'ha, Shelihutah u-Motah* (*Hannah Szenes: Her life, Mission and Death*) (in Hebrew). En Harod: Ha-Kibbutz Ha-Me'uhad.

Cohen, A. 2001. "Hungary." In W. Laquer (ed.), *The Holocaust Encyclopedia*. New Haven: Yale University Press, 314–21.

8   This seminal poem was partly translated into English by Vivian Eden (Alterman 1989).

Deromi, U. 2004. "Medinat ha-Kasztnerim Shelakhem" ("Your Land of Kasztner") (in Hebrew). *Ha'aretz*, 28 January.

Dinur, D. 1987. *Kasztner: Giluyyim Hadashim al ha-Ish u-Fo'olo (Kasztner: New Revelations on the Man and his Deeds)* (in Hebrew). Haifa: Gestlit.

Lahav, P. 1997. *Judgment in Jerusalem: Chief Justice Agranat and the Zionist Century*. Berkeley: University of California Press.

Laor, D. 1995. "The Jewish Uprising and the Role of the Judenrat: A Re-evaluation." In F. H. Littel, A. L. Berger, and H.G. Locke (eds), *What Have We Learned? Telling the Story and Teaching the Lesson of the Holocaust: Papers of the 20th Anniversary Scholars' Conference*. Lewinston: Edwin Mellen Press, 163–91.

—. 1998. "Theatrical Interpretation of the Shoah: Image and Counter-Image." In C. Schumacher (ed.), *Staging the Holocaust: The Shoah in Drama and Performance*. Cambridge: Cambridge University Press, 94–110.

Lerner, M. 1993. "Kasztner." *Modern International Drama*, 27 January.

—. 1994. *Mishpat Kasztner (The Kasztner trial)* (in Hebrew). *The Israel Broadcasting Authority*.

—. 1999. "Lo Medubar bi-Feri Dimyoni" ("I haven't imagined it") (in Hebrew). *Ha'aretz*, 5 September.

Linn, R. 2004. "Ha-Beriha me-Auschwitz: Madu'a Lo Sipru Lanu Al Kakh be-Vatei ha-Sefer?" ("The Escape from Auschwitz: Why were we not told about it in School?") (in Hebrew). *Te'orya u-Vikoret* 24, 163–84.

—. 2004. *Escaping Auschwitz: A Culture of Forgetting*. Ithaca/ London: Cornell University Press.

Masters, A. 1972. *The Summer That Bled: The Biography of Hannah Senesh*. London: Michael Joseph.

Megged, A. 1945. "Kavim li-Demutah" ("A Personal Sketch") (in Hebrew). *Hannah Szenes: Devarim le-Zikhra (Hannah Szenes: In her memory)* (in Hebrew). Sedot Yam, 63–71.

—. 1993. "Hannah Szenes," translated by Michael Taub. *Modern International Drama*. 27 January.

Megged, M. 1955. "Bein ha-Keni'a veha-Gevurah" ("Between Surrender and Heroism") (in Hebrew). *La'merhav*, 1 July.

Palgi, Y. 1946. *Ru'ah Gedolah Ba'ah* (*There came a Great Wind*) (in Hebrew). En Harod: Ha-Kibbutz Ha-Me'uhad.

—. 2003. *Into the Inferno: The Memoir of Jewish Paratrooper behind Nazi Lines*. New Brunswick: Rutgers University Press.

Porat, D. 1990. *The Blue and Yellow Stars of David: The Zionist Leadership in Palestine and the Holocaust, 1939–1945.* Cambridge: Harvard University Press.

Porat, L. 1998. "Hannah Szenes be-Habimah" ("Hannah Szenes in Habimah") (in Hebrew). *La'merhav*, 6 June.

Rosenfeld, S. 1955. *Tik Plily 124: Mishpat Gruenwald-Kastner* (*Criminal Trial 124, the Gruenwald-Kastner trial*) (in Hebrew). Tel Aviv: Karni.

Segev, T. 1993. *The Seventh Million: The Israelis and the Holocaust.* New York: Hill and Wang.

Stauber, R. 2006. *Ideology and Memory*. New York: Valentine & Mitchell.

Tamir, S. 2001. *Ben ha-Aretz ha-Zot* (*Son of this Land*) (in Hebrew). Tel Aviv: Zemora Bitan.

Tidor-Baumel, J. 1996. "The Heroism of Hannah Szenesz: An Exercise in Creating Collective National Memory in the State of Israel." *Journal of Contemporary History* 31 (3), 521–46.

Weitz, Y. 1993. "Ha-Shinui be-Dimuyo shel Kasztner ke-Edut la-Shinui be-Dimuyah shel ha-Shoah" ("The transformation of Kasztner's Image as a Reflection of the Transformation in the Image of the Holocaust") (in Hebrew). *Cathedra* 69, 133–51.

—. 1995. *Ha-Ish she-Nirzah Pa'amayim* (*The Man who was murdered twice*) (in Hebrew). Jerusalem: Keter.

Chapter 10

AMIA LIEBLICH

The Second Generation of Kfar Etzion: A Study of Collective Memory

1 Introduction

Since the phenomenon of memory is normally associated with an individual, the question arises: what is collective memory? Where does it reside? Is it a real phenomenon or just a metaphor? What are the rules that govern it?

The concept of collective memory, which crosses fields of history, psychology, sociology, education, communication, anthropology and more, has received much theoretical and empirical attention in the last decades. The scholarship is vast,[1] and is naturally beyond the scope of the present paper to review. Suffice it to say, for our modest purpose, that it is presently well accepted that the subject of memory should be studied not only through a "within person" approach but as a phenomenon of the social world we live in. The members of a community to which they belong in fact share part of what people recognize as their personal, individual memory. This creates a common store of information and ideas, which are part of what we would define as "tradition," "culture" or "collective identity."

Whereas personal memory is the entire store of what an individual remembers, consciously or unconsciously, collective memory is an aspect of the social-cultural reality. It consists of the shared memories of individuals who belong to a certain group, real or imagined. Thus it

---

1   The major sources for my understanding of the topic are listed in the bibliography at the end of the chapter.

has a major role in the definition of national, social or religious identity. It points to past events, which happened or did not happen, and strives to remind individuals of these ideas and events. Collective memory is often oral, yet it uses various material sites and rituals for its manifestation. In literate societies, it tends to be put in writing too, eventually. When writing takes place, one passes to the realm of "history," which produces fixed, normative versions of subjects that were earlier the domain of the more flexible collective memory.

How are these three realms of memory – individual memory, collective memory and history – related to the issue of truth or factuality? Scholars from various disciplines, from history to psychology, agree that selective and interpretive processes occur at all three levels, which are shaped and reshaped by a multitude of factors through time. Power positions and political interests naturally influence the selection processes of collective memory and history. To put it bluntly: due to these forces, the hegemonic narrative of past events is implicitly chosen – and named "truth" – so that the current social regime and its aims are reinforced. However, as culture is not monolithic, alternative, competing memories or narratives survive as recessive, subversive voices, which may surface in the proper time and circumstances.

The study of the second generation of Kfar Etzion, which is summarized below, provides an interesting angle for the exploration of some of these issues concerning collective memory. Following the outline of the study and its main results, this paper will focus on three interrelated subjects: what are the factors that contribute to the construction of a collective memory (and to the obliteration of alternative narratives), how is it preserved, and how is it related to the social world of the remembering community?

2 The Research Study

Kibbutz Kfar Etzion, on the hills between Jerusalem and Hebron, was founded by a group of religious pioneers in 1943. The common history of the first generation started, however, in the mid-thirties, when they formed training groups for collective farming (*kvutzot hakhshara*) and started their communal existence as Kvutzat Avraham – a commune of agricultural workers who lived near Kfar Pines, at the center of Israel. For five years they prepared themselves, grew in number, and waited for the allocation of land for their settlement as a separate kibbutz, which finally happened in 1943. The short history of this community in its permanent location spans only five years; Kibbutz Kfar Etzion was conquered and destroyed by Arabs during the early stages of the War of Independence, in May 1948. Among the 240 casualties of these bloody days, 70 members of the kibbutz, most of them men, were killed in battle, while trying to defend their settlement. Many of them were murdered after their surrender.

The second generation of the kibbutz, with which the present study is concerned, still call themselves "the children of Kfar Etzion." They consist of 60 men and women; the oldest of them were born in 1939, and the youngest – in 1948. Their survival was ensured by the painful decision to evacuate non-fighters from the settlement. Four months before those tragic events, when life in the kibbutz had become extremely dangerous, all the children, their mothers[2] and some pregnant women, were evacuated from the kibbutz to a monastery in Jerusalem, which sheltered them. Most of them never saw their fathers or husbands again. Their life as a commune continued for a while in Jaffa, where they were given temporary housing; but after 1952 the collective way of life was abandoned, and each family went its own way. This brief history of the community has an additional important chapter, namely the resettlement of Kfar Etzion at its original site after the Six Days War of 1967. Again, this significant finale is more part of the collective than individual memory, since only about 12 of the

---

2   One mother refused to separate from her husband and sent her baby boy away
     with her closest friend. She is the only mother who died in battle.

second-generation group joined the new kibbutz and settled there permanently.

Fifty-five years later, I decided to study the life stories of these
individuals, namely the "children" of Kfar Etzion. At this time, their
addresses are spread all over Israel, with two of them living abroad;
but most of them maintain at least superficial contacts among themselves and see each other annually in the memorial ceremony for their
deceased fathers.

In launching a qualitative, narrative research, I did not start off
with particular hypotheses but had two general aims in mind: from a
psychological perspective, to explore life after a major loss and trauma
as experienced by this group's members; and from a historical perspective, to study the construction of collective and individual memory in these selected individuals. The present paper deals only with the
second aim.

The material for the study was obtained by individual interviews
with 51 members of the second-generation group, which I myself
conducted during 2003–4. Each conversation lasted between 1.5 and 4
hours, conducted in one or two meetings, and fully recorded and
transcribed. In approaching these individuals – now 55 to 65 years old
– I was asking each one separately to tell me her or his life story. No
specific instructions were given, but the men and women knew I was
interested in their unique history, and this obviously affected their
response. Almost all of the interviewees started their personal story
from their common history as "children of Kfar Etzion," including
their serial number within the children's community. The first part of
the interview almost always included a presentation of the collective
story of Kfar Etzion, its establishment, struggle and demise. It also
recounted the story of the father's death – or miraculous survival –
events that were not part of the personal memory of the narrators in
most cases, but based on stories they had heard or read since
childhood. Furthermore, many of the narrators provided a long and
detailed history of their parents' families of origin in East Europe,
their parents' whereabouts during World War II and the circumstances
of their immigration to Palestine or Israel. Their individual life stories
were often only a negligent portion of the family or collective
narrative provided in their interviews.

3 The Relevance of the Study for Understanding Collective Memory

The narrative materials obtained from the second generation of Kfar Etzion provide an interesting and challenging case study for exploring collective memory, its construction and preservation. Following are some of the numerous reasons for this: the participants all belong to a distinct group, with a unique history and identity. Thus it is possible to investigate how a common history, some shared past experiences, are processed, recorded and constructed in the memories of individual members of the group. Furthermore, the story about their past is partly "primary" (that is, based on their own memory), but mostly it is "secondary" (that is, the outcome of what they have heard, learned and absorbed throughout their lives). This combination is highly meaningful for the study of memories of historical events. The story takes us back 60 or 70 years – a length of time that is quite significant, yet not too long to study in detail. Moreover, a group of 50–60 individuals[3] can be contacted and interviewed in its entirety, thus sampling and representation issues are avoided. Moreover, the story has clear political implications (especially at the time it was conducted) regarding the links of nation and homeland, peace versus occupation – and in general, the power struggle between right-wing and left-wing ideologies and interests in Israel. As I gradually discovered, the group made intentional efforts to preserve its collective memory in its hegemonic shape and form, and the means employed for this effort can teach us much about the process of preservation of collective memories everywhere. Finally, as will be elaborated later on, some striking similarities exist between the history of Kfar Etzion, as recounted by its second generation, and the major outline of Jewish history at large. It is therefore undoubtedly interesting to study the collective memory of this community.

---

3   Of the 60 individuals who originally belonged to the group, four were dead by the time I conducted my study: two died in military service in war, and two had died of natural causes. Four individuals refused to meet me: the topic is too painful for two of them; for the remaining two it is insignificant.

While the empirical data available to me were the records of individual life stories,[4] I could see that collective memory penetrated the narrated stories in four distinct ways:

(1) Some of the most profound parts of the collective memory were manifested by *not being articulated* at all. These are the events or ideas that the narrators take to be self-understood and assume "everybody knows," so "it goes without saying." As people who tell a story to an audience, the narrators assumed that I knew these basic facts – first, because everybody knows them and even more so myself, since I had already interviewed a number of informants on the subject. For example, when a woman told me that her father was "killed in the bunker," she assumed that I knew this part of the collective saga – how the last defenders of the settlement had been hiding in the bunker, waiting for further commands, and – when they had come out to sur-render – were murdered by the Arabs. The parts that narra-tors assume are well known by all are clearly components of the collective memory.

(2) Different narrators manifested collective memory in recur-ring *repetitions* of certain parts of their narratives. Thus col-lective memory emerges out of the common denominator in many individual accounts. For example, almost all the participants said that their childhood as orphans in Jaffa was not at all sad or miserable.

(3) Some interviewees *quoted authorities* or written sources to support their personal narrative. They often referred to Knohl's history book,[5] saying "all I know about this is from Knohl's book," and then proceeding by retelling the episode as remembered from that source… This evidently indicates

4   I could of course have collected and studied historical documents about Kfar Etzion, but being a psychologist and not a historian, I decided to base my con-clusions on memories as provided in oral interviews.

5   Dov Knohl, one of the survivors of the last battle in Kfar Etzion in 1948, col-lected many sources and wrote a large book in Hebrew called *Gush Etzion Be-Milhamto* (*Gush Etzion and its War*). The book was first published in 1955, with a second, more widely known, edition in 1957.

the penetration of collective memory into personal realms. Another source of authority often quoted by the narrators is Ben-Gurion's famous eulogy of Kfar Eztion and its fallen defenders, in which he said that Jerusalem, the capital of Israel, was saved due to the heroic struggle of Kfar Etzion.

(4) Finally, some of the collective memory emerges by *expressing counter-narratives*, by arguing that "in fact, things did not happen as they tell us" (or "tell you"). A painful comment of this sort relates to the decision not to evacuate the men and soldiers from the settlement, even though the chances for their survival became very slim. "It is not true, as they write in the history books, that the presence of, and struggle in, Kfar Etzion in its location at that time was essential for the survival of Israeli Jerusalem. It is not true! In fact, my father and all his friends died in vain!"

4   Presenting the Collective Memory of Kfar Etzion

Using the above means, I was able to extract from the rich individual narratives a ten-stage collective scheme, which represents the collective memory of the second generation of Kfar Etzion. This scheme can be recognized as well in some of the public manifestations of the collective memory, which can be used to "verify" it. Among the external sources, first and foremost is the text of the audio-visual show, which is presented in the Commemoration Center in Kfar Etzion. But many other texts repeat the same schema – texts used for school performance on Memorial Day, texts inscribed in stone in the military cemetery where the defenders of Kfar Etzion are buried, and in metal in the location of the Lonely Oak in Gush Etzion, and texts that may be found in history books, military encyclopedias and Internet sites. However, the following collective memory schema is based on my own interviews with the second-generation members, and its stages are the following:

(1) *Historical location*: Kfar Etzion's location, between Jeru-
    salem and Hebron, always belonged to the Jewish ancestors
    and the Judean kingdom. It played an important role in
    ancient Jewish history, as documented in the Bible.
(2) *Exile*: during the long exile of the Israelites from their land,
    this part of the land was desolate and uninhabited.
(3) *Attempted settlement*: the land of the kibbutz was legally
    purchased from the local owners. Two attempts to settle
    were undertaken for brief periods in the twentieth century –
    Migdal Eder in 1927 and the first Kfar Etzion (a moshav) in
    1935. Both settlements were abandoned due to Arab riots.
(4) *Founding the kibbutz*: the foundation of Kibbutz Kfar
    Eztion in the same location in 1943 was a brave act of
    pioneering, resulting from pressure from the pre-state insti-
    tutions, because of strategic considerations. It was under-
    taken in spite of the serious doubts of about a third of the
    group members.
(5) *The shadow of the Holocaust*: the vast majority of the kib-
    butz members were single survivors from large families that
    were eventually exterminated in Europe.
(6) *The shadow of the Arab neighbors*: isolation[6] within a
    hostile environment and continuous tension marked the five
    years of the kibbutz's existence.
(7) *Success and prosperity*: during its short life, the young
    kibbutz was highly successful spiritually, socially and mat-
    erially. It became a model of a religious pioneering com-
    munity.
(8) *Struggle and loss*: this stage consisted of the gradual
    deterioration of the situation during the winter and spring of
    1948 as the kibbutz was continually attacked, the evacuation
    of the mothers and children, and the final loss of the

6   To be accurate, the establishment of three additional kibbutzim in the area
    alleviated some of the isolation, yet as a block of settlements they were still
    pretty detached from the center and lived in the midst of hostile Arab com-
    munities.

settlement as well as many lives, which finally happened on the eve of the Declaration of Independence.

(9) *Exile again*: for 19 years the site of the kibbutz was un-approachable, beyond hostile borders. It became a military camp of the Jordanian army. The memory of the place was, however alive in the hearts of the former members.

(10) *Return*: a miraculous return became possible after the victory of the Six-Day War. Kfar Etzion was the first settle-ment[7] approved by the government in the liberated[8] territor-ies. The "children" of Kfar Etzion who redeemed the land and revived the spirit of their dead parents initiated this just return.

(This story is told, naturally, from the point of view of the Jewish survivors and excludes other possible narratives – e.g. of the Arab neighbors. For a discussion of this issue see the last section of this article.)

The remaining part of this paper is dedicated to the exploration of the powers and processes that support this constructed memory.

5   Factors Contributing to the Emergence and Survival of this Collective Memory

a   Mythical Underpinning

First among the factors that reinforce this collective memory, rather than its conflicting possible versions, is the mythical underpinning of Kfar Etzion's narrative. It is easy to see that the story as described

---

7   This part of the collective memory is factually wrong, as the first settlement after the Six-Day War was Merom HaGolan, in the Golan Heights.

8   The term *liberated* reflects of course the language of this particular group, whereas many Israelis would have said *occupied* instead. This political effect on the collective memory will be discussed in the last section of the chapter.

above reflects and repeats famous mythological patterns, both Jewish and general. The basic narrative of Jewish history is a story about short-lived freedom or kingdoms, destruction, exile and redemption. The root narrative about the destruction of the First Temple, followed by the destruction of the Second Temple; of the various exiles and the return to the land, as well as the more recent narrative about the Holocaust and the establishment of the State of Israel – all demonstrate the prevalence of this type of narrative pattern in Jewish mythology. In presenting the short history of Kfar Etzion as a stage in a series of episodes of construction-destruction, ending with the victorious return of the just to their land, the narrators echo a well-known plot and narrative form.

Furthermore, Jewish history is replete with stories about martyrs who sacrificed their lives for God, his people and religion. Martyrdom always consists of worthy suffering and death; it provides causes for tragic events. The men and women who defended Kfar Etzion and the road to Jerusalem to the end, and with their lives, paved the way for the establishment of the State – which occurred exactly a day after their sacrifice and loss – thus joining a long and respected chain of Jewish martyrs throughout history.

However, the story of Kfar Eztion as constructed in collective memory manifests also a pattern of myths, prevalent all over the globe, which tell the story of birth, life, death and rebirth, or the U-shaped narrative about building, destructive obstacles and successful coping. It demonstrates the just rule of God, history or nature, where redemption is the fate of the worthy and punishment is meted out to the evil ones. It is the desired story, concluding with a happy ending.

These clear similarities between the Kfar Etzion story and the famous myths of both Judaism and cultures in general made it much more likely for the story to be selected and survive. This link between mythical underpinning and survival is multi-faceted: (1) The collective memory has been constructed in this fashion because of the availability of cultural narrative patterns for the story to be molded in. (2) Its survival is an outcome of this "good story" form. (3) Simultaneously, the emergence of such a story reinforces the cultural patterns of the mythological plots as explicated above.

b   Active Attempts

The study of the second generation of Kfar Etzion teaches us a lot about the active steps a community may take to create and preserve a certain collective memory, and at the same time repress other possible narratives. The more I heard the life stories of the participants, the more aware I became of numerous active means that have been pursued for that purpose, especially during the exile period (stage 9 above) – but also to this very day. Among them are:

Education of the children. Since the children went to regular schools, the educational efforts of the community were limited to a variety of afterschool activities, and especially field trips and summer camps, which enacted the history of Kfar Etzion, imitated its topography and reinforced the children's hope to return there. Trips to view the Lonely Oak from a distance were among the annual activities of the children of the group.

Creation of art and literature. Books, plays, poems and paintings repeated the story of Kfar Etzion in various forms, and praised the heroism of its defenders.

Preserving and writing history. In addition to the literary or artistic work, great effort was invested in collecting documents, photographs and all kinds of artifacts to preserve the memory of Kfar Etzion and the individuals who died it its defense. These consisted of the archives of Kfar Etzion, which were later moved and installed in the new settlement. The history of the kibbutz and its struggle was documented in Knohl's book, which became the canonical text of the community (further discussion in the next section).

Commemoration sites. As proposed by Pierre Nora, culture preserves its collective memories by creating memory sites, which symbolize past events in space and in which the community may gather for rituals or to retell their tales and listen to each other. Kfar Etzion has several extremely powerful sites that commemorate its past: first of all, the common grave of the deceased defenders in the military cemetery of Mt. Herzl in Jerusalem. In addition, the Commemorating Center at Kfar Etzion, where an audiovisual presentation of the history of the place is displayed for the visitors. Among the additional sites, I will mention only the Lonely Oak and the plaque that depicts its history and role – a site chosen by many young settlers for their wedding ceremonies.

The establishment of symbols and rituals. The community created numerous symbols and rituals (these can hardly be distinguished from the "sites" enumerated above), including hymns and prayers that related to the past loss and the hope to return. The picture of the Lonely Oak, for example, became an important symbol of the group. It was hung in many homes and decorated numerous publications. Traditional prayers, especially of the Sabbath and the High Holidays, were conducted according to the style and melody of the original synagogue of Kfar Etzion.

All the above means were used intentionally and consciously by the community and its leaders to ensure the survival of their collective memory. However, an additional spontaneous and relevant factor relates to the social interaction among the group members. For all these years, many of the members of this community have maintained close contact with one another. In personal visits as well as in social events such as bar mitzvahs and wedding ceremonies or the commemorative visits for the elders who died, people have repeated, exchanged and retold their memories of Kfar Etzion, thus creating a general, shared repository of the group's memories.

c   *Social Roles*

The concept of collective memory implies a more-or-less defined group of people, the "collective," that shares its particular narrative. Moreover, my analysis of the narrators' stories revealed that they have distinct roles, which define their functions within the memory-community. About ten men and women can be termed "memory priests," the majority of the participants can be named "carriers," while the remaining minority are "subversive voices." The main characteristic of the memory priest is a conscious or unconscious overlap of their personal stories and the collective memory. In other words, these people present a narrative that is extremely similar to the collective memory as outlined above. Furthermore, their stories are highly heroic and idealized, without any trace of criticism of the people or the events depicted. Their identity as "children of Kfar Etzion" is emphasized throughout our conversation, and probably in their reality as well – (1) in their personal lives: they are Orthodox (religious), and many of them inhabit settlements or kibbutzim (including several who presently live in Kfar Etzion); and (2) professionally: a number of them work as educators, politicians, historians and archivists. They tend to participate in various public events or activities that are relevant to their particular history and identity. Their social interactions with one another, which occur frequently, reinforce their identity and shared memories.

For the majority of the research participants, however, the individual narratives are more diverse, and clear differences also exist between their personal memory and the collective memory of the group. They carry and appreciate the memory of their common heritage, but it is not as central and dominant in their identity. Several of them live a secular life style, while others are presently ultra-Orthodox. They all seem to endorse right-wing political views. They live in Tel Aviv, Jerusalem and other urban centers, and their relationships with the remaining members of the group are not as frequent or intense. More than any characteristic, their memories can be identified by their emphasis on, or at least reference to, trauma and loss, rather than heroic idealization of the past.

Finally, a small group of participants can be defined as marginal and oppositional. They are all secular and politically leftist. They express two different positions: either subversive – namely, that the shared heroic collective memory is all wrong, political and misleading; or indifferent – i.e. that their past as Kfar Etzion children is insignificant and should be laid to rest. The "subversive" subgroup openly defined themselves as psychologically affected by their traumatic past. I suspect that this is also what stands behind the "indifferent" position, as well as the refusal by some of the people who belong to the group to participate in the interview process.

This role division demonstrates how society allocates different functions to people who belong to the memory community and more generally – how memory is a social and not only an individual phenomenon. Although the small size of the group and the familiarity among them contribute to the emergence of the memory-community, similar processes are probably inherent in all instances of memories of historical events shared by many, and not only in the particular case of the Kfar Etzion children.

The model of a memory community of this sort may be summarized by the metaphor of a hand fan, in which the spine represents the "priests"; the entire wingspace the diverse narratives of the "carriers"; and the very margins, the subversive and indifferent voices.

d   A Canonical Text

Several scholars agree that collective memory is greatly enhanced by the publication of a book or books (scriptures, so to speak), which represent the common history of a community. On the other hand, this written document may fixate the collective memory[9] even more than the oral testimonies, which naturally allow for more flexibility. The case of Kfar Etzion provides an example of this aspect of collective memory as well.

As mentioned earlier, one of the few male survivors of the first generation, Dov Knohl, had started already during his captivity in Jordan to collect all the evidence and write down the history of Kfar Etzion and the three other kibbutzim that had resided in the area. This became his life project, which was finally published in 1955, in Hebrew, under the title *Gush Etzion and Its War*. The book became extremely significant for the survivors and their children, including the next generations. It is a large volume, and its status as being a long time out of print, adds to its aura. It was widely quoted in the interviews as a source of reliability and authority. (In reference to this book, participants did not provide any details, assuming that I am as familiar with the text as they are.) It seemed to me that knowing this book and its contents, or having it on one's bookshelves, defined belonging to the past – and perhaps also present – Kfar Etzion community.

---

9   Some scholars suggest that once history is written down, this means the end of memory.

Several features of this book make it a canonical manuscript that represents and reinforces the collective memory of the group. The book provides a detailed description of the kibbutz and its surroundings, including maps of this "terra incognita" at the time of its publication. Moreover, it details the events of the last months in the life of the community by providing a dated, day-by-day account, including relevant documents, letters and diary sources on each day. This daily report gives readers a sense of the long siege and the growing immensity of the approaching disaster as time goes by. But I think that the book attained its canonical value due to some of its formal aspects. The author, himself a witness to the events, one of the founders of the kibbutz and a prestigious member of the community, plays down his own voice and authority, and presents his report as the shared, common outcome of many voices. Except for the commanding officers, he does not name the heroes of the events described but uses only their initials. Thus a collective voice emerges instead of an assembly of individual stories. On the other hand, an important section of this book is its appendix, in which the naming phenomenon is reversed: an alphabetical list names all the deceased soldiers and inhabitants of the settlements, and provides a short biography of each. This book thus became a site for the *collective* memory of the living as well as the repository of all those *individuals* who had died in the war.

In terms of its message, my interviewees described the book as providing meaning to the loss of the lives of their fathers and the destruction of the place (even during the 19 bleak years of exile from the spot). They felt that the book transmitted the messages of "remember" and "return," which were the two basic commandments of their life and identity. Newer books that can claim better editorial work and more accuracy have not reached the status and acclaim of this particular volume.

6   Discussion: On the Politics of Collective Memory

Above and beyond all the issues presented in this paper so far, the study of Kfar Etzion demonstrates also the political foundations and implications of collective memory, which probably exist behind every example of collective memory but are so transparent in the present case. There are close links between the right-wing political agenda of the people whom I named "memory priests" and the kind of memory they embrace and disseminate. Their story has the aura of a sacred saga one is not allowed to change, doubt or even touch. The moral, historical and legal rightness of the act of settlement in Kfar Etzion in 1943, and again in 1967, is embedded in the entire ten-stage narrative – and provides justification for. This is so clear in the discourse of the narrators that it may be termed a mobilized narrative. Or, in terms of the dialogues that occurred between me and each one of the narrators, many of them may be described – as I often felt – as missionary conversation, aimed to convert me to their views. Did I judge them, did I accept their truths, empathize with their losses? The position of the researcher in such a field is extremely sensitive and demands continuous reflexivity. These sensitivities always exist in studying current affairs; but the merit of the present study is in bringing these subtle trends into the open.

All in all, although variations of length and kind do exist among the research participants' stories,[10] their stories may seem extremely one-sided. The majority of the narrators do not see their history in terms of occupation of another nation and its territories [...] Some of them see Kfar Etzion as a very special place among all the other settlements in Judea and Samaria, due to its unique history. For others, however, it is no different than any other settlement and proves our right to live in any part of the Land of Israel. Each group utilizes the collective and personal memory to defend its position and indicate its justice and logic.

---

10   These variations were not demonstrated in the present chapter, but will be evident in the book that is presently being prepared, based on this research.

Should I have gone, to balance these trends, to other circles or memory communities, where alternative narratives may reside? Should I have interviewed people who object to all kinds of occupation, perhaps even Arabs refugees who had lost their homes and villages? This is perhaps what a historian ought to have done, to get to the truth of the matter. But I am a psychologist, I study memory rather than history, and I do not believe that the "truth of the matter" exists anywhere at all. With all its limitations, the case of the second generation of Kfar Etzion offers us a unique and significant view of the phenomenon of collective memory.

Bibliography

Anderson, B. 1987. *Imagined Communities: Reflections on the Origin and Spread of Nationalism.* London: Verso.

Davis, N. Z. and R. Starn. 1989. "Introduction to a Special Issue on Collective Memory and Countermemory." *Representations* 16, 1–6.

Eliade, M. 1959. *Cosmos and History: The Myth of Eternal Return.* New York: Harper and Row.

Freeman, M. 2002. "Charting the Narrative Unconscious: Cultural Memory and the Challenge of Autobiography." *Narrative Inquiry* 12, 193–211.

Gillis, J. R. (ed.) 1994. *Commemorations: The Politics of National Identity.* Princeton, N.J.: Princeton University Press.

Halbwachs, M. 1992. *On Collective Memory.* Chicago: The University of Chicago Press.

Nora, P. 1984. *Les lieux de mémoire.* Paris: Gallimard.

—. 1989. "Between Memory and History: Les lieux de mémoire." *Representations* 26, 7–25.

Sarbin, T. R. (ed.) 1986. *Narrative Psychology: The Storied Nature of Human Conduct.* New York: Praeger.

Shlesinger, P. 1993. "Wishful Thinking: Cultural Politics, Media and Collective Identities in Europe." *Journal of Communication* 43, 6–17.

Wertsch, J. V. 2002. *Voices of Collective Remembering.* Cambridge, UK: Cambridge University Press.

White, H. 1987. *The Content of the Form: Narrative Discourse and Historical Representation.* Baltimore: Johns Hopkins University Press.

Zerubavel, E. 2003. *Collective Memory and the Social Shape of the Past.* Chicago: University of Chicago Press.

Zerubavel, Y. 1995. *Recovered Roots: Collective Memory and the Making of Israeli National Tradition.* Chicago: University of Chicago Press.

—. 1996. "The Forest as a National Icon: Literature, Politics and the Archeology of Memory." *Israel Studies* 12, 60–99

—. 2005. "Transhistorical Encounters in the Land of Israel: National Memory, Symbolic Bridges, and the Literary Imagination." *Jewish Social Studies* 11(3), 115–40.

Chapter 11

TAMAR LIEBES

"Hear O Israel": Radio, Nationbuilding and Collective Memory

> No other nation has as strong a need as our nation for the medium of radio; as if
> it were created in the six days of creation in order to bridge between one dias-
> pora and another, and between them and the homeland, gradually being built.
>
> Y. M. Davar, 4 June 1947

The medium typically associated with nation building, in the case of the new nations established in the twentieth century, is television (Katz and Wedell 1977). In the case of the founding of the Jewish state, however, radio was the instrument charged with the project of integrating the immigrants from the various diasporas. Television was introduced only two decades later – and even then for the wrong reasons (Katz 1971, 17–23; Liebes 2000, 305–23). Israel's radio took its first steps twelve years prior to the establishment of the state, as the "Hebrew Hour" of the British Mandatory government channel entitled *The Voice of Jerusalem*.[1] During Israel's formative decade, radio turned out to be the central site for negotiating the ideological and cultural identity of the future nation. The Yishuv – the organized Zionist entity in British Mandatory Palestine – made use of the daily broadcasts for inventing modern Hebrew and a civic culture, and for experimenting with acoustic formats and practices for the ritual and functional needs of the nascent society. These were in place when the "Hebrew Hour" re-emerged in 1948 as *The Voice of Israel* (*Kol*

---

1 The name was a compromise between the British suggestion of the "Broadcasting Service of Palestine" and the Jewish leadership's "Broadcasting Service
   of the Land of Israel."

Yisrael), charged with nothing less than the forging of a national culture from the remnants of 2,000 years of dispersion.

1   Privileging Voice over Image: The Hebrews and the Greeks

Although radio played an important part in the public life of Western nations, it was particularly compatible with the culture of the Jewish state. Unlike the Greeks, Judaism favors the voice over the picture, and the sense of hearing over seeing. To quote cultural historian Martin Jay, "It is generally agreed that classical Greece privileged sight over the other senses, a judgment lent special weight by the contrast often posited with its more verbally oriented Hebraic competitor" (Jay 1993). Thus *mind*, for the Greeks, serves as an absorber of images; hence the word "theory" (which shares its root with "theater") means "to *look* attentively and to behold," and *knowledge* in the Greek epistemology is "the state of having seen" (ibid., 24). This visual bias, says Hans Jonas (quoted in Jay, 24), emphasizes the unchanging eternal presence as against the fleeting succession of temporality. "If the Jews could begin their most heartfelt prayer, 'Hear, O Israel!'" says Jay, "the Greek philosophers were in effect urging, 'See, O Hellas!'" The primordial centrality of the voice rather than the image, of hearing rather than seeing, is evidenced throughout the biblical text, where God is revealed as a voice. First heard from in the creation of the physical world, God's voice reverberates in the negotiations with the central characters of Genesis, and again with the Jewish people at Mount Sinai, who suddenly "saw the voices" and promised, in response, to act and to listen. In later times, too, talk is the medium that best characterizes the most vital genres of Talmudic disputation in the *yeshivot* and the sermonizing in the synagogues (Blondheim and Blum-Kulka 2001, 511–41).

Heinrich Graetz, a highly influential historian of Judaism, has argued that the voice is directly relevant to the religious heritage, to

the Jewish national movement and, in particular, to the centrality of
the voice at Mount Sinai, the founding moment of the Jewish people.
Graetz sees the superiority of the voice over the image as an essential
characteristic of Judaism, the one that distinguishes it from paganism.
Whereas pagan religions worship nature, and at the same time are
steeped in it, their gods, just as much as men, are oppressed by its
rules. In Judaism, God is separated from nature and frees man from it.
Accordingly, the Greeks are oriented toward visual art, which person-
ifies gods in the shape of men by making them into sculptures;
Judaism, in which God's spiritual appearance is formed in the human
consciousness, is oriented to poetry, which can connect with God only
by the word.

2 The Relevance of Primordial Culture to Nationalism

On what grounds can a nation's primordial roots be relevant for
contemporary nationalist movements, the nation-states that they found
and the media that act as their mouthpiece? Regarding the Jews,
Graetz makes the connection between the idea of monotheism and
modern Jewish nationalism by anchoring God in historic action. He
sees Judaism as a religion not of individuals but of the collective.
Jewish life, accordingly, turns on religious truth and the social good;
Judaism is both church and state. Thus Benedict Anderson's imagined
communities entail imagining the nation as connected with the
collective past as well as with a continuing future (Anderson 1991). It
is wrong to conceive of nationalism as a conscious ideology, says
Anderson. Rather, like the way in which we think of "family relationship," nationalism should be seen as a cultural system, created vis-à-
vis, and in opposition to, religious community and kingdom. With the
loss of religion and, with it, the loss of comfort in the idea of
redemption, it is nationalism that is expected to fulfill the promises of
continuity and meaning. The nation-states, "widely considered to be
'new' and 'historic,'" cannot do it by themselves. Therefore, "the

nations to which they give political expression always loom out of immemorial past, and [...] glide into a limitless future." Thus "it is the magic of nationalism to turn chance into destiny" (ibid., 12).

The tie between Judaism and Zionism is particularly problematic inasmuch as the Zionist national movement was founded by Jews who broke away from religion, into modernism, enlightenment and socialism. After realizing that the emancipation gained by nineteenth-century Jews in Europe was leading to a new vicious form of anti-Semitism, the Zionists adopted the idea of nationalism. At the same time they also realized that in order to mobilize a national movement they needed to appeal to the largely religious communities, with whom they had only little in common. This tension between the secular Zionist idea and its primordial base was experienced from the outset and continues with the contemporary debate over whether to treat religion as part of the state's cultural heritage. A clue to the secular acknowledgment of the shared past is the case of *The Voice of Israel,* which (to this day) continues the ancient ritual of opening its broadcasts with a ceremonial reading of "Hear, O Israel," in which a deep male voice, with an unmistakable Yemenite Hebrew accent, leads a collective prayer to God for the majority of (non-observant) Israelis. By invoking the ancient voice, it also leans on the compatibility of radio, rather than television, to this heritage. Thus, ironically, whereas the voice was preserved throughout the generations by the written scrolls, radio's transmission by the voice is closer to the original.

3   The Voice and the Word: In Print and on Radio

The voice cannot be separated from the word it carries unless it is a cry of joy or agony – that is, a purely expressive utterance (Jacobson 1972, 73–85). In the spirit of McLuhan's brilliant insight, according to which each mass medium becomes the content of the medium that follows in its wake, radio is the medium for which the voice is the content, with the voice itself serving as medium for the word, the medium for conveying meaning. But the linear succession of media and content is not as neat as McLuhan would have it. Perhaps it would be more precise to argue that the pure word is mass diffused by two kinds of media. One is the older medium, that of the printed text (be it scrolls, books, pamphlets or newspapers), which mediates the word "cold" without the "tone" or "mood" of its expression (sometimes supplementing it with a verbal description – "angrily," "smilingly"). Seen from the perspective of communication technology, print mutes the voice and packages the message, robbing it of being heard in real time and emphasizing its cognitive, organized, controlled aspects. But when the genres of writing and the ways in which the text is read are taken into account, not all is dead. The most prominent example of a written text designed to evoke the speaking voice are Plato's dialogues, intended to overcome the closed finality of the text (which cannot be argued with) by inserting performative elements – a "live" debate among "real" fictional characters. Other texts are written as scripts to be acted. As for variations in the reading and in the context of reception, consider the biblical text, read aloud, in public, in synagogue, its intensity and earthiness reinstated.

The newer medium of radio lifts the voice from the page, resurrects its texture, diffusing it simultaneously – or by simulating simultaneity. Radio is also more directly focused than television's mix of icons and words. Listening means concentrating on the message, not being sidetracked by visual details that may be peripheral or irrelevant to the meaning conveyed by a speaker. There is, however, another possibility. Whereas the texture and "purity" of the spoken word give it focus and authenticity, directing the listener to meaning, the style of delivery leaves room for variation and manipulation. Presenters may address listeners as individuals, conveying intimacy and/or spontaneity, or address the community or the public, conveying ritualistic formality (recall the BBC model of news reading compared to the presenters' style on commercial radio and television; Goffman 1972).

The fact that radio exercised a formative influence on the renascent Israeli culture is not a coincidence of history. Just as television in the 1970s was central to the establishment of the third-world nations and printed pamphlets were the central medium of the American Revolution (Beilin 1992), so radio was the only accessible electronic medium in British Mandatory Palestine in the 1940s. Nevertheless, there is no doubt that its power was enhanced by its compatibility with the culture of the voice and the word as the medium that characterized the various genres of Jewish talk. The fact that radio was an active preference, rather than just an economic or a technological necessity, is evidenced in the political establishment's strong opposition to introducing television for the first two decades of the state's existence. Politicians feared that television would displace reading, Americanize the culture, promote consumerism, undermine the diffusion of the Hebrew language and culture, and personalize and de-ideologize politics (Katz 1971, 17–23). When television was finally approved, it was slipped in through the back door and for misguided reasons.

Given these initial fears, it is no small paradox that both television and radio were founded – or, rather, rushed into being – for external political reasons. In the case of television, the push came in the wake of the Six-Day War of 1967, when Israel (following an attack by Egypt, Syria and Jordan) found itself a conqueror and entertained the somewhat naïve idea of having to "balance" Arab propaganda with "truth" and with positive images of coexistence. Similarly, *The Voice of Jerusalem* was established by the British as an arena in which the Arab and the Jewish communities could let off steam and act less violently. Instead, the "Hebrew Hour" – the space allotted to the *Yishuv* – became the unlikely rallying site in which and around which the Zionist revolutionary movement consolidated its ideological and cultural togetherness.[2]

---

2   *Ezel* and *Lehi*, the more radical anti-British Zionist underground groups, had their own pirate channels, from which they managed intermittent broadcasts.

4   Live Radio versus Live Television: The Voice of
     Trauma, the Site of Ceremony

The Israeli case suggests that radio and television specialize in different types of dramatic genres. In the era in which radio reigned alone
(that is, in the pre-state era of the British Mandate and in the first two
decades of the state), radio broadcasting of public events was associated with moments of crisis and fear, sometimes of existential anxiety.
By contrast, Israelis remember the great events of television for the
performance of ceremonial events (Dayan and Katz 1992). This division of labor has to do both with the different technologies and with
the changing economic, ideological and cultural contexts associated
with each.

The events characterizing the years of radio, even those that
should have been – or at least ended – ceremonial moments, began as
traumatic, anxiety-arousing events, often taking the listeners by surprise. Their outcomes were uncertain, sometimes clandestine, always
in the shadow of risk and failure. Such fateful events, via radio, were
followed with trepidation by listener/witnesses waiting for the verdict.
Unlike today's image of radio as an intimate companion in the quiet of
a car, or in bed at night, Israeli radio's heyday was a time of collective
audiences. At critical moments in the nation's history, people
streamed into the streets to listen together, gathering round public
loudspeakers or car transistors or within earshot of their neighbors'
radios.

The most memorable example of such a fateful event was the live
broadcast of the UN roll-call vote on the partition of Palestine into two
states. In 1947, for the Jewish inhabitants of mandatory Palestine –
most of whom had fled from their countries of origin – this meant
finally having a state of their own. Years later, people still recall the
experience of this broadcast, at midnight Israeli-time. They remember
where, and with whom, they were at the time, how they kept their own
count of the votes as they were being announced, the point at which
they knew the resolution would pass, and the spontaneous dancing that
broke out once it was announced. Movingly documented in the auto-

biographical novel by Amos Oz (2004), this was a transformative moment, fraught with collective anxiety, at the end of which a neighborhood community of (mostly) World War II refugees felt a surge of relief and joy, and a new sense of belonging. The recollection of this moment is commonly visualized in the form of a dense mass of heads crowding around a radio set.

Next in the chain of open-ended landmarks in the history of nation-building events was the declaration of independence six months later. Unlike the UN vote, in which the time of the event was known but the outcome was not, the Declaration of Independence was expected, but the timing remained uncertain. Indeed, neither the society nor the paramilitary armed forces had much advance notice of the decision. The reason, as many knew, was that the announcement would almost certainly be followed by the frightening prospect of a full-fledged war, inasmuch as the Arabs, who had made no secret of their objection to the division of Palestine into two states and their competing claim to the whole of the territory, had already started a violent insurgency to prevent its implementation. The transmission of the broadcast itself was poor, and heard by some to the sound of shooting (*Radio Magazine* March 1961). Far from a ceremonial event, the poor semi-clandestine broadcast of the Declaration of Independence was part of the larger drama of British forces leaving, Arab states invading and Jewish post-World War II refugees streaming in. Prime Minister Ben-Gurion's decisive (surprisingly high-pitched) voice, infiltrating the chaos, was the signal for the beginning of a battle. Only the outcome of the war would determine whether this was the birth of a state.

The third memorable broadcast, typically listened to in public, was the live transmission of the Adolf Eichmann trial in Jerusalem, following his capture in Argentina in 1961 (Eichmann was the senior Nazi bureaucrat in charge of transporting the Jews to the death camps).[3] The trial marked a transformation in the way in which the first generation of native-born Israelis, in particular, perceived their relationship with the Holocaust, and with its Jewish survivors. For the

---

3   A more detailed description of the impact of the live broadcast of historic events may be found in Liebes 2005.

native-born, the Zionist ethos was intended to distance the "diasporic" Jewish existence. The dominant ideology focused on the new Jew – the pioneer, working the land and defending himself against his enemies. For young Israelis, and for thousands of Jewish immigrants from Arab countries who had little acquaintance with the history of European Jewry, the trial was a first confrontation with the collective trauma in which the majority of the Jewish communities in Europe had perished. The voice of the Holocaust had remained mute in the daily life of the Israeli survivors until then. The history books were still unwritten. For some, the Holocaust was seen in the image of half-crazed survivors wandering the streets.[4] Ironically, the Eichmann trial was conducted with an eye to the world outside, to show that Israel can conduct a fair and dignified trial against a senior Nazi war criminal. The major impact on the society in Israel came as a surprise to the organizers, who had not even planned in advance to broadcast the trial live. But from the first day, people huddled around the voices that emerged from radio sets in public buses, children gathered around loudspeakers in school classes and schoolyards, and families gathered at home around the single radio set to relive the incongruously tragic common past.[5] Listening to the voices of the survivors, in their role of witnesses, recalling their life histories, had a shattering effect.

Why were the organizers surprised after the impact of these live broadcasts? Perhaps their failure to anticipate radio's power in this case was rooted in the widely held belief among contemporaries that radio, or any form of mediation, would be only a poor substitute for actual presence at the place in which the event was happening.

---

4   Yossi Beilin, a former government minister and the initiator of the Oslo agreement, spoke in a radio program produced in 2002, entitled "When Eichmann Came into my Home," in which a number of prominent Israelis, teenagers at the time, described how the live broadcast had changed their lives.

5   Menahem Blondheim, a communications scholar at The Hebrew University, Jerusalem, is one of a number of people who recall, as children, listening to the trial on radio, whilst having lunch, for the duration of the trial. In fact, as Ora Herman has shown, in an MA dissertation, "Broadcasting from Another Planet: The Electronic Media, the Government and the Eichmann Trial," at the Hebrew University's Institute for Contemporary Judaism (2005), the trial was broadcast live on no more than eleven of the court's meetings.

Ascending to Jerusalem (as to the Temple in ancient times) demonstrated motivation, a willingness to make an effort; and "being there"
meant exposure to the event in its unique, authentic context. Thus little
thought was given to the live broadcast of the Eichmann trial, even if
much effort was invested in finding and rehabilitating a hall large
enough to contain the audience that was expected to come to Jerusalem for the trial.

Indeed, in the era of radio, the major ceremonial events – notably
the military parades of Independence Day – were organized to
encourage in-person participation, echoing the ancient ritual of festive
pilgrimage. The descriptions in the newspapers focused on the masses
that were gathered along the route. Radio's attempts to conduct "vox
pop" interviews in the streets sound dull, awkward, uninspired, even
pompous, and fail to convey the audience excitement or the mood of
folksy celebration. Ironically, these anniversary parades were discon-
tinued after the introduction of television, following the only victory
parade, broadcast live, in 1968.

Yet another aspect of radio's poor performance in mediating
establishment ceremonies may be the dissonance between the extrava-
gance of public celebrations and the asceticism that characterized
Israel's early years. The dominant value was one of austerity. Indeed,
Davar, the daily of Israel's as yet undefeated Labor party, took pride
in the policy of playing down ceremonies, especially ones that
encouraged a cult of leadership. One self-congratulatory report
(25.1.50) quotes the amazement expressed by *A Zaiad*, a Lebanese
newspaper, over the simplicity with which Israeli radio had reported
the reception given to Israel's ailing president Haim Weizman on his
return from medical treatment abroad. Unsurprisingly, it is difficult to
distinguish between the simplicity of the ceremony itself and of its
report on radio. Headlined, "Such Wonders!""*A Zaiad* continues:

> The State that was just established in the East reports its ceremonies in a most
> simple form. We did not hear any inflated titles, nor did we hear about décor-
> ations and tributes in celebrating the arrival of this great man. The announcer
> did not pour on words of prayer, or of thanks, nor did he express happiness over
> this celebrity's convalescence […]. We should not forget either that this is the
> man who brought back to the promised land the people who had departed and

were dispersed for 2000 years, from all ends of the world, and laid the foundation for a homeland and a government. How ungrateful of Israel, yet how wise.

Thus live radio in its heyday is remembered for its transmission of uncertain, often traumatic events. Unlike radio, the historic moments of television, during the two decades in which one monopoly channel acted as tribal bonfire, are best remembered for the live broadcasts of preplanned, ceremonial, "media events" such as Egyptian President Sadat's visit to Jerusalem, followed by the signing of the peace treaty on the White House lawn. Such ceremonial events, viewed on television, lacked the suspense and anxiety of the fateful events transmitted by radio in its great moments (Dayan and Katz 1992).

5   The Integrative Role of Radio

The centrality of radio in the pre-state life of the Jewish community, and in the first formative years of the state, is evident in the large space devoted to it in the daily printed press. The way in which journalists saw radio can be demonstrated by the following commentary in *Davar* (10.10.48):

> Radio is a tremendous instrument, which, if you will, largely determines the soul of the nation [...] it is endowed with the tasks of educating to citizenship the hundreds of thousands of immigrants coming in, and creating connections with the diaspora.

The paper concludes with the romantic expectation that "the airwaves should also infiltrate waves of love and affection to the state."

Commentators, radio critics and intellectuals expressed profound belief in radio's ability to reinforce (and even to invent) the central aspects of national and cultural identity. They argued about the goals of radio and how well these were being accomplished in light of the various perceptions of the governing principles of the new state. Proposals for improving the performance of the new medium ranged from the way it treated the most fundamental cultural issues to reprimanding announcers for the mistaken use of a Hebrew word, or for mispronouncing it, or even for using the wrong (mostly "too high") register. The heated debates on programming reflected the conflicting views on the ideological, political and cultural dilemmas facing the new nation, and the high expectations that radio, as the only medium accessible to the mass of Israelis, would play a major part in the diffusion of the language and cultural riches considered essential for the new Israelis.

Radio was indeed a central actor in tackling the major issues of identity formation.[6] Anticipating a model of public broadcasting, paternalistic from the outset, the guiding value was to give equal access to cultural heritage and ceremony (Cardiff and Scannell 1987). Functionally, access meant first teaching Hebrew to new immigrants and continuing with "improving their tastes and values" (*Davar* 10.10.48). In spite of the wish to promote cultural unity in broadcasting to a society of immigrants from various cultural backgrounds, and to Jews and Arabs, radio broadcasters faced the classic dilemma of the extent to which to allow for segmented multiculturalism. Should radio allocate separate channels to cultural minorities? How many cultural and linguistic slots should it allocate to the various groups on the one mainstream channel?[7] In spite of the elitist Ashkenazi bias, the predominant voice of both policymakers and public opinion recognized the need for a balance on the shared mainstream channel between the "high" culture (complete with classical music, literature and art) imported by immigrants from Europe, and the Oriental/folk/ popular culture of the Jewish immigration from Arab countries. A partially overlapping dilemma faced by radio broadcasters, regarding themselves as the voice of a liberal, secular, socialist society, was finding ways in which to incorporate religion as cultural heritage

---

6   Liebes (2000) elaborates the three periods in which first radio, then one TV
     channel, and (from the mid 1990s) a plurality of channels, formed and reflected
     the dominant history of the electronic media in Israel.
7   Nathan Rotenstreich, a philosophy professor, wrote an article in *Davar* in
     which he strongly advocated incorporating the Arabic broadcasts into the
     general Hebrew channel.

rather than as normative code (Herzl 1997). There was unanimous agreement, in the spirit of Zionism, about daily readings of a chapter from the Bible, but a bitter continual argument about the identity of the commentators; by the Orthodox community, literary, historical interpretation was seen as a threat. Another basic dilemma that arose in the debate everywhere over public broadcasting was balancing between education and entertainment. Typical of the Israeli anomaly was the constant demand of kibbutz members to have classical music in the evening instead of "salon dancing" music to entertain café-goers in Tel Aviv, who could look after themselves by employing local musicians. Even where there was agreement, the attempt to carry out the various tasks within the limited time of daily broadcasting, mostly on the one channel, entailed impossible choices – such as the one attacked in a furious *Davar* column criticizing radio's substitution of "Hebrew/Jewish music" with "gymnastic lessons for the workers" at 7:30 in the morning.

Radio's immediate tasks included bringing home the formative (and transformative) historic moments – the events that led to the founding of Israel, and its first stormy decades – including wars, political crises and ceremonial events. Often – as in Ben-Gurion's tense Declaration of Independence, accompanied by the sound of shooting, and sadness over the knowledge of the looming war – ceremony and crisis were mixed. Serving as the real-time announcer of history in the making, a courier for mobilizing the troops, and a babysitter for the home front, radio lived up to its role of instructing civilians in emergencies. Even in the era of television it remained the medium to turn to in immediate crisis. The slogan "Yellow cheese" broke the traditional media silence of Yom Kippur in 1973 and put the reserve army on its way; and "Viper Snake," interrupted the broadcast at the start of the first Gulf War, assembling Israelis in their "sealed room" to protect themselves against Saddam Hussein's chemical missiles.

6   Hebrew Radio Talking Yiddish to WW II Jewish Survivors

Whereas radio broadcasters struggled with answering all these needs and values, the most crucial, difficult and miraculously successful task undertaken by radio was that of reviving the Hebrew language, accompanied by its fight against the Yiddish that symbolized life in the diaspora.

Radio's need to undertake the task of reviving, updating and giving voice to the ancient Hebrew language was the result of 2,000 years of diasporic existence, which it had survived mostly as the written language of prayer and study. Yiddish was the vernacular for the masses of Jews in Eastern Europe. Radio rose to the challenge of impressing Hebrew on large sections of the multicultural population of immigrants to Israel, the majority of whom had to learn it from scratch (by daily repeated routines, direct teaching, programs in "easy Hebrew," and slowing down the speed of news reading).

However, the irony of history dictated that following World War II the assignment of reviving Hebrew had to be postponed. Before mobilizing the broadcasts for the Zionist revolution, the most urgent task faced by the "Hebrew Hour" was creating contact with that part of the Jewish people in Europe that had survived the war, whose predominant language was Yiddish. These refugees were now dispersed in displaced people (DP) camps throughout Europe. For the luckier refugees who had managed to escape to Palestine before the war and were desperately trying to establish contact with their loved ones, this attempt to call the survivors and to listen to their voices was crucial. Regarding itself as "a homeland in process" (*Davar* 4.6.47), the community in British Palestine acted in the spirit of the Jewish principle of mutual responsibility, extending the boundaries of the imagined community to give preference to Jews in distress wherever they might be. Broadcasting in Yiddish was done in direct contradiction of the ideological principles of the *Yishuv*. As literary scholar Dan Miron (2004) convincingly argues, the adoption of Hebrew – the ancient language of the Hebrews in the Land of the Israelites – was the symbol of the clear divide between the experience and way of life of Jewish non-revolutionary existence "in exile," and that of the born-again life in *Eretz Yisrael*. Miron argues that separation between the Yiddish and the Hebrew was crucial for serving the goals of the Zionist Hebrew culture, because Yiddish was the most commonly used language throughout the generations in spite of the continuous struggle against it. It was especially important since a large part of life for Jews in pre-Israel Palestine was also marked by a Jewish "exile-like" culture, not fully internalizing that they were "the last generation of slavery, and the first of redemption."

But once the war was won, ideologies had to wait, and the "Hebrew Hour," stretching far beyond the geographic and linguistic boundaries of the *Yishuv*, set out to search for remnants of the Jewish communities in Europe. One obvious way to discover which of them were still alive was to send greetings by shortwave radio to "the Jewish communities wherever they may be" (*Davar* 22.6.47) and to pray for signs of life. These voices transmitting greetings from Palestine, perhaps only by talking into thin air, were sometimes miraculously answered by transmissions received from radio Lublin, Stockholm and Warsaw.

One section of the nation-to-be, still waiting behind fences, were the homeless refugees who, following the war, tried to make their way to Palestine. Regardless of the decision taken by the British, according to which Palestine was declared a national home for the Jewish people, these displaced persons were arrested by the British at sea, or on disembarking on the shores of Tel Aviv. Thus, as reported by *Ha'zofe* (27.8.48), broadcasts to the illegal immigrants imprisoned in Cyprus were intended to "allow them to listen to the voice of the homeland." The demand for special programs in Yiddish had first come from the camp residents themselves (entitled by the paper "the Cyprus diaspora"), who asked "to be brought closer to the life of the state and its problems by broadcasting news, commentary and light talks in a language which is familiar to most of them." One program, entitled *Zabar*, addressed to the new Jewish immigrants on their way to Palestine, was devoted to explaining "what is 'exile' and what is the 'Yishuv,' in a (rather naïve) effort to turn the newcomers into 'real' native '*Yishuvniks*'" (*Ha'aretz* 16.8.45).

Closer to home, the most urgent need for many Jews in Palestine, following the defeat of the Nazis, was the possibility of creating contact with the Jewish soldiers who had taken part in the war. There was particular concern for the fate of the brigade of Jewish soldiers from Mandatory Palestine, who had volunteered to join the British army and were stationed in Europe (*Ha'zofe* 9.4.45). For this task, the Hebrew press encountered only little enthusiasm in its struggle to convince British officials in Palestine to allocate the short waves that had served for anti-Nazi propaganda to the Middle Eastern countries (*Ha'mashkif* 30.1.45; *Davar* 4.2.45). One strategy of persuasion was to remind the British that the Hebrew (Palestinian) soldiers were barred from contact with the homeland – a contact that "every nation tries to keep with its soldiers." Using the occasion of the celebration of Passover, the paper urged "not to impose this exclusion from the *Voice of Jerusalem* on our soldiers and on the diasporic communities in exile" (*Davar* 27.3.45). A few months later the shortwave transmission began broadcasting to the Jewish Brigade.

A glimpse at the newspapers of this period reveals a certain amount of collaboration between the BBC and the Hebrew radio in bringing home voices of Jewish soldiers. For example, the BBC recorded a prayer for Jewish soldiers in a London synagogue for the "Hebrew Hour" (*Davar* 15.8.45), conducted interviews with Jewish soldiers who were imprisoned in Germany (*Ha'mashkif* 12.8.45), and initiated "greetings from the *Golah* (exile)" twice a week. Note that it was the participation of volunteer Jewish soldiers from Palestine in the British army that gave legitimacy to the *Yishuv*'s claim to broadcast to Europe, and in turn to serve as a channel for contacting displaced Jewish survivors.

7 Radio and the Revival of the Hebrew Language

Before establishing itself as the daily spoken language of the first- and second-generation immigrants to Palestine, Hebrew had been preserved in the various Jewish diasporas, through the generations, only as the language of prayer and religious study. Daily life within the community was conducted in Yiddish and was the lingua franca used in its contacts with the rest of the society. Moreover, the choice of Hebrew as Israel's official language was far from self-evident for some of the first Zionist leaders. Because Zionism in Western Europe arose as a national movement within the climate of enlightenment and emancipation, its leaders had broken away from religion, and from the language associated with it. Theodor Herzl, the movement's undisputed leader, was an assimilated journalist, who grew up with German and Hungarian and later acquired English and French. He set out in the latter part of the nineteenth century to solve the Jewish problem (defined as the poverty and persecution of the East European Jews, and the rise of a new kind of anti-Semitism at the onset of emancipation and enlightenment in Western Europe). He envisioned a multicultural state, one in which the Jews from the East and the West would continue to speak in their own languages. He, for one, was convinced that he would continue to speak German. Once Hebrew was decided on, its diffusion became the radio's greatest challenge. Dr. Z. M. (*Davar*, 12.11.48) expressed the expectations from the miraculous new medium in the following words:

> Radio [...] is conquering the world, unlimited in its influence and power [...]
> And if this is true for the world's nations, all the more so in our case [...] It is a
> national educational instrument of the first order, and we have to prepare in
> time so that we will not miss its potential. The Hebrew language is the first and
> foremost element. The rest of the world's nations takes this element for granted,
> which is by no means the case here. And as the language is so central, it has to
> be carefully nurtured [...] both in terms of the culture of speech, and in terms of
> access to the mechanical voice that reaches every ear.

The obsession with teaching Hebrew was accompanied by unrelenting criticism of broadcasting in Yiddish. A forceful example is

A. Ramba *(Ha'mashkif* 20.2.49), who reprimands Kol Yisrael for broadcasting in Yiddish. Even after the camp in Cyprus was dismantled, says Ramba, its Yiddish broadcasts continued "under the guise of broadcasting to Europe":

> The Yiddish supporters should not come to us with demagogic arguments about the tens of thousands of new immigrants who do not understand Hebrew, and the idea that their lives and absorption will be made easier by not leaving them deaf and dumb. There must not be two languages for the Hebrew people in its state. A broadcast in *Yiddish*, a paper, even theatre, all disturb the process of making Hebrew speakers of the new state's citizens. If they can find media in their own language, the language of exile, why should they bother to learn a new language when they are grownup or old? The only task that lies ahead is to use all the possible means in the search for adequate methods for teaching Hebrew to all the immigrants, the young and the old, men, women and babies.

In the relentless fight against Yiddish on radio, the article uses another powerful argument: favoritism toward Yiddish-speakers means discrimination against the rest of the new immigrants. What about the thousands who speak other languages, such as *Spaniolit* (a dialect of Spanish), Hungarian, Polish, English, French and Romanian? "We dearly love all the Israelites. Will we build a new 'Tower of Babel' and broadcast in all the languages still prevalent in our country?" The drive to universalize Hebrew was so extreme that even broadcasting to the Yemenite Jewish community – whose Hebrew pronunciation was considered the most authentic – in their "particular Hebrew dialect" was considered counterproductive from the perspective of "inculcating the (Hebrew) language" *(Al Ha'mishmar* 20.9.54).

8   Forming Hebrew Speech: Register, Invention, Pronunciation

As a mass medium, radio could address various groups of the population, feature special programs for new immigrants in "easy Hebrew" and develop a common standard for spoken Hebrew by adopting the "right" register for speaking, deciding on the "right" pronunciation, inventing new words (often in collaboration with the Academy for the Hebrew Language) to cover modern concepts and new technologies, and translating necessary words (mostly from the English). Such decisions were carefully considered and often furiously attacked by the daily press. Listeners criticized the radio's use of too high a register, sometimes incorrectly. Others requested slowing the pace of news reading (*Ha'aretz* 3.4.49; *Ha'boker* 3.4.49).

Two examples are significant for demonstrating radio's attempts to invoke the authentic sounds and rhythms of ancient Hebrew. One is the decision to adopt the Oriental (Yemenite) pronunciation, considered to be closest to the original in its preservation of the subtle distinctions between ostensibly similar letters. It was a romantic and heroic attempt, and doomed in advance. Long erased in the Ashkenazi pronunciation of Hebrew, there was no way the bulk of Ashkenazi Zionists could adopt this pronunciation. But it was seriously attempted. Interestingly, it was probably a unique case in which the political and educated elite made an attempt to adopt the accent and pronunciation of a low-class, uneducated group. This meant that the majority of (Ashkenazi) radio announcers had to learn and practice the right way of speaking Hebrew. The tradition was upheld until the decline of public broadcasting and the rise of commercial broadcasting. By then, announcers were using the universally spoken Hebrew, its richness flattened, the distinctions between similar letters (*tet* and *tav*, *alef* and *ayin*) abandoned. Its collapse, ironically, coincided with the rise of multiculturalism and the takeover of (second-generation) popular *Mizrahi* singers.

Another attempt at resurrecting the sound of spoken biblical Hebrew was the station's choice of a musical ID, meant to invoke the ancient cantillation of public reading from the Torah. For the vast majority of Jews, the language of the Bible lasted throughout the diaspora solely as the language of prayer. The choice of a musical theme was another way of demonstrating the strong Zionist motivation to connect with the common religious roots, even if only in the form of "cultural heritage." The choice of sounds that allude to the ancient intonation of the biblical text in the synagogue, for summoning listeners to tune in and stay with the station, strengthened the symbolic meaning of the choice of Hebrew. It could of course be argued that in making these choices, the radio programmers aimed to skip over the period of the diaspora and connect directly to the ancient Canaanite roots. And indeed, the choice of the signal gave rise to another heated debate. "It should be known," said Menashe Ravina (*Ha'dor*) "that this signal is not as ancient as many believe [...] It is well known that different ethnic groups read by different musical motifs." The author concluded that it was impossible to decide which group of tunes could be declared "the most ancient," as long as there was no authoritative committee that would support it. Nevertheless, the fact that the motif chosen was alleged to have been read aloud in synagogues for hundreds of years justified the decision to declare it uniquely Jewish.

9   Sounding Out a Homeland

Hebrew radio at its birth was truly an "imagined homeland," a new medium in which to try out the Zionist utopia. Unlike *Altneuland*, Herzl's utopian novel, frozen in book form, radio could experiment continuously with various genres and formats, speak in various languages, receive regular feedback from its various target audiences (mostly in the press) and report daily developments. Its imagined communities – including Jewish immigrants at home and abroad – had no continuous geographic territory. Its voice was heard in a plurality of languages, by diasporic communities at home and abroad, and by Jews in the neighboring Arab countries. Thus, under the auspices of an ambivalent colonial government, Hebrew radio became the site of a state-in-the-making and a virtual home for the *Yishuv.*

Twenty-five years after the establishment of Hebrew radio, Prime Minister David Ben-Gurion celebrated its dramatic achievement in building the cultural identity of Israelis. He underlined "the place of the broadcast Hebrew word in the miraculous act of the revival of the Hebrew language and Hebrew speech." The biggest proof of its success, said Ben-Gurion, was the paradox of how difficult it is to explain to a generation of teenagers who had lived their whole lives in a Jewish state that the revival of Hebrew should not be taken for granted. It would not have succeeded, said Ben-Gurion, "if we did not work on this revival with all our hearts every day [...] What few can imagine is that each step of talking Hebrew was a deed of a new creation, a conquest."

Looking at the linguistic transformations that accompanied Zionism, literary critic Dan Miron (2004) pointed to the phenomenon of Yiddish, the language spoken in the homes of the masses of Jews (in Europe and after immigrating to Israel), becoming a comic language in Israel. In public life, said Miron – that is, in social meetings, in the Yiddish theater and in the media, Yiddish is used as a language for ridiculing, for telling (and listening to) jokes. Miron saw the ideological function of this distancing as achieving one of the main targets of the Zionist Hebrew culture – that of raising a clear buffer between the primordial, non-continuous, life of redemption in *Eretz Yisrael* and the non-revolutionary Jewish life "in exile." The sweet revenge of Yiddish, he claimed, is that for the third and fourth generation of Israelis, the pathos of the Hebrew Zionist language as it was spoken by the founding generation became itself an object of ridicule, turning into a second Yiddish, and "put into double quotation marks." And indeed, the Hebrew heard on Israeli media half a century after independence, is a far cry from the ideal of the Zionist founders. One television critic (*Ha'aretz* 21.1.2005) counted 12 mistakes in Hebrew in songs that came first in the hit parade. Speaking from the Knesset podium (to an almost empty assembly hall) Prime Minister Ariel Sharon lamented what he saw as the deterioration of spoken Hebrew, including the fashionable use of English words. In a period in which new television channels are named "HOT" and "YES," and

"Shalom," the most common Hebrew greeting, has been replaced by
the Arabic/English "*yalla bye*," the media, as usual, represents ideological and cultural changes and, thereby, reinforces them.

Bibliography

Anderson, B. 1991. *Imagined Communities: Reflections on the
    Origins and Spread of Nationalism*. London: Verso.
Beilin, B. 1992. *The Ideological Origins of the American Revolution*.
    Cambridge, MA: Belknap Press.
Blondheim, M. and S. Blum-Kulka. 2001. "Literacy, Orality, Tele-
    vision: Mediation and Authenticity in Jewish Conversational
    Arguing, 1–2000 C.E." *The Communication Review* 4(4), 511–
    41.
Cardiff, D. and P. Scannell. 1987. "Broadcasting and National Unity."
    In J. Curan et al. (eds), *Impact and Influences*. London/New
    York: Methuen.
Dayan, D. and E. Katz. 1992. *Media Events: The Live Broadcasting of
    History*. Cambridge, MA: Harvard University Press.
Goffman, E. 1972. *Forms of Talk*. Oxford: Blackwell.
Herzl, T. 1997. *Altneuland*. Jerusalem: Akademon.
Jakobson, R. 1972. "Linguistics and Poetics." In R. T. De George and
    F. M. De George (eds), *The Structuralitst: From Marx to Levi-
    Straus*. New York: Anchor Books, 73–85.
Jay, M. 1993. *Downcast Eyes: The Denigration of Vision in 20th-
    Century French Thought*. Berkeley: University of California
    Press.
Katz, E. 1971. "Television Comes to the People of the Book." In
    I. L. Horowitz (ed.), *The Use and Abuse of Social Sciences*. New
    Brunswick, NJ: Transaction Books, 17–23.
Katz, E. and G. Wedell. 1977. *Broadcasting in the First World*.
    Cambridge, MA: Harvard University Press.

Liebes, T. 2000. "Performing a Dream and Its Dissolution: A Social History of Broadcasting in Israel." In J. Curran and M. Myung-Jin Park (eds), *Dewesternizing Media Research*. London/New York: Routledge.

—. 2005. "Acoustic Space: The Role of Radio in Israeli Collective History." *Jewish History* 20, 69–90.

Miron, D. 2004. *The Dark Side of Sholom Aleichem's Laughter* (in Hebrew). Tel-Aviv: Am Oved.

Oz, A. 2004. *A Tale of Love and Darkness* (in Hebrew). Tel Aviv: Am Oved.

Chapter 12

Doron Mendels

A Model of Public Memory and a note on Günter Grass's *Crabwalk*

As shown in detail in my recent book *Memory in Jewish, Pagan and Christian Societies of the Graeco-Roman World*, we can speak of a range of various "kinds" of memories in historical groups, from individual through "comprehensive" to "collective." For instance, Augustine's *Confessions* is an example of individual memory written down by the "rememberer" himself, whereas Thucydides' *Peloponnesian War* represents the "comprehensive" kind of memory, a synthesis made up of many memories collected from many sources (oral and written). A "collective" memory can be found in Sparta of the classical and Hellenistic periods and even (with certain reservations) among the first Christians. An imposed collective memory can be found in the *Res Gestae* of Augustus, and the finest instances of a durable "public memory" can be found in ancient and Ptolemaic Egypt.

There exists in ancient societies, as I have attempted to show in the model, a correlation between (1) the *nature* of the society (open, as in a democracy, or rigid and closed, as in Sparta or the communities of the first Christians); (2) its *memories* (comprehensive, fragmented, etc.); (3), *the media* (theater, inscription, historiography and their position in the public space), which are the mediators of memory; and (4) *time*. Time plays a significant role in these considerations – the point in time that an oral memory is written down. Are we speaking of memory that is written down by the generation that experienced the event or by a generation (or more) after the event? Or are we speaking of a memory that has crystallized and been unchanged for generations and centuries? Here I will concentrate on the *media and the means of communication* that preserve memories and sometimes even mold them. The agents and means I would like to consider are based on my published study, with some minor afterthoughts. I will then demon-strate the model with a test case that is very far removed from the societies I have examined so far.

Let me now briefly outline my ideas concerning canonization as a means that transmits a memory of a certain period to later ones (Mendels 2004, 1–29). A fragmentary historiography, stored in archival material, has shaped the memory of the Western world concerning ancient history. It took more than a thousand years to be established in its present form. This stored memory is constantly studied by later generations, and although its reception may change in nuance from period to period, it remains available in its basic form – namely, the canonical texts, handed down to us by ancient historians from the early Middle Ages. Western civilization has for hundreds of years memorized classical Athens and the Roman Republic, as well as the period of Alexander the Great, because of this channel of commu-nication, the canon of historiography. Such an effect of historiography on a public memory can also be found in modern Israel. In the first decades of the state's existence, the national historic memory was inter alia molded by the school curricula – a point not emphasized by Yael Zerubavel in her excellent book *Recovered Roots*, 1995. This history was taught on the basis of the histories written by such scholars as Graetz, Dubnow and Gedaliah Alon. I cannot agree on this point with Yerushalmi, who draws a sharp contrast between Jewish memory and Jewish historiography.[1]

The theater is an example of an important medium within the public sphere which can create new sets of memory that may turn into alternative memories coexisting with prevalent collective, fragmented, individual and comprehensive ones (Mendels 2004, 48–59). Aes-chylus' *Persians* was staged eight years after the battle of Salamis in 480 B.C.E. The Greeks gained a victory over the invading Persians, and that victory gave an impetus to the rise of radical democracy in Athens. Aeschylus in fact attempted to change the collective memory of Salamis in the minds of the audience, some of whom were soldiers

---

1   See the reaction of Olick and Robins concerning Yerushalmi 1998, 110–11.

and sailors in the battle and still had their "original" individual memories of it.

Aeschylus shifted the attention of his audience to the defeated Persian court and thereby modified the memories of this same audience concerning the centrality of this dramatic event in their lives. Whereas the "original" collective memory associated the victory with democratic ideas, Aeschylus, by taking his audience to a fictitious scene in the defeated Persian court, shifted their attention to kingship. It is important to emphasize here that although a relatively short span of time (eight years) elapsed between the event (the battle of Salamis, which was crucial to the society) and the attempt to change the collective memory of it (which was probably still in its oral form), henceforward three sets of memory were available in Greece, a "formal" one (perhaps formulated later in the narrative of Herodotus), an alternative (proposed by a theatrical medium) and the individual memories of the veterans. Whereas the individual memories were lost in the course of time, the other two versions were written down and thus imprinted in the collective memory of the West as an original memory (Herodotus') and an alternative (Aeschylus'). In a fragmentary cultural heritage, these existing memories are all we have.

The regulation of communication agents by a state can lead to an extreme situation in which the state itself is prevented from having a collective memory. Many modern examples spring to mind, but I have chosen the case of Plato's *Politeia* (Mendels 2004, 60–8).

Plato's ideal state has been criticized in many quarters, and particular attention has been given to its system of education (*paideia*). In fact, Plato proposed two systems of education, one in books 2–3 and the other in book 10. In the earlier books he suggests introducing poetry into the city but in a censored form. In book 10 he proposes eliminating all forms of poetry from the ideal city-state (595b); all study of literary material is banned from the state because Plato believes that imitation of the stories by the hearers will cause harm (through the process of *mimesis*). Yet in books 2–3 he still thought that a censored literary heritage could be introduced because its "good part" would not harm the souls of the children and adults of the ideal city-state. Many attempts have been made to explain this

Doron Mendels

discrepancy, the more recent ones striving to harmonize the two
sections of *Politeia*.

But why is Plato so negative about the teaching of mythology? In
fact, the act of mimesis is what causes people to recycle, passionately
and actively, the deeds of heroes that (they believe) occurred in their
own past. Thus, putting it in our terms, Plato did not intend his ideal
city-state to have a cultural or historical collective memory at all (if
we follow book 10), or perhaps he wanted it to have only an extremely
dull and selective collective memory (if we follow books 2–3). The
ideal city-state, according to Plato, should have a system regulating
the flow of past information into the memories of the citizens. Today
we would say that his state would regulate what people should
remember (and forget), up to the most trivial details of the common
cultural "collective memory."

Yet a collective memory or any fragment of it is not transmitted
by an education system alone but also by other media within the communication systems of the state. This is why Plato in his "totalitarian"
state "shuts down" those media that are instrumental in preserving and
keeping alive past memories. The media that functioned in the societies of antiquity as communication channels for the manipulation of
memories of various kinds are accorded a limited role in Plato's new
city-state. First, the lack of any sort of bureaucratic system (including
central political institutions) is crucial, since a bureaucracy provides
the state with mechanisms and agents that communicate between the
regime and its citizens, and vice versa. For instance, there is no
mention of a central state assembly. Such an "assembly" – as it was
known in classical Athens – is a constant reminder of the common
identity and is one of the many vehicles enabling this kind of corpor-
ation to preserve a changing collective memory.

Second, in the real city-state of Greece many rituals – daily,
weekly, monthly and yearly – were performed, constituting a significant medium for transmitting the traditions of common experiences.
This role may in fact be one of the reasons that Plato eliminated rituals
from his ideal state. The few that were performed for the conception
of the new generation – hymns to the gods and public commemoration
for deceased guardians – were geared to the special aims of the state.

Third, Plato's ideal state operates without a codex of laws, since these have become superfluous in such a peculiar political structure. Law is an important mechanism for the preservation of collective memories and fragments thereof. Plato eliminated almost all laws from his ideal city (534d), hence this important communicative channel, which links individuals in the state and constitutes parts of its memory, is altogether absent from *Politeia*.

Fourth, the deities in pagan societies constituted a lively reminder of active pasts. They played an important role in the shaping of individual, collective and fragmentary memories within societies and states in antiquity. Plato says that temples will remain untouched in his ideal state, yet he defines "god" as "not responsible for everything, but only for what is good" (380c). God does not change and, I would add, is quite boring according to Plato's definition:

> God is certainly single in form and true, both in what he does and in what he says. He does not change in himself, and he does not deceive others – waking and sleeping – either with apparitions, or with words, or by sending signs (382e).

Plato censors the gods so thoroughly in books 2–3 that he alters their nature completely when compared to the mythological gods who had entered the collective memory of the Greeks. And if we accept Plato's description in book 10 of the total elimination of all references to gods (except hymns to them), then a very crucial communicative discourse concerning the narrative of memory is erased from the ideal city.

In short, as long as the *Politeia* functions, little of what we call collective and public memory will remain unaltered, and it will live with a defined unchanging and minimal collective memory (or no memory at all). Most totalitarian states in modern times have lived according to such a pattern.

But how did a central authority manage to guard the collective memory against change, misunderstanding and elimination (Mendels 2004, 69–80)?

Ptolemaic Egypt constitutes a good example, since there the messages sent from the central authority created, affirmed and supported the "collective memory" of the society. But what means did the

Ptolemaic kings employ to make sure that the messages they sent to their subjects were received as intended? To examine this issue I adopted a set of criteria regarding this means recently developed by E. Katz and M. Popescu (2004, 19–39). Here I shall touch on three of them.

The first mechanism borrowed from Katz and Popescu's typology of supplementation (as they call it) is the one declaring that communicators who wish to guarantee that their message will be received *create an environment* (space construct) that ensures the acceptance of the message as it is intended. Examples: God telling Moses that he is standing on holy ground is a symbolic construction; as are Memorial Day ceremonies in Israel broadcast from the enclosure of the Wailing Wall and Independence Day ceremonies broadcast from the Mount Herzl memorial in Jerusalem. (Television brings the Israeli audience into these "constructed places.") Space may also be constructed by decorum control, and there are constructions – physical or symbolic – that reinforce messages for those who are admitted by keeping others out. The Ptolemaic kings were masters of space construction. They built temples for the native inhabitants that were in fact imitations of Egyptian originals with some Hellenistic modifications. The Horus temple in Edfu looks like a pharaonic temple. These spaces, needless to say, with all their traditional symbols and paintings, created a mode of communication familiar to the native Egyptians. The latter were, as it were, "locked" within a physical framework in which the message transmitted to them from the court could hardly be wrongly decoded. Hence a well-defined, clear-cut public memory was embedded, unchanged and guaranteed for centuries. The Ptolemaic kings took care to preserve the ancient pharaonic memories that were deeply rooted within the native society, while adapting them to their own public propagandistic needs.

Another mechanism is the one concerned with *constructing time*. Broadcasts have the power to declare time out – to say that society should hold its breath [...] Television is proposing a holiday to celebrate an event which it has constructed from the raw material of another event [...] thereby assuming that the re-presentation will be properly received, collectively remembered, and [...] institutionally retained. (The Superbowl and the ritual equivalents of Superbowl Day are an invention of television.) Hellenistic monarchs were aware of this technique and used it effectively. The procession (*pompe*) introduced by the Ptolemaic kings, the "Ptolemaieia," was meant to convey a message to the Greek population (as opposed to the natives of Egypt). The procession was decidedly meant "to interrupt the cycle of life, to lead [the Greeks in Egypt] to commune with a shared value" (Katz and Popescu 2004, 26) and it was in fact a staging and representation of the familiar mythological events of the Dionysus cycle. Alexander the Great was associated with Dionysus, and Ptolemy II (who initiated the festival) was associated, via Alexander, with Dionysus. In other words, the state, on a seasonal basis, staged mythological events (or scenes) to be collectively remembered by the Greek population of Egypt.

Another mechanism is that of *constructing identities*. Broadcasters have the power to tell us who we are: we are "at war," we are "mourners," or we are a "jury" (as in the case of O. J. Simpson). "Public broadcasting [...] wishes to evoke our identity as citizens, as do media events" (Katz and Popescu 2004, 28). If we examine the Rosetta Stone we can see examples of how an identity (double or even triple) is created in three languages. It tells the native Egyptians who they are and who they should be, by evoking mythological associations and memories concerning them.

These and other mechanisms made it possible in Ptolemaic Egypt to preserve an already embedded public collective memory for hundreds of years.

Law as memory was illustrated in my book by the laws of the Christian emperors concerning the Jews during 300–450 C.E. (Mendels 2004, 114–29).

A law dated 29 May 408 C.E. states that

> the governors of the provinces shall prohibit the Jews from setting fire to Haman in memory of his past punishment, in a certain ceremony of their festival, and from burning with sacrilegious intent a form made to resemble the saint cross in contempt of the Christian faith.

Such laws are good formulations of fragments of Christians memories about Jews (some of them are even positive). Laws, especially when clearly dated, are an ideal medium for the preservation of memories and their presentation within the public arena. They are able to freeze memories since they are relatively concise, precise and repetitive, and use a language that is full of signals emanating from the real world. At times they are a mirror of a society and confirm its realities. Laws create clear boundaries within societies and within segments of the societies themselves, since they most effectively define groups (Dan-Cohen 1984, 625–77). They are not only formulations of but also reactions to realities. They are not necessarily cultural constructs. They are the memories, however fragmentary, that a society leaves behind it of social conditions and situations. Laws constitute the evidence of what members of a society do to each other, for conduct and misconduct. They are perhaps the most objective of memories. And in some instances laws preserve the final memory of a long process that is consolidated in a single law. The law courts have been an important medium as well; Socrates' trial is our only memory of that important media event.[2]

Physical monuments and formal propagandistic documents are an obvious domain of memory and memorials. For instance, the political testament of Augustus, written in 12 C.E., two years before the emperor's death, is a good example of a memorial monument since it was probably erected in several parts of the Roman Empire. One copy was found in Ancyra (modern Ankara, Turkey). It is engraved on stone and conveys the memoirs of the new *princeps*. Augustus formulated his memories and imposed them on his subjects in the Roman Empire to become the formal collective memory of his regime (Mendels 2004, 37–41).

The Book of 1 Maccabees is an example of a formal propagandistic publication. It reflects an "official" document of the Hasmonean rulers (whose public burial place became an important lieu of pilgrimage). The book – a "lieu de mémoire" according to Nora's definitions (1997) and an "Errinerungsort" according to Francois and Schulze (2001) – which commemorates the regime of the Hasmoneans (second and beginning of first centuries B.C.E.). Through it I would like to demonstrate how the collective memory of a crucial time in the history

2   For media events see Dayan and Katz 1992.

of a nation is formed and how decisive certain media are in its preservation for future generations.

The author of the Book of 1 Maccabees filtered memories into a fragmentary set. In fact, he himself considers memory an important factor in daily life (1 Maccabees 1.49; 2.51; 4.1–10; 5.4; 6.12; 7.38). However, the Jews did not have a Thucydides to form a "comprehensive memory" of their war of independence in the second century B.C.E. Following are some of the factors that made it so fragmentary a memory (Mendels 2004, 81–8):

(1) The problem of time and the selection of memories to be inscribed: the 16 chapters of 1 Maccabees narrate events that occurred during approximately forty years. The author himself realizes his extreme concision and says in 9:22: "The rest of the acts of Judas, his battles, the exploits which he performed, and his greatness are not written down; for they were many." Such a strategy had serious implications, because after the generations that still remembered the events in their oral form ceased to exist, the national memory surviving in an inscribed form remained extremely fragmentary.

(2) The memories of many of the narrated battles are "contaminated" by the biblical descriptions that the author (and his audience) had in mind. The numbers engaged in the battles mentioned are partial and typological, and no "statistical reality" can be found.

(3) The "site of memory" (to use Nora's expression) created by the author of 1 Maccabees in this book reflects relevance to Jews at the time it was inscribed, as can be discerned throughout the author's historical narrative and through his use of terminology. But this fact makes the act of remembrance of this heroic period extremely partial. Future generations may be misled by their own memories – as for instance in the case of the early Zionist movement, which used the memories of 1 Maccabees incorrectly. The conquest of the Land of Israel was equated in many instances with the conquests of the Maccabees. But the circumstances had changed, and this was not always taken into consideration

when such romanticized memories became a mimetic force behind the wars led by the founding fathers of modern Israel, instead of remaining passive memories of ancient times.

(4)   The site of memory, in 1 Maccabees lacks *diversity* – namely, an attempt to express the whole picture and all its details.

(5)   1 Maccabees uses different orders of discourse that are intertwined in the descriptions; it is anything but a serious, comprehensive site of memory; one can find here some historical narrative, but also hymns, documents, eulogies, fiction, praise. These and other factors caused this *lieu de mémoire* of a crucial period in Jewish history to become extremely fragmentary. Yet this inscribed memory of the Hasmonean period is (except for the alternative fragmented memory concerning part of the period that we find in 2 Maccabees) the only collective memory preserved from that time.

Conclusions (see figure 12.1)

(1) A correlation exists between the *nature of the society* – namely, its political organization (i.e. open societies [democracies], rigid and closed societies, religious groups within a larger political organization) – and the *nature of the memories* it, or its components, maintain in terms of morphology and ideology.

(2) The *media* – namely, the mechanisms or agents through which memories reach the public domain – have a great impact on the diffusion, durability and modification of public memories.

(3) *Time* is crucial. Memories change and undergo transformation in the course of time. Generations come and go; memories are affected by changing circumstances and changing viewpoints. They can be oral or inscribed. What was a memory for a certain generation becomes dry narrative, or forgotten tradition, for later ones and frequently even

disappears altogether. Yet a common experience that disappeared or was suppressed for a while, might resurface unexpectedly.

(4) *Ideology* plays a role in the formation, preservation or change of memories or their disappearance. Ideology is meant here as any body of knowledge or ideas that affects the memorizer and /or his media at one particular moment of the "history" of a certain memory.

Test Case. A Modern Event and Its Memories: Memory in Günter Grass's *Crabwalk*

As we shall see, the scheme can be applied to a complex society that has to come to terms with a horrendous past: postwar Germany. Here I have chosen a recent book by Günter Grass, *Crabwalk*, which was published in 2002.[3] The central theme is the issue of memory. I am not going to discuss memory in postwar Germany, which has recently been treated from different perspectives and concerning different sectors of the present German population (Moeller 2003, 147–81). My purpose is much more limited – namely, to demonstrate through this novella how Grass, a significant figure in the preservation and maintenance of German memory after the war, tackles memories and their media in contemporary German society. We shall see that the media of memory, their morphology and ideological setting within the society, play a critical role in certain segments of German society. Public memories in their various facets depend on the media that transmit them during a given time span.

Thus the media that figure in Grass are the Internet, historiography (i.e. historical narrative), monuments and models of historical artifacts, the "theatrical stage" (here film), the oral and written evidence of people who experienced the event and are still around to tell their story, and law (court procedures). Grass narrates the interplay and tensions that exist between all kinds of memory (collective,

3   See *Der Spiegel* 6 (2002). For the reader's convenience I use the 2002 translation by Krishna Winston, *Crabwalk* (London: Faber and Faber).

comprehensive, fragmented, individual, imposed and defined) and tells the story of their media within a small part of German society some decades after the end of World War II. He presents one fragment of memory, based on the sinking of the *Wilhelm Gustloff* on 30 January 1945, alongside many individual memories. The central character, Paul Pokriefke, who was born during the sinking of the ship recounts many personal memories of his mother as well as his own memories that were acquired from her and from other sources (p. 55 ff. and elsewhere).

The memory of this disaster achieved significance in modern Germany, being associated with the German expellees from the East at the end of the war.[4] Grass builds the narrative of the event itself, proceeding like a historian, using all kinds of sources. He constructs the historiography through surfing the Internet as well as combing other sources – personal, oral and written. There is something ironic about the fact that a single fictional historian (his hero is a journalist who wants to get the events straight) is capable of shaping a memory by walking like a crab (backwards, forwards and sideways). He concocts three main, different, historical narratives: one of Wilhelm Gustloff, the original victim; one of David Frankfurter, his murderer; and one of Marinesko, the Russian commander responsible for the sinking of the *Gustloff*. Working with this "trio," he attempts to combine them into a single coherent narrative, intertwining their stories with the memories he collects from survivors and other sources. The result of this strategy is that from under the surface of a recitation of events (the historical level), a written history of the memory of the event emerges. The sequence of events in this latter narrative of memory is linked by "stations" of commemoration (physical and spiritual), dispersed at certain junctures of time and space. For instance, David Frankfurter kills Wilhelm Gustloff, who falls down under the photographs of the Führer (p. 24); Gustloff's burial ceremony turns into a "media event" (pp. 31–6) and is followed by a public staging of Frankfurter's trial in Switzerland (p. 44). Then comes the ritual of the launching of the *Gustloff* on 5 May 1937 (pp. 50–3); the memorial

---

4   See Moeller 2001, 2003; and Confino 1998, esp. concerning the memories of the expellees.

service for the 50th anniversary of the sinking at Damp (p. 96: "No one mentioned publicly that this date happened to coincide with the takeover in '33 and the birthday of the man whom David Frankfurter had shot [...]."). There is frequent mention of the commemoration monument in Schwerin that was demolished (p. 168). Yet the main theme remains the history (or narrative) of a commemorative object, the ship *Gustloff*.

The story told by Grass deals with the murder of Wilhelm Gustloff, a senior member (*Landesgruppenleiter*) of the Nazi party in 1936, in Davos, Switzerland, by a Jew, David Frankfurter, and the legal procedures that led to his prison sentence. When Frankfurter was asked why he committed the crime he said: "I fired the shots because I am a Jew. I am fully aware of what I have done and have no regrets" (p. 25). A ship was later named after Gustloff, and its subsequent history is told in detail (a tourist boat, a hospital, etc.) until it was finally destroyed by a Soviet submarine in the Baltic on 30 January 1945. Nine thousand German expellees including children and elderly people perished in the freezing water:

> On 30 January 1945, fifty years to the day after the martyr's birth, the ship named after him began to sink, signaling the down-fall of the Thousand-Year Reich, twelve years – again to the day – since the Nazis' seizure of power (p. 6).

Perhaps not surprisingly, the four Russian torpedoes, three of which sank the ship, had a clear commemorative aspect:

> I must insert into this report a legend that has been passed down. Before S-13 left Hangoe Harbor, a crew member by the name of Pichur allegedly took a brush and painted dedications on all the torpedoes, including the four that were now ready to be fired. The first read for THE MOTHERLAND, the torpedo in tube 2 was marked for STALIN, and on tubes 3 and 4 the dedications painted onto the eel-smoothed surface read for THE SOVIET PEOPLE and FOR LENINGRAD (p. 138).

Yet the sinking of the *Gustloff* is but a tiny fragment (although an important one since it is the deadliest sea disaster in history) of the collective memory embedded in German society concerning its experiences in World War II. But this fragment became the principal memory of a small segment of that society (the few survivors and

some refugees), whereas the collective experience of the war became
vague (and distorted) in certain circles even soon after the war (the
process of *Verdrängung*); fragments such as the sinking of the ship
became their most meaningful memory for certain parts of the population. In the words of Grass:

> No one wanted to hear the story, not here in the West, and certainly not in the
> East. For decades the Gustloff and its awful fate were taboo, on a pan-German
> basis, so to speak. (p. 29) [...] All past, gone with the wind! Who still recalls
> the name of the leader of the German Labour Front? Along with Hitler, those
> whom people mention nowadays as all powerful are Goebbels, Goering, Hess.
> On a television quiz show, if questions came up about Himmler or Eichmann,
> some contestants might have heard of them, but most would draw a total
> historical blank [...] but who today, besides my Webmaster, bouncing around in
> the Net, knows anything about Robert Ley? (p. 36) [...] I don't want to go into
> all the circumstances that caused the doomed ship – forgotten by the entire
> world or, to be more accurate, repressed, but now suddenly roaming the Internet
> like a ghost ship [...] (p. 127).

Fragments of memory are either selected from a large arsenal of
past events or in some instances simply adopted because an oppositional group has selected them for its own purposes. (Some are unaware of certain memories.) This process of selection and adoption of
memories of various sorts is presented in *Im Krebsgang* in a masterful
manner. Pro- and anti-Nazi groups as well as individuals who have
access to the Internet and to other media such as books and cinema,
have selectively memorized what ideologically motivated them in the
first place to adopt this particular fragment from the German past.
One group commemorates the person of the Nazi official Wilhelm
Gustloff; another focuses on the memory of David Frankfurter, his
killer. Grass shows how memory is manipulated not only by individuals and ideologically oriented groups but also by time factors and
ideologically motivated officials. For instance, Grass illustrates with
ironic enjoyment that physical commemoration is not durable:

> That's how it goes with monuments. Some of them are put up too soon, and then, when the era of their particular notion of heroism is past, have to be cleared away. Others [...] remain standing (p. 177).[5]

It is no accident that the three commemorative monuments created for Wilhelm Gustloff during the narrative are destroyed (the ship, the monument and the model ship bought by the son of the narrator, Konny Pokriefke, a model that had stigmata symbolizing the three torpedoes that hit the *Gustloff*). Yet the memory remains.

Grass, as yet another of the voices writing about Germany as a victim of the war that have emerged recently (Friedrich 2002; Moeller 2003), emphasizes the victimization of Germans during World War II (in this case the drowning of thousands of refugees). But even more so, he points out that groups in the German society became the victims of their own fragmented memory. In the Federal Republic of Germany after the war, collective memory has undergone a process of fragmentation, and the accessible media (especially the Internet and films) are transforming this strong collective memory into alternative fragmented memories that sometimes even take its place or have their own life alongside it and become embedded in segments of the society. In modern times the media have received the role of archivist for forgotten memories that have to compete with other more famous events (that perhaps have received more publicity). This comes to the fore in Grass's remark concerning the film *Night Fell over Gotenhafen* (which tells the story of the *Gustloff*):

> Even when a film was made at the end of the fifties – *Night fell over Gotenhafen* – for which Schoen served as an adviser, it achieved only a modest echo. Not long ago a documentary was shown on television, but it still seems as though nothing can stop the *Titanic*, as if the Wilhelm Gustloff had never existed, as if there were no room for another maritime disaster, as if only the victims of the *Titanic* could be remembered, not those of the Gustloff (p. 63).

And later: "Banned in the East, the film [...] is now forgotten, like the unfortunate ship itself, submerged in the depths of archives" (p. 119).

Yet the modern media make memories and their fragments available at any time. They are just stored, to be selected by individ-

5   For monuments in Germany, see Koshar 2000.

uals or groups. The media have always been agents that transmitted memories but also had the effect of molding and distorting them. Grass makes his narrator complain:

> My son's web site made no mention of a Paul Pokriefke, not even in abbreviated form. Absolute silence about anything having to do with me (p. 157).

False and true, alternative and contaminated, memories are frequently imposed by the media. As with Aeschylus, who leads us to the imagined defeated camp of the Persians (false memory), it is a fictitious film that makes us imagine and memorize the last minutes of the victims of the sinking *Gustloff*. Real memory as opposed to false is here contaminated by fictitious pictures filmed in a studio long after the event:

> Such an attempt was undertaken by that black-and-white film, with images shot in a studio. You see masses of people pushing, clogged corridors, the struggle for every step up the staircase [...]. And you see children in the film. Children separated from their mothers. Children holding dangling dolls. Children wandering lost along corridors that have already been vacated. Close-ups of the eyes of individual children. But the more than four thousand infants, children, and youths for whom no survival was possible were not filmed, simply for reasons of expense; they remained, and will remain, an abstract number [...]" (p. 145).

The nature of present-day German society, socially and politically, and the length of time that has elapsed since the war, are factors to be taken into account when changes in collective and other kinds of social memory are discussed. And here I return to a connection one can make between Plato's objection to mimesis and Grass.

Memory according to Grass has a strong mimetic impact that may become dangerous. The son of the narrator, Konny, who sympathizes with a neo-Nazi group, takes on himself the role of Wilhelm Gustloff, whose history he learns from the Internet and from his grandmother's stories (pp. 95–100). Decades after the latter's murder, he kills a non-Jewish teenager who took on the role of the Jew Frankfurter during an Internet chat. The murder is performed where the ruins of the monument to the "martyr" Gustloff could still be deciphered:

Not until they were standing on the foundation of the old hall of honor, and my son explained to his guest exactly where the large memorial stone had stood [...] only then, when he indicated the sight line for the granite boulder, and recited the martyr's name on the front of the stone and then, word for word, the three lines inscribed on the back, did David Stremplin allegedly say, "As a Jew, I have only this to say," whereupon he spat three times on the mossy foundation – thereby, as my son later testified, "desecrating" the memorial site. Right after that, shots were fired (p. 187).

Fragmented memory in this story becomes fatal, since it moves a chain of events that makes history repeat itself. In fact, Grass shows that the Nazi past cannot just turn into normality, even if the Holocaust is eliminated from any postwar narrative. He mentions the Holocaust only briefly and in passing (pp. 13, 29, 50, 111, 160, etc.). For instance, at one point he says: "And when you in the West talked about the past, it was always about other bad stuff, like Auschwitz and such" (p. 50). The slight mention of the Holocaust is not because he wishes to show how normal Germany has become. On the contrary, since he is a novelist and not a historian, he wishes to present a realistic picture of groups in contemporary Germany – namely, segments that have adopted a single fragment of a collective memory, and ignore the other components of this collective "package deal."

To conclude this short survey: by emphasizing a narrative of memory of an event, Grass has played down its history. He shows how, within a pluralistic society, a minute fragment taken from the bigger collective memory can be activated by a segment. The breaking down of the collective memory into its components has taken its toll. Unpredictable consequences can arise from this very fragmentation and the wild adoption of memories by groups within the society.

Bibliography

Assman, A. and U. Frevert. 1999. *Geschichtsvergessenheit/ Geschichtsversessenheit: Vom Umgang mit deutschen Vergangenheit nach 1945*. Stuttgart: Deutsche Verlags-Anstalt.

Confino, A. 1998. "Edgar Reitz's *Heimat* and German Nationhood: Film, Memory, and Understanding of the Past." *German History* 16, 185–208.

Dan-Cohen, M. 1984. "Decision Rules and Conduct Rules: On Acoustic Separation in Criminal Law." *Harvard Law Review* 97, 625–77.

Dayan, D. and E. Katz. 1992. *Media Events: The Live Broadcasting of History*. Cambridge: Harvard University Press.

Francois, E. and H. Schulze (eds). 2001. *Deutsche Erinnerungsorte*. 3 vols. Munich: C. H. Beck.

Friedrich, J. 2002. *Der Brand: Deutschland im Bombenkrieg 1940– 1945*. Munich: Propyläen.

Hartman, G. H. (ed.). 1994. *Holocaust Remembrance: The Shapes of Memory*. Oxford: Blackwell.

Katz, E. and M. Popescu. 2004. "Supplementation: On Communicator Control of the Conditions of Reception." In I. Bondebjerg and P. Golding (eds), *European Culture and the Media*. Oregon: Intellect Books, 19–43.

Koshar, R. 2000. *From Monuments to Traces: Artifacts of German Memory, 1870–1990*. Berkeley: University of California Press.

Marcuse, H. 2001. *Legacies of Dachau: The Uses and Abuses of a Concentration Camp, 1933–2001*. Cambridge: Cambridge University Press.

Mendels, D. 2004. *Memory in Jewish, Pagan and Christian Societies of the Graeco-Roman World*. London/New York: Continuum and T&T Clark.

Moeller, R. G. 2001. *War Stories: The Search for a Usable Past in the Federal Republic of Germany*. Berkeley: University of California Press.

—. 2003. "Sinking Ships, the Lost *Heimat* and Broken Taboos: Günter Grass and the Politics of Memory in Contemporary Germany." *Contemporary European History* 12(2), 147–81.

Mueller, J.-W. 2000. *Another Country: German Intellectuals, Unification and National Identity.* New Haven/London: Yale University Press.

Nora, P. 1997. *Les Lieux de Mémoire.* 3 vols. Paris: Gallimard.

Olick, J. K. and J. Robbins. 1998. "Social Memory Studies: From 'Collective Memory' to the Historical Sociology of Mnemonic Practices." *Annual Review of Sociology* 24, 105–40.

Yerushalmi, Y. H. 1982. *Zakhor: Jewish History and Jewish Memory.* Seattle: University of Washington Press.

Zerubavel, Y. 1995. *Recovered Roots: Collective Memory and the Making of Israeli National Tradition.* Chicago: University of Chicago Press.

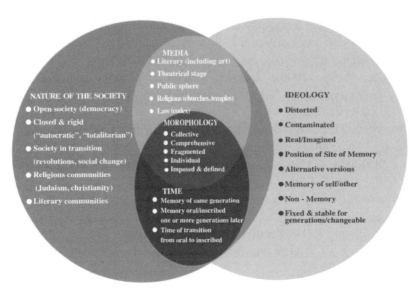

Figure 12.1 Public Historical Memory in Antiquity

Chapter 13

MOSHE SHOKEID

Anthropological Texts: Mirrored Memories of Researchers and Subjects

Abstract

This paper discusses the changes that have taken place in the status and use of memories in anthropological writings. From a strict avoidance until the late 1970s, we have witnessed a growing presence in contemporary ethnographic texts of accounts of both individual and collective memories. This exposition addresses some theoretical and ethical problems inherent in the ethnographic method when memories become part of its reports. I use my own works to illustrate some of the issues involved in this consequential transformation.

1

Received anthropological wisdom warns against using statements that people make about their past lives in constructing their histories.

Renato Rosaldo 1980, 31

In their ethnographic explorations, anthropologists encountered indigenous memory forms that did not seem to fit the European idea of historical time: an objective, unmediated, linear account of past events. By a focus on myths, ritual, oratory, and body practices, they uncovered the narrative and performance possibilities of a history of the present.

Linke 2001, 2220

When the conveners of the Jerusalem Interdisciplinary Meeting on Memory invited me to present a paper on anthropology and memory, I did not remember that I had already planned to write on the issue some fifteen years ago. It was only after I completed the Hebrew version of my paper that I found the aging handwritten pages and the attached bibliographical notes I had assembled for that earlier attempt. I do not recall now the reason I left that paper unfinished.[1] In any case, my first attempt must have been motivated by the experiences I endured during my two-year fieldwork (1982–4) among Israeli immigrants in New York. I was engulfed at that time by my informants' nostalgic, painful, or resentful memories of their lives prior to their departure from Israel. I also found, in the old envelope of my notes for the unfinished paper, a letter that had been sent to me by a close friend among the Israelis I had studied there. He was relating to the happy, as well as the aggravating, experiences my family must be going through on our return home. It was a letter based on his memories of the pleasures and pains of life in Israel. In the ethnography that presented my research in New York (Shokeid 1988), however, there is no indication of the term "memory" in the index.

My method regarding the use – or rather non-use – of memories in professional writing reflected the unique position of anthropology, in Britain in particular, in its treatment of memory as a social phenomenon. As expressed by the above opening excerpts from Rosaldo and Linke, the modern ethnographic tradition that started with Malinowski (1922) and Radcliffe-Brown (1952), and their colleagues and students since the 1920s had made a claim to offer descriptions and interpretations of human behavior based on direct observation. That method enabled its special viewpoint to be compared with other disciplines in the humanities and the social sciences, such as history, sociology and psychology. "Participant observation" endowed the ethnographic

---

1 It may well have been the difficulty of identifying a clear theoretical context that caused me to abandon the subject at that time. This drawback was also expressed recently by anthropologists engaged in research of memories: "One could characterize the field as being in a liminal state, a state of creativity and searching, on its way to a more comprehensive theoretical approach" (Cattell and Climo 2002, 36). See also a review article by Golden (2005).

fieldworker with data and understanding that could be gained only by researchers who made a commitment to live for a long period (at least one year) together with people they had not known before, but with whom they had come to share their lives as individuals, as family, as community members. That intimate knowledge was compared with the historian's reliance on documents, the sociologist's work based on surveys and questionnaires, or the psychologist's deep interviews that recorded memories from infancy onward.

That absolute reliance of anthropologists on direct observations seemed a flawless method. The subjects of their research in New Guinea, Africa and other Third World locations were mostly illiterate. They had no written tradition to record past events or other forms of cultural creations – such as religious texts or monuments that related their ancestors' deeds. These were the "savages" in the titles of Malinowski's influential ethnographies.

The stories and other oral presentations made by the people anthropologists studied, which came to display, for example, their specific group identities and narratives of creation, were interpreted as cultural traditions, myths, rituals and sacred taboos that confirmed such present-day forms of social life as the norms of kinship, the allocation of power and domination. The natives' reports were not perceived as evidence of past events to be counted as reliable historical records. This treatment of human memory as highly manipulative and malleable to serve changing circumstances and human needs was supported by the psychological research in particular (e.g. Bartlet 1950; Schachtel 1959; Strauss 1969).

2

These were some of the basic terms of research I emulated when I transferred in 1964 from sociology at the Hebrew University, dominated at that time by Parsonian theories, to social anthropology at the

University of Manchester.[2] The teachers and students at Manchester
were probably even more stringent than other British schools about the
careful collection of accurate field material. The prevailing mantra of
professional education at Manchester was: "Have your data right!"
Here was developed the "extended case-method," a way of presenting
field material in a series of related events observed by the ethnographer (e.g. Van Velsen 1967; Burawoy 1991). That method of
detailed and interrelated descriptions of observations in various
domains of social life enabled theoretical interpretation that combined
micro reality with macro environmental, economic, and political constraints and developments. The "past" in that perception of sociological structure was closely related to the period of fieldwork.

My apprenticeship as an anthropologist had been much influenced by an assignment given to me to report on an exemplary ethnography, *Lugbara Religion,* by John Middleton (1958). It related in great
detail a series of about thirty events of ghost invocation that Middleton
observed during a stay of one year in Uganda. This complicated story
of ritual machinations revealed a political process that culminated in a
change of leadership, the segmentation of a lineage and a new
allocation of economic resources. The head of the newly established
sublineage challenged the officially narrated story of the group's
genealogy and its legitimate leadership. Thus "history" was revised in
front of the diligent anthropologist, aimed to suit the changing economic and social circumstances of his subjects. I still consider
Middleton's ethnography a masterpiece demonstrating the intercon-
nections between religion, economy and politics. It also displayed the
flexible nature of what might be called "historical records."

For my own research project, I conducted eighteen months of
fieldwork in a village in Israel whose Jewish residents had immigrated
ten years earlier from a community in the Atlas Mountains of
Morocco. I joined them in the synagogue for daily prayers. I was a
guest at their tables for many meals and during family and communal
celebrations. I observed the meetings of the village cooperative organization and recorded the hectic discussions and often the more aggres-

---

2   The anthropology department in Manchester was founded and led for many
     years by Professor Max Gluckman.

sive conflicts that dominated relationships between the three kin groups that composed the community. I observed them regularly as they worked on their farms and went with them to visit their relatives in other parts of the country. I joined them on journeys to pay respect to famous rabbis or on pilgrimage to attend crowded celebrations at the tombs of saints. I went to bed after chatting with the sentries patrolling at night on their security duties.

However, when I returned to Manchester from the "field" with a load of "fieldnotes" and came to write my ethnography, I discovered that my thesis was focused on a time and social reality I did not and could not observe. As it turned out, major parts of my dissertation and later publications were engaged with the constant confrontation in the settlers' discourse about the stratification ladder that had existed in their community in Morocco prior to immigration to Israel (Shokeid 1971, 1985; Deshen and Shokeid 1974). I reached the conclusion that much of the conflict that I observed among the settlers in the Negev was actually a result of the constant role played by the past in their present lives. The farmers who were divided into three family groups, tried – each according to its members' benefit – to reconstruct or rather to undermine the former social status structure based on the occupation and economic position its members had enjoyed in Morocco. The family of traders, who had been considered wealthy and powerful in Morocco, made efforts to maintain their advantageous economic and social position in the new Israeli environment. At the same time, the craftsmen, who had had a lower status in Morocco, seemed determined to prove equal, or even superior, to their formerly better-off compatriots. When my turn came to report on my research at the Manchester departmental seminars, I felt I was caught in a difficult situation. I believed it was unacceptable in the forum of my teachers to treat the Moroccan Jews' references to their lives in a past time as indicating a social "fact." It seemed a sort of charlatanism to rely on data that could not be confirmed by official documents or written reports left by visitors to their community in the Atlas Mountains.

I found a solution to that predicament by defining my reference to the immigrants' past as a myth of some sort. Employing a measure of intellectual gymnastics, I denied the empirical dimension of my basic argument:

> On no account do I treat reports of the past by these people as implying an
> objective historical account; rather I employ the approach of Malinowski and of
> later studies to social history [...] as a social phenomenon whose "truth" may
> often be based in the logic of its relevant social context. (Shokeid 1971, 7 and
> 16)

I had no doubt, however, that what one would call "memories," alive and potent in the minds of my Moroccan subjects, were not a late manifestation of a somewhat invented reality suited to the immigrants' present circumstances. My perception of the stratification of kin groups in Morocco was supported by the stories – memories – continuously related to me by all parties to that social conflict. True, each side added a perspective that embellished the position of its membership in economic, social or moral terms; but I was convinced about the hierarchy that had dominated the lives of individuals and groups in their Atlas Mountains community. Thus my research of observations of the present life of former peddlers and craftsmen turned into farmers in Israel was much engaged in the record and analysis of memories from Morocco that continued to raise strong feelings of pride, resentment, vengeance, sorrow and pain.

My worries about the true nature of my sociological reconstruction of the immigrants' past lives were relieved a few years later when a linguist at Ben-Gurion University carried on research in the same community. Yaakov Ben-Tolila (1983) discovered that the different forms of speech he tracked in the daily habits of conversation and reading between subjects of the same age and gender could be explained by my thesis of the past social stratification between kin groups in Morocco. Members of the former wealthier group and their children had given up an accent closer to Arabic and adopted, instead, the more prestigious accent of Israelis of veteran Ashkenazi background. The memories I was careful to disguise under the shield of myth seemed now a reliable means of social reporting. At the same time, however, those memories carried a dynamic dimension, since they gave meaning to present circumstances of individuals and groups and were prone to manipulation in the service of new social needs.

3

The absence of memory from the anthropological dictionary is clearly visible in the *The Anthropology of Experience* (Turner and Bruner 1986). That collection of essays included a list of vanguard anthropologists who greatly contributed to new genres, concepts and metaphors in ethnographic writing. The term "memory," however, does not appear in the index of that volume. Nor can one find "memory" in the most detailed indices of the many books by Victor Turner, a towering figure in modern anthropology – who started his career in Manchester and developed some major concepts in the anthropological codex (such as "social drama," "liminality," "anti-structure"). It is puzzling: a method that was designed to study human behavior in close proximity to everyday demeanor and its banalities, yet denied in its records the importance of a major intellectual and emotional capacity as manifested in memory. No doubt, the founding generations of the study of anthropology made great efforts to separate the personal narratives they collected, and their interpretations, from the scientific domain of their colleagues, the psychologists. They were no less careful to avoid the risk of revealing a hidden temptation for a literary career, even though they all had the stuff for many exciting novels.

There were, however, a few "deviants" who were less strict in their perception of ethnographic writing. Oscar Lewis, in particular, reached a wide audience as he employed a literary model and style to present his subjects and their memories, adding only short introductory or concluding chapters that reflected his sociological viewpoints. For example, *La Vida* (Lewis 1967), a book of 800 pages that told the story of a Puerto Rican prostitute, Fernanda, and her family history across four generations. Only fifty pages of that captivating narrative of the economic struggles, family affairs and erotic life of Fernanda, her offspring and their partners were dedicated to the methodology employed by the author and his sociological conclusions. Nevertheless, his thesis about the "culture of poverty" raised much interest regardless of the unconventional ethnographic account. Lewis represented a minor genre in anthropology – that of life history – though

it sometimes also engaged mainstream ethnographers, particularly among American anthropologists. I mention in particular Mintz
(1960), Crapanzano (1980), Shostak (1981) and Eickelman (1985).
These life histories of ordinary or eccentric figures were chosen in
order to display a social type or a lifestyle that seemed to represent an
important element in the local culture. Life histories were based on a
mixed method – direct observations during a period of fieldwork, but
no less the reconstruction of past experiences of the subject and his/
her social environment (e.g. Langness and Frank 1991). The heroes of
these ethnographies were often unusual characters, such as Fernanda,
the assertive prostitute; Tuhami, the Moroccan man married to a
demon, presented in Crapanzano's ethnography; and Castaneda's Don
Juan, the most problematic character and a mystery in anthropology.
He is the shaman whose existence no one has ever confirmed. The
serious doubts about the nature of Castaneda's work did not affect the
marketing of his series on the life and teachings of his reported subject
and spiritual mentor, Don Juan (e.g. Castaneda 1968).

Although tempting, the method of life history was not adopted as
an important mode for ethnographic writings. The works and writing
style of Lewis and, in particular, Castaneda, raised suspicion and dis-
dain. Also Crapanzano's psychoanalytical orientation aroused some
uneasiness. Most anthropologists have been anxious to display in their
texts the sociological dimension they identified in the stories told by
individuals they encountered in the field. We have therefore witnessed
the anthropologists' continuing search for the connecting thread
between private memories and "culture." They have explored the
transformation of the stories relating to past experiences in terms of
myth, ritual, tradition, social conflicts and codes of behavior.

4

From the late 1970s, however, anthropologists started publishing ethnographies based on memories and making no effort to disguise the use of the term. This trend has recently been described as "the memory boom in anthropology" (Berliner 2005). I mention only a few that have aroused my interest: Myerhoff (1978), Rosaldo (1980), Herzfeld (1991) and Boyarin (1991). The titles of these ethnographies announced their engagement with time, something missing in earlier works. Myerhoff's ethnography, about the life of aging Jews who made their homes in Los Angeles after retirement, was widely acclaimed among anthropologists and reached also other audiences. Her book *Number Our Days* concentrated on the memories that took her subjects, members of a Jewish club, back to their earlier days of work and also prior to their immigration to America. Reconstructing the stories of their lives in America as well as in the East European *shtetel* created a social text shared by the participants in Myerhoff's study. That story of collective memory, though representing a somewhat idealized reality, helped them to display a coherent existential identity that overcame the difficulties and disappointments of their present life.

Rosaldo presented the sources of collective consciousness of a group of men in New Guinea based on their traumatic memories from the days of the Japanese occupation during World War II. These memories had been rooted in their minds as a period of violence marked by a series of headhunting expeditions. The stories displayed a formative stage in the life of twenty young men connected through marriage ties, who met the ethnographer about twenty years after that turbulent period.

Herzfeld's ethnography introduced the residents of a town in Crete who were engaged in the preservation of their old homes. They confronted the government and municipal rulings that disallowed changing the façade and structure of buildings considered a national heritage and a tourist attraction. The personal and family history – namely, memories and their close social context – seemed far more important in that discourse than official history and national pride of the Greek people.

Boyarin's ethnography, which told the story of Polish Jews who migrated to Paris before and after World War II, is reminiscent of Myerhoff's research among Jewish retirees in Los Angeles. The subjects – members of various *landsmanschafts* – were attracted to the ethnographer because they were anxious to communicate and save their memories of the loss of family, community and homeland.

Unwittingly, I got involved in a professional confrontation concerning the research of memories when I published a critique (Shokeid 1992a) of a study on the memories of elderly male residents of the West Bank (under Israeli control since 1967), who had participated during the 1930s in the Arab Revolt in Palestine (Swedenburg 1989). That revolt had been ignited against the rule and armed forces of the British Mandatory power, as well as against the growing presence of Jews in Palestine. In all the other studies mentioned above, the ethnographers were aware of the dynamics of their subjects' reconstruction of memories under the impact of circumstances and the social context of their present lives. But in this case, motivated by a personal commitment to his subjects and his own conception of the "truth" concerning the history of events that culminated in violence during the 1930s (causing the loss of life and property of Jews in particular), the ethnographer took the liberty to correct the text of collective memory as commonly recorded in Palestinian society. He decided to help create a myth not held by the urban elites of Palestinian society:

> The aim of my research was to uncover a popular memory of the 1936–39 revolt [...] I hoped that this obscured local remembrance might serve as a kind of corrective to the official Palestinian nationalist representations that tend to project a unified picture of the revolt and gloss over the importance of the popular classes (Swedenburg 1989, 266).

Moreover, Swedenburg admitted (and seemed to congratulate himself thereon) that his interviewees, by way of repeated sequences of silence in his presence, had concealed those memories that might have exposed their active participation in incidents of attacks on the bodies or property of their Jewish neighbors:

My study of these memories of revolt, related, in unstable present, has required an effort on my part to unlearn academic training in anthropology and history that compels one to unveil objective truth. The silences, resistances, dissimulations, avoidances, and hedging about the past that I encountered in fact have a greater "truth" value than supposedly neutral historical facts. This truth lies in an unequal relation to power, between occupier and occupied, between researcher and subject (p. 270).

I share Swedenburg's resentment of the Israeli occupation of the West Bank. Nevertheless, I could not condone the unabashed claim that an anthropologist is permitted to disregard the "truth" in order to prove his empathy for his subjects. By this method, the study of old Palestinians' memories turned into a text consciously rewritten by the ethnographer, who became an active partner in the reconstruction of memories guided by his own ideological beliefs.

In retrospect, one can comprehend that both Rosaldo and Swedenburg witnessed a similar phenomenon as the people they observed were going back in memory to reconstruct a violent traumatic period in their lives. The memories of violent acts – of stripping the heads of Japanese soldiers or those of members of other tribes in New Guinea – did not seem to present a moral or politically distressing issue for the researcher and his subjects. But the "honest" reconstruction of the history of violent acts of the 1930s aimed against unarmed Jewish neighbors presented a risky situation for the Palestinian interviewees now under the domination of a powerful Jewish state. I assume that readers remote from Swedenburg's field, yet sympathetic to the Palestinian cause, might not have greatly censored the ethnographer for the freedom he took in his eagerness to conceal or revise his subjects' memories.

I believe that the gained recognition of memories as a promising vehicle for ethnographic work was encouraged by the growing impact of reflexivity in anthropology. The genre demanded the researcher's increased presence in the ethnographic text to allow for better information about his relationships with the people he studied, as well as about his/her own feelings and role in the field (e.g. Rabinow 1977). Among those most visible in that popular stream in recent years, I relate to the writings by Ruth Behar. Behar made her reputation on the reports of her return journeys to the sites and society of her childhood in Cuba, from where her Jewish parents emigrated to the U.S. after the Castro revolution. This ethnographic trend is marked, sometimes by an emotional overtone. Behar claimed that the experience of loss and the preservation of a vanished world constituted a major achievement of the ethnographic project:

> Loss has been a classical trope of ethnography [...] Ethnography engaged in a language of loss, of preventing loss, of mourning loss. (Behar 2003, 20)

In all the texts mentioned above the authors transformed the memories that nourished the personal stories assembled in their field-notes into a coherent document that produced a collective memory representing the ethos of a particular group. This method applied a sociological strategy when the writers chose the framework for a para-digmatic narrative that suited their leading thesis (e.g. Hawlbachs 1992; Zerubavel 1996). It seems inevitable that they omitted from the final text those memories that did not harmonize with that leading conception. The researcher is thus always an active partner, whose role in the construction of the "collective memory" cannot be fully appreciated. In any case, the volume of memories included in the text and the rhetorical voice of the writers assure the impact of their ethnographic authority and the terms of their acceptance among the readers.

5

I return to my own ethnographies. In the studies that followed my work among the immigrants from Morocco, I also recorded observa-tions of behavior that continuously echoed memories of past existen-tial experiences. The Arab men I studied in Jaffa early in the 1970s (Shokeid and Deshen 1982) have endured the loss of national honor, the disintegration of their community and a change of personal status. My observations introduced a mixed group of Muslims and Christians who remained in Jaffa in 1948 when the majority of the local population evacuated their town (as they escaped to Gaza, Lebanon, Jordan, etc.). The quarter and its society presented a shabby replica of a major Arab city in Mandatory Palestine. The losses were evident at every corner of the streets of the poor suburb they had occupied since 1948, as well as in the type of leadership that replaced the former elites. Appointed by the government, a committee of trustees controlled the communal Muslim *wakf* property (endowments of land and buildings). My work focused on a group of young Muslims who tried to replace the corrupt leadership and retrieve some of the past reputation of their town.

The study of Israeli emigrants, nicknamed y*ordim*, in New York (Shokeid 1988) was much engaged in memories. A chapter I consider central to the ethnography described gatherings dedicated to the singing of Israeli folk songs. I observed Israeli men and women meeting in crowded halls, in community centers or elsewhere, excitedly singing old songs that raised images of such attractive sites, as the Lake of Galilee, Jerusalem, the Golan Heights and Mediterranean beaches in summertime. The songs and the participants' comments revived memories of experiences they cherished from their days of youth movements and army service. These were memories of a world left behind, now untainted by the less attractive facets of daily life.

In all these studies, I organized into conceptual frameworks the memories related in my presence, which gave them a timeless sociological meaning. Thus the Moroccans' memories of their community life prior to immigration to Israel were transformed into a theoretical vehicle I defined as the "reference situation." According to my interpretation, the Jaffa Arabs' expressed (and probably accommodated to) the trauma of the escape of the majority of their neighbors and becoming a minority in their home town, in the various manifestations of the Arab "code of honor." The Israeli y*ordim,* in their virtual journeys to their lost homeland, were presented in my text as engaged in a ritual activity, though of a secular character, which I identified as a type of "cultural performance."

6

Committed to a rigorous tradition of fieldwork, I believe that throughout my ethnographic work I have tried to maintain the role of a neutral
and uninvolved observer, the recorder of memories. I feel I was only
minimally influenced by my own personal interests. Naturally, I might
have harbored some social or ideological biases of which I was unaware. Recently, however, I confronted a situation of personal involvement when I prepared to report on the changes that had taken
place in Congregation Beth Simchat Torah (CBST), the gay synagogue in New York – a fieldwork project I started in 1989. That field
was very different from my earlier ethnographic sites. No longer a
separate ethnic community or a residential neighborhood, but an
institution that constituted a voluntary association.

During the major period of my work at CBST, the synagogue had
had no salaried employees. All tasks of organization and all roles of
religious leadership were performed by volunteers. The ethnography I
published in 1995 ended its description with my observations of the
process that had initiated the appointment of CBST's first full-time
salaried rabbi. I am presently writing an article designed to be the last
from that field. It records not only the transformation of a lay-led
synagogue into an institution run by salaried professionals (rabbis,
cantors and administrators), but also my own feelings about these
changes. I combine my reaction to the new situation, however, with
the responses of some among my close veteran informants (Shokeid
2007).

The changes of leadership and the new style of operation in the
religious and other domains of the organization have had far-reaching
effects. The composition of the congregation has changed dramatically
with the rapid increase of women in all ranks of the synagogue
structure. The patterns of activity and the status of the lay congregants
were radically altered, as were most positions of power; and all major
roles in ritual and liturgy were now being filled by the professional
staff.

I recorded the varied responses of several congregants to these changes; however, my own personal comfort and my position as a privileged observer had been affected by these recent events. On my renewed visits, I missed an important cohort among my friends – those who had died of AIDS or left for other places in the United States. Moreover, not a few among the veteran congregants had reduced their participation in the synagogue's affairs because they could not accommodate themselves to the changing social atmosphere and religious style at CBST. I discovered that, like my old acquaintances, I could not help comparing and judging the present social climate and religious style with my memories of life at CBST in the late 1980s and early 1990s. As a matter of fact, I often asked my interviewees: "What would Mel Rosen have said had he seen the present changes at CBST?" Rosen was the president who orchestrated the change of leadership, and he invested all his dwindling energies into convincing a reluctant congregation to hire a full-time rabbi. He passed away one week before the inauguration ceremony of the rabbi he had so wished to see as a promise for greater stability and clear direction at his cherished synagogue. The appointment of the rabbi served as a trigger for unanticipated changes in synagogue life.

Thus my laconic question, raised for the purpose of ethnographic interest, revived memories of the days when I had witnessed hectic arguments at public and private meetings about the pros and cons of the formal appointment of a full-time pulpit rabbi. All my acquaintances left from those days had no doubt that this was the turning point for all other changes. They acknowledged that they had gained a far more gentrified synagogue. They had gained public recognition also among mainstream Jewish constituencies; but they had lost the *heimish* (homey) atmosphere of a lay-led association of dedicated individuals who had created a Jewish space against all odds. Some male participants also felt the loss of what seemed in the earlier days to be a society dominated by gay men.

My field of research and my style of presentation differ from Behar's experiences and literary strategy, as manifested in the narrative of her return journeys to her lost homeland. I am more restrained in the display of emotions, but I experience a flush of memories when I recall, for example, Mel's (Rosen's) friendship, his warm reception of my presence and his openness as he revealed to me his plans and hopes for the synagogue. By the end of my first year of observations, and later during my visits in the early 1990s, I had felt I was welcome to attend all meetings and be privy to the guarded secrets and gossip of various factions at the synagogue. I felt I was treated as an intimate and respected friend. Now I feel that I have exchanged the robe of a neutral observer for that of a participant who naturally compares the present situation to a time past. The CBST field of today is radically different from that which I had observed about fifteen years ago. It is now an institution run by experts, who must be somewhat ambivalent, even reluctant about cooperating with an independent observer who might criticize their work.

A researcher coming today to conduct ethnographic work at CBST would reveal another world. He would also be relieved of my memories. Moreover, he would possibly relate to the memories of the veteran congregants of the cohort I had studied as a spiteful group, representing men, in particular, who relate to a refurbished past in order to justify, for example, their resentment of women. In any case, the notion of engagement with my subjects' memories seems much different than that revealed by Swedenburg. His involvement with the memories of elderly Palestinians was prescribed by an ideological position introduced by the ethnographer's political agenda. In contrast, my recent engagement originated from the experiences I had shared with my subjects. I "went native," to an extent. My "otherness" – a basic assumption in anthropological tradition, meaning the ethnographer's position of outsider – has been mutated to some extent. I share memories with veteran congregants and I therefore perceive the present reality at CBST, partly at least, screened through the same worldview as my subjects.

7

Beyond the special circumstances of my work today, however – as well as that of the more conventional ethnographic situations discussed above – I posit that the ethnographic text is – from an early stage of its creation – based on memory. The fieldnotes secured by the majority of ethnographers are already based on memory when they are composed in their notebooks or laptops. These fieldnotes are usually recorded soon after the observers' return to their residences in the communities they are studying, or elsewhere nearby at the end of a day or after a few hours of work. I confess that I was sometimes too tired to stay up and record my observations. I delayed the recording until next morning. Whenever that operation takes place, however, memory selection is involved. Moreover, since the ethnographic text is written much later, after the completion of the fieldwork journey, the anthropologists rereading their observations are again doing a work of memory. There is no way to examine the extent of selection, of emphasis and of omission in that process. That issue has been addressed by the contributors to a volume entitled *Fieldnotes* (Sanjek 1990):

> Fieldnotes as selective records of refracted past occurrences may not always accord with memory [...] Fieldnotes are part of a complex personal and collective negotiation of some past reality that contributes to the recounting and making of history, not just to its description and analysis. (Bond 1990, 276–8).

Ethnographic texts have been characterized in this article as accounts of memories of both the studied individuals and their researcher, screened through the impact of time, fieldwork circumstances and theoretical positions. These "memory ethnographies," however, differ also from the memory texts of sociologists and historians, because they do not explore contested memories – they are not involved with "mnemonic battles": "The most mnemonic battles are the ones fought over the 'correct' way to interpret the past." (Zerubavel 1996, 295).

By and large, anthropologists still maintain a methodological tradition of presenting a single compact collective image of the community they are studying. This is a community of memory that carries, for example: the shared identity of genealogical and marriage ties of headhunters in New Guinea; aging Americans in Los Angeles becoming representatives of the ethos of a reconstructed *shtetl* society; the shared memories of Polish-Jewish *landsmanshaft* communities in Paris; the veteran citizens representing the authentic owners and carriers of tradition of a town in Crete against the defenders of a Greek national heritage. Rosaldo and Swedenburg, for example, were associated throughout their research with one kinship or ethnic group. They developed a deep commitment to its membership, absorbed its conception of identity and identified with its traumatic memories. They were not engaged with the life and narratives of other local groups that might have contested the memory claims of the ethnographer's chosen people.

The method of personal participation in the lives of other people and their organizations denies the ethnographers – as honest and articulate as they might be – the restrained and "cool" position that sociologists or historians, though not necessarily neutral, can maintain in their work. The latter's obtainment of their research material does not engage them in a personal obligation to the subjects of their texts. The ethnographic text, however, does not allow a separation between the personality and memories of the researcher from that of his/her subjects. Using Victor Turner's style of metaphors, I would conclude with the following image:

> Had the participants of the ethnographic drama looked into a mirror, it would have been difficult if not impossible for the accidental onlooker to separate between the actors and their director.

8

One is naturally puzzled: what is the merit of ethnographic texts if, as I claim, they are so deeply compromised by memory? We should not, however, assume that historical descriptions are memory-free. As explicated by Mendels (2004) in his examination of the historical canon of the Graeco-Roman period, the canon based on stored memory is constantly studied and interpreted by every generation as needed for its collective memory at that time. Moreover, he concludes:

> The memories created or formulated within a group, a nation or any other organization for that matter, are at times independent and isolated from the realities in which they grow (ibid., 102).

Humans have been defined by various disciplines according to the unique characteristics that constitute their social and cultural being. In anthropology, it was often the innate skill to create symbols that seemed the jewel in the social crown. The more I think about it now, the more I feel that the capacity of individuals and groups to store memories – or rather the inability to forget the traumatic as well as the pleasurable events and sequences in their lives – are crucial indicators among the basics of our social being. Early in the last century, the founders of modern anthropology were anxious to de-lineate clear borders between their new subject and other neighboring disciplines, psychology in particular. Revolting against the generation of evolutionists in anthropology, they were also careful to avoid giving the impression of being pseudohistorians. Memories must have appeared to them as part of the kit of the psychologist, or the stuff of mythology, rather than reliable records of social history.

Today, however, the borders of anthropology are no longer secure from attack by outside or inside forces that might risk its disciplinarian purity and uniqueness. As much as other intellectual fields have borrowed, if not kidnapped, some of the domains of anthropology (cultural studies in particular), anthropologists have also borrowed from other methodologies and theoretical canons.

9

I began this paper with a story of finding the forgotten notes of an unfinished manuscript on memory in anthropology. I end with another recollection of an earlier presentation, but this time of a paper published about the same time –"Exceptional Experiences in Everyday Life" (Shokeid 1992b). It remained an unusual piece of writing in the record of my work, as it was not based on ordinary ethnographic observations in the company of "other people." Not only was the material for that paper based entirely on memories, it was also based upon my own self. My experiences and memories were the subject of the research. As argued earlier, it was acceptable in the late 1960s to interpret the memories I had gathered among Moroccan Jews as a sort of mythic discourse; but I would not have imagined at that time the possibility of ever contemplating writing a serious paper based on my own life experiences/memories and having it published in a mainstream professional journal. It took another twenty years before I could take that step and claim in the opening paragraph:

> The definition of fieldwork and the context of anthropological enquiry has been expanding rapidly in recent years [...]. I wish to take this liberty to record and try to comprehend a type of ethnographic experience [...] which I believe has not yet been considered a field for anthropological research (Shokeid 1992b, 232).

"Exceptional Experiences in Everyday Life" recorded a series of uncanny and often traumatic episodes, from childhood to adulthood, stuck in my memory though rarely revealed to family or close friends. I analyzed these unforgettable and eventful experiences as forming a type of hidden rite of passage that most men and women go through individually; they remain planted in people's consciousness as part of the process of social education. I suggested that these types of mini-dramas in our lives supplement the grand staged dramas that Victor Turner analyzed in his seminal essay on the liminal period in the *rites de passage* (Turner 1967). While the "grand staged dramas" (the ceremonies and tests prescribed by society) are visibly shared and similar in content, the "mini-dramas" stay with us as personal memories.

I assume that only a few of the people who are familiar with my work are aware I wrote that paper. It apparently represents a complete deviation from the professional ethos of the Manchester education "Have your data right!" How right would it be when you rely on the memories selected from your own life experiences?

I would certainly keep away from a memory flood or memory mania in anthropology. The new professional fads and genres are fruitful as long as they offer additional tools and perspectives to ethnographic work based on close proximity to the life *in vivo* of the people we study. Memories form an essential element in the lives of the people anthropologists meet on their fieldwork journeys, as much as those they meet in their own lives. How, then, can they afford to neglect these elementary facts of life in their texts?

Bibliography

Bartlet, F. C. [1932] 1950. *Remembering: A Study of Experimental and Social Psychology.* Cambridge, UK: Cambridge University Press.

Behar, R. 2003. "Ethnography and the Book That Was Lost." *Ethnography* 4(1), 15–39.

Ben-Tolila, Y. 1983. "The Sociophonology of Hebrew as Spoken in a Rural Settlement of Moroccan Jews in the Negev." PhD Thesis (in Hebrew). The Hebrew University of Jerusalem.

Berliner, D. 2005. "The Abuse of Memory: Reflections on the Memory Boom in Anthropology." *Anthropological Quarterly* 78(1), 197–211.

Bond, G. 1990. "Fieldnotes: Research in Past Occurrences." In R. Sanjek (ed.), *Fieldnotes: The Makings of Anthropology.* Ithaca: Cornell University Press, 273–89.

Boyarin, J. 1991. *Polish Jews in Paris: The Ethnography of Memory.* Bloomington: Indiana University Press.

Burawoy, M. et al. 1991. *Ethnography Unbound: Power and Resistance in the Modern Metropolis.* Berkeley: University of California Press.

Castaneda, C. 1968. *The Teaching of Don Juan: A Yaqui Way of Knowledge.* Berkeley: University of California Press.

Climo, J. J. and M. G. Cattell (eds) 2000. *Social Memory and History: Anthropological Perspectives.* Walnut Creek, CA: Alta Mira Press.

Craparzano, V. 1980. *Tuhami: Portrait of a Moroccan.* Chicago: University of Chicago Press.

Deshen, S. and M. Shokeid 1974. *The Predicament of Homecoming: Cultural and Social Life of North African Immigrants in Israel.* Ithaca/London: Cornell University Press.

Eickelman, D. 1985. *Knowledge and Power in Morocco: The Education of a Twentieth-Century Notable.* Princeton, NJ: Princeton University Press.

Golden, C. 2005. "Where Does Memory Reside, and Why Isn't It History?" *American Anthropologist* 107(2), 270–4.

Hawlbachs, M. 1992. *On Collective Memory.* Chicago: University of Chicago Press.

Herzfeld, M. 1991. *A Place in History: Social and Monumental Time in a Creatan Town.* Princeton: Princeton University Press.

Langness, L. L. and F. Gelya. 1981. *Lives: An Anthroplogical Approach.* Nevato, CA: Chandler & Sharp.

Lewis, O. 1967. *La Vida.* London: Martin Sacker & Warburg.

Linke, U. 2002. "Collective Memory, Anthropology of." In *International Encyclopedia of Social and Behavioral Sciences.* Oxford: Elsevier Science 4: 2219–23.

Malinowski, B. 1922. *Argonauts of the Western Pacific.* London: Routledge & Sons.

Mendels, D. 2004. *Memory in Jewish, Pagan and Christian Societies of the Graeco-Roman World.* London/New York: T&T Clark International.

Mintz, S. 1960. *Worker in the Cane: A Puerto Rican Life History.* New Haven, CT: Yale University Press.

Myerhoff, B. 1978. *Number Our Days*. New York: Simon and Schuster.

Rabinow, P. 1977. *Reflections on Fieldwork in Morocco*. Berkeley: University of California Press.

Radcliffe-Brown, A. R. 1952. *Structure and Function in Primitive Society*. London: Cohen & West.

Rosaldo, R. 1980. *Ilongot Headhunting 1883–1974: A Study in Society and History*. Stanford: Stanford University Press.

Sanjek, R. (ed.) 1990. *Fieldnotes: The Makings of Anthropology*. Ithaca: Cornell University Press.

Schachtel, E. G. 1959. "On Memory and Childhood Amnesia." In E. G. Schachtel (ed.), *Metamorphosis*. New York: Basic Books, 279–322.

Shokeid, M. (1971), 1985. *The Dual Heritage: Immigrants from the Atlas Mountains in an Israeli Village*. Manchester: Manchester University Press, (augmented edition, New Brunswick: Trans-action Books).

—. 1988. *Children of Circumstances: Israeli Emigrants in New York*. Ithaca: Cornell University Press.

—. (1995), 2003. *A Gay Synagogue in New York*. New York: Columbia University Press (augmented edition, Philadelphia, PA: University of Pennsylvania Press).

—. 1992a. "Commitment and Contextual Study in Anthropology." *Cultural Anthropology* 7(4), 464–77.

—. 1992b. "Exceptional Experiences in Everyday Life." *Cultural Anthropology* 7(2), 232–43.

—. Forthcoming 2007. "When the Curtain Falls on a Fieldwork Project: The Last Chapter of a Gay Synagogue Study." *Ethnos*.

Shokeid, M. and S. Deshen 1982. *Distant Relations: Ethnicity and Politics among Arabs and North African Jews in Israel*. New York: Praeger and Bergin.

Shostak, M. 1981. *Nisa: The Life and Words of a Kung Woman*. Cambridge, MA: Harvard University Press.

Strauss, A. L. 1969. *Mirrors and Masks: The Search of Identity*. London: Martin Robertson.

Swedenburg, T. 1989. "Occupational Hazards: Palestinian Ethnography." *Cultural Anthropology* 4(3), 265–72.

Teski, M. C. and J. J. Climo (eds) 1995. *The Labyrinth of Memory: Ethnographic Journeys*. Westport, CT: Bergin & Garvey.

Tonkin, E. 1992. *Narrating Our Past: The Social Construction of Oral History*. Cambridge: Cambridge University Press.

Turner, V. W. 1967. "Betwixt and Between: The Liminal Period in Rites de Passage." In V. Turner, *The Forest of Symbols*. Ithaca: Cornell University Press, 93–111.

Turner, V. W. and E. M. Bruner. 1986. *The Anthropology of Experience*. Urbana: University of Illinois Press.

Van Velsen, J. 1967. "The Extended Case Method and Situational Analysis." In A. L. Epstein (ed.), *The Craft of Social Anthropology*. London: Tavistock, 129–49.

Zerubavel, E. 1996. "Social Memories: Steps to a Sociology of the Past." *Qualitative Sociology* 19, 283–99.

Chapter 14

JONATHAN H. SLAVIN[1]

Personal Agency and the Possession of Memory

1 Memory

Consider the following episodes: in the late 1970s a professional man, B (not a psychotherapist), in his mid-50s, whom I had known casually for several years, asked to consult me. This was at a time before the topic of childhood sexual abuse and trauma, and the debate about whether memories of trauma could be forgotten and later recovered, had captured the attention of the public or the psychoanalytic community.

As he began, his eyes filled with tears. He said he didn't know what to make of what had happened to him or what to do about it. His daughter, he said, a woman in her mid 20s, had been seeing a therapist and had developed the belief that she had been sexually abused by him. She claimed to have memories of the abuse, although she had not said specifically what she thought had happened. As a result of her work with this therapist she had become very angry and had cut off communication with him.

1   An earlier version of this chapter was originally published as "Memory, Dissociation and Agency in Sexual Abuse" in: R. Gartner, *Memories of Sexual Betrayal: Truth, Fantasy, Repression, and Dissociation.* New York: Aronson 1997. Some of the central ideas discussed here emerged in work with my colleagues Linda Pollock, PsyD, and Miki Rahmani, MA. Thanks are due to Patricia Hertz, LICSW, Mary Loughlin, Laura Heideman, LICSW and Jessica Slavin, MSW, who were exceptionally generous in their substantive suggestions on this discussion.

B was distraught at the breakdown in his relationship with his daughter and felt totally bewildered by the accusation. He knew of nothing, he told me, that would even hint at the development of memories such as his daughter was claiming. As he sobbed quietly and talked, he began to wonder, could it be that he had done something that he didn't know about? How else could he account for what his daughter was saying? His despair was palpable, as he looked not only at the destruction of his relationship with his daughter but also at the destruction of his own sense of the believability of his own mind and experience. B was not a drinker, he had suffered no known trauma in his own development, and he had achieved a position of prominence and trust in public affairs. And he didn't know what to do. He felt helpless, immobilized and trapped in the face of these accusations. It was as though reality had taken a weird, sick turn and he was looking at the world and his own experience through a bizarrely distorted mirror, as if at a carnival, but a carnival of horror.

Ten years later a young woman, L, is sitting in a psychology course listening to a lecture about the now increasingly public issue of sexual abuse. She listens, riveted, as the professor talks about the pervasiveness of sexual abuse, about the phenomenon of dissociation,[2]

2   The phenomenon of dissociation, discussed in detail later in this chapter, refers to what happens when an individual experiences a kind of "split" or fracturing in his or her conscious attentiveness. It has nothing to do with schizophrenia. Normal, everyday correlates of dissociation occur when we are, for example, riding in a car, bus or plane and suddenly attend to the fact that we had been lost in thought for some time, minutes or longer, without noticing the time or scenes passing by, and often not remembering exactly where our minds had been. Often thought to occur in reaction to unbearable trauma, the individuals who dissociate may feel as though they are watching themselves experience something, but at the same time feel removed from it. Sexually abused children will often remember their minds floating to some corner of the room while the abuse was occurring but not attending to, or remembering the details of, the abuse itself. Survivors of violent trauma, soldiers as well as other victims, may remember the trauma in a removed way, as if in a dream state. They may recall going through the aftermath, even performing heroic deeds, without feeling fully present. More severe versions of dissociation can be found in cases of significant psychogenic amnesia, multiple personality states and fugue states (a person may wind up in another city, many hours or days away and not know

and about the loss of memory in trauma. As she listens she remembers, for the first time since it happened, experiences of abuse by a male relative twelve years older than herself, when she was between the ages of five and ten. In the moment of recollection her mind splits. One part of her "knows" that she is remembering something real, something that actually happened, that she had not remembered before. Another part of her mind disbelieves it. It couldn't have happened. She must be remembering it wrong. And she feels completely crazy because there will be no way to resolve this question.

Indeed, L had felt almost completely crazy all of the time since the age of ten. Although she was a brilliant student, who presented an outwardly engaging and competent persona, she engaged in emotionally hungry relationships, which ultimately became abusive, in an effort to stabilize herself. For twenty years she had lived in a world where her perceptions swirled, and in an experience of never being able to know, let alone assert, her own point of view, will or desire. Now her life is one of constant, deep and overwhelming panic and frantic clinging to any relationship in sight.

Three years later L is in a treatment in which the history of her abuse is understood as related to her experience of internal chaos and fragmentation. She is haunted by her memories. Should she believe them? She feels enraged when she thinks they are true. Should she confront the relative? What if he denies it? It will destroy her mind even more if he denies her reality. Yet the need to verify her memory obsesses her. With the encouragement of her therapist, and with the greatest panic she has ever felt, L finally confronts her abuser and tells him what she remembered. He acknowledges it fully.

For L there is enormous immediate relief and her therapist feels that just as important as the verification was L's capacity to undertake

how they got there, or perhaps even who they are). In contrast to the psychoanalytic concept of "repression," which includes the idea that thoughts and feelings are actually repressed or forgotten, buried in the depths (a kind of horizontal split with some conscious thoughts on top and unconscious ones below), dissociation often implies a "vertical" split, in which one may move from one state of consciousness to another, sometimes aware of, but not truly "present" in, the other state. An experience of dissociation is described in the next example described here.

the confrontation. Yet, to the surprise of both of them, there is no real change in L's internal condition. Although she is well on her way to becoming an effective, even gifted professional, her internal world is still experienced as utterly fragmented, frightening, haunted and swirling, with an inability to locate her own reality and her own experience in some reliable way. And it continues to be reflected in the disturbed and disturbing relationships she has. The therapist is deeply troubled. What more needs to be done to restore L's psychic integrity?

Some months later an episode occurs (Slavin, Rahmani and Pollock 1998) in which L and her therapist are in a moment of acute confrontation about something that has occurred between them. In one of those moments in which thoughts race blindingly across one's mind, the therapist recognizes the truth of L's perception and, although it is acutely discomforting for him, he takes responsibility for his role in what has occurred. Although in some ways similar to the confrontation with the abuser, in this instance the work around the resolution of what had happened between L and her therapist produces a dramatic and permanent change. In the ensuing months L finds a sense of anchorage in the world, and in her own mind, that she had never known before.

Another episode: a graduate student, M, a woman of unquestionable decency and integrity, is telling her therapist about the child care she does to earn extra money for her graduate studies. She recounts a recent instance in taking care of a three-year-old boy. The boy feels abandoned by his parents, both of whom are away much of the time while they are consumed in starting a new business. The student has established a very warm rapport with this little boy and enjoys taking care of him. She is appalled at the emotional coldness and even harshness she sees in the way the parents respond to him when they are around. She is troubled by an episode that had happened that very day. The boy had been very upset in the morning when the parents left. But afterwards he had calmed down and he and M had spent their usual time together. When the parents returned he became frantic, ran to his mother and said that M had hurt him on his penis. M was amazed when she heard this. She surmised that in some way this had to do with a desperate effort to re-engage the parents. As the therapist heard this he had no question there was any possibility that M would have abused this child. He imagined that her hypothesis about the dynamics of this episode was correct. Yet he also imagined that at some time in the future this boy could retain as a "memory" a recollection of a time when he had been taken care of by a babysitter, or someone, who had abused him genitally and that this recollection could be held with very genuine conviction about its veracity.

One final vignette: a therapist is meeting with the mother and aunt of a young woman recently hospitalized after severe dissociative and suicidal episodes. During these episodes the patient had visions of being sexually abused by her mother when she was 7 and 8 years old. In the meeting with the therapist the mother seems a bit too happy, under the circumstances, that "this has finally come out." She says she had asked her daughter, "whose face is it that did this to you? It's not my face you are seeing, honey." She says that when she finds out who did it, "with my face," she will, "kill them." The therapist feels deeply suspicious of the mother, but, he thinks, "Who knows?" At the conclusion of the meeting the mother, a very large woman, rushes up to therapist, throws her arms around his neck, and plants a huge kiss on his face. "You have saved my daughter's life," she says. The therapist feels angry, intruded upon with this uninvited, almost assaultive, physical intimacy and leaves the meeting convinced that the mother was, indeed, the abuser.

So what is going on here? Whom shall we believe? The mother, the daughter, or the therapist's angry conviction in the wake of what just happened to him? Shall we believe the professional man, or his daughter? The graduate student babysitter, or the three-year-old boy? And who will this boy's therapist believe if he carries this "memory" with him into his adult life? And what shall we understand from the failure of L's absolute verification of her memory to alter the damage done to her internal experience and her psychic integrity?

This entire issue is about the need – of the therapist and of the patient – to know what happened, and the need to resolve the question of memory, true or false. Therapists from all perspectives are trying to address this question and approach some way of resolving it; or if not resolving it, finding some stable way of viewing it. But as Davies (1997) states:

Both sides have proven their point; (1) the details of memory are unstable and subject to change over time, particularly influenced by the interpersonal situation in which they are articulated; and (2) the differences between normal memory and traumatic memory are significant, and overwhelming evidence for [...] traumatic amnesia [...] exists throughout the trauma and experimental-cognitive literature (pp. 49–50).

But if both sides prove their point, we are left in a quandary: what shall we do about the patient's memories and the patient's urgent need to validate them? Part of our problem has to do, I believe, with how little we actually know about memory, traumatic or otherwise. Yes, there is increasing research; but if we think about the study of memory in a historical context, human memory has been studied by psychologists for only a very brief period of time. In a sense we can say it began a little over a hundred years ago with Freud's early explorations and understandings of trauma. One hundred years, and not very consistent ones at that. Is it safe to assume, on the basis of the way scientific exploration tends to develop, especially current and future brain research, that in 100 or 200 or 500 years our current struggle to understand memory will seem primitive to our successors? There is so much we don't know and we are only beginning to learn.

Yet we need to know. We need to resolve the issue. Some need to find the truth in the memories and others need to believe in their falseness. Still others try to deal with the problem by suggesting that memory is not the central issue; rather, that the issue is about narrative, or about multiple self-states, or about politics. But whether one addresses the problem of memory in abuse as either true or as false, or tries to resolve it in some other way, there is an urgency about the matter. Clarifying what we understand about memory, especially memory in trauma, seems very important.

Why is memory so important? It seems we, those of us who are therapists, share with our patients some feeling of profound urgency to resolve the question: our patients' question about what happened; and our question, about whether we can believe them. Perhaps it is possible here to frame a larger question: not only what this urgency is about, but what actually happens to people to make them "lose" their memories, and what that tells us about the function of psycho-therapists. Is the therapist's task to help patients retrieve their memories or to resolve or relinquish their urgency, or is it something larger?

2   Narrative Memory and the Development of Agency

In this discussion I will try to address one reason why the question of memory and its believability stirs such an intense urgency in our patients and in psychotherapists' view of their professional endeavor. In developing this perspective I will suggest a way of understanding the search for validation and proof in which patients engage, as well as our own search for proving and validating something about memory. I will relate this perspective to what I believe is one of the core issues affecting therapists and their patients in working with the question of sexual abuse as well as other forms of trauma.

In an earlier paper, a colleague and I (Slavin and Pollock 1997) suggested that the attainment of a capacity for narrative memory – that is, the ability to verbally articulate an account of our own history and of the story of our selves in a way that is experienced with a sense of coherence and continuity – emerges out of complex developmental processes in infancy and early childhood. The capacity for narrative memory requires that the individual develop a sense of self as separate from others and as separate from his or her immediate engagement in some affectively motivated action. Framing our discussion in the terms of Irene Fast's (1985) "event theory," we suggested that although the infant is, from birth, highly engaged with her environment – something that has been amply demonstrated in infant observation research – the infant is initially not internally differentiated from her immediate engagement in whatever highly charged, affectively motivated action is taking place. For example, the infant suckling hungrily at the breast is embedded in that activity and is not capable, initially, of thinking of herself in some other event or action, such as the one that may have momentarily preceded it (the infant crying hungrily in need) or the one that might follow it (the infant calmly sated).

Only as cognitive processes mature, in the context of reasonable and predictable interpersonal experiences, does the infant become capable of extracting herself, so to speak, from her embeddedness in an immediate event and thinking about herself as separate from that moment. At the same time she becomes capable of thinking about others in her environment as also separate from the moment and from herself. In a gradual maturational process, the infant becomes capable of standing somewhat apart from her own immediate needs and urgencies, thinking about her actions before immediately acting on them – that is, being able to be separate from the action – and thus is able to become a motivated, rather than simply a driven, being.

Put in other terms, we were suggesting that the development of a cohesive and coherent sense of self corresponded to that level of self-other differentiation, and emotional and cognitive maturation, which is represented by a sense of personal agency.[3] Fundamentally we sug-

3   The experience of personal agency, as a psychological concept, is adapted from the usage of the terms "agency" or agent in daily English language usage (it is of interest that some languages do not have such a term and they may simply borrow the English language term and meaning. What this implies about cultural differences and mindsets is for another discussion). In an everyday sense, an agent is an individual or entity that acts on one's behalf, or is capable of acting on behalf of another person. Thus we have travel agents who act to arrange our travel itineraries, talent agents who act to secure contracts for our performances, or other "agents," such as lawyers, who act as advocates for us. The Indo-European root of agent is "ag" with the primary connotation "to drive, draw, move," [author's note: "draw" used as in "draw or pull in," connoting a sense of force and movement] (eReference Suite, 2004). The concept of personal agency implies the ability to act for oneself, on one's own behalf; however, the term is not about concrete action but rather the ongoing feeling or experience that one can be one's own agent in the world and in one's own experience of it (whether we actually accomplish what we wish or not). It is the mental or psychological sense of mattering, of being able to have an impact, that indicates a developed or mature sense of personal agency.

The concept of agency can perhaps be more clearly delineated in its absence or disruption. When patients come for psychotherapeutic treatment, their concerns can often be understood as statements about the disturbance in their sense of agency and of the feeling that they can be agents in their own lives. For

gested that it is the capacity to experience one's self as an agent of one's actions, feelings and interpersonal relationships that enables the individual to feel not simply at the mercy of either internal urgencies or the will of others. Most centrally, we suggested that it is the establishment of a sense of agency which permits the individual to have the ordinary capacity for narrative memory in which one can tell one's own story. It is not that the individual needs to be the causative agent in all remembered events. Rather, it is the capacity to experience oneself as an agent, as separated from the events and from the others in them – indeed as separate to some extent from, and something more than, one's own motives – that allows one to articulate and tell a story that feels as though it is about one's self.

Although some of the current psychoanalytic literature written from a "relational" perspective suggests that earlier ideas of the self as a cohesive unit may be less useful than thinking about the development of non-pathological multiple self-states – that is, different self-states in different relational configurations (Bromberg 1994; Mitchell 1993) – I am suggesting something more basic to ordinary human experience – namely, that most of the time, most people *think* of themselves – and experience themselves – as having a cohesive and coherent self; and that such a self-experience is equivalent to experiencing one's self as an agent in one's own life as well as to having the capacity for narrative memory.

In our articles (Slavin and Pollock 1997; Pollock and Slavin 1998) we also suggested that what most fundamentally occurs to the

example, when an individual says that she feels things she wishes she were not feeling, or she finds herself doing things she wishes she did not do, or when an individual says he cannot do the things he wants to do and knows he should do – whether it is as trivial as coming on time to an appointment or as important as making a serious commitment in work or in a relationship – all these kinds of issues are, on the face of it, disturbances in agency. These include concerns about how one relates in one's personal and business life, failure to move ahead in certain ways, inhibitions, repetitive self-defeating actions – indeed, the full gamut of conflicts patients present when seeking therapy. These concerns represent an inability to feel the agency or authorship of one's feelings and actions, or the inability – the lack of agency – to put them into action and try to accomplish what one hopes to accomplish.

psychic integrity of someone who has been sexually abused (as well as in some other forms of trauma) is not primarily the confounding of memory but the destruction of the core experience of personal agency that forms the foundation for a secure sense of narrative memory. In the confusion of the child's motives, the obfuscation of reality ("It's not my face you are seeing, honey."), the toying with meanings and events, the crazy-making redefinition of pleasure and pain – in the moment of experiencing one's self instantaneously as both the helpless victim and the omnipotent perpetrator – the child's maturing and differentiated sense of self and of self as agent, and consequently self as able to securely remember, is irrevocably damaged.

Viewed in this context, memory is extraordinarily important. It is important not simply in terms of establishing the "truth" or validity of some past experience. *Rather, memory is important because it carries our sense of self, our sense of a cohesive self, our story as a person in some cohesive fashion.* But is it memory that coheres us, or is it agency? Davies (1997) comes closest to describing the narrative sense of memory that I am equating with an experience of personal agency when she states that "those experiences that can be […] affectively modulated and […] encoded linguistically within memory systems... will essentially come to form the 'glue' of psychic integrity […]." But for memory to be "linguistically encoded," for it to be able to form the "glue of psychic integrity," requires a sense of "I," a sense of a self as an agent in relation to others. This is the kind of memory we talk about in ordinary conversation: "*I* did this or *I* did that, or that happened to *me*."

Several writers in this area (e.g. Gartner 1997) suggest that part of what happens to memory in cases of traumatic sexual abuse is that the events that have occurred are not known, as Davies puts it, "in the traditional way, because they have never succeeded in being fully known in the first place." In traumatic abuse, the events have never been, "allowed to be linguistically encoded, constructed and discussed" (Price 1997). In developing a perspective of agency as a core experience in the attainment of a mature sense of a differentiated self, I am suggesting that the problem with memory in traumatic sexual abuse is *not* a failure of linguistic encoding per se. Rather, the failure to linguistically encode the memory is part of the symptom of something far more basic. What has happened is that the events have not been integrated into the individual's sense of self and sense of agency. There can be no meaning without a sense of personal agency, and no way of cognitively organizing events where agency has been damaged. Price (1997) states that "language provides us with a way of describing and signifying experiences"; but for the sexually abused and traumatized patient to be able to describe the experience in language requires being able to take some agency in it – and this is what has been lost, or rather, destroyed.

In this context, I am suggesting that we reverse the equation found in discussions of the effects of trauma in which the instability of memory is seen as giving rise to an instability in the self. I am suggesting that when agency is taken away or toyed with, it is memory that then becomes unstable. As Davies notes, memories are particularly influenced "by the interpersonal situation in which they are articulated." The interpersonal situation in sexual abuse and trauma destroys agency. And memory, common narrative memory, disappears in its wake.

A published case discussion (Price 1997) is especially illustrative of the way the issue of agency – masked as a discussion of memory – comes to predominate in the treatment of patients who have been sexually abused. In that case, the patient had had a dream suggesting that she might have been abused by her father. She brought this to a therapist, who did not take it as evidence that incest had occurred. She then took it to a local women's center who confirmed that her dream indicated an incest history. She was then referred to another therapist who was an expert in this area. What took place in the treatment was a struggle between the patient and her therapist about who would be the agent of her memory. The patient, "demanded certainty and definitive interpretations. She felt she could not work with a therapist who could not validate her or overcome the patient's doubts or blockages to know the truth" (Price 1997). Ultimately, the patient left treatment because the therapist could not validate the patient's history, despite her efforts to explain to the patient why she could not.

In this struggle, the patient wanted the therapist to be an unequivocal agent, something she could not be in her own life. Thus I wonder whether – if the therapist had understood the issue as a

struggle over agency rather than as a struggle over memory or validation – they might have fought this battle out in a more productive
way. The transference-countertransference[4] battle, from this perspective, was not about the patient's memory, but about who was going to
own what as an agent in the treatment relationship.

The urgency of this patient's need for validation of her memory
is not, as I have noted, uncommon and is something many psychotherapists who have worked with patients with an abuse history have
confronted. I believe, however, that therapists may have misunder-
stood something about what this urgency represents. What is it that the
patient so desperately needs and wants? The patient I described
earlier, L, while experiencing some relief, got very little more out of
the full validation of her memory by her abuser.

Let me be clear here: I am not opposed to memories being validated, especially in abuse, and it can be very helpful. Moreover, I
believe the great majority of times that patients sense that something
terrible happened *is* a generally reliable indicator that something
terrible happened, even if we don't know exactly what it is. What I am
suggesting is that often therapists and others, like patients, have
mistaken and substituted the recovery of memory for the recovery of
agency. The urgency to validate and verify the memory, to obtain, as
Etan Lwow, MD (personal communication) has put it: "The groveling
confession of the perpetrator," is not simply an urgency to remember
something that may or may not have happened. Much more
fundamentally, it is an urgency to recover a cohesive and coherent
sense of self with a capacity for efficacy and agency in the world.
Trauma does not just alter memory. In a fundamental way, through
processes of dissociation, the cohesive and coherent sense of self is
changed as well.

---

4   That is, how the therapist and patient were each perceiving the other through the
      lens of their own histories and emotional need states.

3   Dissociation and Agency

What about the phenomenon of dissociation that so frequently accompanies the trauma of abuse? What is dissociation? And how is it related to the issue of memory and agency? Dissociation has been well documented and described in the psychiatric literature. But how do we currently really understand it? Does it differ from repression, and if so, how? Perhaps most importantly, how do we understand the role, or the agency, of the trauma survivor in the dissociative process?

Davies distinguishes between repression and dissociation by suggesting that repression is related to the conception of a "static" unconscious, while dissociation emerges from a picture of a "relational unconscious," in which memory is embedded in the nature of internal and external relational events. In this perspective, dissociation, as a relational event, replaces repression as a more purely intrapsychic one, in terms of how we understand the process by which events and their emotional meaning are put at a distance from ourselves.

However, another way of viewing the difference between repression and dissociation is to examine how we understand the patient's agency in the process of the undoing of their memory. The concept of repression emerges from a psychoanalytic, internal conflict perspective and implies a certain personal, if unconscious, agency in the process. The individual, as agent, represses in order to accomplish a critical internal task, to resolve or try to resolve some difficult inner struggle. In this sense she is the agent of the sequestering of her memory. She does it for a purpose.

Our understanding of the role of agency in dissociation is less clear. In contrast to repression, dissociation seems related to concepts of damage to, or deficit in, the self arising from early relational deprivation and trauma. From this point of view the individual is not seen as the agent in the occurrence of her own troubles. It is something that happens to her because of something that was done to her, rather than something she actively or "agentically" does. An observation by Frawley-O'Dea (1997) captures the loss of agency in the dissociative process: trauma survivors, she says, "cannot remember, [but] they cannot forget [...]" To remember is an active process, requiring agency; to be unable to forget suggests something beyond one's own agency, outside of one's will, control or desire.

Put briefly, the conundrum is this: is the dissociated memory and the kind of fragmentation and internal splits that occur with trauma survivors, *something that happens* to the individual or is it *something they do*? And just who is doing this? Is the patient the agent, or is this an eloquent *description* of something happening to her?

If anything can be said to characterize the phenomenon of dissociation as it occurs in abuse, it is the patient's experience of having no agency in the process. It is something that happens, something they do not, or cannot, control. Thus we are left with a dilemma: should psychotherapists believe their patient's experience or should they believe their theories? The question touches on some of the most fundamental philosophical and theoretical differences in psychoanalysis in terms of how we think of agency, personal responsibility, the sources of our difficulties; in short, as Spezzano (1993) has phrased it, whom shall we blame?

This brief discussion (indeed, even a longer one) cannot attempt to resolve these questions. However, I wonder whether in our efforts to understand dissociation we have not conflated the issues of memory and agency. *The inaccessibility of memory, or at least narrative memory, in dissociation is the end result of the process. It is the symptom.* But the underlying statement, the communication that dissociation makes – whether we see our patients as agentically doing it, or as something that overcomes them – is that they have no control in the process. Whether, in a broad philosophical sense, the patient is or is not the agent of the dissociation, the phenomenon itself – and our difficulty in resolving its motivational sources – is perhaps the most eloquent statement of how agency has been disrupted. Dissociation is the core communication of a loss of the experience of being an agent in one's own experiencing. Viewed in this way, the undoing and healing of dissociation is not about retrieving memory, however encoded. It is about restoring agency.

5 Clinical Implications: The Restoration of Agency

While current postmodern views argue against maintaining absolute dichotomies of knowing versus not knowing and true versus false, the reality of working with patients who may have been sexually abused, and other trauma survivors whose memory is disrupted, is that they either were or were not abused; they do, or do not, remember in some way; and there is no way to overestimate their need to know. Patients who have been abused – perhaps most patients – are not happy with a postmodern resolution of their own histories. They want to be re-connected to their histories in order to feel that they have a cohesive self (whether therapists acknowledge that they do or don't have one).

I believe that, despite their denials, therapists also want and need to know. They want and need to know not so much whether the patient was or wasn't abused – although they want to know that too – but they want to know what they are doing, and that what they are doing is good and useful. Therapists, like everyone else, want and need their own sense of agency; it is only with the greatest difficulty that we all live with uncertainties. To combat them we have symposia, we publish books and papers, we construct theories – we do research, all to accomplish the task not only of forwarding our understanding, but of reassuring ourselves that we are in fact agents in our own professional journey on this planet. Patients and others with traumatic histories want and need no less. In a sense, all individuals must be positivists in some fashion in their personal lives in order to feel whole and feel they have a place in the world. That is, they have to be able to be the definer of their own realities. This is what is robbed from those who have experienced sexual abuse and trauma, and along with that, their memory.

What are the clinical implications of this complex picture? This is the core question for psychotherapists. And it is compounded by the uncertainties therapists face in what they can reasonably claim to know about the effects of abuse at a moment in time when the very fundamentals of their expertise are challenged. The so-called "false memory" movement has had a disturbing effect on psychotherapists.

Therapists too have had their sense of agency damaged by the controversy over memory and, I believe, have taken on the term "false memory" too easily, putting definitional power in the hands of others. The power to define our reality is the power of agency, and at this moment in time the therapeutic community finds itself in something akin to the emotional situation of their patients. The power to define reality has been usurped. How can those of us who are therapists return it to ourselves, reclaim our agency in our own work, without falling into simple dichotomies and solutions?

In a remarkably prescient paper, Sandor Ferenczi (1933) comments on the importance of the psychoanalyst's ability to be able to acknowledge error, to say what has been left unsaid in the relationship with the patient. The pivotal effect of that, he says, is:

> The setting free of [the patient's] critical feelings, the willingness on our part to admit our mistakes and the honest endeavor to avoid them in the future, all these go to create in the patient a confidence in the analyst. *It is this confidence that establishes the contrast between the present and the unbearable traumatogenic past,* the contrast which is absolutely necessary for the patient in order to enable him to reexperience the past no longer as *hallucinatory reproduction but as an objective* memory (ibid., 160; latter emphasis added).

Ferenczi's observation suggests a way in which we can begin to think about what, from the point of view presented here, seems to be the primary task in treatment of patients who have been abused: the restoration of the patient's agency and psychic integrity. In his comments, Ferenczi is talking not about the confirmation of dimly remembered, or unremembered, past events, but about what currently transpires between patient and therapist and how it is dealt with. Ferenczi is suggesting that what was traumatogenic in the past was not simply due to the abuse and the intrusion, but to the mind game that was played by the abuser and by the family system, which wreaked havoc on the patient's sense of reality. In this formulation, it is not for the therapist to validate a memory about which she has no direct experience or knowledge. It is, rather, for the therapist to validate, in an authentic way, *an experience that she can know about – namely, what has happened between the therapist and the patient, in the moment.* The negotiation and processing of the disruptions and miscommunications that occur in every psychotherapeutic treatment are crucial. The patient discussed earlier, L, gained much more in her capacity to trust her mind and feel herself an integrated, cohesive self through the processing of what had transpired with her therapist than she had by the direct affirmation of her memories by her abuser. The injunction here is for the therapist not to repeat the mind game, rather than to be the definer or arbiter of past history. It is in *not* denying what has been apprehended by the patient that the patient regains a sense not only of the potential accuracy of her own perceptions but her agency as a perceiver.

As we put it (Slavin and Pollock 1997) in an earlier paper, what is restored is patients' experience of themselves as objective observers, which is the way most people experience their perceptions. Most people do not conduct their daily lives as though everything they saw and experienced were up for grabs (Grand 1995). People with non-traumatic histories generally experience their perceptions as reasonably objective takes on reality, upon which they can base their future behavior. Patients who have been abused, who become dissociated, who have had their sense of agency in relation to their own minds taken away, can no longer trust in their own objectivity. *I speak here of objectivity not in an external "scientific" sense, but rather the subjective experience of ourselves as competent observers, of a psychological capacity for objectivity.* The implication of Ferenczi's views in this perspective is that the restoration and healing of the integrity of the patient's mind, and the restoration of her agency, will enable her to begin to apply her own perceptions and her own thinking in a more confident way to the experiences of the past, whatever they were, and however she remembers them.

Therapists working with patients who have been abused are facing the same task. The false memory syndrome movement has assaulted our sense of agency in our own perceptions. Our assumptions – about what we understood about development, about human behavior, about memory and about the efficacy of our efforts – were challenged in a way that destabilized our work. How do we go about restoring our own agency? We have done so by having conferences, by publishing papers, by asserting it in a communal context where there is an experience of mutual validation of our reality; where there is an experience of literally – as we quote from the studies and cite the statistics – asserting over and over again the *objectivity* of our own perceptions. When we cite statistics and studies, we are not talking about a narrative, nor are we talking about a postmodern take on reality. We are asserting that there is a material reality that we know about, that it is objective, and that it is true. In this way – as well as in seeing our patients heal as we relate to them in an authentic way that ends the obfuscation of their trust in their own minds – we restore agency to ourselves.

Bibliography

Bromberg, P. 1994. "'Speak! That I May See You.' Some Reflections on Dissociation, Reality, and Psychoanalytic Listening." *Psychoanalytic Dialogues* 4, 517–47.

Davies, J. M. 1997. "Dissociation, Repression, and Reality Testing in the Countertransference: The Controversy over Memory and False Memory in the Psychoanalytic Treatment of Adult Survivors of Childhood Sexual Abuse." In R. Gartner (ed.), *Memories of Sexual Betrayal: Truth, Fantasy, Repression, and Dissociation*. New York: Jason Aronson.

eReference Suite. 2004. Based on print version, *The American Heritage Dictionary of the English Language*, 4th edition Copyright© 2004, 2000 by Houghton Mifflin Company.

Fast, I. 1985. *Event Theory: A Piaget-Freud Integration*. Hillsdale, NJ: Erlbaum.

Ferenczi, S. (1933) 1980. "Confusion of Tongues between Adults and the Child." In M. Balint (ed.), *Final Contributions to the Problems and Methods of Psycho-analysis*. London: Karnac Books.

Frawley-O'Dea, M. G. 1997. "Discussion: P3: Patients, Politics and Psychotherapy in the True/False Memory Debate." In R. Gartner (ed.). *Memories of Sexual Betrayal: Truth, Fantasy, Repression, and Dissociation*. New York: Jason Aronson.

Gartner, R. 1997. *Memories of Sexual Betrayal: Truth, Fantasy, Repression, and Dissociation.* New York: Jason Aronson.

Grand, S. 1995. "Incest and the Intersubjective Politics of Knowing History." In J. Alpert (ed.), *Sexual Abuse Recalled: Treating Trauma in the Era of the Recovered Memory Debate.* Northvale, NJ: Aronson, 235–3.

Mitchell, S. 1993. *Hope and Dread in Psychoanalysis.* New York: Basic books.

Pollock, L. and J. Slavin. 1998. "The Struggle for Recognition: Disruption and Reintegration in the Experience of Agency." *Psychoanalytic Dialogues* 8, 857–73.

Price, M. 1997. "Knowing and Not Knowing: Paradox in the Construction of Historical Narratives." In R. Gartner (ed.), *Memories of Sexual Betrayal: Truth, Fantasy, Repression, and Dissociation.* New York: Jason Aronson.

Slavin, J. and L. Pollock. 1997. "The Poisoning of Desire: The Destruction of Agency and the Recovery of Psychic Integrity in Sexual Abuse." *Contemporary Psychoanalysis* 33, 573–93.

Slavin, J., M. Rahmani and L. Pollock 1998. "Reality and Danger in Psychoanalytic Treatment." *Psychoanalytic Quarterly* 67, 191–217.

Spezzano, C. 1993. *Affect in Psychoanalysis: A Clinical Synthesis.* Hillsdale, NJ: The Analytic Press.

Chapter 15

GABRIEL ZIMMERMAN AND HERMONA SOREQ

Remembering Trauma: The Role of Acetylcholinesterase in the Formation of Fear Memories

1   Introduction

Memories of traumatic events are often more vivid than other memories. This bears evolutionary importance, since sharply remembering aversive stimuli may enable avoiding them in the future. Therefore, we would expect psychological stress to affect the formation and maintenance of memories. Both scientists and naïve observers have indeed noticed that memories from stressful events may display different features from "ordinary" ones: it is known, for example, that drastic traumatic memories can be deliberately forgotten, that collectively experienced emotionally charged events can form *flashback* memories, and that well-known bits of information may fail to be retrieved even during a mildly stressful situation. It is, therefore, of considerable interest to understand when, why and how these differences develop.

Post-traumatic stress disorder (PTSD) is one of the most dramatic expressions of the influence of stress on memory. This psychiatric condition is usually initiated by a single exposure to a terrifying event, after which the victim continues reexperiencing the traumatic incident as a vivid and intrusive memory even several years after its occurrence. The stress-induced memory mechanisms underlying this complex disease are not yet understood; however, research conducted at our laboratory identified an apparent involvement of AChE-R, a usually rare neuronal protein, in the consolidation of fear memories. In what follows, we describe this study in the context of what is currently known as the biology of fear reactions.

2   The Biology of Stress Responses

a   Neural and Endocrine Circuits Involved in Stress Responses

Immediately after an organism perceives itself threatened, a series of events activates a global reaction designed to face or avoid the danger. We could say that the signal that the organism has been exposed to a state of alert is conveyed via three interrelated paths: the message gets across the *central nervous system* (CNS) via *catecholamine neuro-transmitters*[1] – such as *epinephrine, norepinephrine* and *dopamine*. It gets to the different organs through the *sympathetic nervous system* (SNS); and it reaches virtually every cell by secreted hormones.

Several brain regions have been shown to be activated in animal models, following different kinds of psychological stress. Many of these activated regions, often called "nuclei," convey their output to the *paraventricular nucleus* of the *hypothalamus* (PVN), where the different signals are integrated and eventually trigger the *hypothalamic-pituitary-adrenocortical axis* (HPA). Successively, the hypothalamus activates the pituitary gland, which in turns releases a hormone that travels through the circulation up to the adrenal glands. These respond by secreting *corticosteroids* and chatecholamines to the circulation. These secreted substances reach every cell in the body and prepare them to cope with the organismal threat (Fig. 15.1 in colour plate section).

The SNS exerts a more direct and specific activation on the different organs. After receiving activating messages from the CNS,

1   Neurotransmitter is a chemical released by a neuron when activated. The released neurotransmitter interacts with adjacent neurons, which can become activated as a consequence of this interaction.

SNS neurons reach each body organ by slender projections called *axons*. When activated, SNS cells secrete norepinephrine (NE) in the proximity of their target organs. NE secretion increases heart rate, raises blood pressure, constricts blood vessels, widens bronchial passages and produces sweating. All of these reactions prepare the organs to cope with the threat, assisting "fight or flight" responses (McEwen 2002; Sapolsky 2000).

b   *Acetylcholine Involvement in Stress Response*

The neurotransmitter acetylcholine (ACh) is found in several brain areas and has been characterized as a *neuromodulator*: more than directly activating or inactivating a specific neuron, ACh regulates the responsiveness of neuron populations to incoming inputs. ACh has been related to virtually all of the aspects of human behavior and higher brain functions: attention, perception, memory, learning, spatial navigation and aggressive behavior, to name just a few.

Among other functions, ACh has been directly associated with stress responses. In a classic conditioning experiment, a tone and a flashlight were associated with a mild electric foot-shock. After the association was established, exposure to the tone and flashlight – which by now were perceived as stressful stimuli – induced the activation of two cholinergic regions: one at the nucleus basalis, and the other at the septum (Acquas et al. 1996). In other words, these two cholinergic nuclei seem to be activated during psychologically stressful situations. Since cholinergic neurons at these two nuclei send their axons to the PVN in the hypothalamus, it was tested whether their activation could trigger the HPA axis. In such tests, artificial activation of these nuclei induced ACh release at the PVN, which in turn activated the HPA axis (Tajima et al. 1996) (Fig. 15.2).

3   Memory

Human memories are stored in an associative manner: once a certain mental representation is activated, one consciously remembers what this representation stands for, and the activation "spreads" to other mental representations that are somehow related to the first one, switching them on. An extreme oversimplification of information representation in the brain allows us to assume that a single neuron stands for each representation, and that when a neuron is activated, it "tries" to activate the neurons related/connected to it. In associative learning, the strength of these connections changes according to experience: the connection between two related representations becomes strengthened, or "facilitated," while that between two unrelated representations becomes weakened (an example is the American association between Memorial Day and shopping, two seemingly unrelated concepts).

This cognitive process of facilitation has a neurophysiological origin: when two neurons are activated simultaneously, the physico-chemical connection – or *synapse* – between them is strengthened. In contrast, when the activation of these two neurons is uncorrelated, the synaptic connection between them is weakened. If the synapse between two neurons is strong enough, the activation of one of them will inevitably lead to the activation of the other. In a figurative way, we could say that the extent of association between neurons denotes the extent of association between the representations they stand for.

The complex phenomenon of *synaptic plasticity* – termed *long term potentiation* (LTP) in the case of synaptic strengthening – stands at the basis of the above depicted memory processes. LTP can be accomplished in several ways: morphological enlargement of synapse size; increase in the amount of neurotransmitter secreted at the synapse; prolonging the time the neurotransmitter prevails at the synaptic cleft, etc.

Endogenous substances that are not directly related to cognitive processes – for example, stress-related hormones and immune system messengers – have been shown to stimulate or inhibit LTP. This, in turn, implies that changes in the status of our hormonal or immune system may affect different memory processes. However, given the complexity of the memory formation process, it is impossible to plot a simple scheme linking memory formation with other physiological processes.

4   AChE, Stress and Memory

a   AChE-R Represents an Active Pathway in Stress Responses and in the Formation of Traumatic Memories

Cholinergic pathways are activated in stress situations. The first effect to occur is enhanced ACh release. This is followed by an increase or decrease in the levels of the various proteins involved in ACh metabolism, which counterbalances this action.

The synthesis of the ACh-synthesizing enzyme ChAT, for example, is reduced, subsequently suppressing the amounts of ACh available for secretion. Prominent among these expression changes is the induction of *AChE-R*, a modified form of *acetylcholinesterase*, the enzyme responsible for ACh breakdown. AChE-R is normally rare, but its levels increase under multiple stressors. Intriguingly, AChE-R by itself has been found to modulate different pathways involved in stress responses, at the cellular as well as at the whole organism level (Soreq and Seidman 2001).

Several different insults, among them psychological stress and cholinergic over-activation, have been shown to increase AChE-R levels in different brain areas (Fig. 15.3 in colour plate section). Moreover, a single, acute exposure of an animal to a threatening stressor will induce chronically high levels of AChE-R in brain and blood alike (Kaufer et al. 1998; Meshorer et al. 2002; Grisaru et al. 2006). This fact encouraged us to consider the possibility that this molecule could be involved in the chronic consequences of a single stress exposure and, more specifically, that it could be involved in PTSD.

To challenge our innovative hypothesis, we performed a series of experiments in which we tried to recreate PTSD conditions in laboratory mice. Stressed mice show a facilitation of their capacity to remember aversive stimuli, a phenomenon resembling PTSD symptoms. We used this fact to test whether AChE-R is involved in this stress-induced learning facilitation. Mice were placed in a novel context and heard a tone followed by a mild foot-shock, after which they were returned to their original cages. Twenty-four hours later, mice were again placed in a context in which the foot-shock was delivered, the threatening sound was repeated and their *conditioned freezing response*[2] was measured. Stressful stimuli are known to facilitate aversive stimuli learning (Blank et al. 2002). Therefore, when mice are immobilized for one hour before being placed in the novel cage, i.e. before the learning event, they show an increased freezing response when returned to that cage.

To test whether AChE-R was causally involved in this process, we created four different experimental conditions. In the no-stress condition, mice were exposed to the learning paradigm – the tone followed by the foot-shock – and their conditioned freezing response was measured as described above. The stress condition was identical to the control one, but prior to learning mice were immobilized for one hour, which induced stress in the animals. The third group, aimed to find out whether AChE-R production was causally involved in stress-induced learning facilitation, was treated similarly to that of the stress condition, but before immobilization they were injected with an *antisense*[3] (AS) specific to AChE-R mRNA, which prevented its protein synthesis. A fourth group, aimed to determine whether AChE-R

2   Conditioned freezing response is the animal reaction of prolonged immobilization after the presentation of a stimulus that has been previously associated with some danger (the foot-shock in our case). The length of time through which the animal remains immobilized is an index of the extent to which an association between the stimulus and the employed stressor has been established.

3   An antisense is a short DNA sequence complementary to a specific mRNA, AChE in this case. An antisense attaches specifically to its target mRNA, impeding the formation of the protein it encodes and/or inducing destruction of the target mRNA.

production by itself may be sufficient to facilitate learning of aversive memories, was not stressed before learning, but instead was injected with a short segment of the AChE-R protein (fig. 15.4).

The results showed that, as expected, learning was facilitated in mice that were preexposed to stress. The AS-treated group did not show such facilitation, demonstrating that AChE-R was necessary in order to yield this effect. Moreover, the AChE-R-segment injected mice showed learning facilitation, although they were not exposed to stress, suggesting that a higher level of AChE-R in the brain was sufficient to generate stress-like behaviors (Nijholt et al. 2004) (Fig. 15.5).

In later experiments we showed that, besides affecting memory phenomena related to PTSD, the same AS agent was capable of drastically abolishing the two other symptoms characteristic of the disease: hyper-arousal and avoidance behavior (Zimmerman et al., unpublished data).

b   AChE-R alters Processes Related to Memories at the Cellular Level

Although the pathways by which AChE and AChE-R bring about their stress-related effects are yet incompletely understood, different experiments indicate that this molecule can play a pivotal role in the synaptic plasticity involved in learning. After verifying that AChE-R was capable of facilitating learning at the behavioral level, we asked whether it could do so at the cellular level, altering LTP. It is known that LTP is facilitated in brain preparations from pre-stressed mice; we asked whether this process was mediated by AChE-R. To answer that question, we measured LTP in four groups resembling the ones in which the behavioral experiment was carried out. Previously stressed mice showed LTP facilitation when compared to control ones. This effect was drastically diminished when mice were treated with AS before stress. The fourth group, this time was composed of transgenic mice engineered to constitutively over-express AChE-R. Although they were not exposed to stress, these mice showed the same facilitation found in stress-exposed mice. Thus AChE-R proved to be necessary and sufficient to induce stress-related learning facilitation at the cellular level as well (Nijholt et al. 2004).

The link between stress and memory has been a classical topic of research for the past decades. Nevertheless, several central concepts about it are still unclear. Two apparently unrelated attributes of AChE – its association to the metabolism of a stress-inducing agent and its capacity to modulate neuronal plasticity – position this molecule at the crossroads of stress-induced memory alterations.

Bibliography

Acquas E., C. Wilson and H. C. Fibiger. 1996. "Conditioned and Unconditioned Stimuli Increase Frontal Cortical and Hippocampal Acetylcholine Release: Effects of Novelty, Habituation, and Fear." *Journal of Neuroscience* 16(9), 3089–96.

Blank T., I. Nijholt, K. Eckart and J. Spiess. 2002. "Priming of Long-Term Potentiation in Mouse Hippocampus by Corticotropin-Releasing Factor and Acute Stress: Implications for Hippocampus-Dependent Learning." *Journal of Neuroscience* 22 (9), 3788–94.

Grisaru D., M. Pick, C. Perry, E. H. Sklan, R. Almog, I. Goldberg, E. Naparstek, J. B. Lessing, H. Soreq and V. Deutsch. 2006. "Hydrolytic and Nonenzymatic Functions of Acetylcholinesterase Comodulate Hemopoietic Stress Responses." *Journal of Immunology* 176(1), 27–35.

Kandel E. R., J. H. Schwartz and T. M. Jessell (eds). 2000. *Principles in Neural Science*, 4th edition. New York: McGraw Hill.

Kaufer D., A. Friedman, S. Seidman and H. Soreq. 1998. "Acute Stress Facilitates Long-Lasting Changes in Cholinergic Gene Expression." *Nature* 393(6686), 373–7.

Meshorer E., C. Erb, R. Gazit, L. Pavlovsky, D. Kaufer, A. Friedman, D. Glick, N. Ben-Arie and H. Soreq. 2002. "Alternative Splicing and Neuritic mRNA Translocation under Long-Term Neuronal Hypersensitivity." *Science* 295(5554), 508–12.

McEwen, B. S. 2002. "Protective and Damaging Effects of Stress Mediators: The Good and Bad sides of the Response to Stress." *Metabolism* 51(6), 2–4.

Nijholt N., M. Farchi, E. Kye, H. Sklan, S. Shoham, G. B. Verbeure, D. Owen, B. Hochner, J. Spiess, H. Soreq and T. Blank. 2004. "Stress-induced Alternative Splicing of Acetylcholinesterase Results in Enhanced Fear Memory and Long-Term Potentiation." *Molecular Psychiatry* 9(2), 174–83.

Sapolsky, R. M. 2000. "Stress Hormones: Good and Bad." *Neurobiology of Disease* 7(5), 540–2.

Soreq, H. and S. Seidman. 2001. "Acetylcholinesterase – New Roles for an Old Factor." *Nature Reviews Neuroscience* 2(4), 294–302.

Soreq H., R. Yirmiya, O. Cohen and D. Glick. 2004. "Acetylcholinesterase as a Window onto Stress Responses," In T. Steckler, N. Kalin, and J. M. H. M. Reul (eds). *Handbook of Stress and the Brain*. Amsterdam: Elsevier Science.

Tajima T., H. Endo, Y. Suzuki, H. Ikari, M. Gotoh and A. Iguchi. 1996. "Immobilization Stress-Induced Increase of Hippocampal Acetylcholine and of plasma epinephrine, Norepinephrine and Glucose in Rats." *Brain Research* 720, 155–8.

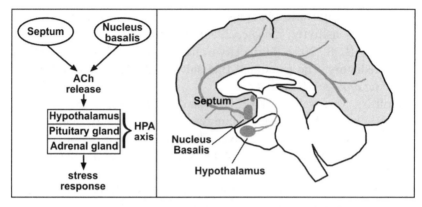

Figure 15.2 The neurotransmitter Ach modulates the activation of the HPA axis

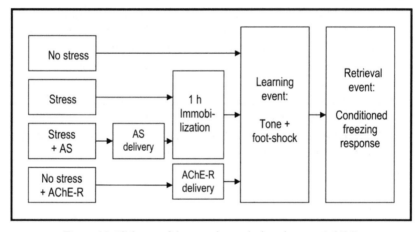

Figure 15.4 Scheme of the experiment designed to test AchE-R
involvement in stress-induced learning facilitation

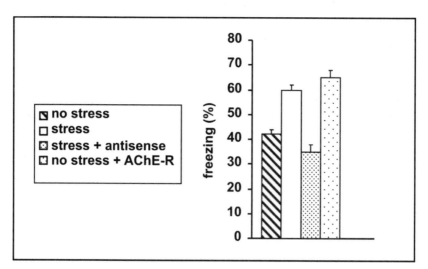

Figure 15.5 AchE-R is directly involved in stress-induced learning facilitation. Shown are observed changes in the freezing reaction of mice exposed to the noted treatments

Chapter 16

YAEL ZERUBAVEL

Antiquity and the Renewal Paradigm: Strategies of Representation and Mnemonic Practices in Israeli Culture

National memory is the product of a dialogue between the present and the past that selectively highlights certain continuities and discontinuities in support of the nation's vision of its collective identity and future development. Collective memory is transmitted through a wide range of mnemonic practices that commemorate specific figures and events and articulate fundamental principles underlying the perception of the past. This essay focuses on the mnemonic practices that advance the Zionist renewal paradigm and highlight the symbolic continuity between antiquity and modern Israeli society.

The concept of renewal offers a useful strategy for negotiating the inevitable tensions between the desire for change and the need to preserve a sense of continuity. Whereas revolutionary ideology advocates a rupture with the past to allow for the introduction of a new historical era, and conservative ideology rejects changes for the sake of preserving the old, renewal ideology attempts to mediate between these two polar positions through a selective reference to the past: it elevates a selected "golden age" from a distant past, which it raises as a model that changes the course of a degenerative process of political, social or moral decline associated with a subsequent period. The term itself denotes this double strategy of encouraging a change (the "new" within "renewal") and defining it as a symbolic return to a chosen past (i.e. "*re*-newal"). Hence, movements promoting the renewal paradigm are identified as "revitalization movements" (Wallace 1972).

Zionism emerged as a revitalization movement whose ideology was centered on a "decline narrative" (Zerubavel 2003, 16–18) associated with the long history of exile and with the vision of national regeneration based on an idealized view of Jewish national life in antiquity (Zerubavel 1995, 13–36). Although the Zionist rhetoric of breaking away from exilic conditions and values at times appeared close to the revolutionary mode, the insistence on a total break with the Jewish past and tradition would have undermined the legitimacy of the Zionist call for a return to the land of Israel on the basis of the historic roots in that land. Moreover, such advocacy would have alienated many followers of Zionism and could have split the movement. The renewal paradigm therefore offered a useful strategy of dealing with these tensions. Zionism continued the traditional periodization of the Jewish past into the golden age of antiquity and the negative view of the period of exile, but the Zionists' master commemorative narrative (Zerubavel 1995, 6–7) shifted the interpretive framework from the traditional-religious to a modern, secular national perspective.

This study focuses on mnemonic practices that were constructed during the formative years of Israeli society and that articulated the premise of regeneration. Operating on various levels of representation simultaneously, the renewal paradigm became a powerful organizing principle of Zionist memory and emphasized the links between the building of a modern Jewish society in the land of Israel and Jews' national life during antiquity. The study of the representation of antiquity within modern Israeli culture examines the various levels – the indexical, the iconic, and the symbolic – drawing on Peirce's tripartite classification of the sign (Peirce 1962, 2: 156–73) and on its elaboration into a semiotic system that moves progressively from concrete to abstract signification (Zerubavel 1997, 68–72). The following discussion thus examines the introduction of the renewal paradigm through the construction of indexical, iconic and symbolic bridges between antiquity and the present, focusing on select examples.

1   The Indexical Representation of Continuity and Regeneration

The indexical representation of continuity between antiquity and the modern Zionist revival is based on the physical presence of artifacts that originated in that distant past. Relics are thus the most concrete and tangible evidence of an otherwise elusive tie connecting the present with the past. The value of a relic is defined by its very association with a past that is marked as significant within the group's master commemorative narrative, and not by its intrinsic value. Indeed, the fine line separating "relics" from "garbage" in the classification of ordinary objects demonstrates the importance of the social attitude toward the past with which they are associated.[1] The dating of the object attributes to it authenticity and affirms its special status as representing a continuous line from antiquity to the present (Shils 1981, 69–70; Lowenthal 1985, 243–9; Zerubavel 2003, 42–4). Relics thus serve as important commemorative artifacts that allow contemporary societies to experience the most direct link to their past.

In the case of modern Israeli society, archeological sites and new discoveries support the national memory of ancient roots in the land of Israel and make it possible to re-experience them as part of its present reality. Consider, for example, the account by Moshe Dayan, the famous general-turned-politician and an amateur archeologist, who was known for his passion for collecting ancient artifacts. Dayan explained his pursuit of relics as a personal quest for bonding with the Jews who lived in the land of Israel during antiquity.

> You sometimes feel that you can literally join their community; though they are
> a bit dead, you can still enter the house of these silent people and perhaps get

---

1   The fine line separating garbage and relics and the importance of relics in supporting national claims is demonstrated in the conflicting attitudes of Israelis and Palestinians toward archeological findings. See Nadia abu El-Haj (2001) for the claim that Israeli archeologists dismiss findings from the Muslim past and the opposite claim by an Israeli archeologist that Muslim authorities on the Temple Mount threw out as "garbage" soil that contains relics from the First Temple (Sheragai 2005).

even more excited by this than when you enter the house of living people. I like
to stick my head into a hole where Jews from Bnei Brak lived six thousand
years ago... and peek into their kitchen, touch the ashes left there from long ago,
or feel the fingerprints which the ancient potter left on the vessel (Elon 1971,
367).[2]

The subtext of Dayan's words is even more poignant. The
location he mentions, Bnei Brak, is today one of the strongholds of the
ultra-Orthodox Jews in Israel. Dayan, a committed secularist, implied
that he experienced a more intense bond with the ancient Hebrews
who had lived there thousands of years ago than with the ultra-
Orthodox Bnei Brak of today. The few relics they had left behind
made it possible for him to smell, feel and touch them, and thereby
establish a direct sensory memory of their past lives. The powerful
impact of a personal, bodily memory (Connerton 1989, 72–104) reinforced his identification with them and contributed to the collective
memory of continuity from that distant past. Another, similar statement reveals the impact of ancient artifacts in providing a concrete
and powerful connection with ancient figures:

> Abraham, Josef, Moses and Joshua, David and Solomon [...] have continued to
> reappear on the stage of history. Yet this time, these are not abstract names that
> originated in early legends. The biblical heroes were flesh and blood, who lived
> and acted in the land of Israel and left their marks on the material culture
> excavated in archeological digs (Etzion 1992, 246).

Relics that remain in their original physical location provide a
double sense of continuity and hence the most immediate and direct
relationship with the past. When relics are removed from their original
setting and placed in museums, they inevitably lose that double
anchoring in time and in place. However, the loss of the authentic
setting may be compensated for to a degree by gaining greater accessibility and visibility in the museum setting. When displayed in a
prestigious museum, the association with the site may further contribute to their sacredness. The Dead Sea Scrolls display in the specially
designed "Shrine of the Book" at the Israel Museum in Jerusalem is a

---

2   This quote draws on the English edition of Elon's book; but I modified it where
     I felt that the translation lost important nuances of the original Hebrew.

case in point: housed at a national commemorative site that is explicitly designated as a sacred civil temple (Roitman 2001), the scrolls are privileged and venerated ancient texts.

The unearthing of ancient relics or sites in the process of building a new settlement, constructing a private house, or working in the fields is not uncommon in Israel.[3] Such discoveries became a literary trope in Zionist settlement narratives, both in literature and in film. A novel for young adults, *The Frontiersmen of Israel* (*Anshei Bereshit*), published in 1933, describes a Zionist pioneer who, in the process of establishing a new farm, finds ancient stones engraved with Jewish symbols buried in the ground. The man calls out to his son: "Do you see these stones? They're the remnants of an ancient settlement. Come on, let's collect a heap of rocks and lay the foundations for our new home" (Smolly (1933) 1964, 15). The incorporation of ancient stones in the construction of a new home provides a concrete and visual manifestation of the Zionist paradigm of national renewal in the land of Israel: the ancient stones that in themselves represent the theme of death and destruction are transformed in their meaning when they become part of a new building. The merging of the past and the present in that new entity thus represents the formula of death and rebirth that underlies the renewal paradigm.

Another Zionist novel, *My Father's House* (Levin 1947), made into a movie by the same title (Herbert Kline 1947), is one of the earliest fictional narratives dealing with Holocaust survivors in Israel. The novel focuses on a child survivor who escapes from the kibbutz to which he is brought after the war in order to look for his father. After a long search he finds out that his father perished in the Holocaust and suffers a mental breakdown. As he begins to show signs of recovery, the child accompanies a group of kibbutz members who engage in the building of a new settlement and discover an ancient stone engraved with the Hebrew name "Halevi." The boy tells the young man from the kibbutz (who acts as his surrogate father) that that was the name of his biological father, and the kibbutznik answers him: "Of all your

---

3   One of the most famous incidents was the discovery of the mosaic of the Beit Alpha synagogue, which was discovered by kibbutz members while digging an irrigation channel. See Elon, 1997, 35.

fathers, David, who once lived here." And he continues: "We'll build our house on this stone here, in this settlement. We'll call it the house of Halevi" (ibid., 192). This ending suggests that the Zionist settlement project will redeem the people from the historical ruptures created by the exile from the land in antiquity and the more recent experience of the Holocaust. Moreover, the novel implies that the ancient stone representing the collective national past will serve as a symbolic compensation for the child's personal loss of his own father and home.[4] In both the Hebrew and the English novels, the ancient relic becomes the cornerstone of a modern building, providing a concrete image of the bridge that serves to connect the modern Zionist revival with the ancient past.

Ritual performances in ancient sites serve as another mnemonic practice of bridging between the past and the present. Although these rituals may vary in their character and commemorative focus, they share a symbolic message that highlights the continuity between the ancient and modern Jews who live (or lived) in the land of Israel. The ceremonial burial at Masada of twenty-seven skeletons identified as the remains of the Zealots who died in defense of the fortress two thousand years ago (as Israel's national radio announced on 7 July 1969) illustrates this function. The official ceremony expressed modern Israelis' moral obligation to provide their ancestors with a final resting place and marks the state's recognition of its official role as the collective representative of its living citizens as well as of past generations. The public funeral symbolically returned the bones to the time and place to which they had belonged, but it also endowed them with a new meaning: the state-sponsored military ceremony, usually limited to soldiers in the Israel Defense Forces, redefined those ancient remnants as part of the modern community of the nation's defenders. The performance of other military ceremonies at the site of Masada has similarly emphasized the symbolic continuity between the ancient

---

4   The name of the kibbutznik who takes care of the child is Avram, alluding to
     his role as a surrogate father, named after the biblical figure Abraham the Patri-
     arch, the father of the nation. The novel suggests the experience of a symbolic
     rebirth in the future family consisting of Avram the kibbutznik, the female
     Holocaust survivor who took care of the child, and the child.

"defenders of Masada" and contemporary Israeli soldiers (Zerubavel 1995, 129–32).

Another recent and highly popular ritual tradition at the site of Masada is the performance of the bat- or barmitzvah ceremony – the traditional rite of passage marking a Jewish youth's transition from a child to a full member of the adult community. The performance of these rituals in the excavated synagogue at Masada emphasizes the ancient roots of Jewish tradition and the continuing use of an ancient sacred space. It is interesting to compare this Masada tradition with the performance of civil rituals at the Western Wall in the Old City of Jerusalem: both are sacred ancient sites, yet Masada is primarily conceived of as an archeological site with a sacred component, whereas the Western Wall, which survived the destruction of the Second Temple in 70 C.E., is considered a religious site, governed by Orthodox rabbinical rules. The Wall represents a continuous memory in Jewish tradition, although at times its function as a religious site was prohibited. Conversely, the site of Masada was forgotten, only to be rediscovered in the nineteenth century, and its development as a commemorative locus began in the twentieth century (Zerubavel 1995, 62–70). In spite of the significant differences in their careers as commemorative sites, both Masada and the Western Wall affirm the patterns of rupture, symbolic death and rebirth that are central to the renewal paradigm. The ongoing performance of rituals at these sites highlights their commemorative function as an indexical bridge within Israeli national memory, representing a line of continuity between the ancient Jewish past and contemporary Israel.

2   The Iconic Representation of Continuity

Unlike the ancient relics that physically mark a direct continuity from antiquity to the present, the creation of modern replicas of ancient objects and phenomena establishes an iconic representation of continuity. The icon offers a *generic* representation that introduces the past into the present through the process of imitation. Like the symbol, then, the icon is new in its origin and currently produced; yet unlike the symbol, it presents physical properties that resemble those of the original, thus attempting to remain closer to the indexical representation of the past. Hence, in spite of its recent origins the icon projects a sense of continuity between Jewish life in antiquity in the land of Israel and its Zionist revival in the modern period.

The adoption of the *menorah*, the ancient seven-branched candelabrum, as the official emblem of the state of Israel in 1949, provides an excellent example of an icon that functions as a bridge between the two periods. The selection of this ancient object for the design of the new state's emblem represents the state's claim for historical continuity from antiquity and underscores its role as custodian of the Jewish national memory. The choice of the particular *menorah* design has an even more resounding meaning: it was modeled after the image of the Second Temple *menorah* that had been taken away by Roman soldiers and paraded by them in Rome as evidence of their victory over Judea. That image, which was displayed on the Arch of Titus in Rome, encapsulated the loss of the Jews' national honor and their uprooting from their homeland (Handelman and Shamgar-Handleman 1990; Mishori 2000, 139–64). The use of the same *menorah* design for the state's official emblem can therefore be seen as a symbolic act of restoration of lost national honor. The large *menorah* monument erected near the Israeli parliament building in Jerusalem constitutes a countermonument to the historic Arch of Titus. The exiled *menorah* has been symbolically returned to the land of Israel; it now serves as a central icon of Jewish sovereignty and represents the Zionist renewal paradigm. The two olive branches that flank the state's emblem represent the hope for peace, thus moving from the past toward the future, while preserving a symbolic continuity between the biblical and post-biblical past and contemporary Israel.

A similar commemorative function is served by the embracement of the ancient Jewish coin, the shekel, as Israeli currency in 1970. The First Zionist Congress's earlier choice, in 1897, to designate its membership fee and card "shekel," had introduced the biblical name as a symbolic bridge to antiquity. The adoption of the shekel as a coin and a monetary unit by the State of Israel preserved both its name and function, thereby establishing the modern shekel as an iconic representation of the old coin. Moreover, this choice echoed the ancient Judeans' decision to issue their own shekels during the revolt against Rome in 66 to 70 C.E (*Encyclopaedia Judaica* 1972, 14:1347–9). This act therefore highlighted the continuity between that short-lived period of renewed independence in antiquity and the Jews' sovereignty over the same land established in the present.

Another important area for the creation of iconic bridges between the present and the distant past developed in modern Hebrew culture is the dramatic performance of scenes representing the biblical and post-biblical past. This mnemonic practice was often used in Hebrew schools as an educational tool designed to enhance students' identification with past figures, ancient customs, and mythical and historical events. During such performances, children become the embodiment of ancient figures and experience a personal bond with the period of antiquity. Thus, on Shavuot, Israeli children perform as ancient Israelites who made pilgrimage to the Temple in Jerusalem, carrying first-fruits baskets; or they act as the Temple priests who received those gifts at the Temple and gave blessings to the pilgrims. During Passover, children become the Israelites walking out of Egypt and wandering through the desert, carrying sacks containing their few belongings. And during Hanukkah, they transform into the Maccabees who resisted the foreign king's forces, liberated the country, cleansed the defiled Temple and observed their religion freely.

Theatrical and dance performances on biblical themes and episodes became highly popular in Israeli culture. The encounters between Abraham's servant Eliezer and Rebecca, Josef and his brothers, or Ruth and Naomi, inspired various artistic forms. Songs and dances depicting ancient and local customs were often performed in kindergartens, schools and various communities during holiday celebrations and other commemorative events (Lev-Ari 1998, 93–7; Eshel 1991, 87–93; Ronen 1999, 262–5). These dramatic performances introduced the ancient past into the present by reenacting key events. The performance metaphorically merged the modern person with the ancient Israelite, creating a new mythical, or transhistorical, figure. As the Passover Haggadah proclaims, each Jew should see himself as personally participating in the Exodus from Egypt, highlighting the significance of the biblical injunction to remember (Yerushalmi 1982, 44–5). The physical embodiment of ancestors represented the symbolic continuity between modern and ancient members of the nation who belong to the same mnemonic community.

Another facet of the iconic representation of continuity between antiquity and the present is the restoration of biblical landscapes and nature. The Neot Kedumim Park (literally, the Ancient Habitat Park) was established "to re-create the physical setting of the Bible in all its depth and detail." As its website indicates, "*Neot Kedumim* embodies the panorama and power of the landscapes that helped shape the values of the Bible and provided a rich vocabulary for expressing them [...]"[5] As a site of ecological restoration, the park presents a claim of authenticity in reproducing the biblical landscape: "*Neot Kedumim* draws on a variety of disciplines – such as Bible scholarship, botany, zoology, geography, history, and archaeology – to bring the Bible and its commentaries to life." Hence the park carries the past into the present and brings contemporary visitors closer to the experience of the biblical people: "Shaded rest areas throughout the reserve offer stunning views of the Israeli landscape just as our forefathers saw it." Although the park attracts many Christian pilgrims and declares that it brings to life "the world of the Hebrew scriptures and the Gospels," its primal significance as a national commemorative site was publicly recognized in 1994, when it was the recipient of the highest honor awarded by the State of Israel – the Israel Prize.

The Biblical Zoo in Jerusalem and the Hai Bar (Wild Life) Park near Kibbutz Yotveta in the southern desert landscape provide two further examples of attempts to restore the ancient natural world in contemporary Israel life. Indeed, the latter project goes further, in its ambitious plan to reintroduce species of animals that disappeared from their indigenous desert landscape and set them free in that habitat. Having successfully raised certain species of wild donkeys and buffalo similar to those that lived in the land during ancient times, the Hai Bar Park has lately succeeded in rearing wild ostriches after 50 years of

5   Quotes and information are from Neot Kedumim's website at www.n-k.org.il, as accessed May 2005, and from its English-language publicity materials at the site, June 2005.

extinction. This project, and the plan to release the ostriches into the wild, were clearly deemed significant enough to merit front-page coverage in the major Israeli daily *Ha'aretz* (Rinat 2005). Like the scholarly credential quoted in support of Neot Kedumim's claim for authentic representation, the Hai Bar's claim to authenticity was based, according to *Ha'aretz*'s report, on archeological evidence of the ostriches' presence in the country in ancient times.

It is interesting to compare the restoration of plants and animals that are considered close to their biblical ancestors with recent news about the astonishing revival of an ancient date seed discovered in an archeological excavation at Masada (Erlanger 2005). Both the contemporary ostriches (as icons of the ancient ones) and the date seed (itself an index of antiquity) constitute important, and perhaps surprising, bridges to antiquity – hence their value as news. Nevertheless, in the case of the ancient seed the achievement is more dramatic, since the regeneration occurred in the specific item originating from that remote past and preserved over the centuries. In contrast, the restoration of biblical landscape is based on growing new plants and animals that have a *generic affinity* with the original specimens associated with that past. The iconic representation therefore conveys that contemporary plants and animals *resemble* their ancestors closely enough to merit their commemorative function as living monuments of the past in contemporary Israeli culture.

3   The Symbolic Representations of Continuity and Regeneration

The construction of symbolic bridges between the present and antiquity is the most extensively used and the most diverse and intriguing process in the gradual shift from a concrete to a more abstract link between historical periods. Rather than relying on objects that survived from the distant past or the creation of replicas that imitate objects or figures from an earlier age, modern Hebrew culture has constructed various forms that are conventionally associated with antiquity and are used to represent the symbolic continuity between the present and that past.

Jewish immigrants' adoption of Hebrew names provides an excellent example of such mechanisms of highlighting the Zionist paradigm of national renewal. The very act of *re*naming an immigrant further dramatizes the symbolic significance attached to the custom of giving Hebrew names to newborn babies. The act of name-changing involves relinquishing a non-Hebrew name and embracing a new Hebrew one, thereby constituting a symbolic rite of passage into Israeli society. In Jewish tradition, naming a child after an older kin or a deceased relative (in the Sephardic and Ashkenazi Jewish traditions, respectively) highlights intergenerational continuity within the family unit. A name not only serves as a marker of one's identity, it also constitutes a living monument of one's family's memory. The commemorative value of names is further evident in the biblical curse, that one's name will be blotted out of history, which implies the obliteration of one's memory.

In a tradition that places such high value on the intrinsic connection between name, memory and identity, the act of *re*naming is a bold symbolic move that reinforces the formula of symbolic death and rebirth.[6] When renaming is performed voluntarily, it conveys the immigrant's motivation to assimilate into the host society; when imposed on a newcomer, it indicates strong social pressure to leave the past behind and become acculturated into the new social and cultural milieu. Immigrants who chose to do away with the non-Hebrew names that bore the stamp of exile demonstrated their commitment to Zionist

---

6   The symbolism of name-changing in Jewish tradition is revealed in an old custom of renaming severely ill persons. By being assigned a new name a critically sick person was perceived as having a new identity; the sick person was believed to be no longer recognized by the angel of death and therefore to have a better chance of survival. Similarly, when a non-Jew converts to Judaism or secular Jews decide to "return to religion" (i.e. to become *baalei teshuvah*), a ritual of name-changing represents the commitment to symbolically erase their past and begin a new life.

collective memory and its renewal paradigm.[7] The desire to enhance the close affinity with the ancient Hebrew forefathers was further articulated in the adoption of the ancient naming pattern of "X the son of Y." Thus Eliezer Yitzhak Perlmann, the so called "father of the Hebrew revival," renamed himself Eliezer Ben-Yehuda, David Grin became David Ben-Gurion and Yitzhak Shimshelevich became Yizhak Ben-Zvi. The symbolism of replacing a family membership with a national one became even more pronounced in those cases in which siblings adopted different Hebrew names.[8] The individual's tie to the nation's memory thus substitutes for (and exceeds) his or her ties to the family. The novelty here is not in the phenomenon of name-changing among immigrants, but rather its creative use as a means of reenacting basic precepts of Zionist national memory and ideology.

The Hebraization of place names provides another example of a mnemonic practice that involved not only the assignment of Hebrew names to newly founded settlements, but also the change of existing names of regions, localities, towns and villages to Hebrew ones, thereby erasing the impact of Jewish exile from the land on the country's landscape (Cohen and Kliot 1981; Azaryahu and Golan 2001). The "born again landscape," to borrow Michael Feige's expression (2007) distances the land from the history of exile as well as from the Palestinians' conflicting claims of ownership. The symbolic act of naming further highlights the significance of the land as an indexical representation of continuity between the ancient past and the present.

---

7 While name-changing emerged as a voluntary act during the early prestate period, immigrants were often expected and encouraged to change their names, and immigrant children were often assigned new Hebrew names. Modern Hebrew names of the prestate and early state periods drew on ancient Hebrew figures. Following the foundation of the state, Hebrew names showed preference for denoting local nature and landscape, highlighting the bond to the land, or denoting power, courage, agility and freedom – qualities that Zionism attributed to the ancient Hebrews and expected to be revived by the new Hebrew youth (Kaganoff 1977, 76–93; Weitman 1988, 148–9). After the foundation of the state, official representatives were required to adopt a Hebrew name. This regulation was abolished in the mid-1990s (Azaryahu and Golan 2001, 190).

8 For example, Yitzhak Ben-Zvi's brother was the writer Aharon Reuveni. Similarly, the famous three Heilperin brothers became Yonatan Ratosh, Zvi Rin and Uzi Ornan.

The poet Rachel (Bluwstein) articulated the power of the Hebrew name in establishing a close connection with her biblical namesake, Rachel the Matriarch. In a poem entitled "Rachel" (1926, 84–5), she describes an intense identification with her biblical namesake, both physically and spiritually: "Her blood runs in my veins,/ her voice sings within me,/ Rachel, the shepherd of Laban's sheep,/ Rachel, the Matriarch." The poet alludes to the mythical fusion of the biblical and the modern Rachels, which turns the latter into a living monument of the former. The modern Rachel, who carries the voice and the blood of her ancient namesake, can be seen as symbolically analogous to the modern building that incorporates ancient stones.

A similar strategy is performed textually in a modern narrative describing the life of the Israeli hero Yosef Trumpeldor, who died in defense of a Jewish settlement in 1920. The biographical sketch provided in a major Israeli textbook of the 1960s and 1970s uses the strategy of borrowing phrases from the biblical narrative of Exodus 2:11–13 to create an analogy between the modern hero and the biblical Moses. According to this text, "Yosef" goes out to see his suffering brethren in exile. Upon witnessing their oppression he is spontaneously moved to defend the weak against the cruel oppressor (Persky 1975, 238).[9] By adopting the Hebrew Bible's language, the narrative suggests not only that Trumpeldor is an heir to Moses' legacy but also that he may be seen as a modern-day reincarnation of the biblical leader (Zerubavel 1995, 87–8). This strategy allows the text to express the broader trend of relating to those who contribute to the Zionist regeneration as the direct followers of biblical or post-biblical heroes. The reference to modern heroes as the "grandsons" of those ancient forefathers (ibid., 26) drew on the genealogical framework to suggest the notion of symbolic continuity from antiquity to the modern Hebrews and thereby emphasized the paradigm of national renewal.

Another narrative genre, which I analyze in greater length elsewhere (Zerubavel 2005), constructs an even stronger message of

---

9   Note that this textbook narrative refers to the hero by his first name, following the biblical custom, using this device to further reinforce Trumpeldor's connection with the earlier biblical figure. Similar versions of this biographical narrative appeared in earlier editions of the *Mikraot Yisrael* textbook.

symbolic continuity between antiquity and modern Israeli society. Children's tales written by known Hebrew writers and published in Hebrew textbooks and holiday anthologies thus describe a trans-historical encounter between ancient heroes and modern-day children during the temporal framework of holidays that are associated with key past events. Narratives for Hanukkah and Lag b'Omer lead to the meeting of symbolic figures from the national past with their modern descendants. In spite of the wide historical gulf separating the participants in this encounter, their common origins and shared attachment to the land provide a strong foundation of intimacy. The narratives thus provide a fictional account of "concrete" evidence of an instantly felt kinship between modern and ancient members of the nation, thereby affirming the otherwise elusive ties that make up the nation (Anderson 1983). The face-to-face meetings disclose the modern child's ability to empathize with his or her ancient forefathers at the same time that they suggest a process of *contemporization* of the dead ancestors (Heilman 1983, 62–6).

In presenting these three levels of representation of antiquity in modern Israeli culture, this article attempts to demonstrate some of the cultural strategies employed in the construction of symbolic continuities and discontinuities within Jewish history. In this case, the strategy is designed to articulate and reinforce the renewal paradigm, which is central to Zionist memory and ideology. The three levels of representation analyzed here convey an idea of continuity between the ancient and the modern experience of the nation that challenges and obscures the existence of nineteen centuries of exile separating antiquity from the modern Zionist revival. The article presents select examples of each of these levels of representation as a means of offering a conceptual framework for a further and broader study of this phenomenon.

Bibliography

Abu El-Haj, N. 2001. *Facts on the Ground: Archaeological Practice and Territorial Self-Fashioning in Israeli Society.* Chicago: University of Chicago Press.

Anderson, B. 1983. *Imagined Communities: Reflections on the Origin and Spread of Nationalism.* London: Verso.

Azaryahu, M. and A. Golan. 2001. "(Re)naming the Landscape: The Formation of the Hebrew Map of Israel 1949–60." *Journal of Historical Society. Journal of Historical Geography* 27 (2), 178–95

Cohen, S. B. and N. Kliot. 1981. "Israel's Place-Names as Reflection of Continuity and Change in Nation-Building." *Names* 29 (3), 227–48.

Connerton, P. 1989. *How Societies Remember.* Cambridge: Cambridge University Press.

Elon, A. 1971. *Israelis: Founders and Sons.* New York: Bantam Books.

—. 1997. "Politics and Archeology." In N. A. Silberman and D. Small (eds), *The Archeology of Israel: Constructing the Past, Interpreting the Present. Journal for the Study of the Old Testament,* Supplement Series 237, 34–47.

Encyclopaedia Judaica. 1972. Jerusalem: Keter.

Erlanger, S. 2005. "After a 2,000-Year Rest, a Seed Sprouts in Jerusalem." *New York Times,* 12 June, 3.

Eshel, R. 1991. *Dancing with the Dream: The Development of Artistic Dance in Israel 1920–1964* (in Hebrew). Tel Aviv: Sifriat Hapoalim.

Etzion, Y. 1992. *The Lost Bible* (in Hebrew). Jerusalem: Schocken.

Feige, M. 2007. *Settling in the Hearts.* Detroit: Wayne State University Press.

Handelman, D. and L. Shamgar-Handelman. 1990. "Shaping Time: The Choice of the National Emblem of Israel," In E. Ohnuki-Tierney (ed.), *Culture through Time: Anthropological Approaches.* Stanford: Stanford University Press, 193–226.

Heilman, S. C. 1983. *The People of the Book: Drama, Fellowship, and Religion*. Chicago: University of Chicago Press.

Kaganoff, B. C. 1977. *A Dictionary of Jewish Names and Their History*. New York: Schocken Books.

Lev-Ari, S. 1998. "Setting the Framework of the Theater Life." In *The History of the Jewish Community in Eretz Israel Since 1882*, Part 1: Zohar Shavit (ed.), *The Construction of Hebrew Culture in Eretz Israel* (in Hebrew). Jerusalem: The Israel Academy for Sciences and Humanities & Bialik Institute, 93–7.

Levin, M. 1947. *My Father's House*. New York: Viking Press.

Lowenthal, D. 1985. *The Past is a Foreign Country*. Cambridge: Cambridge University Press.

Mishori, A. 2000. *Lo and Behold: Zionist Icons and Visual Symbols in Israeli Culture* (in Hebrew). Tel Aviv: Am Oved.

Peirce, C. S. 1962. *Collected Papers of Charles Sanders Peirce*. Cambridge, MA: Harvard University Press.

Persky, N. (ed.) 1975. *Mikra'ot Yisrael Hadashot le-Khita Beit* (*The new Israel's reader: Textbook for the second grade*) (in Hebrew). Tel Aviv: Massada.

Rachel (Bluwstein). (1926) 1985. Translated by R. Friend. In S. Kaufman, G. Hasan Rokem and T. Hess (eds), 1999. *The Defiant Muse: A Bilingual Anthology*. New York: The Feminist Press.

Rinat, T. 2005. "After the Buffalos and the Wild Donkeys, the Ostriches Too Return to the Negev" (in Hebrew) *Ha'aretz*, 17 April.

Roitman, A. 2001. "Exhibiting the Dead Sea Scrolls: Some Historical and Theoretical Considerations." In *Archeology and Society in the 21st Century: The Dead Sea Scrolls and Other Case Studies*. Jerusalem: Israel Exploration Society and the Dorot Foundation, 41–66.

Ronen, D. 1999. "A Dialogue of Belonging: The Search for Local and Native Israeli Identity in the Creation of Folk Dances during the 1950s." In M. Bar-On (ed.), *The Challenge of Sovereignty* (in Hebrew). Jerusalem: Yad Yitzhak Ben-Zvi, 262–74.

Sheragai, N. 2005. "A Fragment of Seal from the First Temple Found in the Temple Mount" (in Hebrew). *Ha'aretz*, 27 September.

Shils, E. 1981. *Tradition*. Chicago: University of Chicago Press.

Smolly, E. (1933). 1973. *Anshei bereshit*. Tel Aviv: Am Oved; English translation by M. Roston, 1964: *Frontiersmen of Israel*. Tel Aviv: Massada.

Wallace, A. 1972. "Revitilization Movements." In W. A. Lessa and E. Z. Vogt (eds), *Reader in Comparative Religion: An Anthropological Perspective*. New York: Harper & Row, 503–12.

Weitman, S. 1988. "Hebrew First Names as a Cultural Measurement: Trends in Israelis' National Identity, 1882–1980." In N. Gertz (ed.), *Points of View: Israeli Culture and Society* (in Hebrew). Tel Aviv: Open University, 141–51.

Yerushalmi, Y. H. 1982. *Zakhor: Jewish History and Jewish Memory*. Seattle: University of Washington Press.

Zerubavel, E. 1997. *Social Mindscapes: An Invitation to Cognitive Sociology*. Cambridge, MA: Harvard University Press.

—. 2003. *Time Maps: Collective Memory and the Social Shape of the Past*. Chicago: University of Chicago Press.

Zerubavel, Y. 1995. *Recovered Roots: Collective Memory and the Making of Israeli National Tradition*. Chicago: University of Chicago Press.

—. 2005. "Transhistorical Encounters in the Land of Israel: National Memory, Symbolic Bridges, and the Literary Imagination." *Jewish Social Studies* 11(3), 115–40.

Notes on Contributors

JEFFREY ANDREW BARASH is professor of Philosophy at the University of Amiens, France. His publications have focused on the themes of political philosophy, historicism and modern German thought and he is the author of three books: *Heidegger et son siecle. Temps de l' Etre, temps de l'histoire* (1995), *Martin Heidegger and the Problem of Historical Meaning* (2003), and *Politiques de l'histoire. L'historicisme comme promesse et commme mythe* (2004). He is currently completing a book entitled *What is a Political Myth?* He is also preparing a comprehensive work on the theme of collective memory.

YORAM BILU is a professor of anthropology and psychology at the Hebrew University of Jerusalem. He published widely on issues related to culture and mental health, dreams in cultural context, and popular religion in Israel. His books include: *Grasping Land: Space and Place in Contemporary Israeli Discourse and Experience* (1997, co-edited with Eyal Ben-Ari), *Without Bounds: The Life and Death of Rabbi Ya'aqov Wazana* (2000), and *The Saint Impresarios: Dreamers, Healers, and Holy Men in Israel's Urban Periphery* (2005) (Hebrew).

NILI COHEN, a member of the Israeli Academy of Science and Humanities and the American Law institute, is the incumbent of the Benno Gitter Chair in Comparative Contract Law and the director of the Beverly and Raymond Sackler Fund for Human Rights in Private Law. She served as Vice-Rector (1994–7) and subsequently as Rector of Tel-Aviv University (1997–2001). She published numerous books and articles on contracts and the interrelations between contracts, torts and property as well as some articles on law and literature. She edited (with Ewan McKendrick) *Comparative Remedies for Breach of Contracts* (2005) and is working now on *Remedies for Breach of Contracts*.

DAN DINER is Professor for Modern European History at the Hebrew University of Jerusalem and Director of the Simon Dubnow Institute for Jewish History and Culture at Leipzig University. His publications are in the field of twentieth-century Europe, the history of the Jews in modern Germany, and in particular he focused on the history of National-socialism and the Holocaust. His most recent book is *Versiegelte Zeit. Über den Stillstand in der islamischen Welt* (2005).

ARYE EDREI is a senior lecturer in Law at the Buchman Faculty of Law at Tel-Aviv University. He received his PhD at the Hebrew University of Jerusalem (1994), and spent the years 1995–7 at Harvard University Center for Jewish Studies. He published numerous articles in leading journals, both in the field of general Law and Jewish Law. His main areas of interest are Talmudic Law and Jewish Jurisprudence of the twentieth century. Recently he published the article "Law, Interpretation, and Ideology: The Renewal of the Jewish Laws of War in the State of Israel," *Cardozo Law Review* 28(2006), 187–227. During his stay at the Institute of Advanced Studies at the Hebrew University of Jerusalem (2005) he co-authored with Doron Mendels the article "A Split Jewish Diaspora: Its Dramatic Consequences," published recently in the *Journal for the Study of the Pseudepigrapha* 16.2. (2007), 91–137.

BIANCA KÜHNEL is Jack Cotton Professor of Architecture and Fine Arts and Director of the European Forum at the Hebrew University. She has published numerous articles and book chapters on medieval art and architecture and is author of *From the Earthly to the Heavenly Jerusalem: Representations of the Holy City in Christian Art of the First Millennium* (1987); *Crusader Art of the Twelfth Century: A Geographical, an Historical, or an Art-Historical Notion?* (1994); *The End of Time in the Order of Things: Science and Eschatology in Early Medieval Art* (2003). She is editor of *The Real and Ideal Jerusalem in Jewish, Christian, and Islamic Art*, special double issue of the annual *Jewish Art* 23/24 (1997/1998).

DAN LAOR is professor of Hebrew Literature at Tel-Aviv University, Israel, and incumbent of the Jacob & Shoshana Schreiber chair for Contemporary Jewish Culture. He served as the chairman of the department of Hebrew Literature and as Dean of Humanities. Among his publications is *Hayei Agnon* (1998) (Hebrew), a biography of Shmuel Yosef Agnon, soon to be published in English in the USA. Professor Laor is the recipient of the Ben Zvi Prize for the history of Erez Israel and the Jacob Buchman memorial prize granted by Yad Vashem.

TAMAR LIEBES is a professor of Media and Journalism at the Hebrew University of Jerusalem, and holds the Carl and Matilda Newhouse Chair in communication. She has published extensively in the fields of media audience, media, war and terror and media and public memory. Among her books: *The Export of Meaning: Cross Cultural readings of Dallas* (1992, with Elihu Katz); *American Dreams, Hebrew Subtitles: Globalization at the Receiving End* (2004).

AMIA LIEBLICH is a professor emeritus of psychology at the Hebrew University of Jerusalem, Israel. Her research work concerns narrative research of a variety of aspects of life in Israel, such as the kibbutz and the military service. She is also an expert on gender differences in various cultural contexts. Among her books in English: *Kibutz Makom* (1982), and *Seasons of Captivity* (1994). Together with Ruthellen Josselson and Dan McAdams, she is the editor of *The Narrative Study of Lives*, an annual series of interdisciplinary work on life stories. The book on *The Children of Kfar Etzion*, which is the basis for the chapter in this book, will appear in Hebrew in 2007.

DORON MENDELS is Max and Sophie Mydans Professor of the Humanities in the Department of History at the Hebrew University of Jerusalem, Israel. He wrote numerous books and articles. Among his books are: *The Land of Israel as a Political Concept in Hasmonean Literature* (1987), *Identity, Religion and Historiography. Studies in Hellenistic History* (1998), *The Media Revolution of Early Christianity* (1999), and recently, *Memory in Jewish, Pagan and Christian Societies of the Graeco-Roman World* (2004). He is currently working on a *Hermeneia* Commentary on the Book of 1 Maccabees.

IDAN SEGEV is a computational neuroscientist working at the Hebrew University of Jerusalem where he heads the Interdisciplinary Center for Neural Computation. His research focuses on nerve cells as information processing and learning microchips. Recently he is involved in the "Blue-Brain projects," aiming at constructing a realistic computer model of a functional piece of the mammalian cortex – the cortical column. He is the co-founder of the *Journal of Computational Neuroscience* and has edited two books: *Methods in Neuronal Modelling* with C. Koch and *The Theoretical Foundation of Dendritic Function* with G. Shepherd and J. Rinzel.

MOSHE SHOKEID is professor of Anthropology at Tel-Aviv University. He has published numerous articles and book chapters. His books include *A Gay Synagogue in New York* (1995/2003), *Children of Circumstances: Israeli Emigrants in New York* (1998), *The Dual Heritage: Immigrants from the Atlas Mountains in an Israeli Village* (1971/1985), and, with Shlomo Deshen, *The Predicament of Homecoming: Cultural and Social Life of North African Immigrants in Israel* (1974) as well as *Distant relations: Ethnicity and Politics Among Arabs and Jews in Israel* (1982).

JONATHAN H. SLAVIN, PhD, ABPP, is currently Clinical Instructor in Psychology at the Department of Psychiatry, Harvard Medical School. He is a past President of the Division of Psychoanalysis (39), American Psychological Association; and was Founding President of the Massachusetts Institute for Psychoanalysis and a member of the faculty of several psychoanalytic institutes. Dr. Slavin has served as Consulting Psychologist, Ministry of Health, State of Israel and Consulting Psychologist, Palestinian Counseling Service. Among his other functions he was Director of the Counseling Center at Tufts University from 1970–2006. He has published on the psychotherapeutic treatment of trauma and sexual abuse, the role of personal agency in human development and in psychoanalytic treatment, adolescent development, psychoanalytic clinical supervision, and psychoanalytic technique.

HERMONA SOREQ is a professor of Molecular Biology and currently serves as Dean of the faculty of Science at the Hebrew University of Jerusalem, Israel. Her research focuses on the molecular mechanisms underlying mammalian stress reactions, with special attention given to the role in these reactions of cellular communication through the neurotransmitter acetylcholine. She has published several books, numerous articles and book chapters and works on the development of novel therapeutic approaches for ameliorating the adverse consequences of traumatic experience.

ALEXANDER YAKOBSON is senior lecturer in the Department of History at the Hebrew University of Jerusalem. His research focuses primarily on late-republican politics, popular participation, public opinion and elections, as well as on political and ideological aspects of the early Principate. He is the author of a number of articles on the late Republic and the early Principate and of the book *Elections and Electioneering in Rome: A Study in the Political System of the Late Republic* (1999).

YAEL ZERUBAVEL is a professor of Jewish Studies and History at Rutgers University, USA. She has published extensively in the area of history and memory, national myths and collective identities as well as on Israeli literature and culture. Her book *Recovered Roots: Collective Memory and the Making of Israeli National Traditions* won the 1996 Salo Baron Prize of the American Academy for Jewish Research. She is currently working on a book entitled *Desert in the Promised Land: Nationalism, Politics, and Symbolic Landscapes* (forthcoming).

GABRIEL ZIMMERMAN is a PhD student at The Hebrew University's Interdisciplinary Center of Neural Computation, where he performs stress-related research under the guidance of Hermona Soreq, teaches molecular neuroscience and has already published four articles on his work.

Index

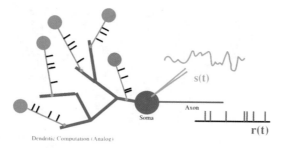

Figure 7.2 The neuron as an input-output electrical device. Many thousands of pre-synaptic neurons (red) contact the post-synaptic neuron (blue) via corresponding synapses (green dots) that are distributed over on its dendritic tree. Each of these red neurons fire series of spikes (black lines), e.g. in response to a sensory input. The spikes arriving to each of these synapses are transformed to a local graded (analog) potential at the blue dendritic tree. These barrage of synaptic potentials from all red cells are summed up at the cell body of the receiving cell (s(t), green line) and (if s(t) is sufficiently positive) a spike train, r(t) is elicited in its axon. Note that each of the red cells also recieves thousands of synaptic inputs. Clearly, changing the strength of the synapses will elicit different output in the blue neuron (and in the network as a whole). This change in synaptic strength is considered to be a major mechanism that underlies memory and learing in the brain.

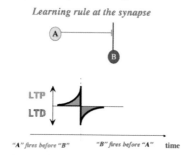

Figure 7.3 "Hebbian" rule for synaptic plasticity. Cell A (the pre-synaptic neuron) is connected via a synapse to cell B (post-synaptic neuron). When cell A fires first and cell B at a later time fires a spike quite consistently, then the synapse is strengthened (LTP – green), whereas when cell B fires first and cell A fires later (so that there is no causal relationship between their firing) then the synapse is weakened (LTD, red). It was experimentally found that the time-window for this type of synaptic plasticity is on the order of 10th of milliseconds. Therefore, this mechanism *per se* cannot explain learning of the type of classical Pavlovian conditioning, in which the time between the ringing of the bell and showing of the food could be at the seconds time scale.

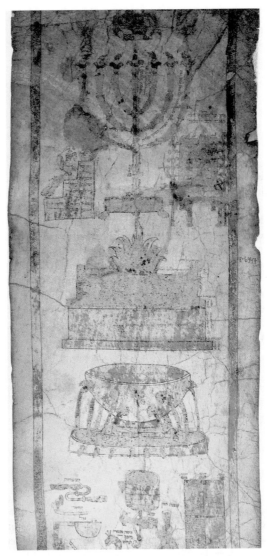

Figure 8.1 JNUL 8° 6947, detail.

Figure 8.2 JNUL 8° 6947, detail.

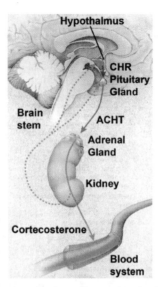

Figure 15.1 Basic neuroendocrine pathways involved in stress responses.

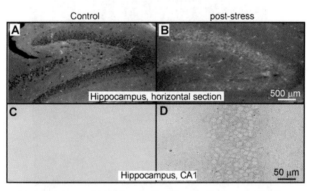

Figure 15.3 AChE-R levels are chronically increased after psychological stress in different brain areas.